KW-329-153

3 0116 00555 8067

MARKETING IN CHINA

The **SAGE Library in Marketing** offers academics the opportunity to access the rich diversity of marketing thinking and research. Drawing on the most influential articles to have been written about marketing, the major works in this series are edited by scholars at the forefront of their fields.

Yonggui Wang is Professor of Marketing and Strategy, and Dean of Business School at the University of International Business and Economy (UIBE) in China. As one of the leading marketing experts in China, he has had numerous articles published in the area of marketing and strategy, in international academic and executive journals including *Journal of Management, Industrial Marketing Management, Journal of Service Management, Decision Support Systems, Journal of Engineering and Technology Management, Information & Management, Management Decision, Journal of Managing Service Quality* and *Journal of Management Development*. He is the associate editor of *Journal of Technology Management in China* and an Editorial Advisory Board Member of *Journal of Chinese Marketing*. He is the Executive member of the China Marketing Association and also a member of American Marketing Association

SAGE LIBRARY IN MARKETING

MARKETING IN CHINA

VOLUME I

Access to Modern Marketing

Edited by

Yonggui Wang

Los Angeles | London | New Delhi | Singapore | Washington DC | Melbourne

Los Angeles | London | New Delhi
Singapore | Washington DC | Melbourne

SAGE Publications Ltd
1 Oliver's Yard
55 City Road
London EC1Y 1SP

SAGE Publications Inc.
2455 Teller Road
Thousand Oaks, California 91320

SAGE Publications India Pvt Ltd
B 1/I 1, Mohan Cooperative Industrial Area
Mathura Road
New Delhi 110 044

SAGE Publications Asia-Pacific Pte Ltd
3 Church Street
#10-04 Samsung Hub
Singapore 049483

Editor: Delia Alfonso
Assistant editor: Colette Wilson
Permissions: Km. Ranjana
Production controller: Prasanta Barik
Proofreader: Vaibhav Bansal
Marketing manager: Kay Stefanski
Cover design: Wendy Scott
Typeset by Boson ITech Pvt. Ltd., Kolkata
Printed and bound by CPI Group (UK) Ltd,
Croydon, CR0 4YY [for Antony Rowe]

At SAGE we take sustainability seriously. Most of our products are printed in the UK using FSC papers and boards. When we print overseas we ensure sustainable papers are used as measured by the Egmont grading system. We undertake an annual audit to monitor our sustainability.

© Introduction and editorial arrangement by Yonggui Wang, 2016

First published 2016

Apart from any fair dealing for the purposes of research or private study, or criticism or review, as permitted under the Copyright, Designs and Patents Act, 1988, this publication may be reproduced, stored or transmitted in any form, or by any means, only with the prior permission in writing of the publishers, or in the case of reprographic reproduction, in accordance with the terms of licences issued by the Copyright Licensing Agency. Enquiries concerning reproduction outside those terms should be sent to the publishers.

Every effort has been made to trace and acknowledge all the copyright owners of the material reprinted herein. However, if any copyright owners have not been located and contacted at the time of publication, the publishers will be pleased to make the necessary arrangements at the first opportunity.

Library of Congress Control Number: 2015947565

British Library Cataloguing in Publication data

A catalogue record for this book is available from the British Library

ISBN: 978-1-4739-1579-4 (set of four volumes)

Contents

Volume I: Access to Modern Marketing

Volume II: Application of Western Marketing in China

Volume III: Rapid Growth of Marketing in China

Volume IV: Prosperity of Marketing in China

Appendix of Sources

All articles and chapters have been reproduced exactly as they were first published, including textual cross-references to material in the original source.

Grateful acknowledgement is made to the following sources for permission to reproduce material in this book.

1. 'Chinese Consumers' Evaluation of Foreign Products: The Influence of Culture, Product Types and Product Presentation Format', *Yong Zhang*
   European Journal of Marketing, 30(12) (1996): 50–68.
   © Emerald Group Publishing Limited all rights reserved. Reprinted with permission from Emerald Group Publishing Limited via Copyright Clearance Center's RightsLink service.

2. 'Emerging Lifestyles in China and Consequences for Perception of Advertising, Buying Behaviour and Consumption Preferences', *Ran Wei*
   International Journal of Advertising, 16(4) (1997): 261–275.
   Copyright © Advertising Association. Reprinted by permission of Taylor & Francis Ltd, www.tandfonline.com on behalf of Advertising Association via Copyright Clearance Center's RightsLink service.

3. 'The Animosity Model of Foreign Product Purchase: An Empirical Test in the People's Republic of China', *Jill Gabrielle Klein, Richard Ettenson and Marlene D. Morris*
   Journal of Marketing, 62(1) (1998): 89–100.
   Republished with permission of American Marketing Association; permission conveyed through Copyright Clearance Center, Inc.

4. 'Marketing and Negotiating in the People's Republic of China: Perceptions of American Businessmen Who Attended the 1975 Canton Fair',
   James A. Brunner and George M. Taoka
   Journal of International Business Studies, 8(2) (1977): 69–82.
   Copyright (1977) published by Palgrave Macmillan. Reprinted by permission from Macmillan Publishers Ltd via Copyright Clearance Center's RightsLink service.

5. 'Chinese Cultural Values: Their Dimensions and Marketing Implications',
   Oliver H.M. Yau
   European Journal of Marketing, 22(5) (1988): 44–57.
   © Emerald Group Publishing Limited all rights reserved. Reprinted with permission from Emerald Group Publishing Limited via Copyright Clearance Center's RightsLink service.

6. 'Advertising, Propaganda, and Value Change in Economic Development: The New Cultural Revolution in China and Attitudes toward Advertising', *Richard W. Pollay, David K. Tse and Zheng-Yuan Wang*
Journal of Business Research, 20(2) (1990): 83–95.
© 1990 Elsevier Science Publishing Co., Inc. 1990. Reprinted with permission from Elsevier via Copyright Clearance Center's RightsLink service.

7. 'Cultural Values Reflected in Chinese and U.S. Television Commercials', *Hong Cheng and John C. Schweitzer*
Journal of Advertising Research, 36(3) (1996): 27–45.
Republished with permission of WARC Ltd; permission conveyed through Copyright Clearance Center, Inc.

8. 'Controllable Factors of New Product Success: A Cross-National Comparison', *Roger J. Calantone, Jeffrey B. Schmidt and X. Michael Song*
Marketing Science, 15(4) (1996): 341–358.
Copyright © 1996, INFORMS (http://www.informs.org). Reproduced with permission from Institute for Operations Research and the Management Sciences (INFORMS) via Copyright Clearance Center's RightsLink service.

9. 'Differences in "Cultural Values" and Their Effects on Responses to Marketing Stimuli: A Cross-Cultural Study between Australians and Chinese from the People's Republic of China', *Anthony Chun-Tung Lowe and David R. Corkindale*
European Journal of Marketing, 32(9/10) (1998): 843–867.
© Emerald Group Publishing Limited all rights reserved. Reprinted with permission from Emerald Group Publishing Limited via Copyright Clearance Center's RightsLink service.

10. '*Guanxi:* Connections as Substitutes for Formal Institutional Support', *Katherine R. Xin and Jone L. Pearce*
Academy of Management Journal, 39(6) (1996): 1641–1658.
Republished with permission of Academy of Management; permission conveyed through Copyright Clearance Center, Inc.

11. 'A Relationship Marketing Approach to *Guanxi*', *José Tomás Gómez Arias*
European Journal of Marketing, 32(1/2) (1998): 145–156.
© Emerald Group Publishing Limited all rights reserved. Reprinted with permission from Emerald Group Publishing Limited via Copyright Clearance Center's RightsLink service.

12. 'Does Culture Matter? A Cross-Cultural Study of Executives' Choice, Decisiveness, and Risk Adjustment in International Marketing', *David K. Tse, Kam-hon Lee, Ilan Vertinsky and Donald A. Wehrung*
Journal of Marketing, 52(4) (1988): 81–95.
Republished with permission of American Marketing Association; permission conveyed through Copyright Clearance Center, Inc.

13. 'Partner Selection and Venturing Success: The Case of Joint Ventures with Firms in the People's Republic of China', *Yadong Luo*
Organization Science, 8(6) (1997): 648–662.
Copyright © 1997, INFORMS (http://www.informs.org). Reproduced with permission from Institute for Operations Research and the Management Sciences (INFORMS) via Copyright Clearance Center's RightsLink service.

14. 'Selling Machinery to China: Chinese Perceptions of Strategies and Relationships', *Norman McGuinness, Nigel Campbell and James Leontiades*
Journal of International Business Studies, 22(2) (1991): 187–207.
Copyright (1991) published by Palgrave Macmillan. Reprinted by permission from Macmillan Publishers Ltd via Copyright Clearance Center's RightsLink service.

15. 'Gift Giving in Hong Kong and the Continuum of Social Ties', *Annamma Joy*
Journal of Consumer Research, 28(2) (2001): 239–256.
© 2001 by Journal of Consumer Research, Inc. Reprinted by permission of Oxford University Press.

16. 'Emerging Market Segments in a Transitional Economy: A Study of Urban Consumers in China', *Geng Cui and Qiming Liu*
Journal of International Marketing, 9(1) (2001): 84–106.
Republished with permission of American Marketing Association; permission conveyed through Copyright Clearance Center, Inc.

17. 'The Impact of Order and Mode of Market Entry on Profitability and Market Share', *Yigang Pan, Shaomin Li and David K. Tse*
Journal of International Business Studies, 30(1) (1999): 81–103.
Copyright (1999) published by Palgrave Macmillan. Reprinted by permission from Macmillan Publishers Ltd via Copyright Clearance Center's RightsLink service.

18. 'The Market Orientation of Chinese Enterprises during a Time of Transition', *Shengliang Deng and Jack Dart*
European Journal of Marketing, 33(5/6) (1999): 631–654.
© Emerald Group Publishing Limited all rights reserved. Reprinted with permission from Emerald Group Publishing Limited via Copyright Clearance Center's RightsLink service.

19. 'Marketing Strategy in Emerging Markets: The Case of China', *Peter G.P. Walters and Saeed Samiee*
Journal of International Marketing, 11(1) (2003): 97–106.
Republished with permission of American Marketing Association; permission conveyed through Copyright Clearance Center, Inc.

20. 'Managing Direct Selling Activities in China: A Cultural Explanation', *Sherriff T.K. Luk, Lorna Fullgrabe and Stephen C.Y. Li*
Journal of Business Research, 45(3) (1999): 257–266.
© 1999 Elsevier Science Inc. All rights reserved. Reprinted with permission from Elsevier via Copyright Clearance Center's RightsLink service.

21. 'Product Stereotypes, Strategy and Performance Satisfaction: The Case of Chinese Exporters', *Lance Eliot Brouthers and Kefeng Xu*
Journal of International Business Studies, 33(4) (2002): 657–677.
Copyright (2002) published by Palgrave Macmillan. Reprinted by permission from Macmillan Publishers Ltd via Copyright Clearance Center's RightsLink service.

22. 'Creating Local Brands in Multilingual International Markets', *Shi Zhang and Bernd H. Schmitt*
Journal of Marketing Research, XXXVIII(3) (2001): 313–325.
Republished with permission of American Marketing Association; permission conveyed through Copyright Clearance Center, Inc.

23. 'Relationship Marketing in China: Guanxi, Favoritism and Adaptation', *Y.H. Wong and Ricky Yee-kwong Chan*
Journal of Business Ethics, 22(2) (1999): 107–118.
© 1999 Kluwer Academic Publishers. Reprinted with kind permission from Springer Science and Business Media via Copyright Clearance Center's RightsLink service.

24. 'Managerial Ties and Firm Performance in a Transition Economy: The Nature of a Micro-Macro Link', *Mike W. Peng and Yadong Luo*
Academy of Management Journal, 43(3) (2000): 486–501.
Republished with permission of Academy of Management; permission conveyed through Copyright Clearance Center, Inc.

25. 'When Does Trust Matter? Antecedents and Contingent Effects of Supervisee Trust on Performance in Selling New Products in China and the United States', *Kwaku Atuahene-Gima and Haiyang Li*
Journal of Marketing, 66(3) (2002): 61–81.
Republished with permission of American Marketing Association; permission conveyed through Copyright Clearance Center, Inc.

26. 'Antecedents of Green Purchases: A Survey in China', *Ricky Y.K. Chan and Lorett B.Y. Lau*
Journal of Consumer Marketing, 17(4) (2000): 338–357.
© Emerald Group Publishing Limited all rights reserved. Reprinted with permission from Emerald Group Publishing Limited via Copyright Clearance Center's RightsLink service.

27. 'E-commerce in China: Changing Business as We Know It', *George T. Haley*
Industrial Marketing Management, 31(2) (2002): 119–124.
© 2001 Elsevier Science Inc. All rights reserved. Reprinted with permission from Elsevier via Copyright Clearance Center's RightsLink service.

28. 'When Does Culture Matter? Effects of Personal Knowledge on the Correction of Culture-based Judgments', *Donnel A. Briley and Jennifer L. Aaker*
Journal of Marketing Research, XLIII(3) (2006): 395–408.
© 2006, American Marketing Association. Republished with permission of American Marketing Association; permission conveyed through Copyright Clearance Center, Inc.

29. 'The Effects of Strategic Orientations on Technology- and Market-based Breakthrough Innovations', *Kevin Zheng Zhou, Chi Kin (Bennett) Yim and David K. Tse*
Journal of Marketing, 69(2) (2005): 42–60.
Republished with permission of American Marketing Association; permission conveyed through Copyright Clearance Center, Inc.

30. 'Resolving the Capability–Rigidity Paradox in New Product Innovation', *Kwaku Atuahene-Gima*
Journal of Marketing, 69(4) (2005): 61–83.
© 2005, American Marketing Association. Republished with permission of American Marketing Association; permission conveyed through Copyright Clearance Center, Inc.

31. '*Guanxi*, Trust, and Long-Term Orientation in Chinese Business Markets', *Don Y. Lee and Philip L. Dawes*
Journal of International Marketing, 13(2) (2005): 28–56.
Republished with permission of American Marketing Association; permission conveyed through Copyright Clearance Center, Inc.

32. 'Relational Ties or Customized Contracts? An Examination of Alternative Governance Choices in China', *Kevin Zheng Zhou, Laura Poppo and Zhilin Yang*
Journal of International Business Studies, 39(3) (2008): 526–534.
Copyright (2008) published by Palgrave Macmillan. Reprinted by permission from Macmillan Publishers Ltd via Copyright Clearance Center's RightsLink service.

33. 'Back from the Brink: Why Customers Stay', *Mark Colgate, Vicky Thuy-Uyen Tong, Christina Kwai-Choi Lee and John U. Farley*
Journal of Service Research, 9(3) (2007): 211–228.
Published by SAGE Publications, Inc. Reprinted with permission.

34. 'When Does the Service Process Matter? A Test of Two Competing Theories', *Michael K. Hui, Xiande Zhao, Xiucheng Fan and Kevin Au*
Journal of Consumer Research, 31(2) (2004): 465–475.
© 2004 by Journal of Consumer Research, Inc. Reprinted by permission of Oxford University Press.

35. 'An Integrated Framework for Service Quality, Customer Value, Satisfaction: Evidence from China's Telecommunication Industry', *Yonggui Wang, Hing-Po Lo and Yongheng Yang*
Information Systems Frontiers, 6(4) (2004): 325–340.
© 2004 Kluwer Academic Publishers. Reprinted with kind permission from Springer Science+Business Media via Copyright Clearance Center's RightsLink service.

36. 'Service Loyalty: An Integrative Model and Examination across Service Contexts', *Xiaoyun Han, Robert J. Kwortnik, Jr and Chunxiao Wang*
Journal of Service Research, 11(1) (2008): 22–42.
Published by SAGE Publications, Inc. Reprinted with permission.

37. 'Determinants of Chinese Hotel Customers' E-satisfaction and Purchase Intentions', *Woo Gon Kim, Xiaojing Ma and Dong Jin Kim*
Tourism Management, 27(5) (2006): 890–900.
© 2005 Elsevier Ltd. All rights reserved. Reprinted with permission from Elsevier via Copyright Clearance Center's RightsLink service.

38. 'Conscious and Nonconscious Components of Superstitious Beliefs in Judgment and Decision Making', *Thomas Kramer and Lauren Block*
Journal of Consumer Research, 34(6) (2008): 783–793.
© 2007 by Journal of Consumer Research, Inc. Reprinted by permission of Oxford University Press.

39. 'Politicizing Consumer Culture: Advertising's Appropriation of Political Ideology in China's Social Transition', *Xin Zhao and Russell W. Belk*
Journal of Consumer Research, 35(2) (2008): 231–244.
© 2008 by Journal of Consumer Research, Inc. Reprinted by permission of Oxford University Press.

40. 'How Do Price Fairness Perceptions Differ across Culture?', *Lisa E. Bolton, Hean Tat Keh and Joseph W. Alba*
Journal of Marketing Research, XLVII(3) (2010): 564–576.
©2009, American Marketing Association. Republished with permission of American Marketing Association; permission conveyed through Copyright Clearance Center, Inc.

41. 'Harmonization Processes and Relational Meanings in Constructing Asian Weddings', *Thuc-Doan T. Nguyen and Russell W. Belk*
Journal of Consumer Research, 40(3) (2013): 518–538.
© 2013 by Journal of Consumer Research, Inc. Reprinted by permission of Oxford University Press.

42. 'Interpersonal Influence as an Alternative Channel Communication Behavior in Emerging Markets: The Case of China', *Chenting Su, Zhilin Yang, Guijun Zhuang, Nan Zhou and Wenyu Dou*
Journal of International Business Studies, 40(4) (2009): 668–689.
Copyright (2009) published by Palgrave Macmillan. Reprinted by permission from Macmillan Publishers Ltd via Copyright Clearance Center's RightsLink service.

43. 'Dealing with Institutional Distances in International Marketing Channels: Governance Strategies that Engender Legitimacy and Efficiency', *Zhilin Yang, Chenting Su and Kim-Shyan Fam*
Journal of Marketing, 76(3) (2012): 41–55.
© 2012, American Marketing Association. Republished with permission of American Marketing Association; permission conveyed through Copyright Clearance Center, Inc.

44. 'Observer Effects of Punishment in a Distribution Network', *Danny T. Wang, Flora F. Gu and Maggie Chuoyan Dong*
Journal of Marketing Research, L(5) (2013): 627–643.
© 2013, American Marketing Association. Republished with permission of American Marketing Association; permission conveyed through Copyright Clearance Center, Inc.

45. 'Firm Value Creation through Major Channel Expansions: Evidence from an Event Study in the United States, Germany, and China', *Christian Homburg, Josef Vollmayr and Alexander Hahn*
Journal of Marketing, 78(3) (2014): 38–61.
© 2014, American Marketing Association. Republished with permission of American Marketing Association; permission conveyed through Copyright Clearance Center, Inc.

46. 'The Effects of Business and Political Ties on Firm Performance: Evidence from China', *Shibin Sheng, Kevin Zheng Zhou and Julie Juan Li*
Journal of Marketing, 75(1) (2011): 1–15.
© 2011, American Marketing Association. Republished with permission of American Marketing Association; permission conveyed through Copyright Clearance Center, Inc.

47. 'How Foreign Firms Curtail Local Supplier Opportunism in China: Detailed Contracts, Centralized Control, and Relational Governance',
Kevin Zheng Zhou and Dean Xu
Journal of International Business Studies, 43(7) (2012): 677–692.
Copyright (2012) published by Palgrave Macmillan. Reprinted by permission from Macmillan Publishers Ltd via Copyright Clearance Center's RightsLink service.

48. 'Other-Customer Failure: Effects of Perceived Employee Effort and Compensation on Complainer and Non-complainer Service Evaluations',
Wen-Hsien Huang
Journal of Service Management, 21(2) (2010): 191–211.
© Emerald Group Publishing Limited all rights reserved. Reprinted with permission from Emerald Group Publishing Limited via Copyright Clearance Center's RightsLink service.

49. '"Tailoring" Customization Services: Effects of Customization Mode and Consumer Regulatory Focus', *Yonggui Wang, Jay Kandampully and He (Michael) Jia*
Journal of Service Management, 24(1) (2013): 82–103.
Published by Emerald Group Publishing Limited. Reprinted with permission.

50. 'A Maslow's Hierarchy of Needs Analysis of Social Networking Services Continuance', *Huanhuan Cao, Jinhu Jiang, Lih-Bin Oh, Hao Li, Xiuwu Liao and Zhiwu Chen*
Journal of Service Management, 24(2) (2013): 170–190.
© Emerald Group Publishing Limited all rights reserved. Reprinted with permission from Emerald Group Publishing Limited via Copyright Clearance Center's RightsLink service.

Editor's Introduction: Marketing in China

Yonggui Wang

The proposal of the major work expands on the basis of the development of marketing in China over the period from 1977 till 2014. Marketing in China closely follows the Western world, and Modern marketing has been introduced from such the western societies as the USA and European countries since 1980s. However, due to the uniqueness of China's economy and politics, it should be noticed that there are great similarities and differences between marketing in China and that in the west. Typical academic articles with great influences (both conceptual and empirical) from top journals in the fields of marketing as well as some managerial oriented articles from leading executive journals, are included in this major work. It must be helpful to contain both connection and variance for students and faculty members who wish to understand the development of Marketing in China. Totally there are four volumes in this major work that are in line with marketing evolution in China.

Volume I (1977–1998)

The first phase refers to the period before 1998. This is the first 20 years since Reform and Opening-up policy in China. During this period, the remarkable feature is significant policy changes and market with a dominant identity. China has started to contact and feel the western marketing economy. In general, researches can be divided into two groups. One group is what China looks like in foreigner's eyes, the foreign companies' efforts have concentrated on the evaluation of economic and industry conditions that influence investment and business decisions in China; the other group is what foreigners look like in Chinese eyes, Chinese's perception of foreign product or advertisement. During this period, China has been regarded as the most potential giant market, therefore, many foreign companies enter into the ancient land. So marketing research puts an emphasis on the evaluation of Chinese environment and business opportunity, how to market their products to Chinese consumers, and explores factors that influence successful marketing activities in China. Based on the aspects mentioned above, six topics are chosen for Volume I, that is, consumer behaviors, marketing environment, marketing tactics, relationship marketing, international marketing, and organizational marketing.

Consumer Behaviors

Isolated from the western world for dozens of years since 1949, China initiates various significant policy changes in an effort to develop its economy and improve the standard of living for her citizens. Due to the reform and opening policy, many new things begin to appear in China, and Chinese consumers have been faced with a variety of foreign products and cultures. Some studies in this period focus on Chinese consumers' attitudes and evaluation of foreign products, and some focus on consumer segmentation and consumer attitudes toward advertising. Here are three typical articles about consumer behaviors in China.

Yong Zhang (1996) investigates what images certain foreign products have in the minds of the Chinese consumers and how such images may influence their product evaluation and purchase decisions. An experiment is designed to study the influence of culture, product type, and presentation format on the COO (country of origin) effect in China. The study employs a quota sample of 300 shoppers in a large shopping center in the north-eastern suburb of Beijing. The shopping center carries many foreign products along with many Chinese made products. The results demonstrate products that enjoy a positive COO image receive more positive ratings from the Chinese consumers and it appears that COO images influence Chinese consumers' decision making independent of cultural influences. This study also indicates that COO effect may be subject to moderation by product type and presentation format and the COO effect has positive relationship with single-cue condition but negative relationship with the presence of additional product information. The findings may help us to gain insights into consumer behaviors in China, which may help Western businesses to market their products in this increasingly crowded market.

In the second article, Ran Wei (1997) successfully segments consumers in China into five groups based on six empirically tested lifestyles: traditionalists, status quo, modern, transitioners and generation Xers. Marked by old age, poor education and poverty, traditionalists lead an old-fashioned life and resist change. Demographically similar to traditionalists, the status quo segment, however, has not reached a stage where life revolves around established routines. Poorly educated with low incomes, transitioners are much younger and open to change. The modern segment is the most affluent and well educated, pursuing a fashionable and materialistic life. Generation Xers, born after the Cultural Revolution, are best educated; they show disrespect for routines and tradition and worry little about money. As consumers, traditionalists and status quo consumers disapprove of advertising, strive to save and prefer all things Chinese. The modern and generation X segments view advertising positively, spend freely and favor a Western lifestyle. Transitioners differ from others, reflecting a lifestyle in transition.

With the implementation of open door policy, a great number of foreign products flourish in China. Klein, Ettenson and Morris (1998), in "The Animosity Model of Foreign Product Purchase: An Empirical Test in the People's Republic of China", provide an initial test of the animosity model of foreign product purchase in the People's Republic of China (PRC). In contrast to Shimp and Sharma's CETSCALE (consumer ethnocentrism scale) (1987), the model predicts that animosity toward a foreign nation will affect negatively the purchase of products produced by that country independently of judgments of product quality. The model is tested using mainland Chinese consumers' attitudes toward Japan and Japanese products. Structural equation modeling supports the model and shows that animosity has a significant impact on buying decisions above and beyond the effect of consumer ethnocentrism. Furthermore, these results are not cohort-specific. The measurement of cross-national hostility enables managers to understand better the purchase behavior of consumers in the international marketplace.

In short, with flourished of foreign product, studies on consumer behaviors basically focus on the emerging phenomenon in China, such as the consumer category, how Chinese perceive, evaluate foreign products and factors influencing consumer behavior.

Marketing Environment

China's economy has experienced tremendous changes since the reform and opening up. Import and export trade has been growing fast. Marketing in China also develops rapidly during this period. As a country with a huge population and unique culture, China shows her own characteristics. Thus, scholars realize the importance of understanding how market works in China. Research on culture values, negotiation, strategy and orientation and other aspects of marketing has emerged in China, for which four typical articles are selected as follows:

Brunner and Taoka (1977) complement a self-administered questionnaire with 218 businessmen who have attended one or more of the recent Canton Trade Fairs as the respondents, to evaluate the various aspects of business opportunities and peculiarities of negotiations in the PRC. It is an innovation to document the perceptions of Americans who have had direct contact with the Chinese mainland and have been able to gain first-hand knowledge of the peculiarities of trading with the Chinese and, at the same time, to develop an appreciation for the types of goods and services they desire by attending the Canton Fairs. Data and interview analysis support many statements that the representatives of the PRC are extremely tough negotiators and group decisions are preferred to individual decisions by the negotiators of the PRC. The final conclusion is that the Chinese are becoming more flexible in their negotiations and are sincerely interested in expanding trade with the United States because of their need for capital goods and the need of United States for many of their products.

To help international marketing managers to understand the Chinese way of life and value systems, Yau (1988) introduces five kinds of culture values and the implications behind them according to Kluckhohn and Strodbeck's classification. The first classification is Man-Nature Orientation. Traditional Chinese generally have low expectations towards the product he/she is going to purchase or consume. The second classification is called Man-to-himself Orientation. Chinese buyers prefer to have their shopping in a free environment without interference and enjoy available things. The third classification is Relational Orientation. Chinese customers with this value are more likely to adopt advice from opinion leaders and the packaging of gift products is extremely important as well. The fourth classification, Time Dimension, reflects the trend of Chinese to have great brand loyalty. The last one is activity orientation whose evidence is conflicting. Chinese buyers accept new fashions or technology, but resist marketing innovations. Chinese culture values, based on the orthodox doctrine of Confucianism, have been changing during these years, especially in Hong Kong, Taiwan and Singapore. The authors choose this right time to investigate the expected relationships between Chinese cultural values and other determinants of consumer behaviors. So it is more different and newer than articles before.

So China is under an amazing transformation in the past three decades. People's thoughts and values have changed a lot, and they have been accepting new things from abroad instead of only sticking to Confucianism. People's consumption view has been changing as well, forcing enterprises to react to it and improve their services and products' quality. China is exploring more cooperation and businesses with other countries.

Marketing Tactics and Strategies

In order to realize "four modernizations" in China, some commercial means, such as advertising, have been viewed as effective instruments to prompt economic development, which were rejected before 1979. Just as Pollay, Tse and Wang (1990) note: 'yesterday's villain is today's hero.' In this period, advertising research focuses on the social and economic changes brought by advertising, the influence of Chinese and western culture on advertising, and the culture values reflected by Chinese ads appealing. Content analysis and comparative analysis are the most popular research methods in domain of advertising before 1999.

With the prosperity of advertising, China's consumer culture has been changing. As a consequence, various social, economic, and legal implications have been formed. Pollay, Tse and Wang (1990) explore a large number of questions about changes of China and advertising based on the data gathered from Beijing, Guangzhou and Harbin. According to the survey, Chinese consumers are very positive about advertising but less satisfied with the style of advertising. And the findings are different from the Chinese manager's. The Chinese managers suggest there should have more information in advertising, but Chinese consumers think there is already enough information contained in advertising. And Chinese consumers score low on artistic, pleasant, amusing, intelligent, hard to forget, honest and convincing, especially aesthetics and entertainment value. By contrast, foreign advertising is excellent to almost all dimensions except understandability. It would be better if the advertising portrays bold, self-oriented and lively lifestyles. The article suggests Chinese consumers are far positive about the impact of advertising on social, economic and legal consideration than western consumers. They consider advertising as an important path to help export efforts, domestic markets, promote competition, and improve product quality.

TV has been the most popular medium in 1990's. Cheng and Schweitzer (1996) examine cultural values reflected in Chinese and U.S. television advertising and compare Chinese ads with U.S. ads in order to seek the dominant culture value reflected by ads. Based on extant literature, the article posits 32 culture values which are divided into symbolic and utilitarian group or eastern culture values and western culture values. Samples are collected from CCTV1, CCTV2, and Shanxi Television. Results show the most dominant values in Chinese TV commercials are "modernity", "youth", "family", "technology", "tradition", the most dominant values in U.S. commercials are "enjoyment", "modernity", "individualism", "economy", and "youth". So "modernity" and "youth" are shared by both countries. Therefore Chinese TV commercial prefers to symbolic rather than utilitarian appeals. The article also reveals that Chinese television commercials tend to use more eastern cultural values than U.S. television commercials, such as "patriotism", "tradition" and "wealth". The article also finds that cultural values have much to do with product categories. In China, "modernity" is used frequently for "automobile", "industrial products" and "household appliance", "individualism", "modernity" and "sex" are most frequently used for imported products and joint-venture product, whereas "tradition" is mainly used for "food and drink" and "medicine". In United States, "enjoyment" is often used for "travel", and "food and drink", and "economy" is usually used for "service" and "medicine".

The two article not only conclude that the attitude of Chinese consumers towards ads is more positive than negative; but also demonstrate the great difference between eastern and western culture and it's implication to ads.

Studies on factors influencing new product success constitute a main research stream of product strategy in this period, and comparative analysis is the most frequently used method by researchers just as in the field of advertising. Calantone, Schmidt, and Song (1996) discuss the controlled factors of new product success by comparing China with USA. This is the first large-scale study that directly tests the similarities and differences of new product success between China and USA. Firstly, they develop a model of managerially controllable factors related to new product success, which includes variable related to the organization, the new product development process, and the product itself. Organizational factors contain marketing resources and skills, competitive and market intelligence, technical resources and skills. Proficiency of marketing and technical activities is the new product development process-related factor whereas product quality is the product-related factor. However, they fail to find positive relationship between proficiency of technical activities and product quality in both USA and China. Then, the article uncovers cross-national differences. The order of importance of these factors in USA is as follows: proficiency of technical activities, competitive and market intelligence, level of marketing resources and skills, proficiency of marketing activities, and the level of technical resource and skills. However, in China, the order is competitive and market intelligence as the most important factor, both product quality and marketing resources and skills rank the second, and proficiency of technical activities ranks the forth followed by proficiency of marketing activities, whereas technical resources and skills are the least important factors. The path from product quality to new product success is not significant in U.S. but significant in China. Except the difference in order, there are some similarities in both countries revealed in the article.

To explore the differences of western and eastern values and their impacts on marketing is a hot topic too. Anthony Chun-Tung Lowe and David R. Corkindale (1998) explore the differences in cultural values and the different responses to some marketing stimuli associated with the difference in culture between Australians and Chinese from PRC. The article analyzes the influence of value on advertising and promotion, branding, sales and retailing, introduction of new/innovative products or services. It assumes there are apparent differences when Australian and Chinese respond to the same marketing stimuli. The findings show that the most important discriminating factors in value orientation, such as relationship with one's parents, modest, going to the extremes, behaving in a socially acceptable manner", tradition, continuity of the family are more important to the Chinese than to Australian. This research also indicates that the most important distinction to response to marketing stimuli, such as, advertisement with "elder people" or "expert", "practical theme", are more persuasive to the Chinese from PRC. And it also reveals that Chinese are more cautious and conservative when making decisions about "new product", and show lower brand loyalty (which contradict with common belief about Chinese) and so on. The article also explores the association among value, attitude and the perception toward marketing stimulus. In a word, some conclusions from this article are similar with prior researchers while some are different, and even contradict.

In conclusion, foreign companies have begun to implement marketing tactics tailored for Chinese marketing, and Chinese consumers and firms unprecedentedly are exposed to various marketing methods in this period.

Relationship Marketing

Guanxi, a unique phenomenon in Chinese society, has also been perceived as a popular research topic, which indicates that the use of personal connections may be an important way to get things done in business activities. Therefore, access to the Chinese market is usually conditioned by the reliance on trust relationships rather than on the enforcement of contracts, since commercial law is almost non-existent, and often arbitrarily enforced at that time. Two typical articles of GUANXI are selected as follows:

Xin and Pearce (1996) explore which executives in the PRC will find personal relationships more important for business and invest more in their cultivation in private-company, state-owned and collective-hybrid companies. Using survey data from China, this study investigates executives of the firm develop personal connections in the condition of underdeveloped legal support for private businesses. The connections in China are called Guanxi. It is found that executives in private companies are more likely to use Guanxi in doing business than those in state-owned or collective-hybrid companies. Furthermore, the executives in private companies also trust government connections and develop such relationships by providing unreciprocated gifts. This is the first empirical test of Guanxi or the circumstance that explores when, where, and with whom sum relationships should be most important to managers.

The evolution of Chinese market brings about the need for a relationship marketing approach to serve more sophisticated consumers who demands better products and services. Understanding the role Guanxi plays in Chinese society and business is part of the process of learning about the Chinese market. Arias (1998) has concluded that there are important commonalities between Guanxi as a typical way of doing business in China, and relationship marketing, both of which need to manage relationships, networks and interactions. However, this research also stresses that identifying Guanxi with relationship marketing might be misleading. Guanxi is essentially a cultural construct with a particular value in doing business in China under its present structural, legal, institutional, political and economic conditions. By contrast, relationship marketing needs to consider the importance of establishment and management of networks. Two managerial implications are provided in this study. First, accessing the right personal connections is useful for doing business well in China as elsewhere. Second, the situation of Guanxi being particularly relevant in doing business in China is changing. Economic and structural conditions have made manage Guanxi more difficult.

In a conclusion, GUANXI is regarded as an important characteristic of China society and business activities. It is often regarded as substitution of formal institutional support. Therefore, GUANXI plays different role in private-company, state-owned and collective-hybrid companies and some researchers try to reveal the similarities and differences between GUANXI and relationship marketing.

International Marketing

In the 1990's, the industrial market in China has undergone a significant change from product shortage to surplus. In the process of industrialization, China is actively participating in international division and international competition. The trend of integration between domestic market and international market transform marketing in China from a closed, monopolized stage into an open and rational development one. Furthermore, the prior low-cost resource advantage has been lost. With more and more foreign capital pouring into Chinese market, the government protectionism is gradually lowered. Firms in China are facing with competition from not only domestic counterparts, but also more multinational corporations (MNCs). Therefore, international marketing in China has attracted much attention from both academic and business areas.

Tse et al. (1988) investigate whether a manager's home culture significantly influences his or her international marketing decisions. They also examine whether the impact of home culture diminishes in an open economy with intense exposure to international markets. Decision making in four simulated international marketing situations is studied with executives from the PRC, Hong Kong, and Canada. The findings show that home culture has a predictable and significant effect on the decision making of the executives from the PRC and Canada. Chinese executives from Hong Kong are affected by a combination of Western and Chinese cultural norms.

Partner selection is an important issue with regard to venturing success. Luo (1997) investigates the relationship between IJVs (international joint ventures) success and the strategic and organizational traits of local partners in the context of an emerging economy (PRC). Newly emerging economies have in recent years become major hosts of direct investment by MNC because the rapidly expanding economies, characterized by an exploding demand previously stifled by ideologically-based government intervention, provide tremendous opportunities that MNCs can preempt. MNCs in such economies, however, face challenges of structural reform, weak market structure, poorly specified property rights, and institutional uncertainty. Right local partners can help MNCs boost market expansion, obtain insightful information, mitigate operational risks, and provide country-specific knowledge. The analysis of the data obtained from China suggests that both strategic and organizational traits of local partners are significantly associated with some individual dimensions of IJV performance.

According to the findings mentioned above, Chinese market has become a potential import target market which foreign companies want to enter. Therefore, the influence of executives' culture and behavior on international marketing decisions has great theoretical and management implications for academics and practitioners.

Organization Marketing

With the reform of Chinese economic system, although the major purchase decision are still centralized within key ministries, local plants and local government agencies have more and more equipment purchases decision. How to sell machines to China becomes an important issue to cope with.

McGuinness, Campbell and Leontiades (1991) examine the impact of marketing strategies and customer relationships on Chinese purchasers of machinery. In their study, Chinese perceptions of foreign machinery suppliers are used to evaluate supplier strategies and the customer relationships formed. The strategy based on product quality and service has the greatest impact on preferences. The relationships formed seem to reflect mainly the perceived value of the product service-package provided. There is much more to do for managing business in China rather than simply being skillful at negotiations. The price, however, is highly correlated with product quality. Lower price is not everything. This study demonstrates that it is a must to combine product oriented, relation oriented with customer oriented to sell machinery to China.

By the end of 1998, Chinese marketing has changed the traditional way of thinking. The discussion and application of marketing theory in China complements the main research streams of western countries. The researches in these areas in 1990's provide a solid foundation for the further investigation in the new century. However, in the future, the combined forces of globalization and digitalization will put forward more new topics that need to be explored in China. As the largest market in the world, can China get competitive advantage in the new era? This provides a critical challenge for both academic researchers and firm managers.

Volume II (1999–2003)

When it approaches the end of 20th century, most scholars in the field of Marketing in China have accepted the modern marketing in the west. In this period, Chinese marketing made a huge progress in terms of both breadth and depth as more and more overseas Chinese students came back to China. One striking feature is that quantitative methods are introduced into marketing research in China, and empirical evidence from China greatly contributes to the integrity of marketing research. Meanwhile, scholars begin to focus on a variety of marketing research topics such as consumer behavior, environment analysis, marketing tactics and strategies, relationship marketing, green marketing and internet marketing based on the accumulation of marketing knowledge.

Culture and Consumer Behaviors

Culture and consumer behaviors are one of the most important parts in Chinese marketing. For example, gift giving is one striking characteristic of Chinese culture. In Hong Kong and the China Mainland, the term "gift" refers to exchanges of products and services that connect people with regard to the concept of reciprocity.

Joy (2001) in "Gift Giving in Hong Kong and the Continuum of Social Ties" explores gift-giving practices based on interview data from Hong Kong. Friends are divided into three types: close friends, good friends and Hi-Bye friends. They represent different ranks of relations of Chinese people. The article explores how gift giving works among them. In family and like-family contexts, reciprocity is discouraged, and there is no need to build relationships through gift giving. The author also suggests, however, that there are various gradations of intimacy in gift relationships against the backdrop of important cultural rules such as reciprocity, sentiment, and face. More researchers' interests are aroused by "gift-giving" phenomenon in Chinese culture after this study.

Scholars are increasingly concerned about consumer behaviors intertwined with Chinese culture, especially after China's entry into WTO. However, it should be noted that most of the studies related to the topic have focused on Hong Kong of China. The context of China mainland should be taken into consideration in future studies of Marketing in China.

Marketing Environments

Marketing environments in China have dramatically changed with the increasing integration of global economy. More and more Multinational Enterprises (MNEs) came to Chinese market during this period. To realize the untapped market potential among various consumer segments in China, MNEs need to realize the market structure and consumer characteristics in China and adapt to the local market conditions.

Cui and Liu (2001) conduct an analysis of China's urban consumers according to a 1997 national survey and reveal several market segments that are different in their demographics, psychographics, lifestyles, media usage, and consumption patterns. The findings provide enough evidence that multinational corporations need to adapt to the local market conditions in China and other transitional economies.

Marketing Tactics and Strategies

Marketing tactics and strategy research in China experiences a long process. During the period across the Millennium, Chinese researchers have been encouraged to adapt marketing tactics and strategies to China's transition economy.

Based on the business activities of a sample of 14,466 foreign firms in China in 1995, Pan, Li and Tse (1999) explore the impacts of the order and mode of market entry into an overseas market. The study finds that early entrants have significantly higher market shares and profitability than late followers. It is also found that equity joint ventures have a higher profitability than either wholly owned operations or contractual joint ventures. A significant interaction exists between the order and mode of market entry. Furthermore, both firm efficiency and size affect the performance of firms.

Aiming at understanding whether market orientation varies across different types of Chinese enterprises, Deng and Dart (1999) raise four hypotheses: H1, private/collectively owned enterprises are more market oriented than state owned enterprises; H2, enterprises in the more open regions (coastal cities) are more market oriented than those located in less open regions (inland cities); H3, enterprises in uncontrolled sectors are more market oriented than those in controlled sectors; H4, small and medium sized firms are more market oriented than larger enterprises. Results show that private and collectively owned enterprises display a substantially greater market orientation in business practices than State-owned enterprises, and enterprises in open, coastal cities with a better inter-functional co-ordination and a greater profit focus are more market oriented than those in inland cities. As for the third hypothesis, strong support is found, and it shows that enterprises in uncontrolled sectors are more market oriented on all components than those in the controlled sectors. And smaller firms exhibit a significantly higher orientation toward all components except inter-functional co-ordination as compared to larger firms, thus partially supporting the fourth hypothesis.

Walters and Samiee (2003) explore barriers to information acquisition in China and focus on the need to understand crucial dimensions of the operating environment with respect to internal protectionism, relationship development, the diversity of the market, and competitive contexts. In particular, Guanxi has been identified as a critical business success factor in China. Therefore, senior managers need to devote considerable time and effort to cultivation and maintenance of a network of appropriate relationships with government and other officials at the national, regional, and local levels.

Direct selling, as a new way of marketing channel in China, by which a great number of foreign cosmetic companies have enjoyed success in China. Luk, Fullgrabe and Li (1999) explain the reasons for success of those foreign cosmetic companies that adopt direct selling as their main selling strategy. They take direct selling as one type of relationship marketing, given that China is a relational society. First, the article analyzes the relationships based on cultural values, such as, group orientation, Renqing, friendship (Ganqing), face and posits that these cultural values have implications for marketing communication and direct selling activities. Then the article classifies all customers into four groups (relatives, friends, referrals, cold call sales) based on extant literature.

With the progress of Chinese economy, more and more Chinese products are exported to other countries. "Made in China" for cheapness has been gradually well known around the world. Many managers decide to adopt low-price strategy. But Brouthers and Xu (2002) point out that employment of price leadership strategy may decrease performance satisfaction whereas branding and positioning strategy will increase performance satisfaction. They choose Chinese firms as primary data to test their hypothesis and analyze several Chinese typical export companies' strategy.

Brand is nearly a constant topic in the marketing literature, and there is no exception in the evolution of China marketing. There exist two outstanding characteristics in the brand management research in China. One is that many foreign-owned enterprises in China pay more attention to how to localize their original brand names; the other is that many domestic and foreign firms pour more efforts to study the relationship between brand and market performance in the transitional economy environment (China).

Whenever a company introduces a product into a foreign market, one of its critical market entry decisions is the choice of a local brand name. Prior research on naming has primarily focused on characteristics and functions of English names. However, because English has specific phonological and morphological characteristics and is represented by a specific writing system, the generalizability is limited. Zhang and Schmitt (2001) propose a framework of the brand-name creation process in multilingual (English and Chinese), international markets, which incorporates (1) a linguistic analysis of three translations methods-phonetic (by sound),semantic(by meaning) and phonosemantic (by sound plus meaning); and (2) a cognitive analysis focusing on the impact of primes and expectations on consumer name evaluations. The authors conducted three experiments to test the hypotheses. This study corresponds to two different managerial decision tasks: One is to decide in what contexts different types of translations will perform most effectively, the other is to decide what types of translations are most effective given contextual constraints.

In this volume, brand research is more involved with comparison between the west and China. Through the comparison, its findings will help foreign firms better understand Chinese market, and Chinese firms strengthen and deepen brand management.

Relationship Marketing

Research on relationship marketing has been on a sharp growth in China especially since 1999. Many insightful scholars adds Guanxi, the Chinese element, to the study of marketing management in the context of Chinese culture. They explore and investigate the impact of Guanxi (tie) on firm performance and relationship between Guanxi and trust, the most noticeable variable in relationship marketing, based on the data collected in China. The three outstanding masterpieces in this regard are as follows:

Since most of the existing research in the early 1990's has been conducted in the context of western culture, the context-specific studies in China have largely unexplored. Particularly, the complex concept of Guanxi in Chinese society needs to be investigated further. Wong and Chan (1999) develop a new framework of Guanxi, and identify four dimensions as follows: adaptation, trust, opportunism and favor. The relationship between Guanxi and relationship quality has been investigated in this study. The study also finds that adaptation and trust are positively related to sales stability and quality. However, adaptation is negatively correlated with relationship termination costs.

Peng and Luo (2000) extend research of GUANXI in the context of China due to Chinese managers' reliance more on the cultivation of personal relationships to cope with exigencies of their situation (Child, 1994). They demonstrate manager's micro interpersonal ties with other firm managers or government officials help improve macro organizational performance. The micro-macro link differs among firms with different 1) ownership types, 2) business sector, 3) sizes and 4) industry growth rates.

Atuahene-Gima and Li (2002) contribute to studies of relationship marketing by investigating the dual roles of sales control and supervisor behaviors as antecedents of salespeople's belief in the benevolence of the supervisor (supervisor trust) and as moderators of the relationship between supervisee trust and new product performance. The empirical evidence adequately illustrates contingent effects of supervisee trust on new product performance. Data from the west and the east helps generalize the findings. As the findings show, supervisee trust may be good, but it is only conditionally good because its antecedents may offer potential conditions for it to hurt sales performance. In addition, the comparison between China and the USA points out some specific and practical implications for enterprises' marketing in China.

Green Marketing

Before the 21st century, an awareness of environmental degradation has taken a long time to emerge in China. In common with industrialization experience of most advanced nations, China has been paying high ecological price for its fast growing economy.

Chan and Lau (2000) try to find out antecedents of green purchases in China. The purpose of the study is to enhance Chinese government's understandings of environmental ethics and the development of green marketing in China, and to assist enterprises to realize the potential of green market in China. Based on Chinese traditional culture review, they adopt man-nature orientation as one of the important forces shaping individual's views about the world. That is to say, man-nature orientation should have a positive influence on ecological knowledge and ecological affect and commitment to green purchase. Findings suggest that Chinese people's level of ecological knowledge and actual involvement in green purchase are still rather low. Fortunately, due to the influence of traditional culture value, Chinese people express a positive ecological affect and green purchase intention. In addition, results also confirm the importance of ecological knowledge and ecological affect in determining Chinese consumer's green purchase intentions as well as their actual purchase behavior.

Internet-based Marketing

E-commerce in the West makes Chinese scholars realize the wide application of internet in business and its profound impacts on the mode of business operation. Here is one typical article as follows:

Haley (2002) explores the route of development of e-commerce in emerging market such as China. He points out that those firms in China cannot mimic policies and strategies employed in advanced economies, because China has no similar existing and mature distribution, financial, advanced communication and computer technologies, distribution and warehousing networks, and communications infrastructure conducive to e-commerce like in the west.

At this stage, the evolution of marketing in China has been at the fast pace. Some new constructs (consumer loyalty, consumer perception, commitment, trust etc. as well as internet context) emerge on the articles with some new perspectives or other theories. With the introduction of quantitative methods, focus has been gradually shifted from conceptual research to empirical research. It has been a trend to test some theories with China's data, which has practical implications for transition economy.

Volume III (2004–2008)

In this period, scholars give a new face lift to marketing in China. With the sharp rise of Chinese economy, marketing in China have gained unprecedented attention home and abroad. Marketing research in China has been on a sharp and diversified trend, and narrowed down to a short distance from the western related research. In this period, scholars conduct a further and rigid marketing research in more detail in such respects as consumer behaviors, marketing tactics and strategies, relationship marketing, service marketing, green marketing, internet-based marketing and marketing environment.

Consumer Behaviors

Many researchers focus on how Chinese consumers behave in Chinese culture, and try to find out similarities and differences in consumers' behaviors in the context of Chinese and western cultures.

Briley and Aaker (2006) explore the effects of personal knowledge on the correction of culture-based judgments with several experiments of both participants in Hong Kong and the United States. Study 1 finds that participants are not affected by cultural norms when they think deeply to arrive at assessments of persuasive messages. Study 2 is to hold constant a potential confound in Study 1, and examine whether culture consistent effects persist when participants are distracted, and therefore are less able to make use of resource-intensive processes. Again, Chinese and North American participants evaluate either a promotion or a prevention Sun Skin advertisement. However, in Study 3, tendencies to deliberate are increased by manipulating the extent to which participants believe that they have little (or plenty of) time to complete their evaluations. To sum up, North Americans are persuaded more by promotion-focused information, and Chinese people are persuaded more by prevention-focused information, but only when initial, automatic reactions to messages are given.

Comparison between Chinese and western consumers could pave the way for the globalization of economy and marketing.

Marketing Tactics and Strategies

In this period, the role of marketing tactics and strategies has been dramatically recognized and strengthened in Chinese marketing. Scholars have conducted a further and more detailed research to get China understood by the rest of the world. In addition, researchers have introduced the new concept of "innovation" in accordance with China's innovation development strategy proposed by Chinese government.

Zhou, Yim and Tse (2005) find that different types of strategic orientation and market forces influence performance, which is mediated differently by breakthrough innovation. To survive the competition, local firms are updating their technologies through internal R&D, knowledge transfer in joint ventures, or direct imports from developed countries in the context of a transition economy. The results find that market orientation has a positive effect on tech-based innovation and a negative impact on market-based innovation. Technology orientation is positively associated with tech-based innovation but is not related to market-based innovation. Both tech- and market-based innovations positively affect firm and product performance. This article grasps the ignored point among strategic orientation and elaborates the influencing mechanism between market orientation, technology orientation and tech-and market based innovations in Chinese market that is characterized by rapid changes.

New product development strategy, as an important strategy in business, has also attracted lots of attention during this period. Of course, innovation is a key point in the process of new product development. However, what kind of capability or resource may influence the outcome of new product innovation? Atuahene-Gima (2005) conducts relevant research to address this question. He integrates some marketing variables with innovation ones together. He proposes that marketing strategy orientation may play a role, such as customer orientation and competitor orientation. But these two variables may not influence innovation directly, and they are linked with some mediated variables, such as competence exploitation and competence exploration. In addition, perceived market opportunity and inter-functional coordination may moderate the main effects. The study incorporates market orientation into the RBV research stream that views firms as response to environmental conditions through existing competencies and the development of new ones. It involves organizational coordination mechanism, knowledge sharing, resource allocation, innovation and marketing theory. Chinese market characteristics make it possible to include exploitation and exploration simultaneously to explain the relationship among these variables.

Relationship Marketing

Scholars go on paying more attention to the antecedents and outcomes of Guanxi, and make comparisons between Guanxi and the contract to find out which one is more suitable in China market.

Lee and Dawes (2005) examine the antecedents and outcomes of buying firm's trust in a supplier's salesperson at both individual and the organizational levels in Chinese Culture. The authors pay special emphasis on the impact of Guanxi, one of three determinants, on trust in salesperson in the context of Chinese culture. Although there are many studies about the Chinese personal relationships, this may be the first to take a measurement approach to Guanxi. Guanxi is defined as a three-dimensional latent construct, which consists of face, reciprocal favor and affect. A key aspect of this research is that authors investigate the impact of each dimension of Guanxi on salesperson trust separately. Findings suggest that personal trust is fostered mainly through the affect component of Guanxi. This conclusion sheds light on the similarities between Guanxi and the western concept "bond". It also suggests that a salesperson should avoid giving the favors to the buyer firm personnel and expect payback in the future because reciprocal favor reduces salesperson trust. Reciprocal favor is a norm in Chinese Culture. However, in buyer-seller relations, reciprocal favor may ultimately lead to the suspicion of corruption.

What are managers more likely to employ to safeguard complex exchanges, relational ties or customized contracts? Zhou, Poppo and Yang (2008) find that managers increasingly rely on the use of personal-based, relational ties for complex exchanges characterized by high levels of specialized asset and uncertainty. At the same time, firms embrace customized contracts for uncertain exchanges but largely resist using more customized contracts for exchanges associated with greater levels of asset specificity. Yet it also indicates that managers tend to customize their contracts when faced with greater uncertainty, because formalized agreements facilitate necessary adaptation. These results illustrate the complicated nature of exchange governance in a transitional economy. While contracts might facilitate adaptation to changes in the supply market, they do not appear to be an effective means to safeguard probable opportunism arising from specialized assets. These findings hold for both local and foreign firms in China.

Service Marketing

According to the National Statistics in China, service sector only accounts for 32% of GDP in China in 2003, even lower than some developing countries, and much lower than those developed countries (60%–75%). Unhealthy industrial structure has been forcing Chinese government to energetically foster the development of service sector. Meanwhile, service marketing starts attracting Chinese scholars' attention. The research involves many different topics such as customer perception in service, service quality, customer decision and customer satisfaction. During the period, much research about service marketing in China has been conducted. Here are three typical articles about service marketing in China.

Colgate et al. (2007) explore the decision of customers to stay or not, and the reasons behind it. The authors apply a combination of qualitative and quantitative methods in this study, which sets a good example in Chinese service marketing. Then, the most important thing is that the article points out that different service context may influence the possible results. Such results help Chinese marketers to understand switching behavior in service industries more deeply and identify the reasons for customers to stay making a comparison with New Zealand. According to the results, the most important staying reasons in China are time and effort. However, it's confidence in New Zealand. The article offers a more complete understanding of the switching process in China, which assists managers in developing strategies and tactics to convince Chinese customers to leave competitors and join their service organizations.

Hui et al. (2004) study the interactive effect of process quality and outcome quality on service evaluation. Results from two experiments confirm that the combined effects of the two types of service quality can be multiplicative rather than simply additive in nature. The results also reveal that in situations in which consumers feel certain about the service outcome prior to consumption, process quality has marginal effects on post-consumption behavior when outcome quality falls short of the expected level. During the period, Chinese marketers have been starting to pay attention to customer perceived quality and customer satisfaction. But most researchers are still on the initial stage. The article can find the crucial connection of two service quality and try to test it based on two theories (fairness heuristic theory and two-factor theory).

Along with the progress of service marketing in China, service quality, customer satisfaction and customer value have become the priority of both manufacturers and service provider in the increasingly intensified competition. Thus, less is known about the relative impacts of quality-related factors on customer value and customer satisfaction up to now and the moderating role of customer value in the relationship between service quality and customer satisfaction has been neglected. Yonggui Wang, Hing-Po Lo and Yongheng Yang (2004) focus on the measurement of service quality based on the SERVQUAL model, and try to demonstrate the moderating effect of customer value between service quality and customer satisfaction. The article develops structural equation models with the software of PLS-Graph. On the one hand, results can be used to explain the competitive behaviors (China Mobile and China Unicom). On the other hand, it also enables firms to compete more effectively and efficiently. Chinese telecommunication industry has been growing very fast, and Chinese market has becoming more and more important in the world. This article leads service marketing research in China toward further steps.

Han, Kwortnik and Wang (2008) derive an integrated framework of service loyalty based on previous paths: quality/value/satisfaction, relationship quality, and relational benefits. The authors test the model with data from various service industries (airlines, banks, beauty salons, hospitals, hotels, mobile telephone) and thousands of customers in China. Results are supportive of a multidimensional view of customer loyalty. Commercial friendship, a construct new to service loyalty models, is added to the key loyalty determinants (customer satisfaction, commitment, service fairness, service quality and trust).

According to these four articles, we have to acknowledge that service marketing research in China combines the theory and practice subtly. However, there is still no systematic framework for Chinese service marketing, and this calls for more attention in the future.

Internet-based Marketing

In this period, some scholars make empirical studies of e-commerce in China, and consumer behavior online is a hot topic.

The Internet meets these demands by allowing potential customers to learn about hotel facilities and to compare prices without contacting a hotel's sales representative. Online reservations can be less expensive than other traditional channels. Considering the nature of tourism products and services (e.g., intangibility, complexity, diversity, and interdependence), consumers are more eager than ever for product-related information to minimize their purchase risk and close the gap between their expectations and the actual travel experience. Kim, Ma and Kim (2006) try to recognize the key factors affecting Chinese hotel customers' online reservation intentions and to evaluate their satisfaction with online hotel reservation. Participants have been selected from 12 Chinese hotels in Beijing, China mainland in March 2003. The results indicate that Chinese hotel consumers are more likely to rely on client information needs and online security rather than hotel branding and price benefits when they become more experienced Internet users.

Marketing Environment

In the period of social and economic transition, the marketing environment plays an increasingly important role, and accordingly it becomes the focus of academic scholars in China. Two classical articles are selected to elaborate on Chinese marketing environment.

Kramer and Block (2008) reveal the influence of superstitious beliefs on consumer behaviors and specify their conscious/non-conscious underlying properties. In particular, the article shows that superstitious beliefs have a robust influence on product satisfaction and decision making under risk. It begins with the impact of superstitious beliefs on consumer satisfaction following product failure by showing that consumers are less (more) satisfied with a product for which they hold positive (negative) superstitious associations based on its color, product quantity, or the digits used in its price. Next, this article demonstrates that the effects of superstitious beliefs are not limited to Asian consumers, showing that participants from the United States make significantly more risk-averse choices when a negative (vs. neutral) superstition is made salient. Finally, it provides evidence that even though the effect of superstitious beliefs on decision making have both conscious and non-conscious components, the contribution of non-conscious processing to the effect is three times the relative size of the conscious effect.

In Western societies, mythical archetypes are often evoked to promote consumption, while Chinese consumer culture in its early development is unmistakably shaped by political ideology. China's ideological transition from a communist country toward a consumer society provides an unprecedented context in which to explore the rise of consumerism in a contemporary society. Zhao and Belk (2008) examine how advertising appropriates a dominant anti-consumerist political ideology to promote consumption during China's social and political transition. They use a semiotic analysis of advertisements in the People's Daily to show how advertising reconfigures both key political symbolism and communist propaganda strategies. Their structural framework of ideological transition extends Barthes's myth model and examines ideological transition in advertising from the macro perspective of political ideology. This framework goes beyond the transfer of cultural meanings and may help to explain ideological shifts in other societies.

At this stage, the evolution of marketing in China has been on the sharp growth. Scholars made more rigid and further detailed studies based on Chinese complex phenomenon instead of one or two simple Chinese elements. The fast growth is mainly due to managerial needs of MNEs and sensitive insight of scholars.

Volume IV (2009–2014)

Boosting domestic demand and the rapid development of information technology from 2009 to 2014 have caused great changes in marketing practices as well as academic fields. Research of consumer behaviors remains to be a hot topic due to consistent attention from academic scholars and practical managers. Besides, research on marketing strategy is not only limited to MNEs in China such as channel expansion, western brands, relational governance, but overseas channel expansion of Chinese companies has been a concern of academic scholars. Furthermore, with the share of GDP of service industry reaches 48.2%, service marketing becomes another popular topic.

Consumer Behaviors

Plenty of research on consumer behaviors has emerged in recent years, such as consumers' characteristics, decision process, response, and so on. The research we list here reflects 'new characteristics' of marketing in China nowadays, and the findings of those studies provide practical suggestions for either entrepreneurs or general consumers. Two articles are selected and analyzed as follows:

Bolton, Keh and Alba (2010) conduct a research to examine consumers' price fairness from a cross-cultural perspective. In their research, two dominant economies, China and the United States, which represent collectivism and individualism respectively, have been selected to address this issue. The results indicate that it is deemed unfair for one consumer paying higher price to an identical good than other consumers. To be specific, Chinese consumers are more sensitive to in-group versus out-group comparisons than those from United States. For example, Chinese consumers experience a greater loss of face when a friend pays a lower price than when a stranger pays a lower price. So, Chinese consumers will not repurchase when they have realized they paid higher price than a friend. They also find that the role of self-construal that interdependent self-construal characterized consumers tend to react more strongly to in-group versus out-group price comparisons than consumers primed with an independent self-construal. Meanwhile, the authors also show that the effects of self-construal, relationship, and price comparison on repurchase intention are mediated by fairness perceptions. Beyond that, the results of their research indicate that Chinese consumers tend to react more strongly to price comparisons in a loyal (vs. first-time) buyer–seller relationship, whereas U.S. consumers respond equally in regarding to the cultural difference.

Harmony is a core social value in traditional and modern Chinese culture, which deeply influences Chinese consumers' behaviors. Nguyen and Belk (2013) explore a series of questions, such as how harmonization happens and the conditions under which harmonization is promoted or defeated. Besides, their research points out that it is dynamic and sustainable to pursue harmonization within individuals, between human beings, and among different entities in the world. The article shows Asian consumers sacrifice individual preferences and bow to collective interests based on the data from Vietnamese weddings, which explains how face may guide Asian consumers' behaviors. Meanwhile it also provides an extension of Richins' categories or levels of consumption meaning. Finally, it indicates that Chinese values such as long-term mutuality, family face, and filial loyalty promote this harmonization process. In addition, it provides a framework for exploring how consumption meanings are layered and negotiated among family members and groups.

Marketing Tactics and Strategies

Marketing channel has becoming one of the major topics for marketing tactics and strategies during this specific period in China. Relevant studies include not only channel communication but also the development of channel capability. Here, both the boundary spanners' interpersonal influence and the senior managers' social capital can be regarded as important factors affecting channel communication and channel capability accumulation. Further, related studies not only investigate the channel expansion of multinational enterprises in China, but also explore the channel expansion of Chinese companies abroad. Last but not the least, the effect of punishment on the observers in the marketing channel has also been taken into consideration, which enriches marketing research theoretically and empirically in China.

Su et al. (2009) mainly explore channel communications between MNE suppliers and their local retailers in emerging markets such as China. Channel relationships in China rely more on interpersonal influence than formal inter-firm communication. Based on embeddedness theory, this study tests the antecedents, moderators, and consequences of interpersonal influence strategies. Particularly, Chinese culture is characterized by informal relationship such as Guanxi, which builds on Confucianism (interpersonal connection). Here, Guanxi includes the elements of Mianzi (saved face when in need) and Renqing (a form of social capital: exchange of favors). Mianzi represents a person's dignity and ability to offer assistance, and Renqing signifies the imperative to offer assistance to friends and acquaintances who face difficulties. Mianzi emphasizes hierarchy and harmony, as helping others highlights the giver's status, and proves the intimacy between the giver and receiver. Renqing emphasizes obligation to pay back, which facilitates Mianzi giving and receiving. Guanxi orientation is defined as "the extent to which people willingly recognize obligations (to offer Renqing), harmony (to save other's Mianzi), and reciprocation (to repay Renqing to maintain long-term cooperation) in their daily socialization".

Firms managing international marketing channels face institutional pressure to gain social acceptance (commonly referred to as legitimacy) and difficulty in evaluating international market, which undermines firm efficiency. There is a dilemma for firms to gain legitimacy and to safeguard efficiency. Yang, Su, and Fam (2012) mainly test how institutional distance may influence the effort of a firm to pursue legitimacy, and how the governance strategies (contract customization and relational governance) deal with legitimacy and efficiency issues to safeguard channel performance. Specifically, institutional environment is an important issue for firms doing business in foreign markets. Institution process includes three elements: regulatory, normative, and cultural-cognitive. The regulatory pillar can be explained as "a nation's laws and regulations and delineates what organizations can or cannot do". The normative pillar is comprised of beliefs, and norms that "specify what people should or should not do" in a society. The cultural-cognitive pillar specifies "what people will typically do". Regulatory instance pertains to the dissimilarity of the laws and regulations, which makes the entrant firms more cautious to the local laws. Normative distance may press the entrant firms to change their established norms into the local norms. Cultural-cognitive distance may press the managers to adopt the belief embraced in the local market to gain legitimacy. Once there exists institutional distance between Chinese market and other countries, for firms to go global, they have pressure to gain legitimacy in foreign markets.

As a typically transitional economy, Chinese market is characterized by Guanxi but insufficient legal protection. So there is no other place better than China to investigate effects of punishment in channel network. Wang, Gu, and Dong (2013) explore the effects of punishment on observers from the viewpoint of social learning, fairness heuristic, and social network theories. The article reveals two mechanisms through which punishment may lead to reduced observer opportunism: (1) a direct deterrence effect and (2) a trust-building process. Moreover, relational embeddedness of the disciplined distributor and monitoring capability of the observer moderate the observer effects differently. The former, which motivates greater information flow to observers, aggravates the problem of information asymmetry against the manufacturer, making punishment less deterrent for observers. In contrast, the latter, which reduces information asymmetry, strengthens observer effects.

Channel expansion has a long-term influence on firm value. Homburg, Vollmayr and Hahn (2014) explore how a firm's announcement of an increase in distribution intensity and the establishment of a new channel influence its firm value contingent on context-specific firm, market, and channel strategy. The hypotheses are tested with an event study of 240 announcements of major channel expansions in the United States, Germany, and China. The two types of channel expansions affect firm value (Abnormal stock returns) differently, and the effects of an increase in distribution intensity on firm value might be attenuated at high level of turbulent or competitive markets.

Relationship Marketing

A variety of relations in the interaction of the enterprise and its upstream and downstream partners, as well as the relationship between government and enterprises, become an important part of the marketing strategy which affects the access to resource for enterprises. Relational governance is absolutely necessary for enterprises in the context of Chinese unique social network culture. The following two articles are related to the relational governance in relationship marketing.

Sheng, Zhou and Li (2011) point out three main aspects of social ties in emerging economies remain underdeveloped, despite increasing attention to the role of social ties in emerging economies. A conceptual framework has been developed that depicts the interplay among social ties, institutional factors, and market uncertainty. The article makes a contrast between business ties and political ties. Meanwhile, it examines the contingent effects of institutional environment and moderating effects of market environment. Random sample of 500 firms from a list of high-tech firms in Beijing, Shanghai, and Guangdong have been selected for the formal survey. The findings from a survey of 241 Chinese firms indicate that business ties have a stronger positive effect on performance than political ties, and both effects depend on institutional and market environments. Business ties are more beneficial when legal enforcement is inefficient and technology is changing rapidly, whereas political ties lead to greater performance when general government support is weak and technological turbulence is low. These findings indicate that firms operating in China should be cautious in their use of business and political ties and adapt their tie utilization to changing institutional and market environments.

The second research examines how relational governance as a social mechanism interact differentially with two distinct types of economic mechanisms – detailed contracts and centralized control – in curbing local supplier opportunism in China. Zhou and Xu (2012) conduct an empirical investigation of the relationship between a foreign subsidiary and its local supplier in China. The article collects data through personal onsite interviews with 336 senior managers from 168 firms from 26 countries or regions. And it refines and assesses the construct validity of multiple-item measures to support its hypothesis of differential interaction effects of relational governance with the two TCE (transaction cost economics)-based mechanisms respectively. Finally, the article concludes that detailed contracts relate negatively to opportunism when relational governance is high, and relate positively to opportunism when relational governance is low. In sharp contrast, centralized control is negatively associated with opportunism when relational governance is low, but is positively associated with opportunism when relational governance is high. In other words, the relational governance complements detailed contracts but substitutes for centralized control in curtailing opportunism.

Service Marketing

The year of 2013 has been a significant milestone of China's development of the service industries, because the share of GDP of service industries reaches 46.1%. It has been the first time for the service industries to surpass the secondary industries. The studies on service marketing have provided impetus and empirical evidence for the development of the service industry.

Huang (2010) examines how organizational recovery responses to other-customer failure may influence a customer's service evaluations of the firm and clarifies what service firms and their employees could and should do. The article developes a 2 (complaint vs. no complaint) × 3 (EE: high vs. low versus no) × 2 (compensation vs. no compensation) between-subject experimental design. Consumers at a large-sized shopping center in Taiwan have been recruited as volunteers. The article draws some conclusions: Customers who have voiced their complaints express lower levels of satisfaction and repurchase intention, and are less likely to indulge in negative WOM than those who do not voice their complaints if other-customer failure discontinues. In contrast, when other-customer failure continues, both complaining and non-complaining customers give similar low scores for satisfaction, repatronage intentions, and high scores for negative WOM. And when participants feel the employees exert a great deal of effort to help solve such problems, they would be more highly satisfied, more willing to come back, and less willing to engage in negative WOM. On the other hand, when participants feel that the employees do not have made a good-faith effort, they would offer low scores for satisfaction and repurchase intention, and high scores for negative WOM, similar to those who do not receive any help from the service employees. The results show that offering compensation is not the cure-all. It provides empirical results that shed some light on the responses of both complainants and non-complainants to organizational recovery efforts after the occurrence of another-customer failure problem.

At the same time, more and more enterprises have involved customers in their product and service design practices nowadays, such as Xiaomi cellphones, Dell computer, and those companies undoubtedly win great success. Wang, Kandampully and Jia (2013) investigate the interaction effect of customization mode and regulatory focus on the 'tailoring' outcomes of customized services. They find that prevention focused consumers, in the context of subtractive customization, will retain more options than promotion focused consumers in the final customized offering, whereas in additive customizations, there is no difference in retaining options between prevention focused consumers and promotion focused consumers. Besides that, they also conclude that product familiarity moderates the effect of regulatory focus and customization, and task enjoyment plays a mediating role in the relationship between the interaction effect and consumers' attitudes. The research extends the literature on decision making and regulatory focus, and provides guidance for managers in designing the customization mode more effectively and efficiently.

Cao et al. (2013) apply Maslow's hierarchy of needs and expectation-confirmation model of information systems to analyze users' continuance intention of social networking services. The finding demonstrates that confirmation, fulfillment of self-actualization needs, and fulfillment of social needs have significant impacts on satisfaction, and satisfaction and fulfillment of self-actualization needs have significant impacts on continuance intentions. Besides, the effect of fulfillment of social needs on continuance intention is fully mediated by satisfaction.

During this period, breakthrough development has taken place in the quantity and quality of research on marketing in China. Indeed, plenty of outstanding articles have sprung up in the worldwide marketing community. The studies not only pay attention to emerging marketing fields, such as social network service, but also combine Chinese unique elements with marketing activities, such as Chinese culture and ideology. Since Chinese business infrastructures and marketing environment are not as systematic as western countries, the research conclusions enlighten practices of marketing in China.

In the past over 30 years, Chinese economy has experienced dramatic changes, and scholars home and abroad have conducted a variety of marketing research in the context of Chinese culture or with a comparison between China and the west. In the process of global integration, uniqueness of marketing in China has been gradually exposed to the world. There is no doubt that this four-volume marketing articles will have some implications for real marketing practices in transition economies and will be useful to those who want to get better understanding of marketing in China.

References

Child, J. 1994. Management in China during the age of reform. Cambridge, England: Cambridge University Press.

Shimp, T. and S. Sharma 1987. "Consumer Ethnocentrism: Construction and Validation of the CETSCALE," *Journal of Marketing Research*, 24 (August), 280–89.

1

Chinese Consumers' Evaluation of Foreign Products: The Influence of Culture, Product Types and Product Presentation Format

Yong Zhang

Introduction

For various reasons, the Chinese market has not been considered a viable market until quite recently. After remaining virtually closed to the rest of the world for 30 years since 1949, China initiated various significant policy changes in an effort to develop its economy and increase the standard of living of its citizens. To these ends, China has achieved remarkable progress in the past 15 years. Meanwhile, China has not only become one of the world's major trading nations with surging exports (International Monetary Fund, 1994), it has also become one of the most sought after emerging markets in the world for a variety of consumer as well as industrial products. China's import of foreign products reached US$67.7 billion in the first seven months of 1995, a 15.3 per cent increase over the same period in 1994 (*People's Daily*, 1995). The total imports of China for 1995 are expected to be well over US$100 billion.

Despite the obvious implications for Western countries from which China sources most of its imports, research in the field of international business and marketing has not kept pace with the development in China's consumer market. While most of the efforts have concentrated on the economic and

Source: *European Journal of Marketing*, 30(12) (1996): 50–68.

industry conditions that influence investment and business decisions in China, little research has focused on the Chinese consumers. As a consequence, knowledge about the Chinese consumers still remains quite scarce. In particular, few research efforts have explored Chinese consumers' attitudes towards foreign-sourced products. This study partly addresses this deficiency by investigating how Chinese consumers evaluate foreign made products. Specifically, the study tries to find out what images certain foreign products have in the minds of the Chinese consumers and how such images may influence their product evaluation and purchase decisions. The findings may help us to gain insights into consumer behaviour in China which may help Western businesses to market their products in this increasingly crowded market.

Literature Review

The Country of Origin Effect

Country of origin (COO) refers to information pertaining to where a product is made. Marketers are particularly interested in the perceived image associated with the COO (Martin and Eroglu, 1993; Parameswaran and Pisharodi, 1994). COO image has been defined as "the overall perception consumers form of products from a particular country, based on their prior perceptions of the country's production and marketing strengths and weaknesses" (Roth and Romeo, 1992). Since Schooler's (1965) seminal study, many studies have acknowledged that consumers have significantly different perceptions about products made in different countries, and that these general perceptions have important effects on consumers' evaluation of the products manufactured in a particular country.

Studies in the COO literature have identified different processes that explain how COO influences product evaluations. One process falls within the framework of the Fishbein model (Fishbein and Ajzen, 1975). That is, beliefs about a product's attributes precede and influence the formation of attitude towards the product. According to this view, when consumers engage in product evaluation, they base their evaluation on various descriptive, inferential or informational cues. Such cues can be intrinsic (such as colour, design, specifications, etc.) or extrinsic (such as price). Research has shown that intangible, extrinsic cues are often used by consumers as surrogate indicators when there are missing and/or difficult intrinsic cues. For example, price may be used to evaluate the quality of a product when other information is lacking (Gerstner, 1985; Olson and Jacoby, 1972;). Other extrinsic cues include those that are controlled by the firm, such as guarantees, warranties, brand reputation (Jacoby *et al.*, 1977), seller reputation (Shapiro, 1982), promotional messages (Klein and Leffler, 1981), and those that are controlled by third parties, such as product rating services and government standard-setting agencies (Cordell, 1988). COO can serve as a controllable extrinsic cue in the sense that sourcing and location decisions are made by the firm.

In contrast to the multi-attribute model conceptualization of the effect of COO on consumer evaluation, a second school of thought has focused on a "halo" effect model which suggests a reciprocal linkage from affect (evaluations) to beliefs (Beckwith and Lehmann, 1975; Han, 1989; Zajonc, 1980). According to this model, beliefs about a product can be influenced by overall evaluations. Such a conceptualization has been applied in the study of COO as an image variable, which is defined as some aspect of the product which is distinct from its physical characteristics, but which is nevertheless identified with the product (Erickson *et al.*, 1984; Johansson *et al.*, 1985; Narayana, 1981). COO is found to influence belief formation rather than attitude (evaluation) in some studies, although the effects of COO are not identical across all product attributes (Erickson *et al.*, 1984). Johansson *et al.* (1985), in particular, noted the existence of a persistent "halo" effect in ratings on specific product attributes.

Regardless of the direction of the influence of COO, empirical evidence suggests that COO perceptions may result from stereotyping (i.e. a positive relationship between country image and levels of economic development) and home country biases (Bannister and Saunders, 1978; Nagashima, 1970; Schooler, 1965; Yaprak, 1978). International marketers are concerned with the effect of COO because consumers may evaluate a product based on their perception of the COO. As new foreign markets emerge, knowledge about COO images in those markets will enable marketers to make wiser decisions. However, to date, it is unclear whether such findings hold for the Chinese consumers. We are not sure to what extent the Chinese consumers would react to COO information in a similar fashion.

Cross-Cultural Studies of COO Effects

The majority of COO studies have been conducted in developed countries in North America and Europe. Evidence from studies that have dealt with cross-cultural comparisons of COO effects (e.g. Darling and Kraft, 1977; Cattin *et al.*, 1982; Nagashima, 1970; Papadopoulos *et al.*, 1990) indicates that consumers' attitudes towards foreign products differ significantly from country to country. For example, such differences were noted between Japanese and American consumers (Nagashima, 1970). National pride, loyalty, and patriotism have been found to influence consumers' reactions to foreign products. Consumers often exhibit a preference for products produced in the home country even though home country products do not necessarily have the best quality or price (Darling and Kraft, 1977; Gaedeke, 1973; Wall *et al.*, 1986).

Evidence also suggests that the image of a country can be perceived differently by consumers in different countries. Cattin *et al.* (1982) reported that Americans perceived French-, German-, and Japanese-labelled products more favourably than the French. According to some authors, such differences may be attributable to the particular economic environment found in each country, the sample characteristics and the intensity of multinational marketing activity undertaken by the companies from the exporting countries (Lin and Sternquist, 1994). The perceived similarity, or the lack of it, with the source country's belief system (Tonberg, 1972) and cultural and political characteristics may also account for such differences (Wang and Lamb, 1983; Yevas and Alpay, 1986). Stronger COO effects may exist for products from a country with dissimilar belief system and socio-cultural climate from for products from a similar country.

Culture is a complex and multifaceted construct. According to some researchers, one of its basic dimensions is the value placed on individualism vs. collectivism (Hofstede, 1980). The individualism-collectivism continuum reflects the relationship between the individual and the collectivity that prevails in a particular society. Marked differences are observed in the characteristics of these two types of culture. Individualistic cultures emphasize independence, freedom, high levels of competition and pleasure; whereas collectivistic cultures tend to embrace interdependence, family security, social hierarchies, co-operation, and lower levels of competition (Triandis, 1989, 1990). The Far Eastern cultures such as the Chinese, Japanese, and Korean cultures share the same collectivistic values and beliefs which are distinct from those of the more individualistic cultures such as the USA. In addition to the individualism/collectivism difference, Hofstede (1980) also sees cultures placing more or less value on what he calls "masculinity," "power distance", and "uncertainty avoidance". Recently, he added to these four aspects a fifth dimension of cultural difference, namely, "Confucian dynamism" or "long-term/short-term orientation" regarding cultural traits such as thrift (saving) and perseverance (Hofstede, 1994). The three eastern Asian countries share this fifth dimension of culture. Obviously, the three Asian countries are more similar to one another than to the USA in these cultural dimensions.

In the light of such similarity and differences, it is expected that the COO images of Japan, Korea, and the USA would be influenced by the degree of shared similarity in the cultural traits of these countries with those of China. In other words, Chinese consumers may react to the COO information of these countries differently based on their perceived cultural and value similarity with these countries. It may be hypothesized that, other things being equal, the more similar the culture, the more favourable the COO image may be. For example, products made in Japan may be perceived more favourably by the Chinese consumers than products made in the USA.

The Influence of Product Type

As pointed out earlier, empirical evidence in COO research has converged on the notion that COO information is often used by consumers as a surrogate information cue in product evaluation. This tendency is strongest if knowledge or awareness of product attributes is low or not very accurate (Johansson *et al.*, 1985). Therefore, it may be expected that when consumers shop for products which possess features that are more complex and difficult to evaluate, they may be more likely to rely on the COO image of a product to aid them in their evaluation and choice processes.

Along this line of reasoning, previous studies have suggested that the COO effect may vary with different products. For example, Kaynak and Cavusgil (1983) investigated whether COO perception biases existed across product classes such as electronics, food items, fashion merchandise and household goods. Responses obtained from a sample of Canadian consumers indicated that, in addition to variation of quality perceptions across the countries studied, quality perceptions also tended to be product-specific. A country may rank high for one product class and low in another. For example, Japan was ranked very high in electronic items, but very low in food products. In a similar way, France was ranked high in fashion merchandise but low on all other product classes.

Some researchers have argued that for consumers in less developed countries, country image is likely to play a more significant role in influencing their attitude and behaviour (Lin and Sternquist, 1994). Unlike their counterparts in more developed countries, this is partly because consumers in less developed countries have less abundant information and purchasing experiences with foreign products. This may be particularly the case with more expensive and complex products. As a result, these consumers may have to rely more heavily on surrogate information cues such as the producing country's image in product evaluation. Therefore, COO information can be more important for a durable product with more complex features than a common non-durable product with simple features. This product type effect may be more salient than that typically found in developed countries. Some researchers have called for more attention to the COO effects across product types (Khanna, 1986). They have argued that comparative assessment of two or more countries and studies conducted across different product classes using different countries of origin to produce a comparison of national images in a specific market would be particularly desirable and fruitful.

The Effect of Product Presentation Format

In previous COO studies, subjects have often been provided only with information concerning the country of origin of the product(s) under study (White, 1979). Other studies have employed either multiple verbal cues or physical products to be evaluated by the subjects (Wall and Heslop, 1986). Researchers argued that, with all other factors held equal, single-cue COO studies should be expected to produce substantially larger COO effects than those employing multiple cues. This is because everything about the products in these single-cue studies must necessarily be inferred from knowledge of the COO (Lim *et al.*, 1994). Further, single-cue COO studies do not allow for the possibility of dissonant product cues, such as verbal or visual product information that may conflict with the subjects' initial perceptions of the products produced by the designated COO.

Research in consumer information processing has argued that when product information (either verbal or visual, such as picture or a physical product) is provided in addition to the COO information, the difference in presentation format becomes a relevant factor which affects consumers' information acquisition strategies, information processing, and choice processes (Bettman and Kakkar, 1977; Bettman and Zins, 1979). Because COO often serves as a cue from which the character of important product attributes is often inferred, it has a greater effect on buyers' evaluative reactions when it is the only cue and is obtrusively presented to the subjects than when this information is presented to them together with other product cues and in a more natural manner (Wall and Heslop, 1986). One recent study has demonstrated that when other product information cues are provided at the time of exposure to the COO information, such product information lessened the effect of COO (Lim *et al.*, 1994). In light of these findings, we would expect that when Chinese consumers are presented with a multi-cue, physical product, a similar difference in the COO effect would emerge.

Method

Design and Procedures

An experiment was designed to study the influence of culture, product type, and presentation format on the COO effect in China. The study employed a quota sample of 300 shoppers in a large shopping centre in the north-eastern suburb of Beijing (see Table I for a profile of the sample). The shopping centre carried many foreign products along with many Chinese made products. With assistance from the shopping centre, the experiment was carried out during a ten-day period of time including two weekends to ensure a representative sample of shoppers and their shopping patterns. A realistic setting and the shopping-mall intercept procedure were used to enhance the realism of the study. Mall intercept has been demonstrated to be a methodologically robust and externally valid technique for generating samples to tap consumer preferences and to uncover consumer judgement

Table I: Sample profile

Sample profiled according to these aspects	*Subgroups*	*Proportion of sample*
Gender (%):	Male	46.4
	Female	53.6
Age (years):	Mean	33.7
	Standard	6.6
Education (%):	Junior Middle school or lower	17.4
	Senior Middle school	47.6
	College or higher	35.0
Employed (%):		95.3
Bought foreign product before (%):		92.2

processes. Adult shoppers were randomly intercepted and recruited to participate in the study which lasted about 15 minutes. On their agreement to participate in the study, they were invited to a booth located in the shopping centre where they were explained what to do and were subsequently presented with the experimental stimuli. The subjects evaluated the product information while seated at a table, and then answered questions contained in a questionnaire. As a reward, they were paid ten yuan (the Chinese currency unit) which was the equivalent of US$1.20 for their participation in the study.

The study had a between-subject design in the COO factor (the USA, Japan, and South Korea) and the product information cue factor (single-cue and multiple-cue/physical product). It also had a within-subject design in the product type factor (non-durable product and durable product). Therefore, this study had a 3 × 3 × 2 factorial design.

Stimuli

Product. Two exemplar products were selected from a pool of candidate products. One product was a shirt, which was a common non-durable product very familiar to the participants and relatively easy to evaluate. The other product was a 19-inch colour television set, which was a common durable electronic product yet more difficult to evaluate. For both products, the original brand names were carefully altered to avoid possible confounding of COO images with brand images. The shirt had a "Century" brand name and the television had a "Polaris" brand name, both of which were fictional. The same product was used throughout the experiment and only the COO information was varied with the experimental condition. It was expected that more salient COO effect would be exhibited for the more difficult to evaluate television set. An additional benefit of using the two products was that the potential confounding effect owing to performance risks (Baumgartner and Jolibert, 1977; Kaynak and Cavusgil, 1983) could be removed. Performance risk has been found to moderate the influence of COO information (Cordell, 1992).

Presentation format. The COO information of the products was presented to the subjects in two different formats. For the single-cue condition, the product type, name, and the "made in" label were printed on an 8×11-inch card and presented to the subjects for evaluation. No other information was provided. For the multiple-cue condition, the subjects were presented with the physical product. The shirt was in its original box with a see-through window. It was placed on a display stand next to the table where the subject sat. On the package, the English brand name "Century" was clearly displayed. The use of English words on packages of foreign products in China is very common. A COO label in Chinese was ostensibly affixed to the package. The subjects were told that they could open the package and examine the product. The television set was placed on a stand and presented to the subject without the packaging. The original brand name was covered with a small professionally-made metal plate with the English word "Polaris" etched on to it. The original COO label on the back of the TV set was concealed. The COO information was printed on a tag and displayed on top of the TV set.

Country selection. The three countries selected for study are all major trading partners of China. Their products are widely available on the Chinese market. The USA and Japan are industrialized countries with more favourable COO images, while South Korea is a rapidly industrializing country with less favourable country image compared with the other two countries. In addition, since culturally China is more similar to Korea and Japan than to the USA, this study would be able to assess whether cultural similarity influences the effect of country image.

Dependent Measures

Several dependent variables were adapted from previous COO studies and used to measure the effect of COO in this study.

Product evaluation. A five-item, seven-point semantic differential scale (unreliable/reliable, common/exclusive, of not careful and meticulous workmanship/of careful and meticulous workmanship, technically not advanced/advanced, of poor/good style) was used to measure subjects' overall product evaluation (coefficient $\alpha = 0.92$). Subjects rated the products separately using this scale yielding two sets of ratings corresponding to the two products. Semantic differential scales have been characterized as "pan-cultural" scales suitable for measuring consumer traits and responses in cross-cultural studies (Osgood *et al.*, 1975). It has been demonstrated that such scales can capture concepts and dimensions used to evaluate stimuli – either objects or subjects – and account for major proportions of the variation in responses. The mean of the multiple ratings served as the measure of product evaluation.

Attitude. Attitude towards the brand was measured with a three-item semantic differential scale anchored by three pairs of adjectives (bad/good, unfavourable/favourable, and unlikeable/likeable). The coefficient a for this scale was 0.88. The mean of these items was used as indication of brand attitude.

Product choice. Product choice was measured by asking the subjects whether they would purchase this product if they were in the market for such a product. Subjects who chose the products were coded as 1 and those who chose the alternative ones were coded as 0.

Several ancillary measures (such as subject demographics) were also taken to check for potential biases in their responses. The questionnaire was translated from English into Chinese through an iterative parallel translation process by several bilingual researchers in China and the USA. Different versions were compared and a final version was agreed on.

Analyses and Results

Repeated-measure MANOVA was used to analyse the product evaluation and attitude data. The product evaluation and attitude scores formed a nested factor (the measure factor) within the product type factor in the within design. Product choice data were analysed with maximum likelihood logit analysis procedure. SAS general linear model and categorical data modelling procedures were used in the data analyses. The cell means and standard deviations are presented in Table II. First, a three-way, repeated-measure MANOVA was conducted with the product evaluation and attitude scores for both the non-durable and durable products as the dependent variables (the Product within-subject factor) and country and presentation format as the independent variables (the between-subject Country and Format factors). Results are presented in Table III.

Table II: Means and standard deviations of the dependent measures

		Shirt				*Television set*			
		Evaluation		*Attitude*		*Evaluation*		*Attitude*	
Country	*Format*	*Mean*	*SD*	*Mean*	*SD*	*Mean*	*SD*	*Mean*	*SD*
USA	Single	5.29	1.28	5.49	1.42	5.54	0.97	5.70	1.24
	Multiple	4.86	1.44	4.69	1.53	5.14	0.76	5.13	1.28
Japan	Single	5.23	1.14	5.20	1.22	6.32	0.34	6.19	0.57
	Multiple	4.89	1.04	4.87	0.98	6.00	0.70	5.90	0.72
South Korea	Single	4.00	1.35	4.12	0.85	4.06	1.80	4.14	1.29
	Multiple	3.92	1.35	4.01	0.92	3.93	1.40	4.19	1.28

Table III: Omnibus MANOVA results

Effects	*DF*	F-*value*	p-*value*
Product[a] (P)	1/294	142.88	0.0001
Measure[a] (M)	1/294	0.69	0.40
Country[b] (C)	2	63.22	0.0001
Format[b] (F)	1	7.25	0.01
P × M	1/294	0.06	0.79
P × C	2/294	56.75	0.0001
P × F	1/294	0.77	0.38
M × C	2/294	1.82	0.16
M × F	1/294	0.47	0.49
C × F	2	1.44	0.23
P × M × C	2/294	0.86	0.42
P × M × F	1/294	1.59	0.20
M × C × F	2/294	1.49	0.22
P × M × C × F	2/294	0.27	0.75

Notes: [a]Within-subject factor.
[b]Between-subject factors.

Table IV: Follow-up analyses: Product effect within country

Effects	*DF*	F-*value*	p-*value*
USA			
Product[a] (P)	1/99	28.77	0.0001
Measure[a] (M)	1/99	0.33	0.56
P × M	1/99	0.41	0.52
Japan			
Product[a] (P)	1/99	137.20	0.0001
Measure[a] (M)	1/99	1.93	0.16
P × M	1/99	0.94	0.33
South Korea			
Product[a] (P)	1/99	1.58	0.21
Measure[a] (M)	1/99	1.96	0.16
P × M	1/99	0.47	0.49

Note: [a] Within-subject factor.

The Product Type Effect

The results revealed a significant product main effect and a significant product by country interaction effect. As can be seen from Table III, the four-way interaction was not significant. The interaction effect indicated that the COO effect was not the same at different levels of the product types, suggesting the existence of moderating effect owing to product type.

To follow up, three analyses were carried out within each level of the country factor (see Table IV). No interactions involving the measure factor were significant, indicating that the product evaluation and attitude scores were consistent. For the USA and Japan, the product effect was significant, whereas for Korea it was non-significant. An examination of the score pattern indicated that when the product was the television set, the COO effect was stronger for both the USA and Japan (product evaluation: 5.34 vs. 5.08 (USA), 6.16 vs. 5.06 (Japan); attitude: 5.42 vs. 5.09 (USA), 6.05 vs. 5.04 (Japan)). This difference indicates that the COO effect was more important for a television set than for a shirt in the minds of the Chinese consumers. However, with Korean products, such a difference was less salient. Both products had relatively low scores compared with those of the USA and Japan.

The Effect of Presentation Format

The MANOVA test results (Table III) revealed a significant presentation format or cue effect. None of the multivariate and univariate interaction effects involving presentation format were significant. This result showed that the COO effect varied with the different format of presentation. In order to examine the exact nature of the cue effect, two separate procedures were run within each product type. Results are summarized in Table V. In both cases, the presentation format effect was significant. The format did not interact with the between-subject Country factor nor with the within-subject Measure factor.

Examination of the marginal means indicated that the COO effect was more salient when shoppers were presented with the single-cue format.

Table V: Follow-up analyses within product types: Univariate tests of between and within subjects effects

Source	*DF*	*Type III SS*	*Mean square*	*F-value*	*Pr > F*
Shirt: (change to new output)					
Between subject effects:					
Country (C)	2	147.68	73.84	27.59	0.001
Format (F)	1	18.16	18.16	8.79	0.007
C × F	2	6.84	4.42	1.28	0.388
Error	294	786.82	2.67		
Within subject effects:					
Measure (M)	1	0.13	0.13	0.35	0.55
M × C	2	0.39	0.20	0.54	0.58
M × F	1	0.64	0.64	1.74	0.18
M × C × F	2	1.06	0.53	1.44	0.23
Error (M)	294	108.24	0.37		
Television set:					
Between subject effects:					
Country (C)	2	419.00	209.50	113.03	0.001
Format (F)	1	11.65	11.64	6.28	0.012
C × F	2	4.98	2.49	1.35	0.262
Error	294	544.95	1.85		
Within subject effects:					
Measure (M)	1	0.28	0.28	0.65	0.420
M × C	2	2.09	1.04	2.39	0.093
M × F	1	0.00	0.00	0.01	0.921
M × C × F	2	0.78	0.40	0.89	0.412
Error (M)	294	128.79	0.43		

Product evaluation scores for the shirt were 4.84 (single cue) vs 4.56 (multiple cue) and, for the television set (TV), 5.31 (single cue) vs. 5.02 (multiple cue). The attitude score pattern resembled that of product evaluation. The scores for shirt were 4.94 (single cue) and 4.52 (multiple cue) and those for television were 5.34 (single cue) and 5.07 (multiple cue). Therefore, the presence of additional product cues in the form of a physical product seemed to mitigate the COO effect.

The Influence of Culture

Given the cultural differences between the three foreign countries and between China and each of the three countries, it was expected that there would be a significant difference in the COO effect between the USA and Japan, although both have a more positive COO image. There should be a less salient difference between the USA and Korea although the USA enjoys a more positive COO image than South Korea. Such effects should be independent of product types. Single degree of freedom, univariate contrast analyses were conducted to compare the differences in COO images between these three countries. Table VI summarizes the results.

The analyses revealed inconsistent results regarding the influence of culture on the perceived COO by the Chinese consumers. While there was a significant difference in the television set scores between the USA and Japan, the scores on the shirt did not show any significant difference. And yet, for

Table VI: Univariate contrast analyses: Difference in COO images between the USA, Japan and South Korea

Contrast	*DF*	*Contrast SS*	*Mean square*	F-*value*	*Pr* > F
Shirt:					
Product evaluation:					
USA vs. Japan	1	0.01	0.01	0.01	0.9298
USA vs. Korea	1	61.82	61.82	37.53	0.0001
Japan vs. Korea	1	60.06	60.06	36.46	0.0001
Attitude:					
USA vs. Japan	1	0.14	0.14	0.10	0.7549
USA vs. Korea	1	52.70	52.70	36.19	0.0001
Japan vs. Korea	1	47.36	47.36	32.53	0.0001
TV set:					
Product evaluation:					
USA vs. Japan	1	32.96	32.96	28.44	0.0001
USA vs. Korea	1	91.12	91.12	78.62	0.0001
Japan vs. Korea	1	233.71	233.71	201.63	0.0001
Attitude:					
USA vs. Japan	1	19.63	19.63	16.81	0.0001
USA vs. Korea	1	78.12	78.12	66.88	0.0001
Japan vs. Korea	1	176.09	176.09	150.76	0.0001

both products, USA was rated significantly higher than South Korea. In addition, subjects rated the products of Japan and Korea differently despite the cultural similarity between the two countries. Both the USA and Japan had a much more favourable COO image than South Korea. It seemed that cultural similarity had little to do with the perceived COO images of the countries in this study.

Product Choice

Product choice data were analysed using logit analysis. The use of the logit model enabled the determination of the effect of the two categorical experimental variables (country and presentation format) on a single dependent categorical variable, product choice. The influence of such independent variables on product choice could be expressed in terms of the predicted probabilities and their associate odds for choosing one level of the dependent variable over another.

Two logit models were fitted using the choice data for each of the two product types. The product choice data on shirt were first analysed with country and format as the independent variables. The experimental conditions were dummy-coded for the analyses. The empirically derived model revealed an expected country main effect (see upper part of Table VII). Format did not make a significant contribution to the model. The model fit appeared to be satisfactory; the residual likelihood ratio chi-squared statistic was 0.11 ($df = 2$, $p = 0.94$), suggesting a good fit to the data. The results indicated that the choice of the experimental product depended primarily on the country of origin of the product. Presentation format did not have much influence on the choice.

Generalized logits were computed for the model. These logits were derived from the log of the ratio of the estimated probabilities of choosing the product to not choosing the product. Thus, with $\pi_{1|ij}$ representing the

Table VII: Maximum likelihood ANOVA results in the logit analysis

Variables	*DF*	*Wald χ^2-value*	*$Pr > \chi^2$*
Shirt:			
Intercept	1	39.58	0.0000
Country	2	20.15	0.0000
Format	1	1.34	0.2475
Likelihood ratio	2	0.11	0.9456
TV set:			
Intercept	1	42.65	0.0000
Country	2	27.75	0.0000
Format	1	0.85	0.3579
Likelihood ratio	2	0.21	0.9019

probability of choosing the product and $\pi_{2|ij}$ representing the probability of not choosing the product, the logit model postulates that:

$$\log\{\pi_{1|ij}/\pi_{2|ij}\} = \alpha + \beta_i^{\text{Country}} + \beta_j^{\text{Format}}$$

where $\pi_{k|ij}$ is the probability of response k, when factor country is at level i and factor format is at level j, so

$$\pi_{1|ij} + \pi_{2|ij} = 1.$$

The generalized logits are exponentiated and reported in odds form. Since in this case interpreting the marginal effect on the odds of an event occurring is tantamount to examining the odds ratio between the odds of each event occurring, a number greater than one implies that the choice of the product is more likely than not choosing the product. The odds emerging out of the results were that Chinese consumers were more likely to choose the shirts labelled as made in the USA and Japan than Korea no matter whether the presentation format was single cue or multiple cue. All the odds ratio were greater than one except in the case of Korea and multiple-cue/physical product. The largest odds ratio was associated with the shirt made in the USA and the single-cue format (4.00). The smallest of the odds ratio was associated with the shirt made in Korea and the multiple-cue format (0.85), indicating a decreased chance of a choice occurring versus not occurring. The shirt made in the USA enjoyed the highest estimated odds of being chosen by the subjects. However, the odds ratios for the Korean made products had an average ratio of close to 1.00, indicating that there was not much difference between the choice and non-choice of the product.

A second logit model was fitted with the data on TV sets. Similar results were obtained. The analyses of variance results are presented in the lower part of Table VII. Again, only country contributed significantly to the model. Assessment of model fit using a maximum likelihood ratio chi-squared statistic indicated a good fit (chi square $= 0.21$, df $= 2$, $p = 0.90$). The estimated odds ratios of choosing the product were subsequently calculated. The largest odds ratio was associated with the Japanese TV set (6.14) with single cue presentation format, substantially higher than those for the shirt. Again, all the US and Japanese products had a ratio larger than one. The odds for choosing a Korean TV set was 0.852 when the subjects examined the TV set. The subjects in the single-cue condition only had a log odds ratio of 1.08. Examination of the predicted probabilities indicated that the probability of not choosing the Korean TV set and that of choosing the same product exhibited little difference (single-cue condition: 0.48 vs. 0.52; multiple-cue condition: 0.54 vs. 0.46).

In summary, the choice data indicated that the product choice was significantly influenced by COO information. Unlike the results on product evaluation and attitude measures, presentation format had little effect on product choice. Therefore, the factors influencing choice behaviours of the subjects appeared to be more parsimonious than those influencing product evaluation and attitudes.

Discussion

This study focused on Chinese consumers' perception of COO images and how such perceptions influenced their product evaluations, attitudes and product choices. In addition, this study also examined the effect of COO in the context of different presentation format and product types. Several results are worth noting.

This study found evidence that COO information influences Chinese consumers' reactions to foreign products. Consistent with studies conducted in Western countries (Bilkey and Nes, 1982; Samiee, 1994), products that enjoy a positive COO image received more positive ratings from the Chinese consumers. Specifically, products from Japan and the USA were preferred to those from South Korea, indicating that COO stereotyping was a factor in the product evaluation process of the Chinese consumers. This result is interesting given the cultural similarity between China and its two neighbours, South Korea and Japan, and the cultural dissimilarity between the USA and Japan. It appeared that COO images influenced Chinese consumers' decision making independent of cultural influences. This is contrary to the arguments by some researchers that similarity in cultural and belief systems may foster a more positive COO image. Given the result that the culturally dissimilar Japan and the USA both enjoyed highly positive COO images in the minds of the Chinese consumers, other factors, such as the perceived degree of economic development, may be more important determinants of their COO images.

Yet, this is not to suggest that COO effect may operate equally across other conditions. Indeed, results from this study indicate that COO effect may be subject to moderation by other factors, such as product type. The impact of COO on Chinese consumers varied with different products. For a more sophisticated electronic product, the COO effect was more salient. Television sets made in Japan and the USA received higher ratings than shirts produced in the same two countries. However, such a product effect was much less salient with Korean made products owing to an overall less positive COO image across both product types. This finding seems to suggest that product type did not matter in the case of poor COO images. In the case of positive COO images, the COO effect was more salient for a more sophisticated product.

The COO effect observed in this study was quite robust in the light of the between-subject design of the study. The findings of this study are consistent with the notion that COO is often used as a surrogate information cue when people process product information and engage in heuristic decision making and stereotyping. Research on stereotyping (Bodenhausen and Wyer, 1985) suggests that when an object belongs to a category whose members typically have judgement-relevant attributes, people may use category membership as a heuristic basis for judgement without considering the object's characteristics. Thus, people who learn that a product originated in a country with a particular COO image may use this information as a basis for evaluation without much consideration of specific product attribute information.

Results of this study also suggest that another factor, presentation format, can potentially moderate the effect of COO image. The single-cue condition was related to a stronger COO effect. Such a stronger cue effect was present for both product types, indicating that the cue effect can be consistent across product classes. When COO is the only information available, buyers may base their evaluative responses on their perception of a typical product produced by that particular country (Lim *et al.*, 1994). Such perceptions may reflect the general stereotype of the source country and may not necessarily reflect the exact quality of the product under consideration. However, the COO effect may be attenuated by the presence of additional product information. This indicates that the presence of a tangible and more credible product information may reduce the need for having to rely on heuristic decision making in product evaluation and attitude formation (Bodenhausen and Wyer, 1985; Johansson *et al.*, 1985).

The COO cue effect can be understood in the context of other COO studies that dealt with the cue function of COO. The extent to which COO image may act as a category membership cue which influences consumer reactions to a particular product may be a function of the amount of other intrinsic cues present in product evaluation. Although this study did not specifically investigate the relationship, the perceived relevance and cogency of such intrinsic cues may very well moderate the effect of COO cues. Intrinsic cues, such as style for fashion goods or technical features for technologically complex products, may play important roles in influencing the magnitude of the extrinsic COO cue effect. Future studies may want to address this issue.

Managerial Implication

The results of this study suggest that consumers in an emerging market and a less developed country are also likely to rely on COO information in their product evaluation and purchasing decision making. Recognizing the income disparity in China, this study offers some managerial implications more meaningful for companies seeking consumers in urban rather than rural areas in China. However, even with this qualification, the size of the urban population in China (over 300 million) is larger than the total population of either the USA or Japan. Although their income level cannot even compare with those of middle-income countries, such as South Korea, their discretionary incomes in purchasing power parity (PPP) terms are rising rapidly, creating a feasible market for a huge variety of products and services. Marketers who are better equipped with knowledge about these consumers may be better able to penetrate such a market with increased chances of success.

Another interesting point emerging from this study is that, despite the per capita income disparity between South Korea and China, Chinese consumers generally exhibited an indifference to Korean made products. Examining their product evaluation and attitude scores indicates that the ratings were at about mid-range on the scales. This finding may have particular implications for Korean companies and, indeed, for companies in other countries that have a less favourable COO image. In their effort to market their products to the Chinese consumers, they may want to stress and build up a stronger brand image for their products instead of relying on or emphasizing the COO image. In view of the cue effect observed in this study, cogent product arguments and persuasive intrinsic cues can lessen the less favourable COO effect.

The findings of this study may shed light on the mentality of urban Chinese consumers about foreign products. Understanding such mentality may help foreign producers to market effectively in China. Although at the current level of income it is still premature to expect an explosive growth in the sales of foreign products, the prospect of a sizeable market for foreign products is becoming more and more realistic. According to a recent United Nations report, the Chinese economy continued to grow at a faster pace than any other nation in the world in 1994 (The United Nations, 1995).

Finally, based on the large COO effect in this study, it appears that the Chinese consumers may be particularly sensitive to COO. This suggests that COO can be a particularly important tool in marketing foreign products to these consumers. Over the past 15 years, more Chinese consumers began to have access to a wider array of consumer products previously unavailable to them. Many of these products are either imported from abroad or produced locally through joint ventures under foreign brand names. Countries enjoying a positive COO image in China certainly are in an advantaged position. For example, US companies may benefit from promotional campaigns highlighting the country of origin of their products since such COO images may signify superior product quality and style to the Chinese consumers.

Limitation and Conclusion

Limitations of this study should be kept in mind. The experimental nature of the study should bring caution to the generalizability of the findings to other settings. However, since the subjects were all actual shoppers in a realistic field setting and the sample was reasonably diverse, the external validity of the study was not unduly jeopardized.

It should be pointed out that only two products were studied. Other products, such as fashion products, may exhibit a COO effect different from those observed in this study. The degree to which products moderate the influence of COO can be different across different products. Therefore, the product effect should be studied across other product types. In addition, the two products chosen for this study were very familiar to the Chinese consumers. Product familiarity may be a factor that can influence the extent to which consumers use COO in their product evaluation and purchase decisions. Future studies may compare the COO effect for products with different degrees of familiarity.

Another limitation of the study is the limited number of countries studied. No European countries were included in this study. The reason for not including European countries was the lack of consumer goods from those countries. Perhaps, as more European consumer products become available in China, it will be feasible to study the COO effects involving such countries.

In conclusion, it is clear that practitioners and researchers alike need to pay more attention to COO images in marketing to the Chinese consumers. Specification of COO effects can enhance the ability to predict consumer reactions to foreign sourced products and help managers to make wiser promotional decisions. The study of COO effects should not be limited to consumers in the developed world only. As the globalization process quickens and more less developed countries join the global market, Western businesses should be prepared to double their effort to enter those emerging markets. Therefore, there is increasingly the need to research and understand consumers in those markets.

References

Bannister, J.P. and Saunders, J.A. (1978), "UK consumers' attitudes towards imports: the measurement of national stereotype image", *European Journal of Marketing*, Vol. 12, No. 8, pp. 562–70.

Baumgartner, G. and Jolibert, A. (1977), "The perception of foreign products in France", in Hunt, K. (Ed.), *Advances in Consumer Research*, Vol. 3, Association for Consumer Research, Ann Arbor, MI, pp. 603–05.

Beckwith, N.E. and Lehmann, D.R. (1975), "The importance of halo effects in multi-attribute attitude models", *Journal of marketing Research*, August, pp. 265–75.

Bettman, J.R. and Kakkar, P. (1977), "Effects of information presentation format on consumer information acquisition strategies", *Journal of Consumer Research*, Vol. 3, March, pp. 233–40.

Bettman, J.R. and Zins, M.A. (1979), "Information format and choice task effects in decision making", *Journal of Consumer Research*, Vol. 6, September, pp. 141–53.

Bilkey, W.J. and Nes, E. (1982), "Country-of-origin effects on product evaluations", *Journal of International Business Studies*, Spring/Summer, Vol. 13, pp. 89–99.

Bodenhausen, G.V. and Wyer, R.S. (1985), "Effects of stereotypes on decision making and information-processing strategies", *Journal of Personality and Social Psychology*, Vol. 48, February, pp. 267–82.

Cattin, P.J., Jolibert, A. and Lohnes, C. (1982), "A cross-cultural study of 'made in' concepts", *Journal of International Business Studies*, Vol. 13, pp. 131–41.

Cordell, V.V. (1988), "Effect of country of origin and other characteristics on product evaluation", doctoral dissertation, University of Houston, TX.

Cordell, V.V. (1992), "Effects of consumer preferences for foreign sourced products", *Journal of International Business Studies*, Vol. 23, No. 2, pp. 251–69.

Darling, J.R. and Kraft, F.B. (1977), "A competitive profile of products and associated marketing practices of selected European and non-European countries", *European Journal of Marketing*, Vol. 11, pp. 521–42.

Erickson, G.M., Johansson, J.K. and Chao, P. (1984), "Image variables in multi-attribute product evaluations: country-of-origin effects", *Journal of Consumer Research*, Vol. 11, September, pp. 694–99.

Fishbein, M. and Ajzen, I. (1975), *Belief, Attitude, Intention and Behavior: An Introduction to Theory and Research*, Addison-Wesley, Reading, MA.

Gaedeke, R. (1973), "Consumer attitudes toward products 'made in' developing countries," *Journal of Retailing*, Vol. 49, Summer, pp. 13–24.

Gerstner, E. (1985), "Do higher prices signal higher quality?", *Journal of Marketing Research*, Vol. 12, May, pp. 209–15.

Han, C.M. (1989), "Country image: halo or summary construct?", *Journal of Marketing Research*, Vol. 26, May, pp. 222–9.

Hofstede, G. (1980), *Culture's Consequences: International Differences in Work-related Values*, Sage, Beverly Hills, CA.

Hofstede, G. (1994), "Management scientists are human", *Management Science*, Vol. 40, No. 1, pp. 4–13.

International Monetary Fund (1994), *International Financial Statistics Yearbook*, International Monetary Fund, Washington, DC.

Jacoby, J., Szybillo, G. and Busato-Schach, J. (1977), "Information acquisition behavior in brand choice situations", *Journal of Consumer Research*, Vol. 3, March, pp. 209–16.

Johansson, J.K., Douglas, S.P. and Nonaka, I. (1985), "Assessing the impact of country of origin on product evaluations: a new methodological perspective", *Journal of Marketing Research*, Vol. 22, November, pp. 388–96.

Kaynak, E. and Cavusgil, S.T. (1983), "Consumer attitudes towards products of foreign origin: do they vary across product classes?", *International Journal of Advertising*, Vol. 2, pp. 147–57.

Khanna, S.R. (1986), "Asian companies and the country stereotyping paradox: an empirical study", *Columbia Journal of World Business*, Vol. 21, Summer, pp. 29–38.

Klein, B. and Leffler, K. B. (1981), "The role of market forces in assuring contractual performance", *Journal of Political Economy*, Vol. 89, No. 4, pp. 615–41.

Lim, J., Darley, W.K. and Summers, J.O. (1994), "An assessment of country of origin effects under alternative presentation formats", *Journal of the Academy of Marketing Science*, Vol. 22, No. 3, pp. 274–82.

Lin, L. and Sternquist, B. (1994), "Taiwanese consumers' perceptions of product information cues: country of origin and store prestige", *European Journal of Marketing*, Vol. 28, pp. 5–18.

Martin, I.M. and Eroglu, S. (1993), "Measuring a multi-dimensional construct: country image", *Journal of Business Research*, Vol. 28, pp. 191–210.

Nagashima, A. (1970), "A comparison of Japanese and US attitudes toward foreign products", *Journal of Marketing*, Vol. 34, January, pp. 68–74.

Narayana, C.L. (1981), "Aggregate images of American and Japanese products: implications on international marketing", *Columbia Journal of World Business,* Vol. 16, Summer, pp. 31–5.

Olson, J. and Jacoby, J. (1972), "Cue utilization in the quality perception process", in Venkatesan, M. (Ed.), *Proceedings of the Third Annual Conference of the Association for Consumer Research,* pp. 167–79.

Osgood, C.E., May, W.H. and Miron, M.S. (1975), *Cross-Cultural Universals of Affective Meaning,* University of Illinois Press, Urbana, IL.

Papadopoulos, N., Heslop, L.A. and Beraces, J. (1990), "National stereotypes and product evaluation in a socialist country", *International Marketing Review,* Vol. 7, pp. 32–47.

Parameswaran, R. and Pisharodi, R.M. (1994), "Facets of country of origin image: an empirical assessment", *Journal of Advertising,* Vol. 23, No. 1, pp. 43–56.

People's Daily (1995), "The steady increase in China's foreign trade", *People's Daily, Overseas Edition,* 16 August, p. 1.

Roth, M.S. and Romeo, J.B. (1992), "Matching product category and country image perceptions: a framework for managing country-of-origin effects", *Journal of International Business Studies,* 3rd quarter, pp. 477–97.

Samiee, S. (1994), "Customer evaluation of products in a global market", *Journal of International Business Studies,* Vol. 25, No. 3, pp. 579–604.

Schooler, R.D. (1965), "Product bias in the central American common market", *Journal of Marketing Research,* November, pp. 394–7.

Shapiro, C. (1982), "Consumer information, product quality, and seller reputation", *Bell Journal of Economics,* Vol. 13, No. 1, Spring, pp. 20–35.

Tongberg, R.C. (1972), "An empirical study of relationships between dogmatism and consumer attitudes toward foreign products", doctoral dissertation, Pennsylvania State University, PA.

Triandis, H.C. (1989), "The self and social behavior in differing cultural contexts", *Psychological Review,* Vol. 96, No. 3, pp. 506–20.

Triandis, H.C. (1990), "Cross-cultural studies of individualism and collectivism", in Berman, J. (Ed.), *Nebraska Symposium on Motivation,* University of Nebraska Press, Lincoln, NB.

The United Nations, *The 1995 World Economic and Social Report,* The United Nations, New York, NY.

Wall, M. and Heslop, L.A. (1986), "Consumer attitudes toward Canadian-made vs. imported products", *Journal of the Academy of Marketing Science,* Vol. 14, Summer, pp. 27–36.

Wall, M., Heslop, L.A. and Hofstra, G. (1988), "Male and female viewpoints of countries as producers of consumer goods", *Journal of International Consumer Marketing,* Vol. 1, pp. 1–25.

Wang, C. and Lamb C.W. Jr (1983), "Foreign environmental factors influencing American consumers' predisposition toward European products", *Journal of the Academy of Marketing Science,* Vol. 8, Fall, pp. 345–56.

White, P.D. (1979), "Attitude of US purchasing managers toward industrial products manufactured in selected Western European nations", *Journal of International Business Studies,* Vol. 10, Spring/Summer, pp. 81–90.

Yaprak, A. (1978), "Formulating a multinational marketing strategy: a deductive cross-national consumer behavior model", PhD dissertation, Georgia State University, GA.

Yevas, B. and Alpay, G. (1986), "Does an exporting nation enjoy the same cross-national commercial image?" *International Journal of Advertising,* Vol. 2, pp. 109–19.

Zajonc, R.B. (1980), "Feeling and thinking: references need no inferences", *American Psychologist,* February, pp. 151–75.

2

Emerging Lifestyles in China and Consequences for Perception of Advertising, Buying Behaviour and Consumption Preferences

Ran Wei

Introduction

Western countries have experienced a proliferation of various lifestyles in the past few decades (Johansson, 1994; Sobel, 1983). Lifestyle theorists argue that when a society accumulates sufficient capital to generate enough leisure time for many people, alternative standards of value and lifestyle become a feature of society (Bell, 1976; Blumer, 1969; Johansson & Miegel, 1992; Lewis, 1973; Zablocki & Kanter, 1976). Given the rapidly improving living standards and the return to 'class values' (O'Neil, 1997) in reformed China, will a variety of lifestyles emerge? If so, what form will they be? And what are the consequences of emerging lifestyles for marketing and advertising?

This study represents an attempt to establish and elaborate the possible formations of lifestyle in Chinese consumers. It will then explore the linkages between lifestyle segments and consumer behaviour, including the perception of advertising. Specifically, this study raises two central research questions: (1) What are the possible formations of lifestyle in contemporary China? (2) Are there any significant differences among lifestyle segments in perceiving advertising, buying behaviour and preferences for consumption of all things Chinese *vis-a-vis* Western products?

Source: *International Journal of Advertising*, 16(4) (1997): 261–275.

The emergence of different lifestyles in reformed China is closely intertwined with the country's momentous economic reform since the early 1990s. More importantly, the creation of lifestyles through differentation of classes and status groups will attest to a rising consumer society in China. At the same time, the growth of different lifestyle groups provides a rare opportunity to witness and study the process of modernization and individualization in Chinese consumers. Thus, research on consumer lifestyles in a Chinese context carries theoretical importance.

In fact, studies on the forming of various lifestyles in China are overdue, for such studies can provide a valuable approach to segment this new and huge market of 1.2 billion. Target marketing strategies can be tested based on the differentiation of lifestyle segments. Products can be better positioned to meet the needs of different segments and groups. Moreover, the identification and classification of consumers according to their lifestyles will help to make advertising in China more effective. Different creative strategies can be developed based on the understanding of various consumer segments.

Literature Review and Conceptual Framework

The concept of lifestyle originates from market research into consumer behaviour (Mitchell, 1983; Pitts & Woodside, 1984; Plummer, 1974; Wells, 1974). The study of lifestyles became more meaningful in the early 1970s when the reduced costs of multivariate analysis enabled the classification of consumers by psychographic dimensions to be added to traditional demographic and behavioural data. This improved market researchers' ability to identify the broad trends (for example, trait aspects of consumers and lifestyle characteristics) that influence how consumers live, work and play (Anderson & Golden, 1984; Moven, 1990; Settle & Alreck, 1989; Williams, 1981).

Defined briefly, lifestyle is about 'how people live, how they spend their money, and how they allocate their time' (Cosmas, 1982; Hawkins *et al.*, 1983) as well as 'patterned activities' of consumers (Pingree & Hawkins, 1994). Zablocki and Kanter (1976) further define lifestyle in terms of 'shared preferences or tastes, where the people sharing a lifestyle as collectivity that otherwise lacks social and cultural identity'. One of the most influential studies in lifestyle research is Arnold Mitchell's book *The Nine American Lifestyles* (1983). Based on Maslow's (1968) hierarchy of needs, Mitchell distinguishes between three categories of lifestyles: need-driven, outer-oriented and inner-oriented.

The psychographic research on consumer lifestyles assumes that individuals' traits and characteristics, namely attitudes, beliefs, habits and behaviour, are enduring and complex; that is, we need to identify patterned activities in which individuals are grouped in multi-dimensional spaces. As Pingree and Hawkins (1994) put it, attitudes, values, behaviour and demographics of consumers need to be measured as they 'co-occur' in groups of interrelated variables.

The 'Activities, Interests, and Opinions' (AIOs) inventory items (Cosmas, 1982; Plummer, 1974; Uusitalo, 1979; Valette-Florence & Jolibert, 1990; Williams, 1981) have been most widely used in constructing an integrated theory of lifestyle by focusing on consumers' values, views, attitudes and activities. 'Interests' items concern the consumers' preferences for job, recreation, fashion and food among other things; 'opinions' questions measure views and feelings on things such as local, world, economic and social affairs; and 'activities' measures are concerned with consumption behaviour of individuals: what they buy, what they do, how they spend their time. Demographic information, the most basic and fundamental characteristics of consumers, is often included in identifying consumer segments or target markets. In this way, a target group or market segment, which is similar enough to one another on a set of AIOs criteria but different enough from other groups or clusters of people, can be identified. Market segments have high value for developing advertising and marketing strategy (Fletcher & Bowers, 1991).

This study intends to expand previous lifestyle research in a Chinese context, in which consumers have increasing freedom in choices coupled with increasing disposable income. The AIOs framework of analysis will guide the present study to explore patterns of lifestyle in Chinese consumers.

Methodology

Sample and Sampling Procedures

The data for this study were based on three parallel consumer surveys conducted in the three most important markets in China: Beijing, Shanghai and Guangzhou in 1995. The surveys relied on random samples using multi-stage stratified cluster sampling procedures; that is, city districts were drawn at the first stage, followed by residential committees. Households were drawn at the final stage. Such demographic variables as age and sex were used as control in finalizing the samples.

The size of the three samples from Beijing, Shanghai and Guangzhou was comparable, targeting urban residents aged between 12 and 60. Respondents sampled from Beijing were interviewed by trained interviewers face to face. Among the 1024 questionnaires distributed in Beijing, 1005 were collected with a response rate of 98.1 per cent. The surveys in Shanghai and Guangzhou were self-administered. A total of 1010 questionnaires were sent out in Shanghai and 998 were completed, producing a response rate of 98.8 per cent. The total of successfully completed questionnaires in Guangzhou was 950 out of 1010. The response rate was also high at 94.1 per cent. Altogether, the final sample size was 2953. At the 95 per cent confidence interval, the sum of sampling errors was plus or minus 4 per cent (for more details, refer to *IMI Consumer Surveys*, 1996).

Profiles of the Sample

The sample for the present study was quite evenly distributed in the three metro cities. One-third came from Beijing (34 per cent). The remaining two-thirds were from Shanghai (33.8 per cent) and Guangzhou (32.2 per cent). The sample was 52.7 per cent male and 47.3 per cent female, ranging in age from 12 to 59 (M = 34.5, SD = 12.15). Thirty-five per cent of respondents were married. In terms of education, no more than 5 per cent finished primary school or less; 11.6 per cent completed higher education. The majority finished at high school (43 per cent). Blue-collar workers were 26.1 per cent; professionals were 18.5 per cent, and government employees were 7 per cent. Service workers, joint-venture employees, teachers/researchers, self-employed, unemployed and students made up the remaining 48.3 per cent. For monthly average income, the distribution ranged widely from zero to a maximum of $8000 (Renminbi Yuan) (M = $504). About 36.4 per cent reported an average income of less than $500, 42.6 per cent between $501 and $1000, and 20.9 per cent more than $1000. More than 40 per cent spent less than $300 on daily living every month, 31.1 per cent spent between $301 and $500, and 26.2 per cent spent more than $500 (see Table 1).

Table 1: Profile of the sample from the three metro cities in China

Region	Beijing	34.0%
	Shanghai	33.8%
	Guangzhou	32.2%
Age	12 to 29	33.7%
	30 to 40	34.1%
	41 to 59	32.3%
Gender	Men	52.7%
	Women	47.3%
Education	Below high school	32.5%
	High school	42.9%
	Above high school	24.6%
Marital status	Single	34.8%
	Married	65.2%
Occupation	Workers	26.1%
	Professionals	18.5%
	Government employees	7.0%
	Service workers	8.7%
	Joint-venture employees	7.7%
	Teachers/researchers	12.7%
	Self-employed	2.7%
	Unemployed	11.9%
	Students	3.9%
Monthly average income	$500 and less	36.4%
	$501 to $1000	42.6%
	$1001 and more	20.9%
Monthly average expenditure	$300 and less	42.7%
	$301 to $500	31.1%
	$501 and more	26.2%

Note: N ranges from 2953 to 2914.

Measures of Lifestyles, Consumption and Attitude towards Advertising

A wide range of inventories and questionnaires were checked in constructing the questionnaire for the 1995 *IMI Consumer Surveys*. The sources included the US AIOs inventories (e.g. Cosmas, 1982; Plummer, 1974; Wells, 1974) and those market surveys completed in Taiwan. Specifically, the AIOs inventories covered buying behaviour, shopping habits, entertainment sought and participation in social and community events. Items totalled fifty-two. The interest items included fashion, food, money and job. The opinion items were those about respondents themselves, on social issues, on products and brands, and on the future, among other things. The total was 132 items on a 5-point Likert scale, including those gauging respondents' perception of advertising.

Analyses and Results

To answer the two research questions, this study used a three-step procedure for statistical analysis. In the first step, a Principle Components Factor Analysis with Varimax Rotation was applied to determine the possible lifestyle dimensions. The second step clustered the respondents on the basis of the factor scores obtained from the earlier step. The purpose of cluster analysis was to sort them into segments that shared a similar lifestyle. In the final step, discriminant analysis was performed to seek profiling of the cluster centres which represented different lifestyle segments.

Factor Analysis of Lifestyle Indicators

Out of a total of thirty items, a six-factor solution emerged (eigenvalues greater than 1.0). It had twenty-four items with a total variance explained of 44.3 per cent. Six items with a communality less than 0.30 were eliminated. Table 2 shows the emerging lifestyle dimensions with factor loadings.

The first factor consisted of six items that were concerned with pursuing fashions as well as a trendy and stylistic living. This factor has been labelled 'Fashionables and sophisticates'. It is the strongest factor of the solution, explaining 13.5 per cent of variance. The second factor, which was labelled 'Restrained and routines', was made up of three items that dealt with what role schedules, plans and diet played in respondents' lives. This factor captured the extent to which schedules and routines were central. The second factor accounted for 10.2 per cent of variance explained.

The third factor had four items concerning the strong desire for making efforts to increase social mobility with accomplishments. It was named

Table 2: Factor analysis of lifestyle indicators

Statements	*Factor 1*	*Factor 2*	*Factor 3*	*Factor 4*	*Factor 5*	*Factor 6*
Fashionables & sophisticates						
1. I'm fashionable in the eyes of others.	0.69	0.03	−0.06	−0.16	0.16	−0.09
2. I dress up to show off my personality.	0.68	0.10	0.00	0.04	0.08	0.03
3. I enjoy having new and fashionable things.	0.65	−0.10	0.04	0.00	0.13	0.04
4. I pay close attention to trends in fashion.	0.64	−0.01	0.04	0.06	0.04	0.01
5. A fancy and distinctive living attracts me.	0.58	0.16	0.12	0.23	0.02	−0.03
6. I enjoy stylistic dresses.	0.50	0.05	0.22	0.06	−0.07	0.08
Restrained & routines						
1. My life centres around schedules.	−0.06	0.73	−0.00	0.09	0.04	−0.07
2. I'm watchful of my diet.	0.07	0.70	0.07	0.02	−0.02	−0.01
3. Planning is my habit of doing things.	−0.05	0.55	0.25	0.10	0.28	0.10
Socially mobiles & life expansionists						
1. Life is meant to take on challenges and risk.	0.14	−0.09	0.65	0.03	0.08	0.08
2. I'll take some courses to brighten my future.	0.07	0.12	0.65	−0.00	−0.02	−0.06
3. Doing nothing will make me uncomfortable.	0.14	0.05	0.56	0.09	0.15	−0.06
4. I have high hopes about what I can accomplish.	0.07	0.11	0.50	0.01	0.15	0.21
Content with status quo						
1. A living space of my own will make me happy.	0.04	−0.01	0.12	0.64	0.06	−0.04
2. I prefer to do nothing but relax during holidays.	0.14	0.02	0.10	0.64	0.02	−0.12
3. Economic security is primarily important to me.	−0.02	0.25	0.24	0.50	0.05	0.37
4. Jobs should not be changed easily if they are OK.	−0.03	0.09	−0.17	0.49	0.14	0.10
5. I prefer stable and secure jobs.*	−0.09	0.40	−0.10	0.42	−0.11	0.15
Social actives & influencers						
1. I can mingle with strangers easily.	0.01	−0.07	−0.03	0.10	0.64	−0.04
2. I'm active at social functions.	0.21	0.03	0.21	0.02	0.63	−0.10
3. Hesitation is not my style in doing things.	0.01	0.28	0.10	0.04	0.58	0.21
4. I have a lot of influence over my friends.	0.27	−0.00	0.14	0.10	0.46	−0.01
Money-conscious						
1. I'd rather work for money than resting.	0.09	−0.16	−0.04	−0.12	0.07	0.80
2. I check my balances periodically.	−0.02	0.24	0.18	0.26	−0.11	0.47
Eigenvalue	3.25	2.45	1.45	1.28	1.14	1.06
Variance explained	13.5%	10.2%	6.1%	5.3%	4.7%	4.5%

Notes: The scale was: 1 = Strongly disagree; 2 = Disagree; 3 = Neutral; 4 = Agree; 5 = Strongly agree.
*Item with cross loadings. (N = 1595).

'Socially mobiles and life expansionists'. The fourth factor consisted of five content-with-the-status quo items. This particular factor captured the tendency of being easily satisfied with life, the predominance of stability and strong resistance to change. It was labelled 'Content with status quo'. The third and fourth factors explained 6.1 per cent and 5.3 per cent of variance respectively. The fifth factor was labelled 'Social actives and influencers' and included four items that indicated respondents' active participation in social events and the amount of perceived influence on others in society. The sixth factor was formed by two items that highlighted the concern for cash flow and the obsession with making money. It was thus labelled 'Money conscious'. The last two factors accounted for 4.7 per cent and 4.5 per cent of variance explained respectively.

In summary, the factor analysis elaborated the emerging different lifestyles in China (the sample size decreased because of missing cases, but it was still large enough, N = 1595, to allow valid factor analysis). Although the indicators are not completely identical, the lifestyles obtained in this study resemble some of the lifestyle categories or typologies developed by Mitchell (1983) and Cosmas (1982). For instance, the 'Restrained and routines' and 'Money-conscious' lifestyles are similar to the need-driven categories of 'Survivors and sustainers' in the Mitchell study. 'Fashionables and sophisticates', 'Socially mobiles and life expansionists' are similar to the 'Mobiles', 'Sophisticates' and 'Life expansionists' lifestyle groups in the Cosmas study.

Cluster Analysis of Lifestyle Dimensions

Cluster analysis was performed next in order to group respondents into lifestyle segments. In this way, homogeneous groups or clusters of respondents who were relatively homogeneous within a cluster centre while heterogeneous to other cluster centres could be identified. Specifically, factors scores on the six lifestyles were entered into a cluster analysis. Because of the large number of respondents, it was not possible to apply hierarchical clusters. Instead, K-Means cluster analysis was used (McRae, 1971). Cluster solutions for four, five and six clusters were compared in selecting the 'best' cluster solution. In doing so, the considerations were based on two criteria: (1) How well did each factor cluster the sample? (2) How interpretable was the cluster solution?

In the initial four-cluster solution, scores on the cluster centres from Factor 2, 'Restrained and routines' and Factor 6, 'Money-conscious' were low. The clustering of lifestyle segments thus mainly came from the other four lifestyles. The six-cluster solution improved the four-cluster solution. All the six factors scored high on the six cluster centres. However, Factor 1, 'Fashionables and sophisticates' scored high on more than three cluster centres, making it difficult to interpret the solution. The five-cluster solution was therefore accepted. It had four similarly sized clusters. Each of the six factors had shown some clustering power, and the solution was much more interpretable. The cluster scores for the five cluster centres are given in Table 3.

The first cluster consisted of 246 respondents who scored high on 'Restrained and routines', 'Socially mobiles and life expansionists' and 'Fashionables and sophisticates'. They scored low on 'Social actives and influencers' and 'Content with status quo'. These respondents were labelled 'Traditionalists' because they strongly agree that life revolves around restraints and routines. They also appeared to disapprove of climbing up the social ladder and experiencing a fashionable and sophisticated lifestyle. The second cluster was made up of 295 respondents whose scores were high on 'Social actives

Table 3: Cluster centres scores on the six lifestyles

	Cluster 1	*Cluster 2*	*Cluster 3*	*Cluster 4*	*Cluster 5*
	Traditionalists (n = 246)	*Status quo (n = 295)*	*Modern (n = 340)*	*Transitioners (n = 382)*	*Generation xers (n = 334)*
Fashionables & sophisticates	−0.48	−0.74	0.82	0.16	0.38
Restrained & routines	0.79	−0.32	0.34	−0.22	−0.91
Socially mobiles & life expansionists	−0.59	0.26	0.58	−0.16	−0.18
Content with status quo	0.17	0.38	0.29	−1.56	0.51
Social actives & influencers	0.12	−1.04	0.48	−0.17	0.33
Money-conscious	−0.20	0.33	0.63	−0.00	−0.82

and influencers' and 'Fashionables and sophisticates', and low on the other four lifestyles. This group clearly indicates a segment in its own right. They were called 'status quo' people, for they tend to be socially inactive, do not take charge, and have little influence on others. A fancy and distinctive lifestyle is not desirable to them either.

The third cluster had 340 respondents who gave relatively high rankings to 'Fashionables and sophisticates', 'Money-conscious', and 'Socially mobiles and life expansionists'. This group bore little resemblance to the traditionalists and status quo segments. Thus, it was labelled 'Modern'. They wish to follow fashions and to pursue a fancy and distinctive lifestyle. At the same time, they are obsessed with making money to expand life upwards. The fourth cluster consisted of 382 respondents, the largest group. These 382 respondents scored highest on the 'Content with the status quo' lifestyle. Their scores on other lifestyles were very low. This group was called 'Transitioners' because they demonstrate discontent with the status quo. The desire for change characterized this segment. The last cluster was made up of 334 respondents whose scores were highest on 'Restrained and routines' and 'Money-conscious'. Scores of this group on other lifestyles were lower, particularly on 'Socially mobiles and life expansionists'. 'Generation X' was the label given to this group, because they are not oriented towards restraints and routines, and not money-conscious. Subsequent analyses reveal this to be the youngest segment as well as the most well educated compared to the other four segments (see Table 4).

Analysis of variance (ANOVA) was performed between the five segments to explore their differences in demographic characteristics. The results, as shown in Table 4, indicate a significant difference in age ($p < 0.001$). Generation X is the youngest, while transitioners, modern and status quo consumers are increasingly older. Traditionalists turned out to be the oldest. The level of education among the five segments is highest for generation Xers, followed by the modern segment. The other three segments are more or less equally lower in education attainment ($p < 0.06$). In terms of monthly average income and expenditure, it seems that the modern segment is the

Table 4: Demographic characteristics of the five lifestyle segments (ANOVA)

	Age	*Education*	*Income*	*Expenditure*
Total	1.99	1.93	1.85	1.83
Traditionalists	2.16	1.89	1.80	1.78
Status quo	2.09	1.89	1.83	1.76
Modern	1.92	1.97	1.91	2.00
Transitioners	1.89	1.89	1.82	1.78
Generation Xers	1.79	2.03	1.86	1.86
F	11.62	2.31	1.06	4.65
Significance	$p < 0.001$	$p < 0.06$	p = n.s.	$p < 0.01$

Age categories: 1 = 12–29; 2 = 30–40; 3 = 41–59.
Education categories: 1 = Below high school; 2 = High school; 3 = Above high school.
Monthly income categories: 1 = $500 and less; 2 = $501–$1000; 3 = $1001 and more.
Monthly expenditure categories: 1 = $300 and less; 2 = $301–$500; 3 = $501 and more.

most affluent, while the traditionalist segment is the least affluent. Not surprisingly, the modern group shows the highest spending and buying power ($p < 0.01$) among the five segments. The buying power of generation X is the second highest, also above the mean. The status quo segment shows the lowest spending, well below the mean.

In sum, demographically, the traditionalists are marked by old age, poor education and poverty. Thus they tend to be old-fashioned, and resistant to change psychographically. The status quo group shares marked demographic characteristics with the traditionalists. However, they differ psychographically from the traditionalists in that they are younger, and have not reached a stage where life revolves around traditions and old-fashioned routines. Transitioners differ little in education attainment and income from the traditionalist and status quo segments. They rather differ significantly in psychographic directions from them, because they are much younger and eager to change the status quo. This segment is highly ambitious. Consumers belonging to this segment strive to get ahead through self-improvement. Since this is a group in transition, Transitioners may stay in this segment for only a short time.

The modern segment moves in another different psychographic direction. Being the most affluent, well educated and probably having a professional job, they are interested in leading a visible and materialistic life. This segment may be the core of the emerging middle class in China. Generation X, on the other hand, consists of those who were born after the Cultural Revolution. Some of them are the single child in the family. Though many are still completing their education, their education level is the highest among the five segments. Psychographically, generation Xers are marked by disrespect for routines and tradition and evince little worry about money. Finally, they are more likely to be hedonistic. To a large extent, these demographic differences validify the segmentation of surveyed respondents into different lifestyles through cluster analysis.

Multivariate Discriminant Analysis of Lifestyle Segments

In the final step, discriminant analyses were employed to establish profiles of the five lifestyle segments. The criterion variables included perception of advertising, buying behaviour, and preferences for consumption of Western products *vis-a-vis* all things Chinese (the ratio between sample size and the number of variables for discriminant analysis is about 20:1, thus discriminant analysis was justified; see Stevens, 1996). The expectation is that respondents who belong to different segments should also differ in those aspects in addition to the marked demographic differences. Discriminant analysis would seem appropriate to analyse the potential differences in viewing advertising, buying and consumption patterns simultaneously. Exploring multivariate patterns of group differences among segments is superior to testing group differences on a single variable at a time (Huberty, 1984, 1994; Stevens, 1996).

Perception of Advertising

Table 5a presents the result of the first discriminant analysis of the five lifestyle segments on their perception of advertising. A total of seven attitudinal variables on advertising were entered as predictors following initial single-variable ANOVA tests. A stepwise procedure of discriminant analysis was used to eliminate those variables without satisfactory discriminating power. This procedure locates the variable that best discriminates among the segments, finds the next best discriminator, and so on, making the five lifestyle segments as distinctive as possible. Four out of the seven discriminant variables showed sufficient discriminating power.

Of the four possible functions that could discriminate among the five segments, only two functions are statistically significant (Wilks's lambda = 0.97 and 0.99, $p < 0.001$). Table 5a describes each function with standardized canonical coefficients (similar to beta weights in multiple regression analysis). It seems that the first significant function is primarily a function of perception of trust in advertising and evaluation of advertising content, to a lesser extent, of trust in advertised brands. High values of Function 1 are associated with a negative view of having trust in advertising and criticism of advertising content, but holding a positive view towards advertised brands. Thus, it can be described as 'practical' (negative about advertising in general but positive about benefits of advertising). It explains the largest proportion of the total variance (59.5 per cent).

High values of the second significant function, on the other hand, are associated with both positive views of advertising in general and advertised

Table 5a: Summary of discriminant function analysis of the five cluster centres on perception of advertising

Statements	*Function 1*	*Function 2*	*Function 3*	*Function 4*
Advertising can be trusted.	−0.61 (−0.53)	0.82 (0.75)	0.22 (0.11)	0.13 (0.38)
Advertised brands are trustworthy.	0.54 (0.35)	0.63 (0.46)	0.02 (0.02)	−0.69 (−0.75)
Good products need no advertising.	0.47 (0.46)	0.06 (0.03)	0.80 (0.85)	0.38 (0.28)
Ads are filled with recycled ideas.	0.58 (0.47)	0.26 (0.37)	−0.52 (−0.58)	0.56 (0.57)
Eigenvalue	0.05	0.02	0.01	0.00
Variance explained	59.5%	24.7%	14.9%	0.1%
Canonical correlation	0.22	0.15	0.11	0.03
Degrees of freedom	9	4	1	–
Wilks's lambda	0.97	0.99	0.99	–
Significance	$p < 0.001$	$p < 0.001$	p = n.s.	p = n.s.

Note: Variables are ordered based on their function loadings. Standardized discriminant function coefficients and structure coefficients (in parentheses) are reported.
Scale: 1 = Strongly disagree; 2 = Disagree; 3 = Neutral; 4 = Agree; 5 = Strongly agree.

Table 5b: Canonical discriminant function centroids of the five lifestyle segments

	Function 1	*Function 2*	*Function 3*	*Function 4*
Traditionalists	0.12	−0.07	0.12	−0.03
Status quo	0.19	−0.19	−0.11	0.02
Modern	0.14	0.21	0.08	0.03
Transitioners	−0.46	−0.07	0.05	0.02
Generation Xers	−0.08	0.14	−0.18	−0.03

Note: Entries are standard scores.

brands in particular. Thus it is likened to 'positive', accounting for 24.7 per cent of variance. High values of Function 3 are positively associated with 'no need to advertise', and negatively with 'ads are filled with recycled ideas'. This particular function, though not significant, can still be characterized as 'negative'.

The mean for each lifestyle segment (group centroids) on each function is shown in Table 5b. The first significant function (practical) discriminates between the transitioners and the other four segments. The implication is that the status quo, traditionalist and modern segments hold a practical view of advertising, while the view of transitioners, and to a lesser extent, generation Xers, is less practical. Function 2 (positive) discriminates mainly the modern, status quo and generation X segments. Such a result indicates that respondents pursuing a modern lifestyle and those belonging to generation X have a favourable attitude towards advertising. In comparison, the status quo segment shows the least favourable attitude about advertising. Although not statistically significant, Function 3 (negative) suggests more differences in perceiving advertising among the five segments. Generation Xers seem to be the least negative about advertising, while the traditionalist segment has the most negative perception of advertising. Such interpretations, however, should be read with caution.

Summary

The directional differences in perceiving advertising of each lifestyle segment can be summarized as follows based on a discriminant plane. The modern segment is the least critical of advertising, for it scores the highest on the 'positive' function and second highest on the 'practical' function. Generation X is similar to the modern segment in holding a positive view of advertising, but it tends to be somewhat critical of advertising content.

The status quo and traditionalist segments share similar characteristics, but show differences to the other three segments. They do not particularly dislike advertising content, but they disapprove of advertising in general. It is interesting to note that the transitioner segment differs from all the other four segments in perceiving advertising. This segment is unfavourable about advertising in general, and sees the least benefit of advertising. Therefore, it reveals its own view. Such results indicate that views on advertising are not necessarily positive across Chinese consumers, as Pollay *et al.* (1990) suggested, but a function of various lifestyles.

Buying Behaviour and Preferences for Consumption

Following similar procedures, the five segments were analysed for differences in buying behaviour and preferences for consumption. A battery of twenty-one shopping and consumption measures, which survived the ANOVA test, were entered for discriminant analysis. These measures concerned various buying activities, such as bargain hunting, shopping for quality and fancy products as well as preferences for a Western lifestyle and products *vis-a-vis* all things Chinese. Table 6a reports the result (nine variables that made no contribution to the discriminant functions in subsequent analysis were eliminated).

Although five segments produced four functions, only Function 1 and Function 2 are significant (Wilks's lambda $= 0.81$ and 0.95, $p < 0.001$). The first significant function seems to represent free spending and a preference for a Western lifestyle. The high values of Function 1 are correlated with buying fancy and stylistic products, frequent visits to night markets, and picky shopping behaviour. At the same time, aspirations to a Western lifestyle are a factor of significant importance in this function. It can be described as 'free-spending and Western-oriented', explaining the largest proportion of the total variance (49.9 per cent). High values of the second significant function, on the other hand, are correlated with preference for Chinese food and shying away from Western fast food such as McDonald's. Moreover, concerns for saving and careful shopping behaviour are correlated to this function. Thus, Function 2 is characterized as 'thrifty and Chinese-oriented'. It accounts for 39.1 per cent of variance.

Table 6b shows the mean for each lifestyle segment (group centroids) on each function. The first function (free-spending and Western-oriented)

Table 6a: Summary of discriminant function analysis of the five cluster centres on buying behaviour and preferences for consumption

Statements	*Function 1*	*Function 2*	*Function 3*	*Function 4*
I enjoy buying stylistic products.	0.28 (0.48)	−0.05 (−0.05)	0.13 (0.07)	0.03 (0.06)
I prefer to buy quality and costly products.	0.43 (0.62)	0.45 (0.44)	−0.21 (−0.14)	0.13 (0.04)
It's worthwhile to spend on vacations.	0.29 (0.46)	−0.20 (−0.21)	0.13 (0.11)	−0.41 (−0.40)
I care about the atmosphere of stores.	0.28 (0.48)	−0.12 (−0.11)	−0.07 (−0.04)	0.08 (0.04)
I read packing information with care.	0.10 (0.28)	0.20 (0.30)	0.34 (0.28)	0.16 (0.10)
Price is my primary consideration in buying.	0.21 (0.14)	0.23 (0.31)	−0.08 (−0.04)	0.24 (0.21)
I enjoy shopping at night markets.	0.31 (0.42)	−0.15 (−0.27)	−0.07 (−0.01)	0.11 (0.16)
I charge a lot of purchases to my credit cards.	0.05 (0.14)	−0.23 (−0.28)	0.39 (0.49)	−0.57 (−0.45)
The Western lifestyle is desirable to me.	0.23 (0.34)	−0.19 (−0.30)	0.03 (−0.05)	−0.14 (−0.11)
I often eat at McDonald's.	0.12 (0.26)	−0.35 (−0.52)	0.10 (0.11)	0.63 (0.52)
I enjoy Chinese operas.	−0.03 (−0.14)	0.20 (0.21)	0.80 (0.81)	0.29 (0.23)
I prefer to eat Chinese food to Western.	0.11 (0.23)	0.41 (0.55)	0.03 (0.02)	−0.29 (−0.29)
Eigenvalue	0.22	0.18	0.04	0.01
Variance explained	49.9%	39.1%	9.3%	1.8%
Canonical correlation	0.43	0.39	0.20	0.09
Degrees of freedom	33	20	9	–
Wilks's lambda	0.81	0.95	0.99	–
Significance	$p < 0.001$	$p < 0.001$	p = n.s.	p = n.s.

Note: Variables are ordered based on their function loadings. Standardized discriminant function coefficients and structure coefficients (in parentheses) are reported. Scale: 1 = Strongly disagree; 2 = Disagree; 3 = Neutral; 4 = Agree; 5 = Strongly agree.

Table 6b: Canonical discriminant function centroids of the five lifestyle segments

	Function 1	*Function 2*	*Function 3*	*Function 4*
Traditionalists	−0.25	0.42	0.18	0.09
Status quo	−0.22	0.38	−0.31	−0.07
Modern	0.82	0.04	0.12	−0.07
Transitioners	−0.57	−0.55	0.15	−0.09
Generation Xers	0.20	−0.51	−0.20	0.12

Note: Entries are standard scores.

largely discriminates between the modern and transitioner segments and the remaining three segments. The interpretation is that the modern segment is high on spending freely and desiring a Western lifestyle. The transitioners are the least in free-spending with the least preference for a lifestyle modelled after the West. Function 2 (thrifty and Chinese-oriented) discriminates mainly the transitioner, generation X and traditionalist segments. Such a result demonstrates that respondents pursuing an old-fashioned and traditional lifestyle care about saving and prefer Chinese products and culture. In contrast, transitioners and generation Xers show less concern for saving in shopping and less preference for things Chinese.

Summary

Characteristics of each consumer segment with distinctive lifestyles can be summarized in a discriminant plane. The key discriminants for the modern consumers are 'big spenders' on the finer things in life to reflect their status and success, and the strongest desire for a Western lifestyle. At the same time, they care about getting their money's worth and have no objection to Chinese products. Generation X is the second highest on the 'free-spending and Western-oriented' function, coupled with little concern for saving as well as avoiding Chinese products. The traditionalist and status quo segments share similar characteristics: both avoid spending freely in shopping and do not desire a Western lifestyle. Moreover, they share the desire to save and favour all things Chinese. The transitioner segment is dissimilar to the other four segments. Transitioners tend to avoid spending freely, but saving is not a primary consideration. At the same time, they favour neither a Western lifestyle nor things Chinese. They thus reflect a typical lifestyle that is in transition.

Conclusions and Discussion

The findings of this study strongly support a conclusion that various lifestyles have emerged in reformed China. Chinese consumers, at least those from metro areas, have grown into different lifestyle segments. This study has empirically established and elaborated five major lifestyle segments based on measures of AIOs indicators: traditionalists, status quo, modern, transitioners and generation Xers. Each segment is homogeneous within itself, but heterogeneous compared to others.

Furthermore, this study found some important differences among the five segments with directional psychographic differences concerning advertising, buying behaviour and preferences for consumption. Traditionalist and status quo consumers disapprove of advertising in general, strive to save and prefer all things Chinese. The modern and generation X segments view advertising more positively than any other segment, spend freely and favour a Western lifestyle. Transitioners differ from the others, reflecting a transitional lifestyle. Thus, the emergence and growth of various lifestyles in contemporary China do have far-reaching consequences for how advertising is viewed, consumption patterns and preferences for Western versus Chinese products.

To conclude, this study provides empirical support for the advent of a consumer society in post-Mao China. China's ambitious modernization drive has led to the rise of different classes and status groups of consumers. More importantly, the results of this study shed some light on how to approach Chinese consumers beyond demographics, to psychographics. Western products and fashions should target those consumers pursuing a modern lifestyle and generation Xers and to a lesser extent, transitioners, who are willing to spend, are favourable towards a Western lifestyle and more receptive to advertising.

This study has established and elaborated five differentiated lifestyle segments. However, it is by no means exhaustive (the number of missing cases may somewhat affect the findings). Furthermore, the sample used for analysis was drawn from the metro areas of China, and the generalizability of the results remains to be tested. Future research, therefore, can expand the present study by attempting a nationwide sample and further refine the lifestyle categories in a Chinese context.

References

Anderson, T. and Golden, L. (1984) Lifestyles and psychographics: a critical review and recommendation. In *Advances in Consumer Research* XI (ed.) Kinnear, T., pp. 405–411. Ann Arbor: Association for Consumer Research.

Bell, D. (1976) *The Coming of Post-Industrial Society*. New York: Basic Books.

Blumer, H. (1969) Fashion: from class differentiation to collective selection. *Sociological Quarterly* **3**, 275–291.

Cosmas, S. (1982) Life styles and consumption patterns. *Journal of Consumer Research* **8**, 453–455.

Fletcher, A. and Bowers, T. (1991) *Fundamentals of Advertising Research*, 4th edn. Belmont, CA: Wadsworth.

Hawkins, D., Best, R. and Coney, K. (1983) *Consumer Behaviour: Implications for Marketing Strategy*. Plano, TX: Business Publications.

Huberty, C. (1984) Issues in the use and interpretation of discriminant analysis, *Psychological Bulletin* **95**, 156–171.

Huberty, C. (1994) *Applied Discriminant Analysis*. New York: John Wiley.

IMI Consumer Surveys in Beijing, Shanghai & Guangzhou (1996) Beijing: China Finance and Economy Press.

Johansson, T. (1994) Later modernity, consumer culture and lifestyles: toward a cognitive-affective theory. In *Media Effects and Beyond: Culture, Socialisation and Lifestyles* (ed.) Rosengren, K., pp. 265–294. London: Routledge.

Johansson, T. and Miegel, F. (1992) *Do the Right Thing: Lifestyle and Identity in Contemporary Youth Culture*. Stockholm: Almqvist & Wiksell International.

Lewis, R. (1973) *The New Service Society*. London: Longman.

McRae, D.J. (1971) Mica, A fortman IV iterative K-Means cluster analysis program. *Behavioural Sciences* **16**, 423–424.

Maslow, A. (1968) *Toward a Psychology of Being*. New York: Van Nostrand Co.

Mitchell, A. (1983) *The Nine American Lifestyles: Who We Are and Where We Are Going*. New York: Warner Books.

Moven, J. (1990) *Consumer Behaviour*, 2nd edn. New York: Macmillan.

O'Neill, M. (1997) Returning to class values. *South China Morning Post*, 24 January, 24.

Pingree, S. and Hawkins, R. (1994) Looking for patterns in lifestyles behaviors. In *Media Effects and Beyond: Culture, Socialisation and Lifestyles* (ed.) Rosengren, K., pp. 76–96. London: Routledge.

Pitts, R.E. and Woodside, A.G. (1984) *Personal Values and Consumer Psychology*. Toronto: Lexington Books.

Plummer, J. (1974) The concept and application of life style segmentation. *Journal of Marketing*, January, 33–37.

Pollay, R., Tse, D. and Wang, Z. (1990) Advertising, propaganda, and value change in economic development: the new cultural revolution in China and attitudes toward advertising. *Journal of Business Research* **20**, 83–95.

Settle, R. and Alreck, P. (1989) *Why They Buy: American Consumers Inside and Out*. New York: John Wiley.

Sobel, M. (1983) Lifestyle expenditures in contemporary America. *American Behavioural Scientists* **26** (4), 521–533.

Stevens, J. (1996) *Applied Multivariate Statistics for the Social Sciences*, 3rd edn. Mahwah, New Jersey: LEA.

Uusitalo, M. (1979) *Consumption Style and Way of Life: An Empirical Identification and Explanation of Consumption Style Dimensions*. Helsinki: The Helsinki Press.

Valette-Florence, P. and Jolibert, A. (1990) Social values, A.I.O., and consumption patterns. *Journal of Business Research* **20**, 109–122.

Wells, W. D. (1974) Life style and psychographics: definitions, uses and problems. In *Life Style and Psychographics* (ed.) Wells, W.D., pp. 354–363. Chicago: American Marketing Association.

Williams, K. (1981) *Behavioral Aspects of Marketing*. London: Butterworth-Heinemann.

Zablocki, B. and Kanter, R. (1976) The differentiation of lifestyles. *Annual Review of Sociology* **2**, 269–298.

3

The Animosity Model of Foreign Product Purchase: An Empirical Test in the People's Republic of China

Jill Gabrielle Klein, Richard Ettenson and Marlene D. Morris

The globalization of markets presents considerable challenges and opportunities for domestic and international marketers. Among the notable trends is that target customers in markets worldwide are exposed to and are selecting from a wider range of foreign brands than ever before. Accordingly, marketers have shown a growing interest in understanding the factors related to consumers' evaluation and selection of imported goods.

Consider the following scenario:

> In the Chinese city of Nanjing, Zhang Li, a 40-year-old professional, receives a substantial bonus from her employer. With this money, she decides to purchase a compact disc player for her family. She shops in a large reputable consumer electronics store. Typical of such stores, considerable product information is provided for each model displayed, including brand name and country of manufacture. Zhang Li has three alternatives from which to choose – Bulong (a domestic brand), Goldstar (a Korean-made brand), and Sony (a Japanese-made brand).

Although researchers in marketing only now are beginning to investigate and understand the marketplace behavior of global consumers (including the Chinese), the Western literature does provide some insight as to how Zhang Li will make her choice among the three brands. Researchers have

Source: *Journal of Marketing*, 62(1) (1998): 89–100.

developed various models to explain how attributes are evaluated and integrated into overall product judgments and purchase decisions (e.g., Bettman 1979; Einhorn 1970; Green and Srinivasan 1990; Lynch 1985). Furthermore, some product attributes, such as price and brand name, are likely to act as cues or signals of the quality of other attributes (Aaker 1991; Carpenter 1987; Dodds, Monroe, and Grewal 1991; Jacoby, Olson, and Haddock 1971). Thus, a high price might lead this consumer to infer that the compact disc player is well made, reliable, and stylish.

The country associated with the product also is thought to influence consumers' quality judgments. Research on evaluations of foreign products has found that inferences about the producing country affect perceptions of a product's attributes. Images of the manufacturing nation have a substantial impact on judgments of product quality (e.g., Bilkey and Nes 1982; Han 1988; Hong and Wyer 1989; Maheswaran 1994; Papadopoulos and Heslop 1993). For example, the consumer may infer on the basis of stereotypes of Korea and Koreans that the Goldstar compact disc player is technologically advanced and of high quality.

Although attribute judgments generally are assumed to influence purchase, most research on consumers' evaluations of foreign products has not measured purchase intentions or decisions directly. A recent meta-analytic review of the foreign products literature shows that a large majority of studies use quality judgments, attribute ratings, or both as their dependent measures (Liefeld 1993). Thus, previous work on foreign product purchase primarily has examined how a country's image (e.g., regarding workmanship, innovation, and technological advancement) is projected onto the features of products produced by that country.

It is possible, however, that a product's origin (signaled by place of manufacture and/or brand name) will affect consumers' buying decisions directly and independently of product judgments. For example, the consumer in the previous scenario lives in Nanjing, a city that endured a terrible occupation and massacre at the hands of the Japanese during World War II. If asked to rate the attributes of the Sony compact disc player, she is likely to give the product high marks. Her country's history does not make her blind to the fact that Sony is a high-end, high-quality brand. But if asked if she would purchase the Sony brand, she might tell us that she would never bring a Japanese product into her home.

The Animosity Model of Foreign Product Purchase

History is fraught with illustrations of the dramatic and damaging effects of hostility between nations. If international tension can lead to armed conflict and atrocities, it seems plausible that animosity toward a current or former enemy also will affect willingness to buy products produced in or by firms from that country. Yet to date, the marketing and consumer behavior literature largely has ignored the construct of animosity between nations and its potential impact on foreign product purchase.

From a strategic perspective, this gap in researchers' understanding is of considerable significance. The international marketing manager has little choice but to include two extrinsic attributes – country of manufacture and brand name – as part of the product bundle. Consequently, managers leverage and exploit these two variables in an attempt to enhance consumer perceptions of their offerings and gain a strategic competitive advantage (Aaker 1991; Johansson 1989; Roth and Romeo 1992). The provision of country-of-origin information is constrained by both the importing nation's labeling requirements and the firm's manufacturing base, and, by definition, this extrinsic attribute directly indicates and identifies country-specific information to the consumer. Similarly, consumers often will deduce country-specific information from a product's brand name by means of association or "mental links" to the brand (see Aaker 1991, pp. 265–66; Ettenson and Gaeth 1991; Han and Terpstra 1988). Managers therefore must understand what effect country-of-origin or brand-related associations are likely to have on consumers who evaluate and select foreign goods.

We propose here that the construct of *animosity* – defined as the remnants of antipathy related to previous or ongoing military, political, or economic events – will affect consumers' purchase behavior in the international marketplace. Furthermore, in contrast to the large amount of extant literature on foreign product purchase, we propose that a product's origin can affect consumer buying decisions independent of product judgments. In other words, consumers might avoid products from the offending nation not because of concern about the quality of goods, but because the exporting nation has engaged in military, political, or economic acts that a consumer finds both grievous and difficult to forgive.

Animosity toward another country can have many sources, from a relatively benign rivalry as a result of sharing a contiguous border (e.g., the United States and Canada) to more serious manifestations stemming from previous military events or recent economic or diplomatic disputes. Examples are numerous and range from reports of Jewish consumers avoiding the purchase of German-made products (see Hirschman 1981) to the boycott of French products by Australian and New Zealand consumers because of the recent nuclear tests by France in the South Pacific. Likewise, nations perceived to be engaged in unfair trading practices also might experience repercussions from consumers in certain foreign markets. Thus, macro-level, nation-specific phenomena are likely to have significant and direct micro-level implications for firms exporting from the offending country. Furthermore, to the extent that the effects of animosity are independent of product judgments and affect buying above and beyond consumers' general beliefs about the appropriateness of purchasing imported goods, managers from countries with controversial military, economic, or political histories must understand how such macro-level phenomena might affect their international marketing activities. This will enable managers to select and target their overseas markets and identify ways to modify their existing marketing and communications strategies in regions where animosity might present an informal but significant barrier to trade.

Distinctions between Animosity and Consumer Ethnocentrism

It is well documented in both U.S. and overseas markets that some consumers have a predilection toward imported goods, whereas others prefer domestic alternatives. Reasons for such tendencies range from beliefs about the quality of imported goods to a patriotic bias against things foreign (Bilkey and Nes 1982; Herche 1992; Netemeyer, Durvasula, and Lichtenstein 1991; Sharma, Shimp, and Shin 1995; Shimp and Sharma 1987). Perhaps the most widely used construct to understand this phenomenon is consumer ethnocentrism, developed by Shimp and Sharma (1987) and measured by their CETSCALE.

Consumer ethnocentrism derives from the more general construct of ethnocentrism, which is defined as people viewing their own in-group as central, as possessing proper standards of behavior, and as offering protection against apparent threats from out-groups (Brislin 1993). Shimp and Sharma apply ethnocentrism to the study of marketing and consumer behavior and have coined the term "consumer ethnocentric tendencies" to represent beliefs held by consumers regarding the appropriateness and morality of purchasing foreign-made products. Studies of consumer ethnocentrism generally have found that scores on the CETSCALE are related inversely to willingness to purchase imports, perceptions of the quality of imported goods, cultural openness, education, and income (Netemeyer, Durvasula, and Lichtenstein 1991; Sharma, Shimp, and Shin 1995; Shimp and Sharma 1987). Consumer ethnocentric tendencies play a significant role when products are perceived to be unnecessary and when consumers believe that either their personal or national well-being is threatened by imports (Sharma, Shimp, and Shin 1995; Shimp and Sharma 1987).

The CETSCALE measures beliefs about buying foreign products in general, whereas animosity is, by definition, a country-specific construct. The present study therefore represents a point of departure from the large amount of research literature assessing foreign product purchase generally and consumer ethnocentrism specifically. Although animosity and consumer ethnocentrism can be related, animosity is conceptually and theoretically country specific. Consumers scoring low on the CETSCALE might find it perfectly acceptable to buy foreign products in general but might eschew products from specific nations toward which they feel animosity. Thus, a consumer might purchase many imported goods but not products from a particular target country. Likewise, if no domestic alternative is available in a given product category (e.g., televisions and video cassette recorders in the U.S. market), some consumers, even though they score high on the CETSCALE, might be willing to tolerate the purchase of products imported from some countries but not others.

For marketers, the distinction between consumer ethnocentrism and country-specific animosity is significant. For example, Shimp and Sharma (1987) find that higher CETSCALE scores among U.S. consumers were predictably related to both a preference for U.S.-made goods and an aversion toward imports. A similar preference for domestically produced goods also was found among German, French, Japanese (Netemeyer, Durvasula, and Lichtenstein 1991), and Korean consumers (Sharma, Shimp, and Shin 1995) who scored high on the CETSCALE. At one level, these results are useful to the practicing marketer: As Shimp and Sharma (1987) suggest, the CETSCALE could become part of a firm's tracking studies of consumer attitudes both domestically and in overseas markets. However, knowing that target consumers (either domestically or internationally) score low on the CETSCALE may be of limited practical value and even misleading if the firm's home country is both apparent to consumers and viewed negatively. Marketing managers might find general measures of consumers' willingness to purchase imports, such as the CETSCALE, less relevant and useful than more focused and precise information that provides specific insight regarding consumer aversion toward a particular target country. Yet researchers assessing consumer ethnocentrism have focused little or no attention on identifying or discriminating the level of aversion toward specific importing nations.[1]

Moreover, consumer ethnocentrism and animosity may have different implications for perceptions of product quality. In Netemeyer, Durvasula, and Lichtenstein's (1991) four-nation validation study, the CETSCALE was found to be correlated with judgments of foreign product quality: Consumers who hold strong ethnocentric beliefs are more likely to evaluate foreign products negatively than are those who do not hold such beliefs. Those who believe that it is wrong to buy foreign goods also tend to perceive those goods as lower in quality than domestic goods; ethnocentric consumers prefer domestic goods not only because of economic or moral beliefs, but also because they believe that their own country produces the best products. In contrast, it is possible that a consumer can harbor animosity toward a specific country without denigrating the quality of goods produced by that country. This consumer might be unwilling to buy these goods but might still believe that foreign products – including the products produced by that country – are of high quality.

The Present Study

In this study, we seek to understand how attitudes toward a country – in particular, remnants of antipathy left by previous military, political, or economic conflict – might affect willingness to buy that nation's products. Specifically, the present research tests the theory that animosity toward another nation can be an important and powerful predictor of foreign product purchase, even when this enmity is unrelated to beliefs about the quality of products produced in that country (see Figure 1).

Researchers have begun to heed the call to extend the study of marketing phenomena to international (non-U.S.) settings. Albaum and Peterson (1984), Lee and Green (1991), and Netemeyer, Durvasula, and Lichtenstein (1991) all note that most consumer behavior models have been developed in the United States and few have been tested empirically outside North America. An emphasis on the United States is problematic for any model that is not intended to be domain specific, including the animosity model, which, by its very nature, is international in scope. Accordingly, the present study is an initial empirical test of the animosity framework carried out in the People's Republic of China (PRC). The target to be evaluated by Chinese consumers is Japan and Japanese-made products.

The PRC is an ideal international setting in which to conduct this initial test of the animosity model. Chinese consumers are likely to harbor both war-based and economic-based animosity (hereafter *war animosity* and *economic animosity*) toward Japan. Over the centuries, Japan often has been an enemy of China, and most recently China fought against Japan in World War II (1931–1945). The Japanese invaded China in 1931, and though

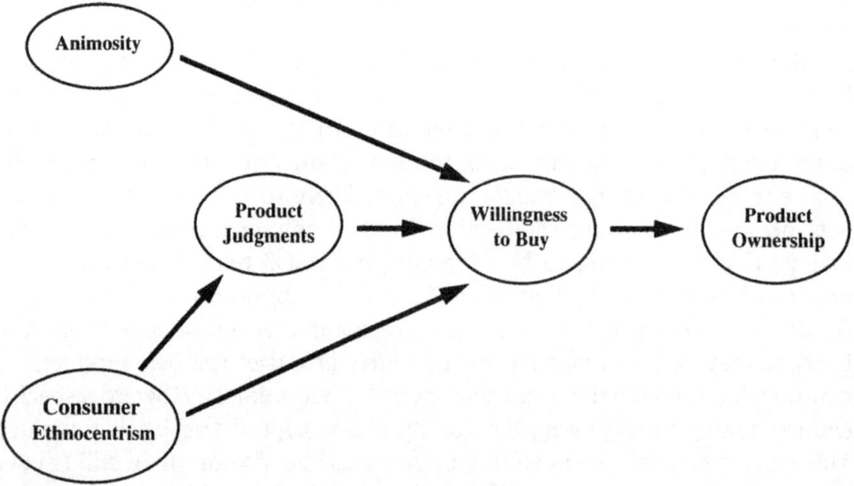

Figure 1: The animosity model of foreign product purchase

the country never was conquered completely, the Chinese suffered under a brutal 14-year Japanese occupation. The city of Nanjing – where the present study was administered – was the site of the horrific slaughter of 300,000 civilians by the Japanese in December, 1937, and January, 1938. Known as the "Nanjing Massacre," it is considered a significant event in contemporary Chinese history and plays a prominent role in geopolitical socialization throughout the PRC.

Coupled with this historical background, Japan today is China's number one trading partner and one of its largest sources of direct foreign investment (Bevacqua 1996; Kaikati et al. 1996). For many Chinese firms, this investment may come at a price. Recent reports indicate that several foreign investors, including the Japanese, are "buying and burying" Chinese brands to champion their own products (Liu 1996). This might result in economic antagonism toward Japan stemming from the proliferation of Japanese products and brands at the expense of displaced domestic brands and industries (*Business China* 1996) or from a perception by the Chinese that Japan engages in unfair trading practices.[2]

Testing the animosity model in the PRC presents several international research challenges. These mainly revolve around the etic/emic dilemma: Should researchers identify pan-cultural universals that can be studied and applied cross-nationally or adapt research instruments in a unique domain-specific manner for each culture or country studied? The latter approach enables researchers to capture attitudinal or behavioral phenomena that may be manifested uniquely across cultures. In this study, we employ a combined or hybrid etic/emic approach in which a universal (etic) concept – animosity – is applied in the PRC but its operationalization is carried out in a culture-specific (emic) manner (Triandis, Malpass, and Davidson 1971; Wind and Douglas 1982, see "Method" section). More precisely, we develop measures of the pan-cultural concept of animosity for specific use in China.

Research Hypotheses

The present study provides an initial test of the animosity model in the context of mainland Chinese consumers and their evaluation and purchase of Japanese products. The following hypotheses are derived from the model:

H_1: Animosity and consumer ethnocentrism (as measured by the CETSCALE) will emerge as separate and distinct constructs in the model.

H_2: The construct of animosity will be indicated by two first-order constructs: war animosity and economic animosity.

H_3: Animosity will have a direct, negative impact on willingness to buy if product judgments and consumer ethnocentrism are held constant.

H_4: Animosity will influence willingness to buy independently of product judgments; that is, animosity will have no effect on product judgments.

These hypotheses focus on consumers' attitudes toward buying Japanese products and their behavioral intentions (i.e., willingness to buy). To assess nomological validity, we also include in the model measures of actual ownership of products from the target country (Japan). Thus,

H_5: Willingness to buy will be a significant predictor of ownership of products from the target country.

We derive hypotheses regarding the CETSCALE from previous research. As discussed previously, consumer ethnocentrism has been found to relate negatively to both evaluations of product quality and the willingness to buy foreign products (Netemeyer, Durvasula, and Lichtenstein 1991). Thus,

H_6: Consumer ethnocentrism will be related negatively to product judgments.

H_7: Consumer ethnocentrism will be related negatively to willingness to buy.

Method

Participants

Data were collected from adult consumers in the Chinese city of Nanjing. Nanjing is China's 11th largest city with a population of 2.5 million (1990 census data, quoted in *The Far East and Australasia* 1996). Our sample was 69.3% female with a mean age of 35 years (and an age range of 18 to 72 years).

Procedure

It was necessary to recruit Chinese consumers in a manner somewhat different from typical recruitment procedures in Western countries. Chinese consumers were approached randomly on the street and asked to complete a brief survey (roughly speaking, the Chinese equivalent of a mall intercept). Solicitation was carried out at several sites around Nanjing by a team of faculty and students from the School of International Business at Nanjing University. Only Chinese nationals were employed for this purpose. In total, 487 Chinese consumers were approached. Of these, 244 agreed to participate, a response rate of 50%. Having agreed to participate, respondents completed the survey in a small booth or office provided at the site. Upon survey completion, participants were debriefed and thanked for their cooperation. On average, the surveys were completed in under 20 minutes.

Measures

Respondents were asked to indicate their agreement (on a 1 = "strongly disagree" to 7 = "strongly agree" scale) with statements regarding four general constructs: (1) Japanese product quality, (2) willingness to buy Japanese products, (3) consumer ethnocentrism, and (4) animosity toward Japan generally and war and economic animosity in particular. Items were coded so that higher ratings indicated more positive product judgments, greater willingness to buy, higher consumer ethnocentrism, and greater levels of animosity. The first three sets of measures were operationalized in a pancultural (etic) manner for the Chinese respondents. The animosity items were developed in a culture-specific (emic) manner to reflect China's unique historical and economic situation with Japan.

Measures of Japanese product quality were culled from previous studies and included the following attributes: workmanship, technological advancement, quality, reliability, design, and value for the money (Darling and Arnold 1988; Darling and Wood 1990; Wood and Darling 1993). Willingness to buy Japanese products was measured next and included such items as "I do not like the idea of owning Japanese products," and "Whenever available, I would prefer to buy products made in Japan" (see the Appendix). Respondents then completed the ten-item CETSCALE (Netemeyer, Durvasula, and Lichtenstein 1991; Shimp and Sharma 1987) to assess their beliefs about buying foreign products. In the fourth part of the survey, participants responded to a series of questions developed specifically for this study to measure animosity toward Japan. The two first-order constructs were measured by items related to war animosity (e.g., "I will never forgive Japan for the Nanjing massacre") and economic animosity (e.g., "The Japanese are doing business unfairly with China"). The second-order construct of animosity was measured by the single item "I dislike the Japanese" (see the Appendix).[3] The final part of the survey solicited respondent demographics and the country of origin of the products they owned in six categories of durable goods: television, video cassette recorder, stereo, radio, camera, and refrigerator. These categories were chosen because Chinese consumers are likely to own these goods and Japanese brands for each are widely available.

The initial survey instrument was drafted in English. Because several measures were included from instruments used in previous studies with Western consumers, it was critical to ensure the appropriateness and adequacy of all measures for administration in the PRC. Accordingly, a systematic approach was taken to develop the research instrument. The initial draft survey was assessed first for cultural compatibility and adequacy for a Chinese sample. In particular, we focused on the relevance of concepts, phrases, and terms used (Douglas and Craig 1984). Two expatriate Chinese nationals fluent in English and teaching Chinese outside the PRC were employed for this purpose. Independently, each Chinese national reviewed the proposed survey items and, in a version of a depth interview, provided detailed feedback on the overall appropriateness of each item. This feedback was provided on several levels: Would a typical Chinese consumer understand what was being asked in the items? Would consumers have experience with or a point of reference for the items? Would the items have a similar/complementary meaning when translated into Mandarin? This was then followed by a similar analysis undertaken in Nanjing by the Dean of the School of International Business at Nanjing University, who is a native of China, is fluent in English, and received his doctorate in the United States. On the basis of the feedback received from all three "key informants," several minor modifications were made. All survey items used in the final instrument were deemed appropriate, adequate, and meaningful for Chinese consumers. In the last step of survey development, the research instrument was translated into Mandarin calligraphy by one of the Chinese expatriates. The Mandarin survey version then was back-translated (independently by the other Chinese expatriate) to ensure linguistic and conceptual equivalence between the Chinese and English versions of the task (Bhalla and Lin 1987). A final check of the Mandarin survey version was undertaken by our Chinese colleague in Nanjing.

Results

Structural Equations Model

Measurement model. Several procedures were used to test the measurement properties of the model using latent variable structural equation modeling (Jöreskog and Sörbom 1993). Each construct in the model was analyzed separately, and the fit of the indicators to the construct as well as construct validity was assessed (see Table 1).[4]

Product judgments. The six items used as indicators of product judgments had significant paths from the construct, and residuals were low. As we show in Table 1, the root mean square error of approximation (RMSEA), goodness-of-fit index (GFI), adjusted goodness-of-fit index (AGFI), comparative fit index (CFI), and Tucker-Lewis index (TLI) all indicate a good level of model fit.

Willingness to buy. All six indicators of willingness to buy were related significantly to the construct and had low residuals. As with product judgments,

Table 1: Results of single-construct measurement models[a]

Construct	χ^2	*df*	*p-level*	*RMSEA*	*GFI*	*AGFI*	*CFI*	*TLI*	*CR*[b]	*VE*[c]	*mean*	*n*[d]
Product Judgments	17.98	9	.04	.066	.97	.94	.96	.93	.73	.32	5.43	6
Willingness to Buy	14.68	9	.10	.053	.98	.95	.98	.97	.79	.39	4.39	5
Consumer Ethnocentrism	13.95	9	.12	.049	.98	.95	.99	.98	.83	.46	2.89	6
War Animosity	–	–	–	–	–	–	–	–	.76	.54	5.53	3
Economic Animosity	2.62	5	.76	.000	1.00	.99	1.00	1.02	.74	.38	5.02	6
Animosity	–	–	–	–	–	–	–	–	.82	.46	5.07[e]	1

[a]Because there were three indicators for the construct of war animosity and one for animosity, the measurement model was identified completely and fit statistics were not computed.
[b]Construct Reliability.
[c]Variance Extracted.
[d]Number of items in each construct.
[e]Animosity is indicated by two first-order constructs (war and economic animosity) and one single-item indicant ("I dislike the Japanese"). The mean reported here is for this single indicant.

the fit indices for the willingness to buy construct consistently reflected a good level of fit.

Consumer ethnocentrism. Although all of the CETSCALE items were related significantly to the construct of consumer ethnocentrism, ten of the residuals were larger than the 2.58 cutoff (Hair et al. 1995), and the RMSEA of .10 was unacceptably high. (Other fit indices were $\chi^2(35) = 121.53$, $p < .001$, GFI = .90, AGFI = .84, CFI = .91, and TLI = .88.) Thus, the CETSCALE was refined to six items that showed low residuals, a low RMSEA, and higher levels of fit (see Table 1 and the Appendix).

War animosity. The measurement model for war animosity showed that all three items were related significantly to this first-order construct. Because there were three indicators for the war animosity construct, the measurement model was identified completely and fit statistics could not be computed.

Economic animosity. All five economic items were related significantly to the first-order construct of economic animosity, residuals were low, and the fit indices were strong.

Animosity. The second-order construct of animosity was indicated by a single item: "I dislike the Japanese."

Product ownership. Respondents indicated the country of origin of the products they owned in six categories of durable goods (television, video cassette recorder, stereo, radio, camera, and refrigerator). Thus, for each respondent, the total number of Japanese products owned could range from zero to six. This number was used as the single indicator of product ownership, with the error variance set equal to the smallest estimated error variance (Θ_ε) in the model (Anderson and Gerbing 1988).

Discriminant validity. Discriminant validity was assessed for the two first-order animosity constructs. A two-construct measurement model was analyzed in which the correlation between war animosity and economic animosity was fixed at 1, as suggested by Bagozzi (1981) and Anderson and Gerbing (1988). This model produced a poor fit: $\chi^2(20) = 147.23, p < .001$. The RMSEA was .17, and the other fit indices were GFI = .84, AGFI = .71, CFI = .75, and TLI = .65. When the correlation between the constructs is unconstrained, the model improves considerably: $\chi^2(19) = 38.31, p < .01$, a significant reduction from the constrained model, $\chi^2(1) = 108.92, p < .001$. Furthermore, the RMSEA = .067, GFI = .96, AGFI = .92, CFI = .96, and TLI = .94.

To test H_1, we examined whether each of the first-order constructs of animosity was distinct from consumer ethnocentrism. First, a measurement model was estimated in which the correlation between consumer ethnocentrism and war animosity was fixed at 1. Model fit was poor: $\chi^2(27) = 207.40$, $p < .001$, RMSEA = .17, and the other fit indices were low: GFI = .84, AGFI = .73, CFI = .74, and TLI = .65. When the correlation between the constructs was unconstrained, model fit improved significantly: $\chi^2(26) = 38.06$, $p < .07$, a significant reduction from the constrained model, $\chi^2(1) = 169.34$, $p < .001$. The other fit indices were RMSEA = .045, GFI = .96, AGFI = .94, CFI = .98, and TLI = .98.

Second, an additional measurement model was estimated in which the correlation between consumer ethnocentrism and economic animosity was fixed at 1. The constrained model again showed a poor fit: $\chi^2(44) = 263.70$, $p < .001$, RMSEA = .15, GFI = .80, AGFI = .69, CFI = .68, and TLI = .60. When the correlation between the constructs was unconstrained, the model was much improved: $\chi^2(43) = 78.44, p < .001$, a significant reduction from the constrained model, $\chi^2(1) = 185.26, p < .001$. The other fit indices were RMSEA = .060, GFI = .94, AGFI = .91, CFI = .95, and TLI = .93.

Thus, there is evidence of discriminant validity between the two first-order animosity constructs. Furthermore, both war and economic animosity are distinct from consumer ethnocentrism, which thereby provides support for H_1.

The full measurement model. The full measurement model was analyzed and exhibited a good level of fit: $\chi^2(331) = 505.68, p < .001$. The RMSEA = .048, GFI = .87, AGFI = .84, CFI = .91, and TLI = .90.

The structural model. The results of the structural equation analysis are shown in Figure 2. Table 2 shows the construct intercorrelations. The model achieved a good level of fit: $\chi^2(343) = 517.34$, $p < .001$, RMSEA = .047, GFI = .86, AGFI = .84, CFI = .91, and TLI = .90. Overall, the model accounted for 55% of the variance in willingness to buy, which in turn accounted for 23% of the variance in ownership of Japanese products. Animosity accounted for 75% of the variance in war animosity and 40% of the variance in economic animosity. As predicted in H_2, the first-order constructs, war and economic animosity, were both significant indicators of general animosity (see Figure 2).[5]

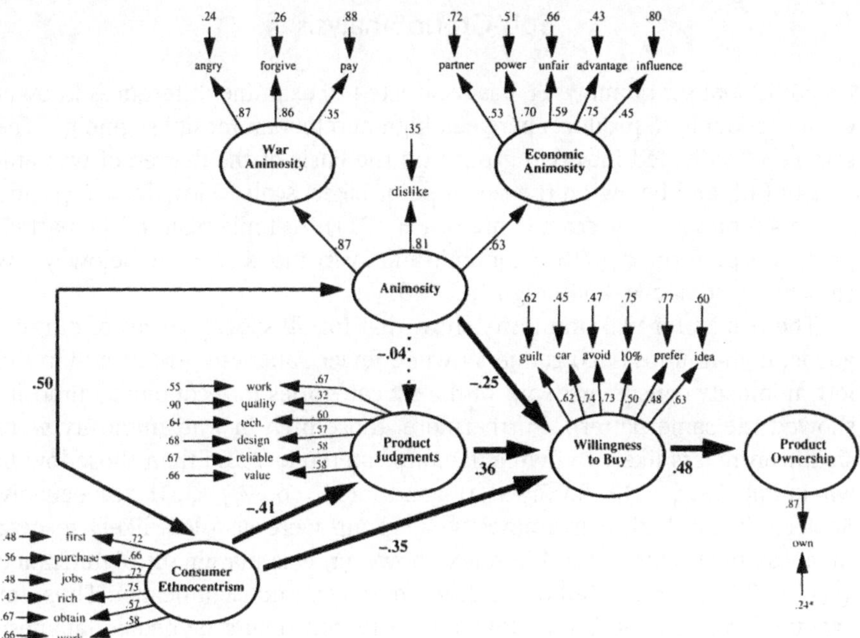

Note: All coefficients are standardized. All solid line path coefficients are significant at $p < .001$. (The dotted line coefficient is nonsignificant).
*This variance was constrained.

Figure 2: Structural equation model results

Table 2: Construct intercorrelations

	Product judgments	*Willingness to buy*	*Consumer ethnocentrism*	*War animosity*	*Economic animosity*	*Animosity*	*Product ownership*
Product Judgments	1.00						
Willingness to Buy	.55	1.00					
Consumer Ethnocentrism	−.40	−.63	1.00				
War Animosity	−.20	−.41	.47	1.00			
Economic Animosity	−.06	−.32	.27	.55	1.00		
Animosity	−.25	−.52	.46	.83	.60	1.00	
Product Ownership	.46	.56	−.28	−.22	−.10	−.20	1.00

As predicted in H_3, the path from animosity to willingness to buy was significant and negative. The high levels of model fit demonstrate support for H_4 because no path was specified between animosity and product judgments. The dotted line in Figure 2 shows that when a path was added to the model between animosity and product judgments its coefficient was −.04 (t = −.41) and nonsignificant. Our results also support H_5; measures of attitudes toward buying were significant predictors of actual ownership of Japanese products.[6]

As predicted in H_6 and H_7, consumer ethnocentrism was a significant negative predictor of both product judgments and willingness to buy.

Sub-Group Analysis

An additional set of analyses was conducted to examine differences in ownership of Japanese products between high-and low-animosity segments. The sample was divided into two groups on the basis of the degree of war animosity (4.5 and below on the seven-point Likert scale = low [n = 51], and above 4.5 on the same scale = high [n = 171]). A similar split of the participants was performed on the economic animosity index (4.5 and below = low [n = 68], and above 4.5 = high [n = 161]).[7]

The results for war animosity show that for all six categories of durable goods, high-animosity consumers owned fewer Japanese products than did low-animosity consumers. Four of the six categories for economic animosity showed the same pattern. Furthermore, those high in war animosity were significantly less likely to own a Japanese stereo or radio than those low in war animosity: $\chi^2(1) = 5.07, p < .03$, and $\chi^2(1) = 6.77, p < .01$, respectively. Subjects in the high war animosity subgroup were also less likely to own Japanese televisions (this difference, however, was marginally significant): $\chi^2(1) = 3.35$, $p < .07$ (all other differences were nonsignificant). Thus, for example, whereas 58.3% of low-animosity consumers owned a Japanese stereo, only 32.4% of high-animosity consumers did. (For radios, the difference was 37.2% versus 18.4%, and for televisions the difference was 49.0% versus 34.3%.)

We also examined whether there were age or gender differences between the animosity subgroups. T-tests were conducted to examine age differences between low- (m = 35.1) and high-animosity (m = 35.3) subgroups for both war animosity (t(220) = .07, n.s.; using the full range of the war animosity variable, r = −.00, n.s.) and economic animosity (low m = 33.8 and high m = 35.8, t(220) =1.11, n.s.; r = .07, n.s.). The lack of a relationship between age and animosity suggests that hostility toward Japan is not cohort specific but instead manifests itself across generations. No gender differences were found between the high and low subgroups for war animosity ($\chi^2 = .02$, n.s.), but there was a tendency for more men than women to be high in economic animosity (77.9% of the men versus 66.0% of the women), $\chi^2 = 4.28, p < .05$.

Discussion

The results of this initial study support each of the research hypotheses and provide several levels of empirical support for the animosity model of foreign product purchase. First, animosity toward Japan and consumer ethnocentrism (as measured by the CETSCALE) were found to be distinct constructs. Discriminant validity was demonstrated, and each construct had different consequences in the model. Second, Chinese consumers' animosity toward

Japan was related negatively to their willingness to purchase Japanese products, and more important, this effect was independent of their judgments about the quality of Japanese products. For those high in animosity, it is not product perceptions that lead to a reluctance to purchase goods from the target country; instead, it is hostility toward that target. Japanese goods were viewed quite positively by Chinese consumers, regardless of the consumers' level of animosity. Apparently, consumers are able to acknowledge the quality of goods from a target country while expressing hostility toward and a marketplace aversion to products from that country. This leads to a third significant finding: Chinese consumers' marketplace behavior (i.e., actual ownership of Japanese goods) was predicted by attitudes toward buying Japanese products, which in turn was predicted by animosity toward Japan. A fourth result was that the effects of animosity on consumer preferences were found to exist even with consumer ethnocentrism held constant. Also of interest was that, for Chinese consumers, historical war-related factors were associated more closely with animosity toward Japan than were contemporary economic concerns. Overall, these findings provide marketing managers and researchers with considerable evidence that factors above and beyond both the quality of foreign products and beliefs about the appropriateness of purchasing imports affect consumers' purchase behavior in the international marketplace. In short, animosity matters.

Managerial Implications

The proliferation of cross-border trade by an increasing number of global firms suggests that intense competition will continue to grow in the international arena. Consequently, international marketers will require an expanding repertoire of tools and constructs to enable them to compete and position their goods more effectively. We argue here that domestic and international marketers might do well to consider animosity as a factor that influences consumer purchase decisions in the global marketplace. The animosity model of foreign product purchase provides several significant and practical implications for practitioners.

First, exporting firms associated with a country whose military, economic, or political histories are enduring and controversial (e.g., Japan, Germany, Russia, the United States, Israel, France, Great Britain) should consider administering research surveys that measure levels of animosity in select target markets. Such studies could be included as part of the standard international marketing research carried out by these firms. Results would show the level of animosity among various segments based on consumer demographic variables as well as the geographic regions where animosity is highest. For example, though the levels of animosity in the present study were found to be relatively high, it is unknown whether similar levels of animosity would be found in other cities or regions across China, such as Beijing or Shanghai, the latter of which is considered to be the most western and cosmopolitan in the PRC. The identification of regional differences in the levels of animosity in a target market holds considerable promise for international marketers because regional differences are easy to measure and amenable to specifically tailored marketing strategies. In the PRC, for example, significant differences exist between urban and rural consumers (Li and Gallup 1995), and large neighboring cities often present dramatically different marketing environments (*Business China* 1994).

Second, the animosity construct can be useful to global and local retailers and their suppliers (e.g., import firms) as they seek and identify potential overseas sources for products and services. It is recognized widely that in the past two decades the global retail environment has become increasingly concentrated and competitive (McGoldrick and Davies 1995). In response, retailers are more customer oriented than ever before and international sourcing plays an increasingly important role in the retail buying function. When sourcing abroad, retailers will benefit by identifying the levels of animosity exhibited toward particular foreign suppliers. This will enable the firm's buying center to concentrate on purchasing goods from producer nations that do not engender animosity from its customers.

The finding that animosity affects buying independently of product judgments is a significant departure from both the long-standing conventional wisdom in marketing practice and the large number of multiattribute models of consumer decision making that have been developed over the past 20 years (Bettman 1979; Green and Srinivasan 1990; Wilkie and Pessemier 1973). Practitioners and researchers often assume a relationship between evaluations of a product's quality and purchase decisions. This assumption is certainly valid in many contexts and provides the rationale for micro-level marketing research that focuses on product attributes, product promotion, and their effects on brand choice. The present study reveals, however, that in many other circumstances, macro-level sociological phenomena also will play a significant role in consumers' decision behavior. If animosity is sufficiently strong, its effect may be so dominant that purchase decisions no longer are influenced by evaluations of the product.

Managers, therefore, must understand that if levels of animosity toward a producer nation are high, it is unlikely that traditional methods of increasing market share will be appropriate or successful. It seems unlikely that sales promotions, brand advertisements, price promotions, or new model design will be effective strategies in attracting high-animosity consumers. Instead, a more appropriate strategic response might be to downplay promotion of the "Made in . . ." aspect of the product and use brand names that are not obviously associated with the target country (Ettenson and Gaeth 1991; Levin and Jasper 1996).

On a broader scale, knowledge of international animosity and its effect on product purchase in select target markets also can guide the development of strategic marketing and manufacturing alliances and the production of so-called "hybrid" products (products manufactured in one country and branded by a firm from another country). Marketers of hybrid products have the benefit of promoting or de-emphasizing their products' origins, as well as flexibility in the selection of the products' brand names (Ettenson and Gaeth 1991; Han and Terpstra 1988; Levin and Jasper 1996). The manufacture of hybrids might prove fruitful to the international marketer whose products or brands have failed to capture satisfactory levels of share in a target market because of consumer animosity. For example, many Japanese firms have established manufacturing facilities in a range of foreign countries (the United States, the PRC, Malaysia, Indonesia, Singapore, and Australia, to name a few). Although economic factors such as the cost of labor and other competitive advantages are likely the primary motivations in these foreign direct investment decisions, Japanese firms now have several strategic options for promoting their goods in overseas markets. Most notably, they can exploit country of origin and alter the brand name in an attempt to de-emphasize (or emphasize) Japan as the source of the good.

International marketers also can choose to address the animosity issue directly in certain markets. One strategy would be to engage in public relations and other communications efforts to improve country perceptions and address sources of international tension. Such efforts might be more effective for minimizing animosity stemming from current diplomatic or economic disputes than from historical and military conflicts.

As the global trend of cross-border trade increases, the animosity construct can be applied by domestic firms seeking to defend their markets against increases in imported goods and, in particular, imported goods from a particular nation. To the extent that levels of animosity are high toward a specific country, local firms can exploit and promote "buy domestic" campaigns, capitalizing on the normative (i.e., social norm) influence of eschewing goods from the offending nation.

In short, the animosity model of foreign product purchase holds considerable promise for domestic and international marketers. The measurement of animosity provides managers with a new and useful strategic tool that will lead to a better understanding of how current and prospective consumers in international markets might react to goods imported from a particular producer nation.

Summary and Further Research

This research identifies and tests the effect of a previously unrecognized factor in the study of consumers' foreign product purchase. A macro-level sociological phenomenon that has received virtually no attention in the research literature in marketing – animosity toward a producer country – is shown here to predict consumers' likelihood of purchasing products from that country. As such, this study provides a basis for developing a better understanding of international consumer and exchange relations. Historical and contemporary government actions and the commercial consequences of such actions appear to be legitimate and important areas of inquiry for researchers in both marketing and public policy. The results in the case we investigate here show that a country's past actions can haunt its international firms many years after the fact.

This initial test of the animosity model focuses on Chinese consumers' views of Japan and Japanese products. Yet the model has far-reaching implications for international competitors from any country with a controversial military, economic, or diplomatic record. Studies should examine other international contexts in which animosity might play a role in consumers' purchase behavior and would include the collection of data on consumer perceptions and attitudes toward other nations and their products. U.S. consumers' evaluations of Japan and Japanese products would be a particularly interesting and relevant area to pursue. Another possibility is the administration of segmentation studies (incorporating additional demographic as well as psychographic variables) in those markets that manifest high levels of animosity toward a particular producer nation. The possibility also exists for experimental work to determine communication strategies that are most effective in reducing animosity in those consumers who manifest high levels of the construct. Another interesting possibility would be to consider the inverse of the animosity construct and explore if, independent of quality judgments, consumers of a particular ethnic heritage express a preference for products from specific countries or regions. Because the present study is the inaugural investigation of the animosity model, the potential areas for further research are considerable.

The implications for U.S. marketers are straightforward. Firms evaluating current or prospective overseas opportunities must develop a better understanding of how the United States is perceived in international target markets. There is little doubt that, as an exporting nation, the United States enjoys a certain stature and high profile abroad. This can be a double-edged sword, however, presenting managers with both benefits and challenges. American marketers with overseas ambitions should not ignore the possibility of negative attitudes toward the United States in some regions of the world. This is particularly important in light of the fact that U.S. exporters must battle for global market share with competitors from a growing list of countries. And though consumers throughout the world are embracing American icons and popular culture, a subset of overseas consumers might avoid the purchase of American brands and goods from American firms. The United States may have sowed the seeds of animosity in markets that are viewed widely as extraordinary growth opportunities. Are consumers in Hiroshima or Hanoi reluctant to buy American goods? The answers lie in future studies.

Appendix

Product Judgments (modified from Darling and Arnold 1988; Darling and Wood 1990; Wood and Darling 1993).

Products made in Japan are carefully produced and have fine workmanship.

Products made in Japan are generally of a lower quality than similar products available from other countries.

Products made in Japan show a very high degree of technological advancement.

Products made in Japan usually show a very clever use of color and design.

Products made in Japan are usually quite reliable and seem to last the desired length of time.

Products made in Japan are usually a good value for the money.

Willingness to Buy (modified from Darling and Arnold 1988; Darling and Wood 1990; Wood and Darling 1993).

I would feel guilty if I bought a Japanese product.

I would never buy a Japanese car.

Whenever possible, I avoid buying Japanese products.

Whenever available, I would prefer to buy products made in Japan.

I do not like the idea of owning Japanese products.

If two products were equal in quality, but one was from Japan and one was from China, I would pay 10% more for the product from China.

Consumer Ethnocentrism (modified from Shimp and Sharma's 1987 CETSCALE).

Chinese products, first, last, and foremost.

Purchasing foreign-made products is un-Chinese.

It is not right to purchase foreign products, because it puts Chinese out of jobs.

We should purchase products manufactured in China instead of letting other countries get rich off of us.

We should buy from foreign countries only those products that we cannot obtain within our own country.

Chinese consumers who purchase products made in other countries are responsible for putting their fellow Chinese out of work.

Animosity.

I dislike the Japanese.

War Animosity.

I feel angry toward the Japanese.

I will never forgive Japan for the Nanjing Massacre.

Japan should pay for what it did to Nanjing during the occupation.

Economic Animosity.

Japan is not a reliable trading partner.

Japan wants to gain economic power over China.

Japan is taking advantage of China.

Japan has too much economic influence in China.

The Japanese are doing business unfairly with China.

Notes

1. Netemeyer, Durvasula, and Lichtenstein (1991) did collect U.S., German, Japanese, and French consumers' attitudes toward purchasing products from the other three countries in the study. Their focus, however, was on the reliability and validity of the CETSCALE and not on assessing animosity and understanding its impact on the evaluation and purchase of foreign goods.
2. In response to this trend, China's Ministry of Commerce Research Center now monitors sales of domestic and foreign brands in several product categories and is encouraging Chinese firms to register and retain their trademarks. A Beijing Brand Strategy Team also has been established to promote and enhance the value of Chinese brands (Liu 1996).
3. As shown in the Appendix, the item "I feel angry toward the Japanese" is an indicator of the war animosity construct rather than the animosity construct. There are two reasons for this, one statistical and one semantic. First, when "angry" is specified as an indicator of animosity, strong residuals result. Furthermore, "angry" was correlated .74 with the item "I will never forgive Japan for the Nanjing massacre" (in fact, this is the highest inter-item correlation in the model). Thus, the separation of the two items into different constructs is counterindicated. Second, according to our Chinese translators, there are two Mandarin characters that can represent "angry." One is a mild form of anger, as in being "cross with a child." The second character (the one used in the translation of the survey instrument) represents an extreme emotion, considerably more so than what might be implied or inferred by the English use of the word "angry" (it was suggested by the translators that this character is closer to the English word "hate"). As a consequence, the use of this Mandarin character is likely to be associated with or stem from some extreme event or circumstance – apparently our respondents related this with animosity stemming from the Japanese invasion of China during World War II. Thus, we have the finding that "angry" and "I will never forgive Japan for the Nanjing massacre" are highly correlated, and "angry" emerges as an indicator for war animosity.
4. Construct reliability was calculated by the following equation: (sum of standardized loadings)^2/[(sum of standardized loadings)^2 + sum of indicator measurement error].
5. An alternative to model estimation was taken in which war and economic animosity were included as predictors of animosity rather than as first-order indicators (i.e., the direction of the paths between the animosity constructs was reversed). This specification produced similar fit statistics: $\chi^2(342) = 517.04$, $p < .001$, RMSEA = .047, GFI = .86, AGFI = .84, CFI = .91, and TLI = .90. The path from war animosity to animosity was .70, the path from economic animosity to animosity was .22, and the path from animosity to buying was −.25. (All of these paths were significant at the $p < .01$ level.) The other paths in the model were unchanged.
6. If paths are added to the model from animosity to product ownership, and from consumer ethnocentrism to product ownership, the results show that these paths are nonsignificant ($\gamma = .09$, t = .76 and $\gamma = .11$, t = .77, respectively). Thus, animosity predicts attitudes toward buying Japanese products, which in turn predict the ownership of these goods.
7. A split at the neutral point of 4 resulted in a sample size for the low-animosity group that was too small to allow subsequent analyses. A median split (at 5.5) would have included high-animosity consumers in the low-animosity group.

References

Aaker, David A. (1991), *Managing Brand Equity.* New York: The Free Press.

Albaum, Gerald and Robert A. Peterson (1984), "Empirical Research in International Marketing: 1976–1982," *Journal of International Business Studies*, 15 (Spring/Summer), 161–73.

Anderson, James C. and David W. Gerbing (1988), "Structural Equation Modeling in Practice: A Review and Recommended Two-Step Approach," *Psychological Bulletin*, 103 (May), 411–23.

Bagozzi, Richard P. (1981), "Evaluating Structural Equation Models with Unobservable Variables and Measurement Error," *Journal of Marketing Research*, 18 (August), 375–81.

Bettman, James (1979), *An Information Processing Theory of Consumer Choice.* Reading, MA: Addison-Wesley.

Bevacqua, Ronald (1996), "Japan and China Cooperation May Bring Increased Stability in the Region," *Reuter Far East Economic News*, (April 30).

Bhalla, Gaurav and Lynn Lin (1987), "Cross Cultural Marketing Research: A Discussion of Equivalence Issues and Management Strategies," *Psychology and Marketing*, 4 (4), 275–85.

Bilkey, Warren J. and Erik Nes (1982), "Country-of-Origin Effects on Product Evaluations," *Journal of International Business Studies*, 13 (Spring/Summer), 89–99.

Brislin, Richard (1993), *Understanding Culture's Influence on Behavior.* Orlando, FL: Harcourt Brace Jovanovich.

Business China (1994), "Market Making," 20 (September), 8–9.

Business China (1996), "From Legend to Reality," 22 (January), 4–6.

Carpenter, Gregory S. (1987), "Modeling Competitive Marketing Strategies: The Impact of Marketing-Mix Relationships and Industry Structure," *Marketing Science*, 6 (Spring), 208–21.

Darling, John R. and Danny R. Arnold (1988), "The Competitive Position Abroad of Products and Marketing Practices of the United States, Japan, and Selected European Countries," *Journal of Consumer Marketing*, 5 (Fall), 61–68.

——— and Van R. Wood (1990), "A Longitudinal Study Comparing Perceptions of U.S. and Japanese Consumer Products in a Third/Neutral Country: Finland 1975 to 1985," *Journal of International Business Studies*, 21 (3), 427–50.

Dodds, William, Kent Monroe, and Dhruv Grewal (1991), "Effects of Price, Brand, and Store Information on Buyers' Product Evaluations," *Journal of Marketing Research*, 28 (August), 307–19.

Douglas, Susan P. and C. S. Craig (1984), "Establishing Equivalence in Comparative Consumer Research," in *Comparative Marketing Systems*, Erdener Kaynak and Ronald Savitt, eds. New York: Praeger, 93–113.

Einhorn, H. (1970), "The Use of Nonlinear, Noncompensatory Models in Decision Making," *Psychological Bulletin*, 73 (March), 221–30.

Ettenson, Richard and Gary Gaeth (1991), "Consumer Perceptions of Hybrid (Bi-National) Products," *Journal of Consumer Marketing*, 8 (Fall), 13–18.

The Far East and Australasia (1996), London: Europa Publications.

Green, Paul E. and V. Srinivasan (1990), "Conjoint Analysis in Marketing: New Developments with Implications for Research and Practice," *Journal of Marketing*, 54 (October), 3–19.

Hair, Joseph F., R. E. Anderson, R. L. Tatham, and W. C. Black (1995), *Multivariate Data Analysis*, 4th ed. Englewood Cliffs, NJ: Prentice-Hall.

Han, C. Min (1988), "The Role of Consumer Patriotism in the Choice of Domestic Versus Foreign Products," *Journal of Advertising Research*, 28 (June/July), 25–31.
——— and V. Terpstra (1988), "Country of Origin Effects for Uni-National and Bi-National Products," *Journal of International Business Studies*, 19 (Summer), 235–56.
Herche, Joel (1992), "A Note on the Predictive Validity of the CETSCALE," *Journal of the Academy of Marketing Science*, 20 (Summer), 261–64.
Hirschman, Elizabeth C. (1981), "American Jewish Ethnicity: Its Relationship to Some Selected Aspects of Consumer Behavior," *Journal of Marketing*, 45 (Summer), 102–10.
Hong, Sung-Tai and Robert S. Wyer, Jr. (1989), "Effects of Country-of-Origin and Product-Attribute Information on Product Evaluation: An Information Processing Perspective," *Journal of Consumer Research*, 16 (September), 175–87.
Jacoby, J., J. Olson, and R. Haddock (1971), "Price, Brand Name, and Product Characteristics as Determinants of Perceived Quality," *Journal of Applied Psychology*, 55 (December), 570–79.
Johansson, Johny K. (1989), "Determinants and Effects of the Use of 'Made in' Labels," *International Marketing Review*, 6 (1), 47–58.
Jöreskog, Karl G. and Dag Sörbom (1993), *LISREL VIII: Analysis of Linear Structural Relations by the Method of Maximum Likelihood.* Chicago: National Education Resources.
Kaikati, Jack G., George M Sullivan, Katherine S. Virgo, and John M. Virgo (1996), "The Role of Japan in China's Economic Development," *Multinational Business Review*, 4 (Spring), 20–28.
Lee, Chol and Robert Green (1991), "Cross-Cultural Examination of the Fishbein Behavioral Intentions Model," *Journal of International Business Studies*, 22 (2), 289–305.
Levin, Irwin P. and J. D. Jasper (1996), "Experimental Analysis of Nationalistic Tendencies in Consumer Decision Processes: Case of the Multinational Product," *Journal of Experimental Psychology: Applied*, 2 (March), 17–30.
Li, Dong and Alec Gallup (1995), "In Search of the Chinese Consumer," *China Business Review*, 22 (September), 19–22.
Liefeld, John P. (1993), "Experiments on Country-of-Origin Effects: Review and Meta-Analysis of Effect Size," in *Product-Country Images: Impact and Role in International Marketing*, N. Papadopoulos and L. A. Heslop, eds. New York: International Business Press.
Liu Jun (1996), "Manufacturers Now Understand What's in a Name," *Washington Post National Weekly Edition: China Supplement*, (August 26–September 1), S6.
Lynch, John G., Jr. (1985), "Uniqueness Issues in the Decompositional Modeling of Multiattribute Overall Evaluations: An Information Integration Perspective," *Journal of Marketing Research*, 22 (February), 1–19.
Maheswaran, Durauraj (1994), "Country-of-Origin as a Stereotype: Effects of Consumer Expertise and Attribute Strength on Product Evaluations," *Journal of Consumer Research*, 21 (September), 354–65.
McGoldrick, Peter J. and Gary Davies (1995), *International Retailing: Trends and Strategies.* London: Pitman Publishing.
Netemeyer, Richard, Srinivas Durvasula, and Donald Lichtenstein (1991), "A Cross-National Assessment of the Reliability and Validity of the CETSCALE," *Journal of Marketing Research*, 28 (August), 320–27.
Papadopoulos, Nicolas and Louise A. Heslop (1993), *Product-Country Images: Impact and Role in International Marketing.* New York: International Business Press.
Roth, Martin S. and Jean B. Romeo (1992), "Matching Product Category and Country Image Perceptions: A Framework for Managing Country-of-Origin Effects," *Journal of International Business Studies*, 23 (3), 477–97.
Sharma, Subhash, Terence A. Shimp, and Jeongshin Shin (1995), "Consumer Ethnocentrism: A Test of Antecedents and Moderators," *Journal of the Academy of Marketing Science*, 23 (Winter), 26–37.

Shimp, T. and S. Sharma (1987), "Consumer Ethnocentrism: Construction and Validation of the CETSCALE," *Journal of Marketing Research*, 24 (August), 280–89.

Triandis, H., R. S. Malpass, and A. Davidson (1971), "Cross Cultural Psychology," in *Biennial Review of Anthropology*, B. J. Seigel, ed. Stanford, CA: Stanford University Press.

Wilkie, William and Edgar Pessemier (1973), "Issues in Marketing's Use of Multi-Attribute Models," *Journal of Marketing Research*, 10 (November), 428–41.

Wind, Yorum and Susan Douglas (1982), "Comparative Consumer Research: The Next Frontier," *Management Decision*, 20 (4), 24–35.

Wood, Van R. and John R. Darling (1993), "The Marketing Challenges of the Newly Independent Republics: Product Competitiveness in Global Markets," *Journal of International Marketing*, 1 (1), 77–102.

4

Marketing and Negotiating in the People's Republic of China: Perceptions of American Businessmen Who Attended the 1975 Canton Fair

James A. Brunner and George M. Taoka

Introduction

Evidence is mounting that the long-run trade prospects between the United States and the People's Republic of China look encouraging even though short-run trade and production problems exist. U.S.-China trade declined from $923 million in 1974 to $464 million in 1975,[1] partly as a result of the nation's desire to reduce her trade deficit. However, there is sufficient evidence to indicate that the decrease in trade will not affect the overall rate of economic growth in the PRC in the next few years. Commencing in 1977, and for the balance of this decade, the petrochemical, fertilizer, and power plants ordered from the U.S., Japan, West Germany, and France totalling $1.2 billion will be in production, and they should contribute greatly toward increased production.[2] It is estimated that by 1977, China's production of petroleum will be approximately one-fourth that of Saudi-Arabia and that as much as 25 million tons of this oil will be available for export, providing the country with foreign exchange that might be used to increase her purchases from the U.S.[3] By 1988, China will become a major producer of oil, according to Selig S. Harrison of the Carnegie Endowment for International Peace.

Source: *Journal of International Business Studies*, 8(2) (1977): 69–82.

American businessmen who recognized the short-run limitations of market development in China have opted to take a long-run view of the market potential. By attending the Canton (Kwangchow) Fairs, they have been able to gain first-hand knowledge of the peculiarities of trading with the Chinese and, at the same time, to develop an appreciation for the types of goods and services they desire. Articles have appeared in various business periodicals concerning the many facets of trade with the PRC, but none has documented the perceptions of Americans who have had direct contact with the Chinese mainland.

The objective of this research is to evaluate the various aspects of business opportunities and peculiarities of negotiations in the People's Republic of China as viewed by businessmen who have attended the Canton Fairs. Some of these men have had the opportunity to view Chinese products that might be imported into the U.S., and others have undertaken serious discussions concerning American capital goods, equipment, and other products that might be exported to the PRC. Since an estimated 50 per cent of all of China's trade is arranged at these Fairs, those in attendance have gained the necessary information to help assess the trade opportunities with the PRC.[4]

In January 1975, a self-administered questionnaire was mailed to 218 persons who had attended one or more of the recent Canton Trade Fairs. One hundred thirty-nine responded prior to the cut-off date of May 1, 1975 – a return rate of 64 per cent. A confidential list of businessmen knowledgeable on trading with China provided an additional 35 respondents, or a total of 174.

Survey Instrument

The questionnaire contained thirty-eight statements pertaining to initial trade effort activities, contracts, negotiations, impediments to trade developments, competitive perceptions, and some of the characteristics of negotiations and social customs in the People's Republic of China. In addition, the recipients were asked to comment about the importance of the PRC market to their companies.

They were requested to indicate their degree of agreement or disagreement with each of the 38 statements on a five-point rating scale. A "strongly agree" response was assigned a value of five and a "strongly disagree" response, a value of one. "No opinion" responses were assigned the median value of three. The greater the difference from three, the greater the magnitude of the opinion expressed by the respondents, either agreeing or disagreeing with the statements. In this analysis the following classification is used:

AGREEMENT	Average Response Values
Strong	4.10 – 3.80
Medium	3.79 – 3.40
Slight	3.39 – 3.00
DISAGREEMENT	Average Responses Values
Slight	2.99 – 2.40
Medium	2.39 – 2.10
Strong	2.09 – 1.80

As might be expected, some of the statements elicited considerable uniformity among the businessmen, but others, sharp disagreement. In this analysis, "low" will indicate that the range of differences in their opinions was relatively slight; if average, the term "moderate" is applied, and, if considerable differences exist, "high".

Initial Trade Efforts

The importance of the awareness of the cultural and philosophical setting and history of the People's Republic of China was emphasized by these respondents and they indicated a strong belief that it is extremely important to acquire such knowledge for the establishment of good business relationships. The aggregate agreement with this statement was the second highest for the 38 statements in this study. Moreover, the results indicate that the differences in opinion were also very low. (See Table 1, Appendix.)

One perceptive businessman in a pamphlet he had written observed that,

> It is undoubtedly true that Western temperament and philosophical perspective result in the celerity in the development of new ideas and their practical application. This orientation is, in some respects, quite alien to China. Yet, while the Chinese perspective is a result of a very different value system, there is just as much concern with maintaining a viable society and thus concerning itself with the need for further development. In neither traditional nor contemporary China is material development a priority, but it is qualified by the context of the particular political and social system. In other words, ideally any development which does take place must not negatively affect the status quo. . . . Thus the Chinese are interested in development – in fact, political and social expedience demand it – but not at the expense of altering their system. Thus, the wholesale introduction of Western technology or plants has not been allowed although a dramatic growth in the areas where this adoption might take place would ideally occur. . . . As a further hedge, a gradualist approach is taken in terms of retooling or introducing new industry. Thus things rarely are allowed to become obsolete and often an old is used next to new. For example, China continues to rely on traditional organic products, human and animal manure, while at the same time builds nitrogen and phosphate fertilizer manufacturing facilities.[5]

There is only slight agreement among businessmen that the China Council for Promotion of International Trade is very helpful to a U.S. firm searching for the proper trade corporation in the People's Republic of China for marketing its product. (See Table 1, Appendix.) Although the Council is a non-government organization, it is an integral part of the PRC's foreign trade machinery. It is comprised of representatives from State trading corporations and experts in law, trade, and economics. It serves in a manner similar to the U.S. Chamber of Commerce in promoting and supporting trade efforts. It arranges trade exhibitions in Peking and supervises some of the trade missions that China sends abroad. It also serves as host to many visiting missions. Presumably, some of these businessmen feel that its value is limited because its role is to aid businessmen who are exploring opportunities in the country, while trade efforts that actually involve business are usually handled by a specific trading corporation.

The United States, in order to encourage trade with the People's Republic of China and to assist businessmen in their initial efforts, has established the National Council for United States-China Trade.[6] The experiences of the respondents with this type of organization have been mixed. There is slight disagreement with the observation that the PRC prefers to initiate trade contracts initially through a private-commercial organization. However, it should be noted that there was a wide difference of opinion on this point, indicating that many believe that this is an effective way to deal with the Chinese while others have found this route to be less than satisfactory. (See Table 1, Appendix.)

Effects of Foreign Competition

Because the United States had not maintained diplomatic relations with the People's Republic of China for over twenty-five years, the opportunities to trade with that country have been limited. What U.S.-China trade there was, necessarily had to be conducted through a third party.

The lack of direct business contact between the U.S. firms and the Chinese has given the, foreign firms an opportunity to establish a strong foothold in China. These businessmen strongly agree that foreign businesses offer very stiff competition in the Chinese markets. There was, however, a moderate degree of difference of opinion among these respondents suggesting that some of them do not feel that they are shut out of the market as long as their goods and services are of satisfactory quality and the prices are competitive. (See Table 2, Appendix.)

Although there was considerable variation in the opinions of these businessmen, most believed that even though they are latecomers, they are not precluded from establishing close trade relationships with the PRC. But the loyalty of the Chinese to suppliers of long standing is recognized by many as a fact (see Table 2, Appendix) requiring special efforts on the part of businessmen if it is to be overcome. Some respondents suggested that this could be accomplished through the use of more liberal terms, products of high quality, and technological competence.

Negotiating Practices in the PRC

Several businessmen, in reflecting upon the parameters involved in conducting business with the Chinese, expressed a sense of frustration. One stated that the Chinese as negotiators have a unique *modus operandi* and observed that their negotiation strategy is dictated by both ideology and business considerations. He noted that their business practices are unique and that profit maximization is not necessarily their primary concern.[7]

Further, there was strong agreement among these businessmen that the Chinese take a longer time to reply to foreign trade proposals than do Europeans, and that the negotiations require more interaction than is expected elsewhere before they fully trust an American firm. Thus, patience evidently is a key ingredient to success, and American businessmen must modify their patterns of negotiation by taking this factor into consideration. Some noted, however, that they were able to complete negotiations rapidly, so circumstances play a major part in the time required. (See Table 3, Appendix.)

The trading corporations which handle all the PRC's importing and exporting activities employ officials who are skilled negotiators. Further, there was general agreement among these businessmen that these officials are technically well trained regarding the products for which they are responsible. This places an extra burden upon the businessman who is interested in dealing with the ultimate end-users as they must also convince the representatives of the trade corporations. (See Table 3 Appendix.) Further, it is important to note that even though the end-users of the products are generally proficient in the knowledge of the technical machinery or systems, in many cases this information is obtained through U.S. journals with which they are totally familiar. In order to gain their confidence, the suggestion was made that technical seminars be established exclusively for these end-users and details be provided concerning performance, construction, maintenance, and the functions of the equipment or systems, part by part.

It is important that an end-user be assured that the equipment will do all that is claimed. This is especially important to counteract what, as one businessman noted, is their belief in the lack of integrity of American corporations as evidenced by frequently overstated claims of U.S. advertisements. The respondents also agreed that it is still necessary for machinery or equipment firms to send technical experts with the firm's negotiators in order to answer the questions of the prospective buyers. However, one businessman noted in his response that, "It is very difficult to get an expression of specific interest in projects for technology so we can prepare a proposal."

The statement with which there was the strongest agreement and the least difference of opinion was that the representatives of the PRC are extremely tough negotiators. (See Table 3, Appendix.) One businessman stated, "At least in our single experience negotiations were pretty much one-sided with the PRC giving us what they wanted and nothing else."

There was strong agreement with the statement that group decisions are preferred to individual decisions by the negotiators of the PRC. (See Table 3, Appendix.) This practice, of course, is foreign to American businessmen, but it is common to some of the countries in the Far East. It eliminates the necessity for one inividual to make a decision and subsequently to be criticized for the action taken. There was also strong agreement with the statement that during negotiations trade officials of the PRC are reluctant to reveal their position or titles. (See Table 3, Appendix.) The experience of some of the respondents indicates, however, that this pattern seems to be changing.

These businessmen are in strong agreement that during the Canton Fairs, the Chinese do not attempt to develop close personal relationships with the representatives of foreign firms. (See Table 3, Appendix.) This is probably due to the differences in ideological philosophy and the language barrier. Furthermore, some of the American businessmen were only observers and did not have machinery or other capital goods to sell and, therefore, did not become involved in direct negotiations.

There was medium agreement with the statement that recent negotiations with the PRC are relaxed and not as tense and drawn out as they had been in the past. (See Table 3, Appendix.) This is undoubtedly a result of the shift in the attitude of the PRC toward trade with foreigners, especially the United States, and a logical outcome of President Nixon's visit to that country. Obviously, closer political relationships will enable the PRC and American businessmen to develop closer ties. (See Table 3, Appendix.)

Contrary to the general belief, representatives of U.S. firms disagreed with the statement that the Chinese negotiators held managerial rank or positions equal to their counterparts from the United States.

There was also slight disagreement with the statement that Chinese negotiators are easier to trade with than those of Western Europe or the United States, (see Table 3, Appendix) suggesting again the accuracy of the observation that the Chinese are extremely tough negotiators, although fair and willing to negotiate on clauses or problems that can be solved amicably. One respondent states that the Chinese negotiators are sophisticated and reliable and are interested in frank discussions concerning solutions to problems that might arise in negotiations.

Other Aspects of Negotiating

One concern frequently expressed by Americans is that the Chinese will not honor patent agreements. There was only slight agreement among these businessmen that this is a problem, but the differences in the opinions of these businessmen on this point were moderate. (See Table 4, Appendix.) This concern is possibly based on their experiences in trading with other recently developed markets.

There was slight agreement among the businessmen that the People's Republic of China discourages the servicing of equipment and other sales follow-up and technical activities after they purchase industrial goods. (See Table 4, Appendix.) Apparently the Chinese are somewhat reluctant to permit foreigners inside their plants, even to ensure the proper functioning of the equipment, indicating they would rather rely upon manuals and their own technological competence. For standardized equipment, one businessman averred, this may be appropriate; but for highly technical equipment in which the Chinese have relatively low competence, this can seriously affect its efficiency and full utilization, leading to a lack of confidence in American capital goods and equipment. Although a knowledge of the history and culture of China is considered to be paramount for successful negotiation in China, the businessmen strongly disagreed with only moderate variation with the statement that social interaction between the Chinese people and the foreign businessmen can be achieved through Canton night life. (See Table 4, Appendix.) There were no suggestions as to how this might be achieved, but several indicated a serious interest in developing closer cultural relationships with the Chinese people as has been done in other countries such as Russia. Unfortunately, social interaction with the Chinese people is restricted because the PRC does not permit businessmen to travel freely in the Canton area at the present time, although there is a great difference of opinion regarding the degree of restriction. (See Table 4, Appendix.)

In the past, suggestions have been made that businessmen quote low prices and take a loss initially in order to establish a foothold in the Chinese market. These businessmen strongly disapproved of this marketing tactic. If adopted, they anticipate difficulties in raising prices at a later date. Furthermore, as will be noted later, the Chinese are very shrewd negotiators who would probably switch to other suppliers if this trading tactic were employed. (See Table 4, Appendix.) In addition, there was general disagreement among these businessmen regarding the use of quantity discounts as an effective negotiating tool. One person averred that this could lead to a request that the price generated by the larger quantity be made applicable to other purchases of lesser quantity, thereby negating the purpose of a quantity discount. This practice, of course, would not be a sound business practice and should be avoided.

ASTON UNIVERSITY
LIBRARY & INFORMATION SERVICES

Some who have done business in China have suggested that to remain after the closing of the Canton Fair in order to complete trade negotiations with Chinese representatives would be prudent. Respondents slightly disagreed with this assertion. (See Table 4, Appendix.)

Specifications of Contracts

These businessmen strongly agree that the Chinese negotiators adhere closely to the terms and conditions specified in their contracts. Thus, to avoid merchandise quality disputes, they believe that it is essential to specify the nature of inspection tests and product standards. The details must be carefully defined because the Chinese will also expect literal adherence to contracts. (See Table 5, Appendix.) One respondent added that it is desirable to conclude a contract before leaving the Canton Fair since to do so by letter or cable at a later date is more difficult.

Writing highly specific and detailed contracts becomes extremely time consuming. Although these businessmen generally agree that Chinese contracts are more specific than those written in the United States, there was a high degree of variation in their opinion on this point. (See Table 5, Appendix.) Evidently, some businessmen are finding the PRC to be more accommodating in writing contracts, a major trade hurdle in the past. This led one person to observe that patience and time are the two key factors to successful United States-PRC trade relations. Another respondent averred, "We found the people friendly and helpful and the negotiators were very interested in learning about technology from the U.S. that we had to offer." One businessman noted that he had made many close friends among Chinese officials and other representatives of firms from Europe, Africa, and Hong Kong while dealing with the negotiators from the PRC.

When disputes arise, however, these businessmen were in general agreement that the Chinese prefer to negotiate settlements rather than to employ arbitration as might be provided in a contract. (See Table 5, Appendix.) If arbitration is necessary, they insist that it be conducted in Europe, preferably in such countries as Switzerland or Sweden, although they are now willing to accept Canada as a site. (See Table 5, Appendix.)

There was also moderate agreement among these businessmen that the Chinese prefer to have prices quoted FOB on imports and CIF on exports, and that the goods be shipped and insured by their own companies. (See Table 5, Appendix.)

Impediments to Trade Development

Differences in technical backgrounds of the Chinese technicians, financial requirements, language differences, and the threat of low cost labor are frequently mentioned as major impediments to the development of trade with

China. Based on their experience, however, the majority of these businessmen do not share these concerns. For example, there was general agreement that the technical background of the PRC technicians and operators would not be a major problem in their training to operate U.S. equipment. (See Table 6, Appendix.) Moreover, these businessmen disagreed with the assertion that the language barrier would prohibit effective training of these technicians, nor did they believe that the language barrier made communications with the PRC representatives difficult. (See Table 6, Appendix.) Highly competent interpreters who can assist in overcoming any language limitation or barriers are available.

The financing of exports has often hampered trade with the Communist nations. The People's Republic of China is no exception. Businessmen have encountered problems relating to the convertibility of currency, the extension of credit, and the insistence that Western-European currencies be used in contract negotiations. These problems have been relieved somewhat with the use of the Japanese yen and the RMB.[8] Use of the U.S. dollar will further relieve the problem. Some businessmen noted that the Chase Manhattan Bank of New York has been invited to become the U.S. correspondent of the Bank of China. That bank will handle foreign remittances and travelers' letters of credit and eventually establish a complete banking relationship with the PRC. While there were wide differences of opinion regarding the financial problems, most businessmen did not foresee this as a major obstacle to the expansion of trade. (See Table 6, Appendix.)

Some opponents of the expansion of U.S.-China trade have alluded to the threat of the development of a major competitive force in the areas of technology if we give the PRC the basic training and tools at this time. A similar argument has been used concerning trade with Russia. However, there was slight disagreement among these businessmen with this fear. (See Table 6, Appendix.) The possibility that the PRC would flood the markets because of its low-cost labor intensive products was, however, strongly rejected. (See Table 6, Appendix.) They noted that the major exports from China in the foreseeable future will be agricultural products, oil, and coal; therefore, the country would not constitute a major threat in the more sophisticated, technological capital goods area. One respondent observed that there is great hostility by the Chinese toward some U.S. governmental agencies such as the Pure Food and Drug Administration which has placed minimum standards regarding quality and other requirements. If the Chinese suspect discriminatory treatment, such problems can be clarified only through greater contact and communications.

Businessmen were asked if labor, consumer, political, and other activist groups who are opposed to the ideological philosophy of China will attempt to prohibit the development of trade with that country. Again there were wide differences in opinion among the respondents, but in general they did not believe that this would be a major barrier to trade development. (See Table 6, Appendix.)

One businessman observed that there was a danger in this type of study in that the findings would only vindicate certain clichés about China trade and would fail to consider the historical significance and long-term dynamics of trade. Fortunately, this problem has not arisen. Many of the statements which were based upon "conventional wisdom" have not been supported by the experiences of these businessmen, and many freely disagreed with other statements in this study.

Industrial Affiliation of Respondents

Although one of the major obstacles to the expansion of trade is the limited nature of the exports from the PRC and their demand for capital goods from the U.S., 78 per cent of the businessmen responding were primarily interested in China as a source of imports while 22 per cent were considering the PRC as a potential market for their products. However, it should be noted that a substantial number of these businessmen were interested in both importing and exporting. (See Table 1.)

Of the firms negotiating on imports, 32 per cent look upon the PRC as a source of light industrial products; 30 per cent, native produce and animal by-products; and 30 per cent, textile products. Fifty-eight per cent of the respondents also indicated their interest in importing metals and materials (21%), chemicals (16%), cereals, oils and foodstuffs (21%). These businessmen have been primarily concerned with importing from China rather than exporting which is contrary to the present trade flow pattern.

The major negotiations for exports from the U.S. were with the machinery and chemical trading corporation of the PRC (30%).

Table 1: U.S. businessmen negotiating import and export trade with the various PRC trading corporations

	Import to U.S. U.S. businessmen		*Export from U.S. U.S. businessmen*	
Product	*Number**	*Per cent*	*Number**	*Per cent*
Cereals, oils and foodstuffs	36	21	5	3
Native produce and animal by-product	53	30	4	2
Light industrial products	55	32	7	4
Textiles	52	30	3	2
Chemicals	27	16	22	13
Machinery	8	5	31	18
Metals and materials	37	21	4	2
TOTAL	268		76	
Respondent's Primary Trade Interest		78%		22%

*Several of the 174 businessmen were interested in negotiating for more than one class of product.

Relative Expectations of PRC Trade[9]

The optimism of these businessmen concerning trade with China is closely correlated with the time period involved. About a third of them were unwilling to make any estimates concerning trade prospects for the two- and five-year periods. Of those who ventured a forecast for the next two years, approximately 50 per cent expect their company's trade to increase between 0 and 25 per cent in the next two years. Another 20 per cent expect it to rise from 25 to 50 per cent. Only 5 per cent expect their trade to increase more than 200 per cent during this period. The average increase expected is 48 per cent. (See Table 2.)

The five-year projections are much more optimistic. Approximately 20 per cent expect their trade to increase from 0 to 25 per cent range, and a similar number expect it to expand as much as 50 per cent. Strikingly, another 23.5 per cent expect an increase of 200 per cent or more, but this highly optimistic level of expansion must be interpreted in the light of a very low level of business at the present time. On the average, the respondents expect a 90 per cent increase in their business with China in the next five years. (See Table 2.)

Generally, these businessmen were cautiously optimistic concerning the growth of trade with China. Insofar as their own companies were concerned, they did not consider it to be highly significant either in the two-year or over the five-year period. Eighty-three per cent thought it would be only moderately significant or less. Approximately 18 per cent of these businessmen who responded indicated their company's trade with China could be very or extremely significant in the next two years. Over the five-year period, one-fourth of the firms surveyed expected their trade with the PRC to be either extremely or very important to their marketing plans. (See Table 3.)

Table 2: Increase expected in PRC trade of respondents' firms (within 2 and 5 years)

		Trade increase forecast (%)						
Time period	*Average %*	*0–25*	*26–50*	*51–75*	*76–100*	*101–150*	*151–200*	*201 +*
2 years (N = 122)	48	49%	18%	11%	11%	5%	2%	5%
5 years (N = 119)	90	24%	23%	5%	15%	5%	4%	24%

Table 3: Respondents' perceptions of the importance of PRC trade to their firms' marketing plans (within 2 and 5 years)

	Degree of importance				
Time period	*Extremely important*	*Very important*	*Moderately important*	*Somewhat important*	*Not important*
2-year plan (N = 151)	9%	9%	22%	37%	23%
5-year plan (N = 145)	12%	14%	32%	33%	9%

A typically cautious view was expressed by one businessman. He stated that:

> International trade will remain a small (5%) volume of the Chinese Gross National Product and will be shared by several Western and Communist countries. U.S promoters of all types make it appear much larger than facts justify. Some make a business out of getting invitations to Canton and bringing a couple of clients who may represent larger companies not invited by the Chinese directly. Keep getting invitations by buying something in China that will keep "half a commune" busy for a year, will do the trick. I call it a big myth.
>
> China has 800 million people. Its living standard is gradually rising. The large population provides the U.S. with a big potential market in the future. We might also expect an increase in imports of labor intensive products such as handicrafts, textiles, light industrial goods, and other manufactured products.
>
> There is no doubt that the PRC trade officials will try to obtain as much information as possible on products in which they are interested from the U.S. representative. The extent of cooperation that is given by U.S. representatives in this area will add much to foster a friendly relationship between the PRC and the U.S. and, in turn, provide greater opportunities for trade between the two countries. Volume depends upon tariffs – Most Favored Nation Clause.

Conclusion

The experiences of these businessmen tend to support the observation that the Chinese are becoming more flexible in their negotiations and are sincerely interested in expanding trade with the United States. Although this trade to date has been heavily one-sided in favor of the United States, their need for capital goods and the U.S. need for many of their products will aid in the expansion of two-way trade. American businessmen should find increasing business opportunities with the People's Republic of China.

Notes

1. U.S. Department of Commerce, *Overseas Business Reports*, May 1976, pp. 24, 28.
2. Ibid., June 1974, p. 13.
3. Ibid., p. 18.
4. *OBR*, October 1974, p.7.
5. Julian M. Sobin, *Bilateral Breakthrough, Discovering the New People's Republic of China* (Praeger Publishers, Inc., 1974), p.3.
6. Established on March 22, 1973.
7. Julian M. Sobin, *China as a Trading Partner: A View After Four Trade Fairs* (Boston: Friendship International Division, Sobin Chemicals, Inc., 1974), p.3.
8. Renminbi is the currency denomination of the PRC used in international trade transactions.

9. The table indicates the degree of optimism with which the respondents view U.S.-PRC trade. However, the expectations must be viewed in light of the fact that current trade figures of the individual firms have not been provided. Thus, an expected increase of 100 per cent might mean an increase from $1000 to $2000. Since the total U.S. exports to the PRC in 1975 amounted to $304 million and imports from the PRC during the same year totalled only $157 million, the expected increase in this trade might be based on these figures. (U.S. Department of Commerce, *Overseas Business Reports*, May 1976), pp. 24, 28.

Appendix

Table 1: Initial trade efforts

Statement	*Businessmen's opinions*	*Average response value*	*Variation among opinions*
In establishing a good business relationship with the People's Republic of China, some knowledge of China's history and culture is helpful.	Strong Agreement	4.04	Low
The China Council for Promotion of International Trade is extremely helpful to the U.S. firm searching for the proper People's Republic of China trade corporations for marketing its products.	Slight Agreement	3.02	Moderate
The People's Republic of China trade corporations prefer to make initial trade contacts through private commercial organizations specializing in People's Republic of China trade.	Slight Disagreement	2.85	High

Table 2: Effects of foreign competition on U.S. trade opportunities

Statement	*Businessmen's opinions*	*Average response value*	*Variation among opinions*
Foreign firms provide U.S. firms with very stiff competition for the People's Republic of China import trade.	Strong Agreement	3.94	Moderate
Because we are late arrivals on the trade scene, it will be difficult to establish a trade relationship (as the Chinese show great loyalty to suppliers of long standing).	Slight Disagreement	2.70	High

Table 3: Negotiating practices of the PRC representatives in the People's Republic of China

Statement	*Businessmen's opinions*	*Average response value*	*Variation among opinions*
The Chinese take a longer time to reply to foreign trade proposals than do Europeans.	Strong Agreement	3.96	Low
People's Republic of China negotiators require more interaction than is expected in the U.S. before fully trusting an American firm.	Strong Agreement	3.85	Low
The People's Republic of China representatives are extremely tough negotiators.	Strong Agreement	4.10	Low

(Continued)

Table 3: *(Continued)*

Statement	*Businessmen's opinions*	*Average response value*	*Variation among opinions*
The officials of the People's Republic of China trade corporations are technically well trained regarding the products they represent.	Medium Agreement	3.73	Moderate
It is necessary that a machine or equipment firm send technical experts with the firm's negotiators.	Medium Agreement	3.72	Low
Group decisions are preferred to individual decisions by People's Republic of China negotiators.	Strong Agreement	3.93	Low
During negotiations, trade officials of the People's Republic of China are reluctant to reveal their positions or titles.	Strong Agreement	3.87	High
At the Canton Fair the Chinese do not attempt to develop close personal relationships with the representatives of foreign firms.	Strong Agreement	3.98	Low
The style of recent negotiations with the People's Republic of China is relaxed; not tense and drawn out as in the past.	Medium Agreement	3.49	Low
The U.S. firm's representatives generally negotiate with People's Republic of China representatives of equal rank or position.	Slight Disagreement	2.85	Moderate
In general, after relations are established, the Chinese negotiators are easier to trade with than those of Western Europe or the United States.	Slight Disagreement	2.77	Moderate

Table 4: Negotiating atmosphere in the PRC

Statement	*Businessmen's opinions*	*Average response value*	*Variation among opinions*
The People's Republic of China can be expected to honor patent agreements.	Slight Agreement	3.09	Moderate
Servicing equipment and other sales follow-up and technological activities are discouraged by the People's Republic of China in the sales of industrial goods, etc.	Slight Agreement	3.02	Moderate
The Canton night life provides social interaction between the Chinese people and the foreign businessmen.	Strong Disagreement	1.84	Moderate
The People's Republic of China permits foreign businessmen to travel freely within the Canton area.	Medium Agreement	3.62	High
In order to make a favorable first impression, U.S. firms are wise to quote low prices initially, with the intention of making up lost profits later by raising prices.	Strong Disagreement	1.86	Moderate
Quantity discounts on goods are an effective negotiating tool in trading with the People's Republic of China.	Slight Disagreement	2.94	Low
It is a prudent practice for trade negotiators to remain after the closing of Canton Fair in order to complete the negotiations.	Slight Disagreement	2.83	Moderate

Table 5: Specifications of contracts

Statement	*Businessmen's opinions*	*Average response value*	*Variation among opinions*
People's Republic of China negotiators adhere closely to the terms and conditions specified in their contracts.	Strong Agreement	3.97	Low
In order to prevent merchandise quality disputes, it is essential to specify the nature of inspection tests and product standards in contracts.	Strong Agreement	3.94	Low
People's Republic of China contracts are highly specific in detail as compared to comparable contracts in the United States.	Slight Agreement	3.12	High
When a contract dispute arises, the Chinese prefer to negotiate settlements rather than employ the arbitration provided in their contracts.	Medium Agreement	3.77	Low
The People's Republic of China prefers that contract terms are f.o.b. for imports and c.i.f. for exports.	Medium Agreement	3.54	Low
The People's Republic of China prefers that goods traded be shipped and insured by their own companies.	Medium Agreement	3.50	Moderate

Table 6: Impediments to trade development

Statement	*Businessmen's opinions*	*Average response value*	*Variation among opinions*
The technical background of People's Republic of China technicians and operators presents a major problem in their training to operate U.S. equipment.	Slight Disagreement	2.85	Low
The language barrier makes communications between People's Republic of China and U.S. representatives very difficult.	Medium Disagreement	2.20	High
Training of People's Republic of China technicians to operate and service U.S. equipment is difficult because of the language barrier.	Slight Disagreement	2.64	Moderate
The People's Republic of China imposes financial requirements on import trade forming definite obstacles to increased trade.	Slight Disagreement	2.75	High
The economy of the People's Republic of China will, in the foreseeable future, become very productive and begin to compete internationally with American companies.	Slight Disagreement	2.60	High
Because of its low-cost labor supply, the People's Republic of China will flood world markets with low-cost, labor intensive product.	Strong Disagreement	2.04	Moderate
The trade of technological goods to the People's Republic of China will erode the U.S. advantage in technology.	Strong Disagreement	2.06	Moderate
The only U.S. products in which the People's Republic of China has shown interest are industrial goods, pharmaceuticals, and agricultural goods.	Slight Agreement	3.14	Moderate
Opposition by labor, consumer, and political activist groups will deter the development of trade with the People's Republic of China.	Slight Disagreement	2.60	High

5

Chinese Cultural Values: Their Dimensions and Marketing Implications

Oliver H.M. Yau

Introduction

With one fifth of the world's population, China has the greatest number of consumers in the world. Businessmen in international trade will often find themselves dealing with Chinese consumers. Waldie (1980) has warned international managers in Hong Kong to examine the cultural differences between Chinese and Western people in general when making management decisions. An English term can have a different meaning in a Chinese situation. For example, in Western culture, maturity means "to be able to express one's genuine self, to be free from the constraints of what other people think, to confront others because of the consequence of being individualised or different" (Waldie, 1980). But, for the Chinese, maturity means a movement towards a harmonious integration into the social fabric of the family, as well as the institute at which one is working. Thus, it is crucial and beneficial for international marketing managers to understand the Chinese way of life and value systems. This is the objective of this article.

Chinese Cultural Values

Researchers in the study of Chinese cultural values may find it amazing that Chinese values have formed a clear and consistent system for generations (Kindle, 1983; Hsu, 1970). Of course, it does not imply that the values and

Source: *European Journal of Marketing*, 22(5) (1988): 44–57.

the system have not been changed. In fact, the Chinese cultural value systems have recently undergone rapid change. For example, during the Cultural Revolution in the People's Republic of China, the orthodox doctrine of Confucianism, which is the foundation of the Chinese value system, was severely criticised and deeds according to the doctrine strictly forbidden. Thus, the classical Chinese value system was disrupted and efforts are now being made to rebuild it. Other Chinese-dominated societies, such as Taiwan, Hong Kong and Singapore, have also shown inevitable changes in the value systems during the process of rapid social and economic change (Shively and Shively, 1972).

Some studies have revealed that Chinese cultural values have indeed changed. In a cross-cultural comparison of human values, Morris (1956) found that there was no noticeable difference in the value systems of sub-samples of university students from four large cities in China. Yang (1977) replicated Morris's study and found that there was a change in hierarchy of the value systems of college students. However, his findings also imply that some of the traditional Chinese values are still held by young Chinese nowadays.

Adopting the methodology from Kluckhohn and Strodbeck (1961), Lin (1966) tried to uncover the value orientations of Hong Kong school students and their parents. He found, within variational limits, that the younger generation had changed considerably, as compared with their parents, with regard to time, man-nature and relational orientations. It would be a mistake, however, to conclude that these findings indicate the traditional Chinese value orientations in Hong Kong have been completely eradicated in the transition to modernisation. Firstly, mastery of traditional Chinese learning is regarded as an important prerequisite for achieving status among the intellectuals in Chinese society (Lin, 1966). Second, strong vestiges of the Chinese heritage are rooted in the family and kinship relations and not in the educational institutes (Hsu, 1947, 1963, 1972). As for individual Chinese, family is a source which constantly diffuses cultural influences on them throughout their lives. Even though they may deviate from the traditional value orientations at some point in their lives, they tend to be assimilated again by their Chinese culture and enjoy their authority and social status as they grow old. Some researchers have argued that education would introduce new values, which would gradually replace the old ones to shape an industrialised society in which family and kinship relationships could not survive (Shively and Shively, 1972). However, this may not be so.

Traditional values will not necessarily be a stumbling block to industrialisation or economic development. The success of the Japanese, which has a similar culture to the Chinese, is a typical example. Hong Kong is another good example of how cultural values have served to make the economy unique. It has been proven during the past 20 years that the prosperity of Hong Kong is not only due to the acumen of the Chinese businessmen, but also to the considerateness and perseverance of the labour force who always try to be in harmony with their employers.

Classification of Chinese Cultural Values

The Chinese cultural values are largely formed and created from interpersonal relationships and social orientations. This is shown in the work of Confucius, whose doctrine is still a basic pillar of Chinese life today. To describe the Chinese culture, it is therefore more suitable to adopt the value-orientation model of Kluckhohn and Strodbeck (1961) which has the same emphasis. The following is a description of each of the Chinese cultural values according to Kluckhohn and Strodbeck's classification, with possible marketing implications discussed for each orientation see Figure 1):

(1) man-nature orientation;
(2) man-himself orientation;
(3) relational orientation;
(4) time orientation, and
(5) personal activity orientation.

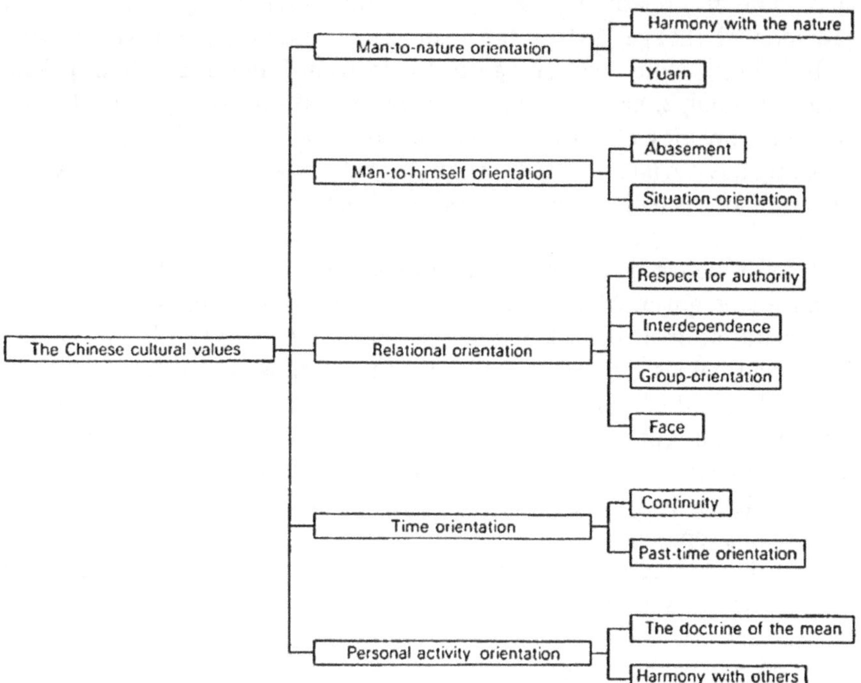

Figure 1: Classification of Chinese cultural values

Chinese Cultural Values and Their Marketing Implications

Man-Nature Orientation

The Chinese regard man as a part of nature, and believe that man should not try to overcome or master nature but has to learn how to adapt to it so as to reach harmony. This is because the Chinese belive that nature has the Way (*Tao*) by which all things become what they are (Chan, 1963). It was said that the Way cannot be told:

> There are existence and destruction, life and death, and flourish and decline . . . What is eternal has neither change nor any definite principle itself. Since it (the Way) has no definite principle itself, it is not bound in any particular locality.

Therefore, it is not wise to hold too tight on to what one has got or lost. There is no such thing as fate or misfortune in life, as they are entangled with each other, as well as causes of each other (Wei, 1980).

Apart from the doctrine of the Way, *Yuarn* (*Karma*) is another important belief which has been rooted in the heart of most Chinese. This belief prevailed well before the time of Confucius (BC 557–479), as he once said: "Life and death are fated; wealth and honours hinge on the will of providence" (Legge, 1960). It resembles the important doctrine, *Karma* in Buddhism, which was spread to China from India in the Han or Tang Dynasty about 2,000 years ago. Hence to a certain extent, it still has the Buddhist meaning of *Karma*. However, after 2,000 years of assimilation, its meaning has deviated from its origin. *Yuarn* can be referred to as predetermined relations with other things or individuals which are far beyond one's control.

The existence or absence of interrelations with the universe is predetermined or governed by a powerful external force. This force could be supernatural, or a social law which is too sophisticated to be understood by human beings. The Chinese believe that friendships or even marriages are predetermined. When *Yuarn* exists, it leads to the chance that two men, living thousands of miles apart, could meet each other and become friends. It also leads consumers to find products with which they may be very satisfied. Further, *Yuarn* will come to an end. When it does, couples have to divorce and friends separate.

Despite its tragic sense, *Yuarn* also has its positive side. The concept of *Yuarn* leads to self-reliance. People cease to complain about their circumstances and try to save themselves from the natural consequences of their own acts before they accept their fate. For example, an individual could beg for *Yuarn* by giving alms and doing charitable deeds in secret so that the interrelations of himself or his family with the universe may be established.

Furthermore, though things are predetermined, he has to try positively to seek for interrelations with others (or things) in order to find out whether he has got *Yuarn* or not. According to the concept, the interrelations among people are always passive. But it is only those who take an active part in searching for, and trying to establish it, who can successfully have *Yuarn.*

The Potential marketing implications for man-to-nature orientation – The man-to-nature orientation has some implications in marketing. According to these two doctrines, it is possible to expect that a Chinese consumer who believes in them would generally have low expectations towards the product he is going to purchase or consume, or that when the performance of the product does not meet with his expectations, he would feel less dissatisfied because he thinks he has to conform to *Yuarn.*

The Chinese have a great tendency to attribute failure of products/services to fate rather than to the company from whom the product was purchased, or even the manufacturer. Hence, they are reluctant to complain about products that do not meet with their expectations. Thorelli (1982) includes this evidence in his recent study on Chinese consumers. Therefore, objective measurement of dissatisfaction, such as frequency of complaints, does not adequately reflect the affective attitude of consumers towards products, and, thus, is not a good measure of marketing effectiveness (see McNeal, 1969; Cavusgil and Kaynak, 1982). Other means of measurement of consumer satisfaction or dissatisfaction are needed.

Man-to-himself Orientation

Abasement – by studying the child-rearing practices of Chinese families, one can observe dramatic differences from Western cultures. From an early stage, a child in a Chinese family is brought up to understand the legitimate role of him/herself in front of others. Chinese are used to believing in modesty and self-effacement, two important virtues that a child, as well as a subordinate, uses to cultivate him/her mind. In the past, individual Chinese would call themselves "the worthless" before their teachers, and "the unfilial" child before their parents. This sort of behaviour is still very common in today's Chinese society. For example, Western people will tend to say "thank you" when praised by others, but Chinese people will be prone to say "No, I am not worthy" in the same situation. Further, Chinese try to avoid saying "No" when asked to express opinions. They believe that saying "No" will embarrass or offend others. Thus, to reply in an indirect or sarcastic way is the best way to express disagreement.

Situation orientation – Chinese today are frequently regarded as situation oriented and pragmatic (Hsu, 1963). Again, this is due to child-rearing practices during which children are taught by parents, uncles and aunts, and other adults in the (extended or joint) family. They are therefore liable to exposure of many points of view. Consequently, Chinese children learn that circumstances have an important bearing upon what is right or wrong, and compromise in most cases is inevitable. Western children, on the other hand, are usually brought up under the guidance of one set of parents, are rarely exposed to various points of view, are kept in a more closed relationship with life's events, and grow up with concepts of one right way to do things (Kindle, 1982). Thus, comparatively, the Chinese are less dogmatic and tend to be more flexible in following a learned principle. The root of this Chinese cultural value is in Lao Tse's doctrine of the Way.

Potential marketing implications for man-to-himself orientation – In marketing, the value of abasement may have possible implications for sales force management. It can be used as a supplement to other sales force selection techniques, such as objective testing, personal interviews and background investigation. If an effective salesman has to be aggressive and positive minded by American standards, Chinese tend to be bad salesmen. However, in Chinese society, aggressive salesmen might frighten customers, who may be humiliated. For example, Chinese buyers like to have their shopping in a free environment without interference. If a salesman in a retail store is too eager to help and approaches a customer who has not decided what to buy, the customer will feel uneasy and go away. The proper thing to do is to deep a distance from the customer, but, at the same time, let him/her know that he is always ready to help.

The value of situation orientation has particular implications for service marketing. Because of this orientation, Chinese tend to enjoy available things. In the United Kingdom or other Western countries, it is commonplace for consumers to queue up Indian file to buy tickets for a movie or to cash a cheque. Customers are requested or assigned to a counter to be served. The Chinese prefer a short queue, even though the waiting time is the same. Moreover, Chinese are anxious to choose the person whom they are familiar with to serve them. Therefore, unless there is no other alternative, Chinese tend to feel more dissatisfied with the serving system and are more likely not to re-purchase than their counterparts in the US. In Hong Kong and even in Taiwan, the multi-line waiting system is usually adopted, except for some English and American banks.

Relational Orientation

Respect for authority – The Chinese have a strong respect for authority. They are prone to trust totally without questioning. In a classroom, Chinese students expect their teachers to "teach" them, as well as guide them. Students will feel they are learning nothing if asked to express their opinions or to solve a problem by themselves. It is the same in psychological therapy. Chinese patients usually request the psychologist to teach them what to do, and do not believe that trying to find out the solution themselves in consultation with the psychologist is a better way to cure their illness.

The early root of the Chinese respect for authority is in Confucius's five cardinal relations, between sovereign and minister, father and son, husband and wife, old and young, and between friends (Hchu and Yang, 1977). These relations have served effectively to control social behaviour in society. Chinese have to observe and act according to the norms prescribed for each instance of interpersonal relations. Thus, the king must be kingly, the minister ministerly, the husband husbandly, the wife wifely, brothers brotherly, and friends friendly. It is not suprising to see that Chinese today still prefer to address someone in more structural or hierarchical-type terms than Westerners. For example, people in the Republic of China used to address Mao as Chairman Mao in order to show respect for his authority. A child is not allowed to call his father's friends by their names. And a venerable man with seniority in an organisation is addressed by adding the term "old brother" before his surname.

This value has particular implications for advertising. Since the Chinese have such respect for authority, directing them to what is right or wrong, advertisements will tend to be more effective when opinion leaders stand up in commercials recommending products/services to their target consumers. Opinion leaders for Chinese consumers include older people, political leaders, family elders and authoritarian types. Kindle (1985) pointed out that Chinese are much more likely to be influenced in their purchasing by opinion leaders than are consumers in the US.

Interdependence – The flexibility of the Chinese in dealing with interpersonal relations comes from the principle of "doing favours", which literally signifies one's honour to another. Favours done for others are often considered what may be termed "social investments", for which handsome returns are expected. The following Chinese proverbs clearly reveal this:

> If you honour me a linear foot, I should in return honour you ten feet.
>
> A horse received must be returned by an ox; a case of presents received is to be acknowledged by a case of presents in return.

Almost every Chinese is brought up to be highly conscious of "doing favours" and to practise it heartily. They believe that the reciprocity of doing favours between man and man should be as certain as a cause-and-effect relationship. It should be continuous so that affinity for each other is well established.

The application of the principle of "doing favours" has a tremendous influence on social, as well as business, behaviour. It maintains relations among Chinese people by the presentation of gifts which they regard as a form of *Li* – propriety. Small businessmen often believe that following the principle of "doing favours" is of utmost importance in making the business go smoothly so as to earn more money. They exchange their favours (help) when supplying goods or credits without signing any legal documents, and believe that the signing of any legal document will terminate the reciprocity of doing favours.

Face – Face is a concept of central importance because of its pervasive influence in interpersonal relations among Chinese. Hu (1944) examined 200 Chinese proverbs and classified face into two types, *lien* and *mien-tsu*:

Lien "represents the confidence of society in the integrity of ego's moral character, the loss of which makes it impossible for him to function properly within the community" (Hu, 1944). *Mien-tsu*, on the other hand, "stands for the kind of prestige that is emphasized . . . a reputation achieved through getting on in life, through success and ostentation" (Hu, 1944).

Mien-tsu can be characterised in both quantitative and qualitative terms (Ho, 1972). The amount of *mien-tsu* a person has is a function of his social status. It varies according to the group with which he is interacting. A manager may have more *mien-tsu* before his subordinates, but not in a group of intellectuals. *Mien-tsu* may be claimed on a variety of grounds. It may be obtained either through personal qualities, or derived from non-personal characteristics, such as wealth, social connections and authority through personal efforts (Ho, 1972).

Mien-tsu can be lost or gained when there are changes which constitute a departure from the quality or quantity of one's claim. *Mien-tsu* can normally be gained by obtaining favourable comments from the interacting group or community, through exemplary behaviour, superior performance or knowledge, or enhancement of status, by formal promotion to higher office, etc. *Mient-tsu* may be lost when conduct or performance falls below the minimum acceptable standard, or when some essential requirements corresponding to one's social position are not satisfactorily met with. Since the standard and requirements are social expectations held by the group with whom he is interacting, the possibility of losing *mien-tsu* may not only come from his own actions or behaviour, but from how he is expected to behave or be treated by other members in the group. Chinese are always under strong constraint to meet the expectations of others so as to maintain their *mien-tsu*, as well as to reciprocate a due regard for the *mien-tsu* of others. The concern for *mien-tsu* exerts a mutual restrictive, even coercive, power on each member of the social network. Thus, the Chinese always try to avoid causing others to lose face, which is regarded as an aggressive act by those whose face has been discredited, but to protect others from losing it, which is an act of consideration.

Lien differs from *mien-tsu* in that *lien* is something that everyone is entitled to by virtue of his membership in society; it can only be lost through misconduct. Thus, it is meaningful to speak only of losing *lien*, but not of gaining it.

The losing of *lien* is more serious than that of *mien-tsu*. This is because when *mien-tsu* is lost, it can more easily be regained. But when *lien* is lost, an individual's integrity of character is cast in doubt, or even destroyed. For example, prostitutes and thieves are all people who renounce their concern for *lien.* The disregard for *lien* can therefore lead to a total transformation of one's social identity.

The significance of *lien* cannot be fully appreciated without realising its close relationship with the concept of *ch'ih,* which, in the Chinese context has literally the same meaning as the word "shame" in English. King and Myers (1977) suggested that in Chinese culture, *lien* (face) is an incomplete concept. They demonstrated a dichotomy between the Chinese face-shame complex, in contrast with the Western sin-guilt complex. *Lien* implies the presence of *ch'ih,* which is one of the fundamental requirements of being human. Thus, Mencius declared that "a man without a sense of *ch'ih* (shame) is not a man" (see Mencius, one of the *Four Books*). Losing *lien* is experienced as *wu ch'ih* (without a sene of *ch'ih*). In cases of complete loss of *lien,* committing suicide may be a final resort to show the presence of *ch'ih.* Even in today's Chinese society, women often commit suicide to demonstrate their innocence following the misfortune of being raped.

Group Orientation

The concept of face is in conflict with individualism, which assumes the individual's well-being or interest. Hofstede (1980), a European scholar, used the term "collective" instead of "group oriented". He indicated that the Chinese, as well as Asians, are collectivistic, although his list of values was incomplete. The collectivistic nature of the Chinese is reflected in the Chinese family and kinship system (Hsu, 1968). Hsu argued that "the primary concern of a majority of Chinese was to protect and enhance their private kinship interests". He indicated that the Chinese regard the kinship system as a basis for relating to others. It means continuous and long-lasting human ties which do not have clearly defined boundaries. For example, in many European countries, the parent-child relationship legally comes to an end when children reach the age of 18 or 21, after which parents lose their say over their chilren's marriages. The Western husband and wife also maintain individual privacy, which cannot be intruded on except by invitation. Efforts at discipline by grandparents and other adults in the family system are regarded as interference. Thus, there exist in the family system dividing lines which make the boundaries clearly defined, and human ties supersede each other rather than being additive (Hsu, 1968).

The Chinese tend to behave in the opposite way. When getting married, children still regard seeking approval from parents as mandatory and necessary (Salaff, 1981). Sometimes, decisions of parents are final. Sons and daughters after marriage are still liable to support the family (in terms of their parents or parents-in-law), even though they may live apart. Further, they spend their leisure time preserving a viable relationship with parents and parents-in-law by a variety of activities, such as having tea in Chinese restaurants, or feasting at home on Saturday or Sunday evenings. Normally, parents live with one of their children (usually the eldest son) even after his/her marriage. Therefore, in contrast with Europeans or Americans, marriage for a Chinese means an increase of psycho-social involvement with his/her parents or parents-in-law. Marriage is not only an affair between the bride and the bridegroom, but an occasion for the family to reciprocate affection to friends and other members in the kinship system (Salaff, 1981).

Chinese may well be able to sacrifice themselves for benefits that largely accrue to a particular social unit, or even to society as a whole. In a poor Chinese family, daughters and the eldest son may have to forgo their educational opportunities by going out to work so as to secure economically the whole family (Salaff, 1981). When making decisions, an individual Chinese should always take into account other members of the family, in contrast with the husband-wife joint decisions in the West. He/she is more motivated towards achieving the goal of the (extended) family or the group that he/she is affiliated with than with individualised self-fulfilment. Wilson and Pusey (1982) have confirmed this in the investigation of achievement motivation and small-business relationship patterns in Chinese society. They found that group orientation correlates more significantly with achievement motivation in the Chinese sample than in the American sample.

However, there is one thing worth mentioning. Chinese are only group oriented towards those social units with whom interactions have been established. They follow the appropriate social norms regardless of their own private views. But they appear to be quite suspicious and cold towards strangers with whom relationships have not been established.

According to the above discussions, it is to be expected that satisfaction with a product may not be derived solely from one's expectations towards, or disconfirmation with, the product, but from other members of the family. This is especially true in an extended family.

Potential marketing implications for relational orientation – The values of interdependence and face are particularly meaningful to the study of gift-giving behaviour. To the Chinese, gift giving is one of the ways to build up relationships with friends. There are festivals in the Chinese Lunar calendar, such as the Chinese New Year, the mid-autumn Festival and the Dragon Boat Festival, when gifts are presented to friends or superiors. Differing from Western societies, there are certain norms that Chinese obey when giving gifts. For example, gifts presented should be expensive enough to match the income of the givers, so that they are giving face to those who receive their gifts, and that they gain face at the same time because they are thought of as being sincere. For friends, gifts of comparable or even higher value should be returned as soon as possible. In marketing products which can be regarded as gifts, the packaging of these products is extremely important. They should be packed prestigiously and beautifully in red, which means happiness and good luck, and priced at a level to match their packaging. When such products are launched by well-known firms or manufacturers, the prices can be set higher than competitors' as the Chinese believe in established brands and companies.

From a different angle, the concept of interdependence is important for Western executives working in Chinese society. They should be reminded that off-duty personal behaviour, through which the relationship with the community is built, is highly important to the firm's image and its effectiveness.

Several aspects of the value of group orientation are noteworthy in marketing, too. First, because the Chinese are strongly collective may imply that informal channels of communications are important in Chinese society, compared with those in the UK. Chinese consumers tend to rely more on word-of-mouth communication. Because of the high contact rate among group members, communications among Chinese consumers for a given product idea may be diffused very quickly. Furthermore, given that informal channels of communication carry both facts and rumour, Chinese consumers are much more likely to rely on, and make use of, the rumour moeity of the informal channel, rather than what is actually claimed for the product officially (Kindle, 1985).

Second, Chinese consumers tend to be more brand loyal than their counterparts in the West. Chinese consumers often endeavour to conform to group norms and therefore tend to purchase the same brand or product other members of the group recommend. In other words, if a reference group has established a product as the normative standard, Chinese consumers are not likely to deviate from the accepted product on their own by switching to a competitive product.

Third, since Chinese are only group oriented towards social units with which close interactions have been established, consumers tend to confine their activities to a small social circle. Hence, they are members of a small number of reference groups. This may be one of the reasons that mass advertising through formal channels (e.g. television) is of limited potential for attracting attention when using reference groups which are often small in size. In Hong Kong, Winston, an American cigarette brand, has been suffering from a continuous decline in sales because of improper use of reference groups in its advertisements.

Fourth, the concept of the extended family is important to advertisements of family products. Unlike consumers in Western societies, the Chinese concept of family is one of the extended family, which includes even distant relatives. Therefore, if an advertisement which attempts to persuade consumers to buy a family product includes only husband, wife and children, it does not really show a picture of a family at all. Other members of the extended family, such as grandfather and grandmother, should be included to make the advertisement more persuasive.

Time Dimension

Past-time orientation – Klukhohn and Strodbeck (1961) noted that the Chinese have a strong preference for past-time orientation:

> Historical China was a society which gave first-order preference to the past-time orientation. Ancestor worship and a strong family tradition were both expressions of this preference. So also was the Chinese attitude that nothing new ever happened in the present or would happen in the future; it had all happened before in the far distant Past.

Van Oort (1970) believed that Chinese people were very history minded:

> A second culture value is the principle of respect for the past, or almost veneration of history. If there is one people in the world that is history-minded, it is certainly the Chinese people.

He did not attempt to explain why it was, but Burkhardt (1953) clearly stated:

> China has always been a conservative country . . . which held to the belief that what was good for their forefathers, and had been tested by countless generations, was sacrilege to tamper with.

No doubt, the Chinese have a strong admiration of their culture, which has a history of thousands of years. The following proverb clearly depicts the feeling of most Chinese: "Among the three unfilial duties, to have no heir is the greatest." There are three reasons why having no heir is unfilial. Firstly, it is necessary to have an heir to extend the biological life of parents and ancestors. To carry this duty is not difficult, but the most fundamental. Secondly, it is necessary to pass down the Chinese culture to the next generation. To do so, parents, have to provide the best education they can for their children. The most important thing is that parents should have a deep knowledge of the Chinese culture. Thirdly, it is necessary to fulfil the hopes that parents or ancestors have failed as yet to accomplish (Yang, 1979).

The salient ethnological fact about Chinese culture is that it is, and always has been, based fundamentally and predominantly on agriculture, which provided the economic margin of security for the people. In contrast with pastoral peoples, the Chinese were prone to be more risk averse and less innovative because, in order to secure a stable or increased food supply, it seemed safer for them to follow the traditional methods which had been proven workable for thousands of years.

Continuity – The Chinese believe that interrelations with things and others are continuous. Once a relation is established, it can hardly be broken. Hence, the Chinese proverb which says: "If you have been my teacher for a day, I will treat you like my father for ever."

Potential marketing implications for time orientation – The values of past-time orientation and continuity also imply that the Chinese tend to have great brand loyalty. Unless the product or brand being used proves very unsatisfactory, they are not likely to switch to purchasing other brands or products. This point of view is also shared by Crow (1937), who pointed out that the Chinese are "the world's most loyal customers", with a high degree of brand consciousness. Furthermore, Chinese consumers, especially married ones, are likely to consider opinions, values and influences of deceased relatives and respected figures in their current consumption choice. Attention should be paid from time to time to these opinions and values when producing advertising copy.

Activity Orientation

As for the activity orientation of the Chinese, the evidence is conflicting. As mentioned earlier, the Chinese have been greatly influenced by the doctrine of the Way which emphasised the "being" orientation. However, the Chinese have found themselves conforming to behaviour according to *Li* (propriety), which denotes a system of semi-formal norms of behaviour. Jarvie and Agassi (1969) gave a description for the predominance of this value orientation:

> The highest value in China is to live properly, which particularly concerns being polite and obeying the rules; and this makes even the social aspect of personal transaction of supreme importance. In other words, in traditional China, being considerate to others is equated with . . . strict observance of the accepted code. To observe the code is to be human; to forget it is to become barbarian.

However, Jarvie and Agassi did not mention the doctrine of the Mean which has been the most important Chinese cultural value (Chu, 1979). The Mean, according to Confucius, was referred to as "being without inclination to either side" (Legge, 1960). Confucius did not believe in suppression of passions and impulses, but in regulation of them so as to achieve internal harmony. The Chinese, therefore, are taught not to let primitive passions and impulses be completely repressed or unrestrictedly satisfied. To explain what is meant by the Mean, Confucius declared:

> The gentleman does what is proper to the station in which he is; he does not desire to go beyond this. In a position of wealth and honour, he does what is proper to a position of wealth and honour. In a poor and low position, he does what is proper to a poor and low position . . . In a low situation, he does not court the favour of his superiors. He rectifies himself, and seeks for nothing from others so that he has no dissatisfactions. He does not murmur against Heaven, nor grumble against men. ("The Doctrine of the Mean, XV", Legge, 1960).

Thus, a concern for the Mean leads to a high degree of moral self-control or self-regulation, at least publicly, for the individual Chinese. His family members or intimate friends are the only channel to whom to express his inner feelings. Hchu and Yang (1979) also supported this point of view in their study on the individual modernity and psychogenic needs of Chinese college students. It was found that more socially oriented Chinese students tended to blame or punish themselves when reacting to frustration. In a similar vein, Yang (1981) also found that traditional Chinese were more cautious and more conforming in verbalising their responses. In retrospect, China has never been an aggressive country in world history. Traditional Chinese were depicted as non-military and self-contented people (La Barre, 1948; Russell, 1922). This can be useful in explaining why, today, only on rare occasions would one see a Chinese lose control and become angry, insulting or threatening in public (Kindle, 1982).

Potential marketing implications for activity orientation – One of the potential marketing implications for the value of activity orientation concerns complaining behaviour. As previously mentioned, Chinese tend not to take public stands, such as complaining to manufacturers, companies or to consumer councils when they encounter unsatisfactory products or services. One of the explanations is that they regard taking public action as something very serious. Careful consideration is given before deciding whether a public action is the proper way to solve the problem concerned. Legal action, which is regarded as extreme behaviour, is normally not considered at all. Marketing managers who wish to obtain data on the satisfaction/dissatisfaction of Chinese consumers should play a more active role, rather than waiting for the consumer to feed back.

The doctrine of the Mean may influence Chinese consumers' attitude to adopting new products. Chinese consumers are slow to accept new fashions or technology, and resist marketing innovations involving complicated features. Of course, it may be because Chinese are more risk averse, as previously mentioned, or because they regard adopting or using a new product as an extreme behaviour which is not proper in their position.

Summary

This article has attempted to investigate the underlying dimensions of Chinese cultural values, in terms of Kluckhohn and Strodbeck's classification, and their potential marketing implications. In recent years, Western thought and ideology have played an important part in the cultural changes of many Chinese societies, especially in Taiwan, Hong Kong and Singapore. It seems that it is time to investigate the expected relationships between Chinese cultural values and other determinants of consumer behaviour. Further,

Chinese cultural values can also be used as an effective basis for market segmentation (Yau, 1986), and help in understanding whether theories of consumer behaviour, which were built on Western premises, can be transplanted to Eastern cultures.

References

Burkhardt, V.R. (1955), *Chinese Creeds and Customs* South China Morning Post Ltd, Hong Kong.

Cavusgil, S.T. and Kaynak, E. (1982), "A Framework for Cross-cultural Measurement of Consumer Dissatisfaction", in Day, R.L. and Hunt, H.K. (Eds.), *New Findings on Consumer Satisfaction and Complaining*, Indiana University, Bloomington, pp. 80–4.

Chan, W.T. (1963), *The Way of Lao Tsu*, Bobbs-Merrill, New York.

Crow, C. (1937), *Four Hundred Million Customers*, Hamish Hamilton, London.

Hchu, and Yang, K.S. (1972), in Li, Y.Y. and Yang, K.S. (Eds.), *Symposium on the Character of the Chinese*, Institution of Ethnology, Academic Sinica (in Chinese), Taipei.

Ho, D.Y.F. (1972), "On the Concept of Face", *American Journal of Sociology*, Vol. 81 No. 4, pp. 72–8.

Hsu, F.L.K. (1947), *Under the Ancestors' Shadow: Kinship, Personality, and Social Mobility in China*, Standford University Press, Standford.

Hsu, F.L.K. (1963), *Clan, Caste, and Club*, Van Nostrand, Princeton, NJ.

Hsu, F.L.K. (1968), "Psychological Anthropology: An Essential Defect and its Remedy", paper presented at the 1968 annual meeting of the American Anthropologist Association, Seattle, Washington.

Hsu, F.L.K. (1970), *Americans and Chinese: Passage to Differences*, 3rd ed., University Press of Hawaii, Honolulu.

Hsu, F.L.K. (1972), "Chinese Kinship and Chinese Behavior", in Ho, P.T. and Tsou, T. (Eds.), *China in Crisis*, Vol. 2, University of Chicago Press, Chicago.

Hu, H.C. (1944), "The Chinese Concept of Face", *American Anthropologist*, Vol. 46, January-March, pp. 45–64.

Kindle, I. (1982), "A Partial Theory of Chinese Consumer Behaviour: Marketing Strategy Implications", *Hong Kong Journal of Business Management*, Vol. 1, pp. 97–109.

Kindle, T. (1985), "Chinese Consumer Behaviour: Historical Perspective Plus an Update on Communication Hypotheses", in Sheth, J. and Tan, C.T. (Eds.), *Historical Perspectives of Consumer Behaviour*, National University of Singapore and Association for Consumer Behaviour, Singapore, pp. 186–90.

King, A.U.C. and Myers, J.R. (1977), *Shame as an Incomplete Conception of Chinese Culture: A Study of Face*, Research Monograph, H.K. Social Research Institute, Chinese University of Hong Kong.

Kluckhohn, F.R. and Strodbeck, F.L. (1961), *Variations in Value Orientation*, Row, Paterson and Co, Illinois.

La Barre, W. (1946), "Some Observations on Character Structure in the Orient", *Psychiatry*, Vol. 9, pp. 215–25.

Legge, J. (1960), *The Chinese Classics*, Hong Kong University Press, Hong Kong.

Lin, W.T. (1966), "Chinese Value Orientation in Hong Kong", *Sociological Analysis*, Vol. 27, pp. 53–66.

Jarvie, I.C. and Agassi, (1969), *Hong Kong: A Society in Transition*, Routledge & Kegan Paul, London.

McNeal, J.M. (1969), "Consumer Satisfaction: The Measure of Marketing Effectiveness", *MSU Business Topics*, Summer, pp. 31–6.

Morris, C. (1956), *Varieties of Human Value*, University of Chicago Press, Chicago.
Russel, B. (1966), *The Problem of China*, George Allen and Unwin, London, Ltd.
Salaff, J.W. (1981), *Working Daughters of Hong Kong: Female Piety or Power in the Family?*, Cambridge University Press, London.
Shively, A.N. and Shively, S. (1972), "Value Changes during a Period of Modernisation: The Case of Hong Kong", working paper, Institute of Social Research, Chinese University of Hong Kong.
Thorelli, H.B. (1982), "China: Consumer Voice and Exit", in Day, R.L. and Hunt, H.K. (Eds.), *International Fare in Consumer Satisfaction and Complaining*, University of Tennessee, Knoxville, Tennessee, pp. 105–10.
Van Oort, H.A. (1970), "Chinese Culture – Values Past and Present", *Chinese Culture*, Vol. 11, 1 March, China Academy, Taipei.
Waldie, K.F. (1981), "Management – Western Ways and Eastern Needs – A Cultural Comparison", *The Hong Kong Manager*, June, p. 19.
Wei, C.T. (1980), *The Wisdom of China*, Cowboy Publishing Co, Taipei.
Wilson, R.W. and Pusey, A.W. (1982), "Achievement Motivation and Small-business Relationship Patterns in Chinese Society", in Greenblatt, S.L. *et al.* (Eds.), *Social Interaction in Chinese Society*, Praeger, New York, pp. 195–208.
Yang, K.S. (1979), "Research on Chinese National Character in Modern Psychology", in Wen, C.I. *et al.* (Eds.), *Modernisation and Change of Value*, Thought and Word Association (in Chinese), Taipei.
Yang, K.S. (1981), "Social Orientation and Individual Modernity among Chinese Students in Taiwan", *Journal of Social Psychology*, Vol. 113, pp. 159–70.
Yau, O.H.M. (1986), *Consumer Satisfaction and Cultural Values*, PhD thesis, University of Bradford, England.

6

Advertising, Propaganda, and Value Change in Economic Development: The New Cultural Revolution in China and Attitudes toward Advertising

Richard W. Pollay, David K. Tse and Zheng-Yuan Wang

Introduction

China has undergone a dramatic cultural change in the last decade in its pursuit of "four modernizations." Since 1979, the official posture against advertising as the essential corruptor of capitalism has been radically revised. A new analysis treats most advertising as at least potentially consistent with traditional Chinese socialist ideals and economic goals. This total reversal of value judgment, complete with propaganda to rationalize and disseminate the new view, is amazing in its speed, and alarming in its indifference to potential cultural upheaval (Pollay, 1986). Even Chinese laws on advertising, developed in 1982, were not very inarticulate on social consequences (Sit, 1983).

The emergent commercial culture promises to change radically both the demand and prospects for economic development. The new advertising prompts the new consumer to want more and more (Belk and Zhou, 1987), and the new ideology preaches that "to get rich is glorious" (Schell, 1984). Advertising, only recently seen as revolting, is now integral to the revolution of thinking implicit in the "Four Modernizations" (*Beijing Review*, 1979). Yesterday's villain is today's hero.

Source: *Journal of Business Research*, 20(2) (1990): 83–95.

Recent efforts to understand better the industry and to realize further the enormous market potential in China are seen in studies on how Chinese managers (Ho and Sin, 1986; Ho and Yao, 1985; Kwan et al., 1983) and advertising professionals (Semenik et al., 1986) perceived the function and social consequences of advertising. Other researchers reported on their professional tours (Rotzoll, 1986) or content analysis of Chinese ads (Rice and Lu, 1988; Stewart and Campbell, 1986; Tse et al., 1989). Most of these efforts provide insights as to how to advertise in China.

The purpose of this article is to review the development of China's consumer culture within the last decade, and to report an exploratory study on the attitudes of People's Republic of China (PRC) consumers toward Chinese ads and their beliefs on the various social, economic, and legal implications of advertising. The results will be compared to the attitudes of "traders" and managers (Ho and Sin, 1986; Kwan et al., 1983; Semenik et al., 1986) and the character of Chinese advertising content (Tse et al., 1989).

Commercialization and a New PRC Consumer Culture

Propaganda for, Not against, Commercial Persuasion

For years advertising had been disparaged as the epitome of self-indulgent, wasteful, and manipulative capitalism. Previous bans on advertising had been rationalized as efficient, a source of tremendous savings for society. But in 1979 advertising was suddenly portrayed as having a number of potential virtues. Advertising could be aesthetic, beautifying the cityscape, while being itself a clean, "smokeless" industry. Advertising could be inspirational, lifting spirits to "make us feel proud of a thriving socialist economy or culture in a cheerful artistic atmosphere" (Anderson, 1983, p. 273). Advertising was now also seen as instrumental to catching up and competing with more developed economies, an essential to becoming more modern and a valuable source of hard currency from foreign advertisers (Kamm, 1979). Chinese enterprises, it seemed, needed to adopt the same aggressive use of advertising as seen in other Asian centers like Honk King, South Korea, Singapore, Taiwan, or Thailand, or risk being left behind and unable to compete in the regional and world economy (Stross, 1988).

Perhaps most significantly, advertising is now perceived as an effective and efficient management tool. Advertising could "promote understanding and cement ties between the masses and production and sales departments (Anderson, 1983, p. 273). The Chinese advertising community argued that the consumer needs "scientific guidance in a socialist system as well as in a capitalist system" (Stross, 1988, p. 9). Their confident pride in being able to "create demand" and "impelling them (citizen consumers) to work harder" is ironic. Such power is assumed, criticized, and feared in the West, and, hence, denied in the public posturing of the industry.

Starting Simple: Advertising Style and Strategies

Most of the trade press (e.g., Ogilvy and Mather, 1979) advises against creative copy and art styles that mirror Western sophistication, indirectness, and reliance upon imagery. Instead, they call for basic pedestrian emphasis on product, price, and information about the firm's history, size, and stability. This advice presumably reflects the industrial character of products offered by some of the pioneer advertisers, but it also reflects Chinese consumers' inexperience at "reading" advertising and fear that Western subtlety might prove opaque to Chinese viewers. Domestic advertising is often described as "basic and unsophisticated" or "uncreative and amateurish" (Reaves, 1985b, 1986a). A less dismissive analysis by Tse et al., (1989) describe a 1979–1985 sample of ads as "utilitarian" (versus hedonistic), as more fitting China's "consumption experience, stage of economic development, advertising philosophy, and political ideology." Occasional trade articles praise the wisdom in the indirect, soft-sell Western styles, as in the classic Chinese expression, "Draw the bow without shooting; just indicate the motions" (Stross, 1988, p. 20).

The common "primitive" ad style may reflect the low importance many Chinese managers place on advertising versus other marketing mix elements like personal selling (Ho and Sin, 1986; Kwan et al., 1983). This managerial perception may not long endure, given dramatic success stories, such as a toothpaste firm's 1984 spending of $100,000, producing $2.2 million in profit (Reaves, 1985c). Simple sales promotion events also seem to have an impact. A contest sponsored by Lever, which entailed guessing the number of bars of soap in a transparent box of a Beijing window display, drew an amazing 500,000 entries (Shao, 1988).

Cultural sensitivity means the de facto ban on the use of some symbols in advertising, and advisement against some strategies. One should not use ghosts and dragons, for reasons unspecified (Hughes, 1985), nor, should maps or flags be used, to prevent compromising the state. Humor risks misunderstanding and puzzlement over the lack of a serious tone (Seligman, 1986). Sexual innuendo risks major offense. Recently, the skimpy costumes of samba dancers in a Lux soap ad blocked clearance of the ad (Shao, 1988). One should not hire Taiwanese or Hong Kong citizens for acting, voiceovers, or written translations because of differences in writing styles and their distinctive accents (Hughes, 1985).

Issues and Criticism

Foreign advertising has from time to time been threatened with more substantial restraints (Curry, 1982), but the concrete action has been to charge all foreign advertisers administered prices (*China Daily*, 1985). These were premium, compared to what local firms pay, but they were very cheap compared to western cost per thousand (cpm). In 1986, the government reacted to the proliferation of outdoor billboards and banned them from Beijing's main street, Changan Avenue. This was interpreted widely as also motivated by anti-Japanese sentiments, as Japanese firms were on 50% of the billboards (Reaves, 1986b).

Most concerns about advertising, however, apply equally to domestic advertising. Initially, there was some concern with advertising creating a materialistic fever, inducing a rising tide of expectations and political impatience (Burstein, 1981). This concern is classic. Current Western analysis suggests that the whole fabric of traditional culture, its value structure, may be jeopardized by commercialization (Pollay, 1986).

Although the Chinese have been neither too articulate nor providing of operationally specific criteria, some guidelines governing advertising took shape early. In 1981, ads should be "for the benefit of socialism and be responsible," with slander, discrimination, and exaggerated claims prohibited. They "should not leave the public with a "negative impression," nor should they be "sexual teasers" or "hypocritical," as in cigarette ads showing healthy people (Curry, 1981). Citizens surveyed in the early 1980s expressed dissatisfaction with the lack of price information in advertising, as well as the displacement of regular programming. A *People's Daily* editorial criticized advertising for improperly forcing itself upon the people, likening prime time TV ads to "a presumptuous guest usurping the host" (Stross, 1988, p. 21). This intolerance may soften, since "worldwide, advertisers engage in pushing back the boundaries of the controversial and permissable as a matter of routine" (Sherry, 1987).

In February 1982, official guidelines were published (Sit, 1983). Of the many articles, the most critical banned "fraudulent" ads and those violating the sanctity of the state (*China Daily*, 1985). Article 6 requires ads to be "clear and understood and true to the facts. Fraudulent advertisements of any form calculated to hoodwink or cheat the end users or consumers shall be prohibited." Article 8 bans publishing, broadcasting, or displaying ads that either "violate state policies, laws and decrees . . . jeopardize the dignity of all Chinese nationalities . . . are counter-revolutionary, obscene, disgusting or superstitious . . . contain libellous propaganda . . . or violate the state security regulations" (Pollay, 1986). Other articles restrained outdoor billboards, and prohibited monopolies and "illegitimate competition."

About the same time, concerns arose about the "spiritual pollution" of capitalism. While it was never defined operationally, the Minister of Culture spoke out in 1983 against portrayals "depraved and sexual in nature, and in stinking bourgeois life-styles dedicated to nothing more than having a good time, drinking, resting, and hedonism" (Schell, 1984, p. 172). The industry displayed some sympathetic self-criticism, but with limited enthusiasm. It argued that female images were helpful, even at times necessary, and should not be treated as spiritual pollution so long as the artistry stressed "health and propriety" (Stross, 1988, p. 27).

Stross (1988) reports that newspapers received a "continuous flow" of misled and cheated readers. Consumers were being victimized by advertised frauds for quack medicines, false employment agencies, and venture schemes, such as earthworm raising. The only recourse open to unhappy consumers consisted of letters to editors of local papers, in hopes of embarrassing firms into restitution or repentance. As in the West, the industry joined the reform fight for truth in advertising, seeing that quackery and fraud threatened the credibility of all advertising.

This led to tightening of some controls, such as the banning of ads that imitate news layouts, and barring individuals from advertising by requiring business licensing (*China Daily*, 1985). One government spokesperson said, "where fake products cause death, those responsible should pay with their lives" (Stevenson, 1985). It was recently decided that both the advertiser and its agency can be held liable for damages (*People's Daily*, 1986). Also prohibited was the coercion of advertisers by media overeager to sell their space and ads that "pander to low tastes" (Reaves, 1986b).

In 1987, the government published a formalization of a long-standing de facto ban on explicit product promotion of cigarette brands. It was not, however, very comprehensive and did not address, e.g., the controversy over sports sponsorships and use of celebrities (*Business China*, 1987).

The precipitous changes in the endorsement and use of advertising in China is a dramatic and perhaps watershed event in the histories of both China and advertising. The changes raise a large number of questions: How prepared is China for the influx of commercialism, especially foreign influenced? Will advertising aid the four modernizations? Will advertising raise expectations and political impatience? Will China manage to regulate advertising to avoid what it once so feared: self-indulgence, profit motives, class conflict, Western values and lifestyles? Will it seek, and be able to foster, advertising that emphasizes information over persuasion and is indigenous over foreign values? How will consumers react to advertising, both domestic and foreign? Will China accelerate through similar phases of advertising history as experienced in the West? Will consumerism be China's next great social movement?

Research Procedure

Sample

Designing a study to explore any of these questions in the People's Republic of China is complicated by the enormous size and regional diversity of the country. A history of government control on surveys and public opinion polls makes respondents inexperienced with surveys. This study reports data gathered from a convenience sample of consumers of three cities: Beijing (China's capital), Guangzhou (a Southern city), and Harbin (a Northeastern city). As residents of the capital, Beijing consumers are consistently exposed to the nation's political events, subject to the straightest government control, and now exposed to increasing foreign commercial and diplomatic traffic. Harbin represents the large and relatively unexposed portion of the country. Guangzhou represents the most prosperous and politically liberal part of China.

In total, 154 respondents were approached in the summer of 1987. Of these, 123, or some 80%, completed the questions. The age distribution of the sample is similar that of the nation, with most respondents young adults' 20–40 years old. Men and women were equally represented, but the sample was more educated (58% had postsecondary education) and more held professional occupations (25.2%) than the population in general. The sample showed high rates of TV ownership (95.9%) and viewing (79% watch TV many times a week or everyday), reflecting the recent rapid development of that medium.

Instrument Design and Administration

The questionnaire contained five parts. The first two evaluated Chinese and foreign advertising separately. The third section elicited normative judgments about their ideals for Chinese ads. A battery of belief statements on the social and economic consequences and legal considerations of advertising composed the fourth part. Last, selective demographic information was obtained. Except for the demographic questions, all items used 5-point Likert scales.

The questions were developed from previous studies in the economic and social issues on advertising modified by studies in Chinese ads (e.g., Ho and Sin 1986; Kwan et al., 1983; Semenik et al., 1986). The questionnaire was translated and back-translated, and a panel of three Chinese researchers (two from PRC and one from Hong Kong) resolved inconsistencies. The questionnaire was further modified after pilot testing on 20 PRC students in Beijing.

Most interviews were conducted in shopping areas while some (about 16%) were conducted during tea breaks in offices and factories. The instrument identified the survey as conducted by a researcher from a university in Beijing. The respondents filled out the questionnaire by themselves. The questionnaire took about 20 minutes to complete.

Findings

Perceptions of Advertising

Three of the five parts in the questionnaire are relevant to understanding how Chinese consumers perceive advertising from domestic sources. These measured perceptions, comparisons with foreign firms' advertising, and normative believes about how Chinese ads should be.

Table 1 displays how the respondents evaluated Chinese ads. In general, Chinese ads were perceived unfavorably, especially for their aesthetics and entertainment value. They scored low on adjectives such as artistic (2.53 on a 5-point scale) pleasant (2.46), amusing (2.28), intelligent (2.43), hard to forget (2.70), honest (2.31), and convincing (2.37), resulting in an unfavorable overall liking for them (2.71). Only informativeness (3.50) and understandability (3.82) were evaluated positively.

How consumers compare Chinese to foreign ads is shown in the exhibit, displaying data on informativeness, aesthetics aspects, and the overall effect. In general, the reactions were one-sided, with foreign ads preferred on almost all dimensions. Foreign ads were better liked and perceived as more honest, more artistically designed, and a more pleasant experience. They are also judged to be more memorable and more convincing. Chinese ads scored

Table 1: Respondents' perception on Chinese Ads

	Mean score	*Standard deviation*
Overall evaluations		
Chinese ads are very good	2.71	1.31
I like them very much	2.31	1.22
Chinese ads are convincing	2.37	1.12
Helpful to society	3.07	1.20
Information content		
Chinese ads are		
Very easy to understand	3.82	1.32
Very informative	3.50	1.38
Very hard to forget	2.70	1.34
Very honest	2.31	1.24
Aesthetic content		
Chinese ads are		
Pleasant to see	2.46	1.24
Artistic	2.56	1.21
Intelligent	2.43	1.25
Amusing	2.28	1.19
Ad style and tone should be/have		
More information	3.00	1.35
Fun	4.36	0.91
Plain	2.29	1.39
Common	3.71	1.54
Attractive	3.94	1.26
Products should be/have		
Expensive items	1.64	1.04
Of higher quality	4.57	0.75
Newer design	4.64	0.74
Role models should be/have		
Shy	2.08	1.21
Humble	3.02	1.31
Hardworking	3.75	1.19
Self-oriented	3.72	1.17
Lifestyles should be/have		
Status quo	2.29	1.30
Lively	4.22	1.04
Simple	3.57	1.21

higher than foreign ads only in understandability. The use of non-Chinese technologies (3.64) and music or art (3.81) in the ads was approved.

Table 1 also reports normative beliefs on how a Chinese ad should be ideally. In contrast to managers' beliefs, consumers were indifferent to the idea of including more information in the ad. They wanted the ads to be less plain (2.29) and more entertaining (4.36). They would like to see ads offering a unique appeal (3.71), more attractive (3.94), and for accessible, not expensive, products (1.64). They wanted ads to emphasize product quality (4.57) and new designs (4.64). While ads should preserve the old virtues of a simple (3.57) and hardworking (3.75) life, ads should not just echo the status quo (2.29). The role models and lifestyles portrayed in ads they wanted to be bold (2.08 on shy), self-oriented (3.72), and lively (4.22).

Economic and Social Consequence and Legal Considerations

Table 2 shows that Chinese consumers were quite favorably disposed to advertising. In particular, they perceived ads as having very positive impacts on the country's economic environment, and they saw ads as helping their export efforts (4.26), domestic markets (4.09), promoting competition

Table 2: Economic and social consequences of advertising in China

	Mean	*(Std. dev.)*
Economic consequences		
Help export marketing	4.26	(1.04)
Help domestic marketing	4.09	(1.02)
Improves product	3.98	(1.24)
Promotes competition	4.25	(0.95)
Expand market, lower prices	3.13	(1.22)
Provides information	4.54	(0.79)
Provides price information	3.97	(1.12)
Helps buying decisions	4.26	(1.00)
Increases power of firms	3.76	(1.18)
Damage competitors	3.04	(1.20)
Makes us proud of our economy	3.42	(1.16)
Makes people work harder	3.53	(1.16)
Social consequences		
People want unaffordable goods	3.31	(1.25)
People buy unwanted products	2.63	(1.35)
Cannot influence consumers	3.00	(1.34)
Influences media content	3.72	(1.18)
Are paid by consumers	3.42	(1.41)
Too many on TV/Radio	4.10	(1.26)
Too many in print media	3.92	(1.28)
Parents control ad to children	3.44	(1.36)
Make people envy others	2.82	(1.24)
Increase dissatisfaction	3.00	(1.31)
Increases trust in authority	3.02	(1.28)

	Mean	*(Std. Dev.)*
Executive's considerations		
Chinese ads should use/display more		
Technical information	4.41	(0.95)
Pictures of beautiful girls	2.37	(1.39)
Testimonials by celebrities	2.37	(1.38)
Affluent lifestyles	2.53	(1.39)
Comparative information	4.24	(1.10)
Ad executions		
Different ads for various markets	3.60	(1.34)
Irritation acceptable if ad works	2.18	(1.31)
Are exaggerated	4.35	(1.11)
Contains deceptive claims	4.07	(0.95)
Use more sexual appeals recently	3.27	(1.28)
Acceptance of foreign elements		
Non-Chinese brand names/slogans	2.28	(1.38)
Non-Chinese technologies	3.64	(1.36)
Non-Chinese models	2.25	(1.40)
Legal considerations		
Disclosure/informativeness		
Government should provide comparative product info	4.52	(0.88)
Government should provide comparative product info	4.22	(1.21)
Should be distinct from news or entertainment	4.63	(0.85)
Hazardous products should have warnings	4.66	(1.66)
Control/regulation		
Industry have self-law	3.98	(1.40)
Government should control ad content	3.76	(1.35)
Government should control size of ad industry	3.37	(1.35)
Ads should prove their claims	4.67	(0.75)
Same laws for local and foreign ads	3.84	(1.24)
Legal liabilities		
Manufacturers should be liable	4.77	(0.68)
Retailers should be liable	4.54	(0.93)
Agencies should be liable	4.42	(1.02)
Media should be liable	4.42	(1.03)
Agencies responsible for ad design	4.52	(0.95)
Virtue (problems) in promoting products		
Alcohol	2.83	(1.34)
Cigarettes	2.24	(1.39)
Medicines	3.86	(1.18)
Film and popular music	3.96	(1.21)
TV and tape recorders	4.07	(1.04)
Imported fashions and cosmetics	3.55	(1.34)
Imported foods and drinks	3.50	(1.26)
Imported household appliances	3.78	(1.30)

(4.25), and improving products (3.98). They also perceived ads as driving them to work harder (3.53) and making them proud of the country's economy (3.42).

Although the Chinese consumers were sensitive to possible negative social consequences of advertising, their reactions were far more positive than typical Western responses. They recognized that ads may lead people to buy unaffordable products (3.31) but slightly disagree that ads would lead them to buy unwanted products (2.63). They were aware of advertisers' influence on the media (3.72) and tended to think that there were too many ads on TV and radio (4.10) and in print media (3.92).

They believed that parents should control the exposure of children to advertising (3.44) but disagree that ads would make people envious of others (2.82). They were quite neutral about whether ads would increase the people's dissatisfaction (3.00) or make people trustful or distrustful about what they hear or read (3.02). Public-policy issues regarding advertising prompted mixed reactions. They have reservations about the promotion of alcohol (2.83) and cigarettes (2.24). They felt that all imported products should be allowed to promote, yet they agreed with having different laws for foreign and domestic ads (3.82).

Chinese consumers were frustrated with the puffery, deceptiveness, and even fraud in their advertising. Our respondents were very aware of exaggerations (4.35) and deception (4.07) in ads, wanted ad claims substantiated (4.67), and believed consumers of health hazardous products should be explicitly warned (4.66); they hold all concerned entities very responsible for the ads. In addition, they would like government (4.22) or consumer advocates (4.52) to provide more efficient comparative product information. With less enthusiasm, they would like the government to exercise more control on both the ad content (3.76) and the ad industry size (3.37). They reacted favorably to the idea of self-regulation in the advertising industry (3.98).

In judging ad executions, the Chinese consumers were conservative, approving primarily the approaches reflecting their existing lifestyle. They agreed somewhat that there was a growing use of sex appeal (3.27) and more clearly disapproved of such approaches (2.37). They were also disinclined toward irritating appeals (2.18), testimonials from celebrities (2.37), portrayal of affluent lifestyles (2.53), non-Chinese brands and slogans (2.28), and non-Chinese models (2.25). Instead, they would prefer more comparative ads (4.24) and technological information in ads (4.41).

Discussion and Conclusion

In contrast to previous findings that Chinese managers perceived the Chinese ads to be interesting and noninsulting but needing to be more informative, the consumers were less than satisfied with the honesty and aesthetic nature of the ads while regarding the informational content adequate. It is not surprising that consumers in China want their ads to be honestly informative, for this is the redeeming virtue of advertising as seen by both classic communism and Western economics. The desire for enhanced aesthetics suggests that the appeals of beauty and enjoyment are more global than many admit. Chinese consumers are enthusiastic and accepting of foreign advertising styles but do not fully embrace the values in capitalistic advertising, and they claim to prefer ads portraying simple and hardworking lifestyles.

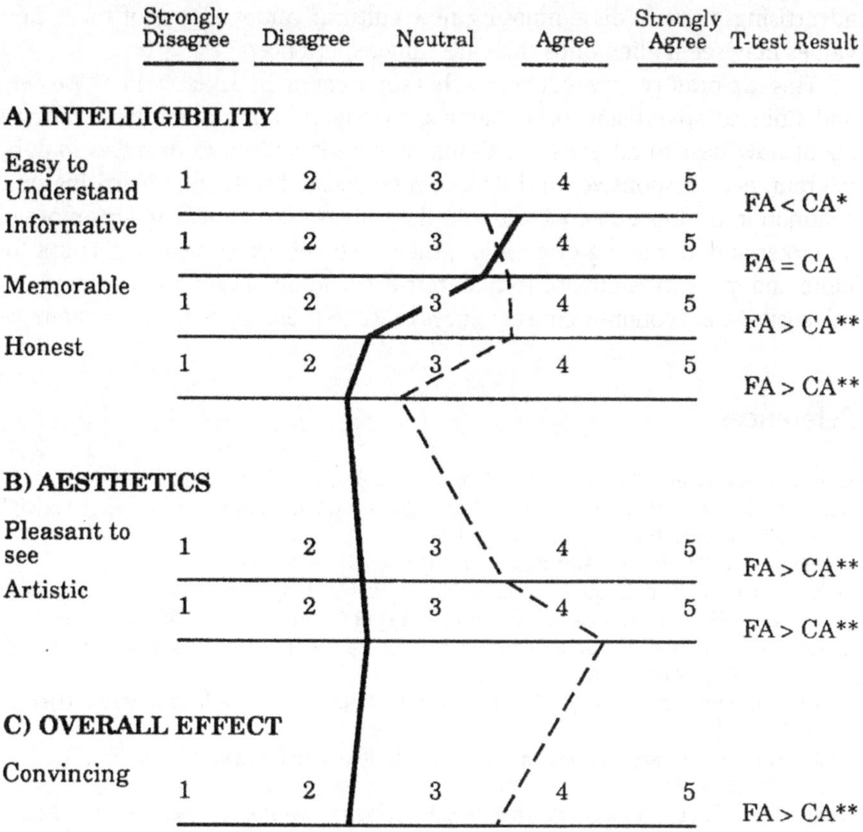

	Strongly Disagree	Disagree	Neutral	Agree	Strongly Agree	T-test Result
A) INTELLIGIBILITY						
Easy to Understand	1	2	3	4	5	FA < CA*
Informative	1	2	3	4	5	FA = CA
Memorable	1	2	3	4	5	FA > CA**
Honest	1	2	3	4	5	FA > CA**
B) AESTHETICS						
Pleasant to see	1	2	3	4	5	FA > CA**
Artistic	1	2	3	4	5	FA > CA**
C) OVERALL EFFECT						
Convincing	1	2	3	4	5	FA > CA**

FA and------denote foreign ads evaluations; CA and ——— denote Chinese (local) ads evaluations. *, ** Significant at 5% and 1% levels, two tailed test.

Exhibit 1: Assessment on ads from China versus other countries

Why Chinese consumers were so positive about advertising compared to consumers of the West is difficult to pinpoint. Advertising, a symbol of capitalism, may be perceived favorably because of a naive enthusiasm prompted more by the latest state propaganda, rather than by extensive experience and reflection. Advertisements that had been barred from 1966 till 1979 have reappeared coincident with the country's recent economic reforms and development, which may be given undue credit for them. In the transformation to a more consumer-oriented society (see Tse et al., 1989), ads may open the eyes of the Chinese consumers and even help them acquire the necessary attitudes and skills to function well in a consumer society.

Whatever the reasons for the current high levels of both official and popular acceptance of advertising, it is essential for advertisers to be aware that a more critical perspective could be just around the corner. If China undergoes rapid economic change, cultural change seems inevitable. By then, policymakers and the general public likely will become more aware of the role advertising plays in disseminating new cultural values. Some of these new values may seem alien once they are fully experienced.

This exploratory survey suggests that some common beliefs held by Western and Chinese advertising professionals, managers, and government officials about how best to advertise in China may be incorrect. Consumers may be tolerant, even responsive, to the more sophisticated styles of advertising now common in developed economies. As the Chinese economy develops more of a market and marketing orientation, the consumer preferences will count for more and more. It is unwise to underestimate a billion Chinese, or the political, social, and economic consequences of widespread advertising to them.

References

Adweek, Once Again, The China Shop Tempts U.S. Bulls, 26 (Sept. 23, 1985): 40.

Anderson, Michael, *Madison Avenue in Asia: Politics and Transnational Advertising*, Farleigh Dickinson Univ. Press, Madison, NJ, 1983.

Beijing Review, Reinstating Advertisements, (March 9, 1979): 31.

Belk, Russell W., and Zhou Nan, Learning to Want Things, in *Advances in Consumer Research*, Vol. 14. Wallendorf, Melanie, and Paul Anderson, eds., 1987, pp. 478–481.

Bolton, Lois, Chinese Ad Unit Determines Society's Needs, Not Wants, *Advertising Age* (August 20, 1979): 8–13.

Burstein, Daniel, Chinese Offer Critique of Ads, Consumerism, *Advertising Age* (Dec. 4, 1981): S-4.

Business China, New Regulations Ban Tobacco Ads, Redefine Content Prohibitions, (Nov. 30, 1987): 169–171.

Cavusgil, S. Tamer, *Advances in International Marketing*, JAI Press, Greenwich, CT, 1986.

Chase, Dennis, U.S. Stumbles at China's Wall, *Advertising Age* (May 3, 1984): 1, 5.

Chiasson, Gail, Taking a Look Over the Great Wall, *Marketing* (Feb. 1, 1988): 27.

China Daily, State Bans Deceptive Advertising, (July 11, 1985): 3.

Cohen, Stanley, Advertising in China, *Advertising Age* (Sept. 8, 1980): 43.

Cragin, John P., Kwan, Y. K., and Ho, Y. N., Social Ethics and the Emergence of Advertising in China: Perceptions from Within the Great Wall, *Journal of Business Ethics* 3 (1984): 59–71.

Crow, Carl, *Four Hundred Million Customers*, Harper & Row, New York, 1937.

Curry, Lynne, China Likely to Curb Foreign Product's Ads, *Advertising Age* (July 12, 1982): 29.

Curry, Lynne, Marx to Mao: New Ad Book Looks Ahead, *Advertising Age* (Dec. 14, 1981): S-8.

Gelb, Norman, China's New Materialism, *The New Leader* (April 8, 1985): 3–6.

Girdwood, Sue, Western Products Score Hit in China, *Advertising Age* (Jan. 14, 1985): 40.

Goldsmith, Carol J., The Art of Advertising, *The China Business Review* (May/June, 1982): 15–16.

Ho, Suk-Ching, and Sin, Yat-Ming, Advertising in China: Looking Back at Looking Forward, *International Journal of Advertising* 5 (1986): 307–316.

Hughes, Lyric, Why and How to Advertise in China, *Advertising World* (June, 1985): 14–16.

Kamm, J., Advertising in China, *The China Business Review* (March–April 1979): 8.

Kwan, Y. K., Ho, Y. N., and Cragin, J. P., Contemporary Advertising Attitudes and Practices Among Executives in the People's Republic of China, *Journal of the Marketing Research Society* 25 (January 1983): 59–71.

Ogilvy and Mather (Hong Kong), *How to Advertise in the People's Republic of China*, Ogilvy and Mather, Hong Kong, 1979.

People's Daily, Clearing and Checking Deceptive Foreign Ads, (March 6, 1986): 4.

Pollay, R. W., Quality of Life in the Padded Sell: Common Criticisms of Advertising's Cultural Character and International Public Policies, *Current Issues and Research in Advertising* 9 (1986): 173–250.

Reaves, Lynne, China: A New Frontier for Advertisers, *Advertising Age* 56 (Sept. 16, 1985a): 74, 78.

Reaves, Lynne, China's Domestic Ad Scene a Paradox: Communist Ads Lack Pizzazz, *Advertising Age* 56 (Sept. 16, 1985b): 76.

Reaves, Lynne, Cure-All Toothpaste Borrows from West in Ads, Promotions, *Advertising Age* 56 (Sept. 16, 1985c): 77.

Reaves, Lynne, China Market Hot Despite Setbacks, *Advertising Age* 57 (June 9, 1986a): 56, 59.

Reaves, Lynne, Government Pinches Ad Industry, *Advertising Age* 57 (June 9, 1986b): 40.

Reaves, Lynne, World Cars: Chinese Auto Scene Mixes Rich and Poor, *Advertising Age* 57 (March 24, 1986c): 86.

Rice, Marshall D., and Lu, Zaiming, A Content Analysis on Chinese Magazine Advertisements, *Journal of Advertising* 17 (1988): 43–48.

Rotzoll, Kim B., Advertising in China: Reflections on an Evolving Institution, working paper, Dept. of Advertising, Univ. of Illinois, 1986.

Schell, Orville, *To Get Rich is Glorious: China in the 80's*, Pantheon Books, New York, 1984.

Schmuck, Claudine, Broadcasts for a Billion: The Growth of Commercial Television in China, *Columbia Journal of World Business* 22 (Fall 1987): 27–34.

Seligman, Scott D., Corporate and Product Promotion, *The China Business Review* 13 (May–June 1986): 8–13.

Semenik, Richard J., Zhou, Nan, and Moore, William L., Chinese Manager's Attitudes Toward Advertising in China, *Journal of Advertising* 15 (1986): 56–62.

Shao, Maria, Laying the Foundation for the Great Mall of China, *Business Week* (Jan. 25, 1988): 68–69.

Sit, Victor, *Commercial and Economic Regulations of the People's Republic of China*, MacMillian Publishers Ltd., Hong Kong, 1983.

South, China's Infrastructure: Facts and Figures, *South: The Third World Magazine* (brochure from Third World Advertising Congress, Beijing, June 16–20, 1987.

Stevenson, H. L., Chinese Worried About Ad Growth: Government Issues Regulations, *Advertising Age* (Sept. 16, 1985a): 79.

Stevenson, H. L., Shanghai Agency Taking Its Own Great Leap Forward, *Advertising Age* 56 (Nov. 11, 1985b): 46, 48.

Stewart, Sally, and Campbell, Nigel, Advertising in Mainland China: A Preliminary Study, *International Journal of Advertising* 5 (1986) 317–323.

Stross, Randall, The Return of Advertising in China: A Survey of the Ideological Reversal, working paper, San Jose State University, CA, 1988.

Television/Radio Age, Commercials: Advertising to China, 33 (Oct. 28, 1985): 50.

Tse, David K., Belk, Russell W., and Nan, Zhou, Becoming a Consumer Society: A Longitudinal and Cross-Cultural Content Analysis of Print Advertisements from Hong Kong, People's Republic of China and Taiwan, *Journal of Consumer Research* 15 (March 1989): 457–472.

Wang, James C. F., Values of the Cultural Revolution, *Journal of Communication* 27 (1983): 41–46.

7

Cultural Values Reflected in Chinese and U.S. Television Commercials

Hong Cheng and John C. Schweitzer

Despite three decades of scholarly interest in the need to relate advertising to culture (Cheng, 1994), inadequate attention has been paid to the cultural content of advertising in China, the largest market in the world. Between 1981 and 1993, advertising business volume in China increased at an average rate of more than 40 percent (*Guoji Guanggao*, 1993). The rapid growth of Chinese advertising is expected to continue. It is estimated that annual advertising spending in the country will hit $4.8 billion by the end of this century (*Wall Street Journal*, 1993; Yuan, 1993). In 1986, the business volume of Chinese advertising ranked thirty-fourth in the world (Xu, 1989) but had climbed to fifteenth place by 1993 (*Zhongguo Daobao*, 1994). As Parsons (1993) put it, "China's advertising industry is witnessing its fastest growth ever."

Advertising is not an abstract field of study but an aspect of the real world. It is the same with advertising in China. As a result of the downturn in economic conditions worldwide, we are seeing transnational advertising agencies reevaluating their advertising strategies. We believe that it is of great importance to analyze the cultural values reflected in Chinese advertising, which is a large-scale experiment with Western "capitalist" commercial practices in the fastest-growing market in the world.

Cultural Values in Advertising

Research into cultural values reflected in advertising content gained great momentum from the debate over standardization or specification of

Source: *Journal of Advertising Research*, 36(3) (1996): 27–45.

international advertising messages in different countries around the world (Mueller, 1987, 1992).

The cultural values reflected in advertising content in such countries as Brazil (Tansey et al., 1990), India (Srikandath, 1991), Japan (Belk et al., 1985; Belk and Pollay, 1985; Belk and Bryce, 1986; Lin, 1993; Mueller, 1987, 1992), the Philippines (Marquez, 1975), and the United Kingdom (Frith and Sengupta, 1991; Frith and Wesson, 1991; Katz and Lee, 1992) have been investigated. Most of these studies compared advertising from those countries with advertising from the United States.

Defined as "the governing ideas and guiding principles for thought and action" in a given society (Srikandath, 1991), *cultural values* conveyed through advertising messages are regarded as powerful forces shaping consumers' motivations, lifestyles, and product choices (Tse et al., 1989).

In 1994, Cheng content analyzed a total of 572 Chinese magazine advertisements from 1982 and 1992 and identified "modernity," "technology," and "quality" as three predominant cultural values manifest in Chinese advertising over those 10 years. The results also indicated that while the values less frequently used in the early 1990s were utilitarian in nature and centered on product quality, the values increasing in occurrence were more symbolic and suggestive of human emotions. The group of symbolic values reflected Western as well as Eastern culture.

Still, some important questions about the cultural values portrayed in Chinese advertising remain unknown. For instance, it is not yet certain if there are any differences between the predominant cultural values manifest in Chinese advertising and advertising in other countries. Although the symbolic cultural values used more often in Chinese advertising now are typical of Western as well as Eastern culture, it is still unclear how "Western" Chinese advertising has become.

Why Compare China with the U.S.?

With these unanswered questions, a comparative study of advertising in China and in at least one other country appeared necessary and important for a deeper understanding of Chinese advertising. We selected the United States for our comparison for several reasons. First, the United States, "the advertising capital of the world" (Baudot, 1989), has the largest and most influential advertising business in the world. In 1993, the U.S. advertising turnover was $107.3 billion – about 50 percent of the world's total advertising expenditures (Endicott, 1994). In the same year, all the top 10 advertising organizations in the world had U.S.-based agencies, and six of them were headquartered in the United States (*Advertising Age*, 1994b). So, a comparison of advertising in China, which is still a "small but robust child" in the world of advertising (Xu, 1989), with the advertising giant will undoubtedly enhance our understanding of Chinese advertising.

Second, most studies of the cultural content in advertising in different countries are conducted either between the United States and another high-income country or between the United States and another upper-middle-income country. Since China is a developing and low-income country, and the United States is a developed and high-income country, a comparative study of advertising in these two countries is even more important. Part of the purpose of this article is, therefore, to find out if the level of economic development in a country has anything to do with the advertising content of the country.

Furthermore, China is a major socialist country and the United States a leading capitalist country in the world. The social realities for advertising in these two countries are quite different. For instance, most advertisements in China still need governmental sanctions.[1] So, a comparative study of advertising in China and in the United States is even more meaningful. It is also part of the purpose of our study to see if ideological reality has any impact on the cultural values carried in advertising messages, which might be an area worthy of exploring in other advertising studies.

Most important of all, the United States is regarded as typical of Western culture. The bulk of the comparative studies of cultural content in advertising have used the United States as either a "reference frame" or a "model" of Western culture (Belk et al., 1985; Belk and Pollay, 1985; Belk and Bryce, 1986; Frith and Sengupta, 1991; Frith and Wesson, 1991; Hong et al., 1987; Katz and Lee, 1992; Lin, 1993; Mueller, 1987, 1992; Tansey et al., 1990). Only through a comparison with advertising in the United States can the "Westernness" and "Easternness" of advertising in China be convincingly decided.

Tradition versus Modernity

Because the East is believed to be tradition-oriented, it was assumed that advertisements in China would be more likely than Western advertisements to use appeals to traditional values such as group consensus, veneration of the elderly and tradition, status, and oneness-with-nature. In contrast, advertisements originating in the West would be more likely to reflect such values as individualism, appeals to youth and modernity, and manipulation or control over nature.

In the United States, "traditional society" has often been defined as static with little specialization, a low level of urbanization, and low literacy. "Modern society" is defined as having a very high level of differentiation, urbanization, high literacy, and wide exposure to the mass media. In the political realm, traditional society is depicted as having an authoritarian political system, whereas modern society is characterized by wide participation on the part of citizens. Above all, traditional society is bound by the cultural horizons established by old customs and conventions, while modern society is culturally dynamic and oriented to change and innovation (Eisenstadt, 1973).

In the U.S. marketing literature, tradition is defined as historical and standing for the past (Frith, 1991; Pollay, 1983; Pollay and Gallagher, 1990). It is often symbolized by the elderly in advertising. As Mueller (1987) observed, advertisements using traditional appeals often show the elderly "being asked for advice, opinions, and recommendations. Models in such advertisements tend to be older."

On the other hand, modernity is regarded as future-oriented, emphasizing the notion of being new, up-to-date, and ahead of the times (Frith, 1991; Pollay, 1983; Pollay and Gallagher, 1990). In advertising, modernity is often associated with "the depiction of younger models. Stress is on contemporariness and youthful benefits of the products" (Mueller, 1987).

While sharing its basic meaning with U.S. culture, tradition has other connotations in Chinese culture. First, it often includes being time-honored and a long history. In their assessment of the current status of 18 traditional Chinese cultural values, Chu and Ju (1993) found that an overwhelming majority of their respondents (91.2 percent) were "proud of China's long historical heritage." The cultural value of a long historical heritage has been passed down generation after generation in China. Even during the Cultural Revolution (1966–1976), when many traditional values were swept away, the value of a long historical heritage was upheld (Chu and Ju, 1993). Second, pride in China's long historical heritage is often associated with patriotism, which has been endorsed as a core value by Chinese leadership from Mao Zedong to Deng Xiaoping to motivate the Chinese people "to march toward a common goal" with a sense of unity (Chu and Ju, 1993). As Eisenstadt (1973) pointed out, "the Chinese heritage was of great importance in shaping the destiny of its encounter with modernity."

In contemporary China, modernity is simply specified as the ongoing "Four Modernizations" program started in the late 1970s. From then on, China's primary national goal has been to achieve the basic modernizations of industry, agriculture, science and technology, and national defense by the turn of the century (*Beijing Review*, 1978). So, modernity in today's Chinese culture stands for a strong national tendency to adopt management and marketing skills as well as advanced science and technology from industrialized countries. In fact, modernity has provided great momentum for Chinese advertising's revival in the late 1970s and unprecedented growth since then.

But, to Chinese leadership, modernization does not mean Westernization. Since the inception of the "Four Modernizations" program, Chinese leadership has tried to draw a line between modernization and Westernization with a strong preference for modernization without Westernization. While the nationwide adoption of advanced technology and management skills from industrialized countries is regarded as a major step to achieving the Four

Modernizations, Western lifestyles and political systems are either discouraged or prohibited. This demarcation line is also clearly drawn in China's advertising regulations. For example, in the Regulations for Advertising Management that were released in 1987 and still in effect when the data for this study were collected, it was clearly stated that advertising in China should be used for "the promotion of socialist construction" (Xu, 1990), and an advertisement "shall not be released if it is reactionary, obscene, superstitious, or absurd in content" (Xu, 1990).

In addition to the "Four Modernizations," modernity stands for "building socialism with Chinese characteristics" (*Beijing Review*, 1987). The most important of those "Chinese characteristics" is what is currently called "a socialist market economy" (*China Daily*, 1993), which combines central planning and market mechanisms.

In short, we hope that this initial analysis will contribute to the growing research literature on the cultural content of advertising, as no other empirical study has compared television advertising in China and in the United States.

The rationale for analyzing television commercials is that television is the major advertising medium in both countries. In 1993 when the data for this study were gathered, television was the second largest advertising medium in both China (*Baokan Guanggao Wenzhai*, 1994) and the United States (*Advertising Age*, 1994a).

Research Question and Hypotheses

Based on the above considerations, one research question and two hypotheses were formulated for the comparison.

Research Question: What are the dominant cultural values manifest in Chinese and U.S. television commercials?

The answer to this question will determine the similarities and differences in the dominant cultural values reflected in the television commercials from these two countries.

Several studies on Chinese advertising have indicated that China has a long way to go before becoming a full-fledged advertiser's dream (Lo and Yung, 1988; Okechuku and Wang, 1988; Pollay et al., 1990; Schmuck, 1987). This implies that advertising in China is still "immature" when compared with its U.S. counterpart.

Leiss et al. (1990) divided the evolution of advertising in the United States into four stages: *production information, product image, personalization*, and *lifestyle.* These four phases took seven decades from the 1910s to the 1980s to develop. Only in the production-information stage was the primary emphasis on the product itself, explaining its benefits and use. The other three stages resorted more and more to symbolic values. Since

China's current stage of development most resembles the United States at an earlier stage of development, when advertising was much more utilitarian and product-oriented, one hypothesis in our article is formulated as follows:

> H I: Chinese television commercials tend to use more utilitarian cultural values than U.S. television commercials.

As the "immaturity" of Chinese advertising industry could also imply a low degree of Westernization in Chinese advertising content, another hypothesis is generated as:

> H II: Chinese television commercials tend to use more Eastern cultural values than U.S. television commercials.

Data Analysis

This section reports how data were collected, coded, and analyzed in our comparative study of Chinese and U.S. television commercials.

Sample Collection

Three Chinese television channels – Channels One (CCTV1) and Two (CCTV2) of the China Central Television and Shanxi Television (STV) – were selected for this analysis. While both CCTV1 and CCTV2 are broadcast nationwide, STV mainly serves the viewers in Shanxi Province, one of the industrial bases in China. Economic development and living standards in Shanxi Province are about average for the nation, so we believe STV is representative of television commercials broadcast by provincial television stations in China. All three Chinese channels were available where the recording was done.

The three U.S. television networks selected for this analysis were ABC, CBS, and NBC, which were "conventionally" selected for all major research on U.S. television commercials (Lin, 1993; Ramaprasad and Hasegawa, 1992; Resnik and Stern, 1977; Stern and Resnik, 1991).

Television commercials from the three Chinese channels and the three U.S. networks constitute the sampling universe. Two weeks' worth of prime-time television was videotaped simultaneously in China and in the United States in June and November 1993. Two hours a night of commercial broadcasting were collected, giving a total of twenty-eight hours for each country. Only network commercials broadcast during these sample periods were collected. The sample commercials were videotaped in color.

The time frames for the recording in both countries were during the last week of June and the first week of November in 1993. There were no important holidays in either country during the two selected weeks, so we believe that they are quite representative of the "average" commercials on the air in the two countries. Meanwhile, we hoped that the selection of one week respectively from the months of June and November would give an equal chance to any possible seasonal differences such as different product categories promoted in different seasons.

The dates for the sample included all seven days of the week, and the same sample dates were used for both countries. The time blocks for the sample were from 6:00 to 7:00 p.m. and from 9:00 to 10:00 p.m. each day for both countries. The selected two hours during prime-time included the daily major national newscast as well as the major entertainment programs. Using the rotation principle developed by Katz and Lee (1992), taping of both Chinese and U.S. commercials was rotated over the 14 days of the two sample weeks. Thus, for example, only ABC commercials were taped from 6:00 to 7:00 p.m. on Sunday, only NBC commercials were taped from 9:00 to 10:00 p.m. on Tuesday, and so on through the two sample weeks. This procedure was used "in order to fully represent" all six channels (Katz and Lee, 1992).

Coding Instrument

The unit of analysis was each complete television commercial. Any duplicate commercials for the same brand were excluded from the sample "in order to eliminate any redundancies which may have skewed the results" (Stern and Resnik, 1991).

The coding design in this analysis was largely based on Cheng's (1994) framework, which was originally built on Pollay's (1983) typology of the cultural values manifest in advertising and many others' studies on cultural values (Bond et al., 1987; Chu and Ju, 1993; Frith and Wesson, 1990; Mueller, 1987, 1992; Rokeach, 1973; Srikandath, 1991; Tse et al., 1989; Xu, 1990).

A pretest of about 10 percent of the usable commercials (50 from Chinese and 60 from U.S. channels) in the database was conducted to test the applicability of Cheng's (1994) framework. As a result of this pretest, three values, "knowledge," "ornamental," and "practicality," in the former coding scheme were eliminated while seven values were added to the current framework. These seven additions are "adventure," "competition," "enjoyment," "natural," "nurturance," "wisdom," and "work." Thus, the coding scheme for the current analysis consists of 32 cultural values. Together with a coding sheet, a codebook with operationalizations for each of the 32 cultural values was prepared (see Table 1).

All 32 of these cultural values can be divided into two groups – utilitarian and symbolic. By *utilitarian values,* we refer to those emphasizing product features or qualities, such as "convenience," "economy," and "effectiveness."

Table 1: Operationalizations of cultural values examined in Chinese and U.S. television commercials

Values	*Operationalizations*
Adventure[a]	This value suggests boldness, daring, bravery, courage, or thrill. Sky-diving is a typical example.
Beauty	This value suggests that the use of a product will enhance the loveliness, attractiveness, elegance, or handsomeness of an individual.
Collectivism[b]	The emphasis here is on the individual in relation to others typically in the reference group. Individuals are depicted as integral parts of the group.
Competition[b]	The emphasis here is on distinguishing a product from its counterparts by aggressive comparisons. While explicit comparisons may mention the competitor's name, implicit comparisons may use such words as "number one" or "leader."
Convenience[a]	A product is suggested to be handy and easy to use.
Courtesy	Politeness and friendship toward the consumer are shown through the use of polished and affable language in the commercial.
Economy[a]	The inexpensive, affordable, and cost-saving nature of a product is emphasized in the commercial.
Effectiveness[a]	A product is suggested to be powerful and capable of achieving certain ends.
Enjoyment[a]	This value suggests that a product will make its user wild with joy. Typical examples include the capital fun that beer or soda drinkers demonstrate in some commercials.
Family[a]	The emphasis here is on the family life and family members. The commercial stresses family scenes: getting married, companionship of siblings, kinship, being at home, and suggests that a certain product is good for the whole family.
Health[a]	This value recommends that the use of a product will enhance or improve the vitality, soundness, strength, and robust of the body.
Individualism[b]	The emphasis here is on the self-sufficiency and self-reliance of an individual or on the individual as being distinct and unlike others.
Leisure[a]	This value suggests that the use of a product will bring one comfort or relaxation.
Magic[a]	The emphasis here is on the miraculous effect and nature of a product, e.g., "Bewitch your man . . ."; "Heals like magic."
Modernity[a]	The notion of being new, contemporary, up-to-date, and ahead of time is emphasized in a commercial.
Natural	This value suggests spiritual harmony between man and nature by making references to the elements, animals, vegetables, or minerals.
Neatness[a]	The notion of being clean and tidy is stressed in a commercial.
Nurturance[a]	This value stresses giving charity, help, protection, support, or sympathy to the weak, disabled, young, or elderly.
Patriotism	The love of and the loyalty to one's own nation inherent in the nature or in the use of a product are suggested here.
Popularity[a]	The focus here is on the universal recognition and acceptance of a certain product by consumers, e.g., "Best seller"; "Well-known nationwide or worldwide."
Quality	The emphasis here is on the excellence and durability of a product, which is usually claimed to be a winner of medals or certificates awarded by a government department for its high grade or is demonstrated by the product's excellent performance.
Respect for the Elderly[b]	The commercial displays a respect for older people by using a model of old age or asking for the opinions, recommendations, and advice of the elders.
Safety[a]	The reliable and secure nature of a product is emphasized.
Sex[a]	The commercial uses glamorous and sensual models or has a background of lovers holding hands, embracing, or kissing to promote a product.
Social Status[a]	The use of a product is claimed to be able to elevate the position or rank of the user in the eyes of others. The feeling of prestige, trendsetting, and pride in the use of a product is conveyed. The promotion of a company manager's status or fame by quoting his words or showing his picture in the commercial is also included.
Technology[a]	Here, the advanced and sophisticated technical skills to engineer and manufacture a particular product are emphasized.
Tradition[b]	The experience of the past, customs, and conventions are respected. The qualities of being historical, time-honored, and legendary are venerated, e.g., "With eighty years of manufacturing experience"; "It's adapted from ancient Chinese prescriptions."

Values	*Operationalizations*
Uniqueness[a]	The unrivaled, incomparable, and unparalleled nature of a product is emphasized, e.g., "We're the only one that offers you the product."
Wealth	This value conveys the idea that being affluent, prosperous, and rich should be encouraged and suggests that a certain product or service will make the user well-off.
Wisdom[a]	This value shows respect for knowledge, education, intelligence, expertise, or experience.
Work	This value shows respect for diligence and dedication of one's labor and skills. A typical example is that a medication has regained a desperate patient his or her ability to work.
Youth[a]	The worship of the younger generation is shown through the depiction of younger models. The rejuvenating benefits of the product are stressed, e.g., "Feel young again!"

[a]Adapted from Pollay (1983).
[b]dapted from Mueller (1987, 1992).

Table 2: Frequencies of product categories coded by country

	Country				
	China (n = *489*)		*U.S.* (n = *616*)		
Product categories	*Frequencies*	%[a]	*Frequencies*	%[a]	X² *Values*[b] (df = *1*)
Automobile	19	3.9	100	16.2	43.255***
Beauty and personal care	96	19.6	86	14.0	6.372*
Clothing	21	4.3	5	8.0	14.392***
Food and drink	81	16.6	205	33.3	39.701***
Household appliances	116	23.7	55	8.9	45.608***
Medicine	118	24.1	32	5.2	83.318***
Services	16	3.3	102	16.6	50.451***
Travel	0	0	14	2.3	11.256***
Industrial products	18	3.7	3	.5	14.916***
Miscellaneous	4	.8	14	2.3	3.600

[a] Percentages may not total 100 percent because of rounding.
[b] X^2 values indicate differences in the frequencies of each product category regarding countries.
*$p < .05$; ***$p < .001$.

By *symbolic values*, we mean those suggesting human emotions such as "enjoyment," "individualism," and "social status." Many of these values can be regarded as typical of either Eastern or Western culture. For instance, while "collectivism" and "tradition" are typical Eastern cultural values, "individualism" and "modernity" are typical Western cultural values (Lin, 1993; Mueller, 1987, 1992).

While commercials from both countries were coded according to which product categories they fell into (see Table 2), Chinese commercials were also coded according to their product origins classified as "domestic," "joint-venture," and "imported," as shown later in Table 8.

Coding Procedure

The dependent variables in this analysis were the cultural values depicted by the Chinese and U.S. television commercials. The independent variables were China and the United States that were hypothesized to indicate the

Table 3: Frequencies of commercials coded by television networks/stations

Chinese TV stations	Frequencies
CCTV1	192
CCTV2	151
STV	146
Total	489
U.S. TV networks	Frequencies
ABC	212
NBC	206
CBS	198
Total	616

cultural value differences in the television commercials from the two countries. In addition, product categories and product origins were employed as two control variables to help examine the cultural value differences.

A total of 1,105 television commercials – 489 from China and 616 from the United States – were coded by two pairs of selected and trained Chinese and U.S. coders, respectively (see Table 3).

During the coding procedure, the coders tried to identify the most dominant value in each commercial, which was decided mainly by the overall first impression or the key elements of the commercial's "gestalt" – the end result or total message possibly received by viewers (Srikandath, 1991). The dominant values are manifest in the visuals depicted such as the setting or the model of the commercial, accompanied by audio messages, background music, or captions. All the coders focused on the cultural values manifest in a given commercial rather than the qualities that flowed out of the advertised product itself.

Intrajudge and interjudge reliabilities of the coding were calculated by using a per item agreement method suggested by Kassarjian (1977) and Stempel and Westley (1989). To check the intrajudge reliability, 10 percent of the commercials of each country (a sample of 49 commercials from China and 62 from the United States) were systematically selected and respectively coded for all variables by the two pairs of coders. This procedure was repeated three times with a one-month interval between each repetition. After the third coding was completed, a percentage of agreement was calculated, item by item for each two coding sessions. An average was then taken as a composite intracoder reliability, which ranged from 88 to 100 percent for the different variables.

At the end of the coding procedure, the same samples used for intracoder reliability were recoded independently for all variables by one of the authors. Similarly, this procedure was repeated three times with a one-month interval between each repetition. This author's results were compared item by item with those obtained by the two pairs of coders. The coefficient of reliability between the Chinese coders and this author ranged from 87 percent to 100 percent for the Chinese commercials regarding the different variables of this analysis. The coefficient of reliability between the U.S. coders and this author ranged from 85 percent to 100 percent for the U.S. commercials.

Every figure above reaches or exceeds the minimum interjudge reliability of 85 percent suggested by Kassarjian (1977). Thus, the coefficients of reliability obtained are believed to be satisfactory.

Findings

In this study, it is found that the dominant values reflected in the Chinese commercials are "family," "technology," and "tradition." The dominant values reflected in the U.S. commercials are "enjoyment," "individualism," and "economy." Common to both countries are "modernity" and "youth."

The results fail to support the first hypothesis that Chinese television commercials would tend to use more utilitarian cultural values than U.S. commercials. But, the second hypothesis that Chinese commercials would tend to use more Eastern cultural values than U.S. commercials is supported.

The results also indicate that cultural values depicted in television commercials from both countries have much to do with the product categories advertised in the commercials.

Dominant Cultural Values

Table 4 presents the frequencies of the 32 cultural values found in Chinese and U.S. television commercials and the differences between the two samples. It is evident in this table that the most dominant values in Chinese television commercials are "modernity" (32.3 percent), "youth" (7.5 percent), "family" (6.9 percent), "technology" (6.7 percent), and "tradition" (5.3 percent). The most dominant values in U.S. commercials are "enjoyment" (15.3 percent), "modernity" (11.9 percent), "individualism" (7.0 percent), "economy" (6.2 percent), and "youth" (6.0 percent). "Modernity" and "youth" are the only two dominant values shared by the commercials from both countries.

Since two dominant cultural values in the commercials from both countries overlap, there are actually eight cultural values that dominate either Chinese or U.S. television commercials. A comparison of these eight cultural values with regard to their differences in frequency comes to three important findings. First, the values "modernity" ($X^2 = 68.534$, $p < .001$, $df = 1$) and "tradition" ($X^2 = 24.557$, $p < .001$, $df = 1$) are both used significantly more often in Chinese than in U.S. television commercials. The value "modernity" is used even more frequently in Chinese television commercials (32.3

Table 4: Frequencies of cultural values manifest in Chinese and U.S. television commercials

	China (n = *489*)		*U.S.* (n = *616*)		
Cultural values	*Frequencies*	%[a]	*Frequencies*	%[a]	X^2 *Values*[b] (df = *1*)
Adventure	1	.2	2	.3	.153
Beauty	15	3.0	27	4.4	1.372
Collectivism	19	3.9	16	2.6	1.394
Competition	13	2.6	33	5.4	5.140*
Convenience	0	0	6	1.0	4.842*
Courtesy	4	.8	4	.7	.098
Economy	1	.2	38	6.2	28.817***
Effectiveness	5	1.0	23	3.8	8.271**
Enjoyment	10	2.0	94	15.3	56.643***
Family	34	6.9	31	5.1	1.694
Health	2	.4	1	.2	.597
Individualism	22	4.5	43	7.0	3.188
Leisure	11	2.2	23	3.8	2.104
Magic	6	1.2	6	1.0	.147
Modernity	159	32.3	73	11.9	68.534***
Natural	4	.8	5	.8	.00002
Neatness	0	0	3	.5	2.414
Nurturance	7	1.4	19	3.1	3.340
Patriotism	4	.8	0	0	5.002*
Popularity	5	1.0	0	0	6.258*
Quality	14	2.8	16	2.6	.573
Respect for the elderly	12	2.4	6	1.0	3.632
Safety	1	.2	7	1.1	3.346
Sex	7	1.4	31	5.1	10.856***
Social status	11	2.2	19	3.1	.771
Technology	33	6.7	25	4.1	3.793
Tradition	26	5.3	3	.5	24.557***
Uniqueness	1	.2	2	.3	.153
Wealth	7	1.4	2	.3	4.062*
Wisdom	15	3.0	14	2.3	.625
Work	6	1.2	5	.8	.452
Youth	37	7.5	37	6.0	.963

[a] Percentages may not total 100 percent because of rounding.
[b] X^2 values indicate difference in the frequencies of each cultural value regarding countries.
* $p < .05$; ** $p < .01$; *** $p < .001$.

percent) than in U.S. commercials (11.9 percent). On the other hand, the values "economy" ($X^2 = 28.817, p < .001, df = 1$) and "enjoyment" ($X^2 = 56.643, p < .001, df = 1$) are both used significantly more often in U.S. than in Chinese television commercials. Third, the differences in the frequencies of "family," "individualism," "technology," and "youth" in Chinese and U.S. television commercials are statistically insignificant.

We had hypothesized that Chinese television commercials would tend to use more utilitarian values than U.S. commercials. Hypothesis I was not supported by the findings when the occurrences of the 32 cultural values were observed. It is evident that of the six values used significantly more often in U.S. television commercials, three ("competition," "enjoyment," and "sex") are symbolic while another three ("convenience," "economy," and "effectiveness") are utilitarian. Conversely, the five values ("modernity," "patriotism," "popularity," "tradition," and "wealth") that occur significantly more often in Chinese television commercials are all symbolic in nature.

In the meantime, none of the six values used significantly more often in the U.S. television commercials is typical of Eastern culture. However, of the five values which occur significantly more often in Chinese television commercials, three ("tradition," "patriotism," and "wealth") are from Eastern culture, while only one ("modernity") is typically Western.[2] These findings, therefore, support Hypothesis II.

Product Categories

We have also found that cultural values portrayed in television commercials from both countries have much to do with product categories. Based on partial correlation analyses, we have noticed that the coefficients, positive and negative alike, between most cultural values and the two country origins tend to become weaker when product categories are partialled out. Of the 30 coefficients computed respectively for television commercials from the two countries, 22 cultural values show a more or less weaker correlation with China and 18 with the United States when product categories are held constant (see Table 5).

For instance, the coefficients between the cultural value, "modernity," and country origins are .3679 for China and .2579 for the United States before product categories are controlled for. But after product categories are partialled out, the coefficients reduce to .3555 for China and .2522 for the United States (see Table 5). The lowered coefficients after product categories are removed indicate that the correlations between cultural values and

Table 5: Partial correlation coefficients between cultural values and country origins

Cultural values	*China (Uncontrolled†)*	*China (Controlled††)*	*U.S. (Uncontrolled†)*	*U.S. (Controlled††)*
Adventure	−.0278	−.0286	.0181	.0188
Beauty	.0645*	.0596*	.0714*	.0667*
Collectivism	.0796**	.0782**	.0281**	.0269**
Competition	−.0761**	−.0769**	.0773**	.0780**
Convenience	–	–	.0919**	.0904**
Courtesy	.0040	.0012	−.0029	−.0003
Economy	−.2478***	−.2493***	−.2378***	.2391***
Effectiveness	−.0731*	−.0743*	.0744*	.0755*
Enjoyment	−.2348***	−.2345***	.2499***	.2478***
Family	.1265***	.1258***	.1247***	.1240***
Health	−.0121	−.0125	−.0130	−.0134
Individualism	−.0476	−.0465	.1243	.1247
Leisure	.0313	.0310	.0327	.0325
Magic	.0283	.0280	−.0199	−.0196
Modernity	.3679***	.3555***	.2579***	.2522***

(Continued)

Table 5: (*Continued*)

Cultural values	*China (Uncontrolled†)*	*China (Controlled††)*	*U.S. (Uncontrolled†)*	*U.S. (Controlled††)*
Natural	−.0851**	−.0861**	−.0859**	−.0868**
Neatness	–	–	.0654*	.0664*
Nurturance	.0205	.0180	.0196	.0173
Patriotism	.0269**	.0258**	–	–
Popularity	.0782**	.0773**	–	–
Quality	.0518	.0514	.0505	.0511
Respect for the elderly	.1303***	.1293***	−.1292***	−.1284***
Safety	−.0845**	−.0866**	.0851**	.0870**
Sex	.0025**	.0009**	.0938**	.0923**
Social status	.0073	.0064	.0132	.0123
Technology	.0454	.0451	.0436	.0433
Tradition	.1455***	.1448***	−.1442***	−.1436***
Uniqueness	−.0762*	−.0771*	.0767*	.0775*
Wealth	.0281	.0278	−.0271	−.0284
Wisdom	.0191	.0187	.0180	.0175
Work	.0024	.0020	−.0017	−.0013
Youth	.0338	.0307	.0306	.0279

† Product categories are not partialled out.
†† Product categories are partialled out.
"-" is printed if a coefficient cannot be computed.
*$p < .05$; ** $p < .01$; ***$p < .001$.

two country origins are partly due to the presence of product categories. Note that the statistically significant differences found in uncontrolled data remain significantly different with the partial correlation removed.

The findings in Table 5 are more meaningful when jointly observed with the findings generated in other tables. For example, "modernity," the most dominant cultural value in Chinese television commercials (see Table 4), is used most frequently for "automobile" (63.2 percent), "industrial products" (44.4 percent), "clothing" (42.9 percent), and "household appliances" (42.2 percent). In the meantime, the value "tradition" is mainly used for "food and drink" (12.2 percent) and "medicine" (10.2 percent) (see Table 6).

"Enjoyment," a value depicted significantly more often in U.S. than in Chinese television commercials, is mainly used for "travel" (28.6 percent) and "food and drink" (28.2 percent).

"Economy," another value that occurs significantly more often in U.S. than in Chinese television commercials, is mainly used for "service" (16.8 percent) and "medicine" (9.4 percent) (see Table 7).

"Individualism," "modernity," and "sex," three typical Western cultural values portrayed in Chinese television commercials, were most frequently used with imported products, followed by joint-venture products (see Table 8).

The findings presented in Tables 5 to 8 will be referred to in the following discussion section to enhance our understanding of the findings generated in Table 4, which directly answer the research question and are closely relevant to the two research hypotheses for this study.

Table 6: Frequencies of cultural values manifest by product categories in Chinese television commercials[a]

Cultural values	*AU* (%)	*BP* (%)	*CL* (%)	*FD* (%)	*HA* (%)	*ME* (%)	*SE* (%)	*IP* (%)	*MI* (%)	X^2 *Values*[b] (df = 8)
Adventure	0	0	0	0	0	.8	0	0	0	3.151
Beauty	0	12.6	0	3.7	0	0	0	0	0	39.195***
Collectivism	0	2.1	0	8.5	3.4	2.5	12.5	5.6	0	11.278
Competition	0	1.1	4.8	7.3	2.6	1.7	0	0	0	10.278
Courtesy	0	1.1	0	0	0	0	18.8	0	0	66.597***
Economy	0	0	0	0	0	0	0	0	.8	3.151
Effectiveness	5.3	0	0	0	0	3.4	0	0	0	13.547
Enjoyment	0	2.1	4.8	3.7	.9	8	0	0	25.0	16.657*
Family	0	3.2	4.8	8.5	8.6	11.0	0	0	0	10.359
Health	0	0	0	0	0	1.7	0	0	0	6.314
Individualism	0	7.4	0	1.2	10.3	1.7	0	0	0	18.933*
Leisure	0	3.2	4.8	2.4	3.4	.8	0	0	0	4.097
Magic	0	2.1	0	0	1.7	0	6.3	5.6	0	9.986
Modernity	63.2	38.9	42.9	22.0	42.2	17.8	31.3	44.4	0	34.873***
Natural	0	1.1	0	3.7	0	0	0	0	0	10.793
Nurturance	0	3.2	0	1.2	0	2.5	0	0	0	5.882
Patriotism	0	1.1	0	0	1.7	0	0	0	25.0	32.329***
Popularity	0	1.1	0	0	2.6	.8	0	0	0	4.492
Quality	0	0	14.3	4.9	1.7	2.5	0	11.1	0	19.987*
Respect for the elderly	0	0	0	1.2	1.7	6.8	0	5.6	0	14.627
Safety	0	0	0	0	0	.8	0	0	0	3.151
Sex	0	3.2	9.5	0	.9	.8	0	0	0	14.323
Social Status	0	0	0	2.4	1.7	4.2	0	5.6	0	7.298
Technology	26.3	2.1	0	2.4	11.2	5.9	6.3	16.7	0	25.653**
Tradition	0	2.1	0	12.2	.9	10.2	0	5.6	0	23.116**
Uniqueness	0	0	0	0	0	.8	0	0	0	3.151
Wealth	5.3	0	0	3.7	0	0	18.8	0	0	44.272***
Wisdom	0	3.2	0	1.2	1.7	6.8	6.3	0	0	9.624
Work	0	0	0	0	0	5.1	0	0	0	19.099
Youth	0	9.5	14.3	9.8	2.6	10.2	0	0	50.0	22.305**

AU = Automobiles BP = Beauty and personal care CL = Clothing
FD = Food and drink HA = Household appliances ME = Medicine
SE = Services IP = Industrial products MI = Miscellaneous

[a] Percentages for each product category may not total 100 percent because of rounding.
[b] X^2 values indicate differences in the frequencies of each cultural value regarding product categories.
* $p < .05$; ** $p < .01$; *** $p < .001$.

Table 7: Frequencies of cultural values manifest by product categories in U.S. televison commercials[a]

Cultural values	*AU* (%)	*BP* (%)	*CL* (%)	*FD* (%)	*HA* (%)	*ME* (%)	*SE* (%)	*TR* (%)	*IP* (%)	*MI* (%)	X^2 *Values*[b] (df = 9)
Adventure	0	1.2	0	.5	0	0	0	0	0	0	3.172
Beauty	1.0	14.3	0	5.8	0	3.1	1.0	0	0	0	30.566***
Collectivism	3.0	0	0	2.4	1.9	0	5.9	7.1	0	0	9.572
Competition	10.0	0	0	2.9	5.6	0	10.9	0	0	16.7	25.080**
Convenience	0	1.2	0	0	0	0	3.0	7.1	0	5.6	17.579*
Courtesy	0	4.8	0	0	0	0	0	0	0	0	25.499**
Economy	6.0	0	0	5.3	0	9.4	16.8	7.1	0	5.6	29.473***
Effectiveness	2.0	0	0	5.3	13.0	0	0	14.3	0	5.6	28.302***

(Continued)

Table 7: (*Continued*)

Cultural values	*AU* (%)	*BP* (%)	*CL* (%)	*FD* (%)	*HA* (%)	*ME* (%)	*SE* (%)	*TR* (%)	*IP* (%)	*MI* (%)	X^2 *Values*[b] (df = 9)
Enjoyment	11.0	7.1	0	28.2	5.6	3.1	9.9	28.6	0	11.1	45.009***
Family	1.0	1.2	0	8.7	1.9	15.6	5.0	0	0	0	22.639**
Health	0	0	0	.5	0	0	0	0	0	0	1.994
Individualism	2.0	9.5	0	11.7	0	18.8	1.0	0	0	11.1	30.085***
Leisure	2.0	11.9	0	.5	7.4	3.1	1.0	14.3	33.3	5.6	38.633***
Magic	0	0	0	1.0	0	9.4	0	0	0	5.6	30.873***
Modernity	25.0	7.1	0	6.8	27.8	6.3	7.9	7.1	0	11.1	40.187***
Natural	0	0	0	.5	1.9	0	0	0	0	16.7	59.966***
Neatness	0	0	0	.5	1.9	0	1.0	0	0	0	3.851
Nurturance	1.0	0	25.0	1.5	0	3.1	12.9	0	0	0	47.576***
Quality	7.0	0	0	1.9	5.6	0	1.0	0	33.3	0	26.166**
Respect for the elderly	0	0	0	.5	1.9	0	4.0	0	0	0	12.789
Safety	0	0	0	0	1.9	0	5.9	0	0	0	26.295**
Sex	4.0	11.9	0	7.3	1.9	3.1	0	0	0	0	19.510*
Social status	16.0	0	0	.5	1.9	3.1	0	0	33.3	0	73.173***
Technology	6.0	4.8	0	1.0	20.4	0	2.0	0	0	0	47.143***
Tradition	0	0	0	1.5	0	0	0	0	0	0	6.000
Uniqueness	0	0	0	0	0	0	1.0	7.1	0	0	23.125**
Wealth	0	0	0	0	0	0	1.0	7.1	0	0	23.125**
Wisdom	1.0	7.1	0	1.5	0	6.3	2.0	0	0	0	14.798
Work	0	2.4	0	.5	0	6.3	0	0	0	0	17.003*
Youth	2.0	15.5	75.0	3.4	1.9	9.4	6.9	0	0	5.6	55.933***

AU = Automobiles; BP = Beauty and personal care; CL = Clothing
FD = Food and drink; HA = Household appliances; ME = Medicine
SE = Services; TR = Travel; IP = Industrial products
MI = Miscellaneous

[a] Percentages for each cultural value may not total 100 percent because of rounding.
[b] X^2 values indicate differences in the frequencies of each cultural value regarding product categories.
* $p < .05$; ** $p < .01$; *** $p < .001$.

Table 8: Frequencies of cultural values manifest by product origins in Chinese television commercials[a]

Cultural values	*Domestic* (%)	*Joint venture* (%)	*Imported* (%)	X^2 *Values*[b] (df = 2)
Adventure	.3	0	0	.251
Beauty	2.8	6.3	0	3.474
Collectivism	4.3	1.6	2.9	1.214
Competition	3.1	0	2.9	1.214
Courtesy	1.0	0	0	1.011
Economy	0	.3	0	.251
Tradition	6.6	0	0	6.883*
Effectiveness	1.3	0	0	1.266
Enjoyment	2.0	1.6	0	.770
Family	8.2	3.2	0	4.922
Health	.5	0	0	.503
Individualism	3.1	6.3	17.1	15.386***
Leisure	2.6	1.6	0	1.100
Magic	1.0	1.6	2.9	.969
Modernity	27.9	49.2	54.3	19.392***
Natural	1.0	0	0	1.011

Cultural values	*Domestic* (%)	*Joint venture* (%)	*Imported* (%)	X^2 *Values*[b] (df = 2)
Nurturance	1.5	0	2.9	1.449
Patriotism	1.0	0	0	1.011
Popularity	1.3	0	0	1.266
Quality	3.3	1.6	0	1.700
Respect for the elderly	2.8	1.6	0	1.289
Safety	.3	0	0	.251
Sex	.5	1.6	11.4	27.147***
Social status	2.0	3.2	0	1.132
Technology	7.4	4.8	2.9	1.515
Tradition	6.6	0	0	6.883*
Uniqueness	.3	0	0	.251
Wealth	1.5	1.6	0	.549
Wisdom	3.1	3.2	2.9	.008
Work	1.5	0	0	1.523
Youth	7.7	11.1	0	4.003

[a] Percentages for each product origin may not total 100 percent because of rounding.
[b] X^2 values indicate differences in the frequencies of each cultural value regarding product origins.
* $p < .05$; *** $p < .001$.

Discussion

Modernity and Youth

As stated in the research question, we intended to ascertain the dominant cultural values manifest in Chinese and U.S. television commercials and to determine the differences between them. Results indicate that "modernity" and "youth" are two dominant values shared by commercials from both countries (see Table 4). This similarity suggests that television commercials in both China and the United States hold that the essential "characteristics" of advertising are to promote things that are new and to encourage change rather than maintain the status quo (Rotzoll et al., 1976). And advertising in both countries is used to target young consumers more often than people of other demographic segments in the marketplace (Hovland and Wilcox, 1989).

Values Dominant in Chinese Commercials

"Family" is the third most dominant value used in Chinese television commercials (see Table 4). This finding is consonant with the leading empirical study of contemporary cultural values in China. In a large-scale survey of cultural change in China's rural and urban areas of the late 1980s, Chu and Ju (1993) used their subjects' goals in life as one indicator of the cultural values prevalent in contemporary China. The results indicated that the most important among 14 goals was "a warm and close family."

A warm and close family has always been high on the list of desirable values for the Chinese and still is. The major reason for the importance of this value in China is because families are regarded as societal cells, and the harmony of families is deemed essential for maintaining social stability, in the past and present alike. Understandably, commercials with "family" as the dominant theme are very appealing to Chinese consumers.

"Technology" is the fourth most dominant value used in Chinese television commercials (see Table 4). As sophisticated high-tech often adds charm to "modernity," it is natural that the value "technology" is also important in Chinese commercials.

"Tradition" is the fifth most frequently used value in Chinese television commercials (see Table 4). This is probably because China has a long history. In their assessment of the current status of 18 traditional Chinese cultural values, Chu and Ju (1993) found that an overwhelming majority of their respondents (91.2 percent) were "proud of China's long historical heritage."

The favor advertisers in China have given to the value "tradition" is not only consonant with the contemporary mentality of the Chinese but is also part of the national heritage itself. Chinese leadership from Mao Zedong to Deng Xiaoping has endorsed this value in many political campaigns (Chu and Ju, 1993). The favor given to "tradition" suggests that this value is not only attractive to Chinese consumers but also fits nicely into the political reality in China.

Product Categories

When this finding is looked at together with product categories, it becomes more meaningful. The value "tradition," is more frequently used for "food and drink" and "medicine" (see Table 6). It is evident that both product categories often have a long historical heritage, which, to a large extent, suggests good quality and wide popularity of these products.

Modernity in China

The finding that the two values, "modernity" and "tradition," are both used significantly more often in Chinese than in U.S. television commercials (see Table 4) is very important and interesting. These two seemingly incompatible findings, in fact, truthfully reflect both the mentality of the contemporary Chinese and reality in today's China. As we have given considerable attention above to "tradition," we will focus on "modernity" below.

The finding that "modernity" is used even more frequently in Chinese than in U.S. television commercials (see Table 4) is understandable in context.

Most products promoted in Chinese television commercials are either new or fashionable to Chinese consumers, who we believe are still commercially naive. These products range from "automobiles" to "industrial products," and from "clothing" to "household appliances" (see Table 6). So, it is natural to use "modernity" in advertising campaigns to promote the "newness" of these products in China.

To attract U.S. consumers, who are commercially more sophisticated than their Chinese counterparts, it is not enough to merely depend on the value "modernity." Thus, advertisers may often find they need to include other values. For instance, while automobiles are mainly promoted as a modern rarity in China, they are often portrayed in U.S. television commercials as a means for personal "enjoyment" and an indicator for "social status" (see Table 7).

However, the reasons for the predominance of "modernity" in Chinese advertising are more complicated and are both internal and external. Internally, modernization is an overwhelming national theme currently promoted by Chinese leadership. So, those advertising campaigns having "modernity" as the dominant value are in accord with government policy. Therefore, it is easy for them to win approval of the Administration for Industry and Commerce which supervises advertising business in China at both national and local levels.

The most important point here is that to Chinese leadership, modernization does not mean Westernization. As we mentioned earlier in this article, Chinese leadership has always tried to draw a line between the two notions, with a clear preference for modernization without Westernization. This policy has a great impact on China's advertising regulations. As a result, those cultural values promoting Western lifestyles are, on the whole, infrequent in Chinese television commercials. This list of "disfavored" values includes "adventure" (.2 percent), "competition" (2.6 percent), "enjoyment" (2.0 percent), "individualism" (4.5 percent), "leisure" (2.2 percent), and "sex" (1.4 percent) (see Table 4).

The external reason for the predominance of "modernity" in Chinese television commercials is the influence from the transnational advertising agencies which mainly run the campaigns for imported and joint-venture products in the Chinese market. The value "modernity" in Chinese television commercials is most frequently used for imported products and secondly for joint-venture products (see Table 8).

This finding is more meaningful when cross-examined with other findings. In addition to "modernity," both "individualism" and "sex," two typical Western cultural values depicted in Chinese television commercials, are used mainly for imported products, followed by joint-venture products (see Table 8). These findings suggest that transnational advertising is exerting a considerably strong influence on Chinese television commercials and is the pace-setter for Western cultural values portrayed in China's advertising.

Traditional Values in China

In the late 1980s, the Chinese Cultural Connection, an international network of social scientists, identified 40 traditional Chinese cultural values (Bond et al., 1987). But as clearly documented in several more recent studies on contemporary Chinese culture, only part of those traditional values are prevalent in the country today (Xu, 1990; Chu and Ju, 1993; Hinkelman, 1994; Pan et al., 1994).

The reason for China being "less traditional" than some other areas under the influence of Confucianism such as Taiwan and Korea (Pan et al., 1994) is multifaceted. In addition to orthodox traditionalism and Western culture, the third powerful ideological force that shaped cultural values in contemporary China is Marxism and Maoism, which primarily took the form of political campaigns like the Cultural Revolution and government propaganda via the mass media. As a result, such typical Confucian values as "differentiation between men and women" and "a house full of sons and grandsons" have largely been abandoned by the Chinese in the 1990s. Nevertheless, some traditional values have survived. The value, "strong family ties," for example, still remains popular in China today (Chu and Ju, 1993; Pan et al., 1994).

Despite some "thought liberation" effects in contemporary China, ideological force is believed to continue to suppress change in the country. As Pan et al. (1994) pointed out, "Changes in the economic sphere, and in people's life experience, are expanding the boundaries of the dominant ideology, but they operate only within the prescribed ideological framework." Unlike the United States where cultural values change in a steady pace that Pan and his collaborators called "dynamic evolution," cultural change in China is characterized by hesitant steps that risk authoritarian suppression, which they termed "suppressive instability."

Although the cultural values prevalent in contemporary China are shaped by three ideological forces, some traditional values do exist and even continue to be widely held by the Chinese. Such a list at least includes "diligence," "face-saving," "frugality," and "tolerance" (Chu and Ju, 1993; Pan et al., 1994; Xu, 1990). But based on our study, none of these values is found in contemporary Chinese advertising. We believe that this is due to the nature of these cultural values – they do not help sell products.

Values Dominant in U.S. Commercials

Among the eight most dominant values depicted in either Chinese or U.S. television commercials, there are no statistically significant differences in the frequencies of "family," "individualism," "technology," and "youth." Three of these four values are from Western culture.

The Eastern cultural value, "family," was found to have occurred in U.S. television commercials (5.1 percent) almost as frequently as in Chinese commercials (6.9 percent) (see Table 4). Interestingly, the "family" value is most frequently used for the same product category – "medicine" (see Tables 6 and 7). This finding indicates a universal need for a warm and close family, especially when one is not feeling well.

Among the eight most dominant values carried in either Chinese or U.S. television commercials, "enjoyment" and "economy" are used significantly more often in U.S. than in Chinese television commercials (see Table 4). It is not surprising that "enjoyment" is the most dominant cultural value depicted in U.S. television commercials, as hedonism is currently still more common in the United States than in China.

The dominance of the value "economy," however, is worthy of attention. In their historical analysis of U.S. advertisements, Leiss et al. (1990) initiated a pattern for advertising growth, namely, there was a general "shift from informational to symbolic presentation" of human values in advertising, as this industry grew "mature" and started to explore new communicative forms.

Human history often develops in spirals, and similar happenings in history are not infrequent. The current dominance of some utilitarian cultural values like "economy" in U.S. advertising may be suggesting a partial shift from symbolic values back to utilitarian values in advertising. This assumption is supported by the finding that the value "effectiveness" is also used significantly more often in U.S. than in Chinese television commercials (see Table 4). This shift is probably because the U.S. consumers have also become "mature." Advertisers might have realized that if they want to survive in the highly competitive U.S. market, they need some more solid information in advertising to cater to their target consumers, who are living in a low-context culture (Hall, 1989) and prefer directness in speech (Frith and Wesson, 1991).

Implications

The findings in this article have several implications for international advertising professionals as well as researchers. First, Chinese television commercials currently tend to use symbolic cultural values, while U.S. television commercials like to use both symbolic and utilitarian values. This finding implies that the historical model of advertising development initiated by Leiss et al. (1990) is applicable to the Chinese context. With a rapid growth for more than a decade, advertising in China has become far more sophisticated than before, having obviously stepped beyond the product information phase described in Leiss et al.'s model.

Nevertheless, this finding does not necessarily suggest that when Chinese consumers in the future have become as sophisticated as their counterparts in developed countries, advertisers in China will inevitably resort to utilitarian values as frequently as U.S. advertisers are doing today. The rationale for this position is that the adoption of utilitarian and symbolic cultural values in advertising sometimes has as much to do with cultural heritage as economic development. This view has been suggested by other researchers in their comparative studies of cultural differences reflected in Japanese and U.S. advertising (Lin, 1993; Mueller, 1987, 1992).

Whether Chinese advertising will adopt more utilitarian or symbolic values or preserve the status quo in the years ahead depends, to a large extent, on how it will keep the heritage of its high-context culture (Hall, 1989). It appears that an extended comparative study of the cultural content among Chinese, Japanese, and U.S. advertising will be necessary and important in order to monitor the development of Chinese advertising in the future. Culturally, China has more to share with Japan which is economically more comparable with the United States.

Second, the finding that both Eastern and Western cultural values are playing important roles in Chinese television commercials implies that advertising in China is a "melting pot" for cultural values, which has been built over the last 10 years. The building of the "melting pot" for Eastern and Western cultural values in China, in fact, started in the mid-nineteenth century when China's door was forced open by the Opium War (1840–1842) with the United Kingdom and continued through the early twentieth century. The May Fourth Movement of 1919 could be called the first cultural revolution in China, which was aimed at destroying some traditional Chinese cultural values while introducing some Western ones. The founding of the People's Republic of China in 1949 commenced a new chapter in cultural changes in a way unprecedented in modern Chinese history. Mao Zedong waged nationwide campaigns assaulting many traditional values. The attack became frantic during the Cultural Revolution (1966–1976). Millions of Red Guards smashed anything regarded as "feudalism, capitalism, and revisionism," which contained both traditional and Western cultural values. What the Chinese people experienced in those years was a "cultural void" (Chu and Ju, 1993).

Recent years have seen the return of some traditional cultural values in China, which, mixed with certain Western values, are forming a "semi-traditional" and "semi-modern" culture. The current building of the cultural "melting pot" in Chinese advertising keeps abreast of the national trend of reviving those "good" traditional Chinese values and accepting those "good" Western ones, which are believed to benefit the ongoing "Four Modernizations" program. The current openness, the widest ever in Chinese history, is signaling a golden opportunity for transnational advertisers who intend to step into this huge market.

Third, we have noticed in this study that cultural values depicted in the television commercials from both China and the United States have much to do with the product categories advertised in these two countries. This finding implies that while transnational advertisers should be sensitive to the effects of country difference on cultural values used in their advertising campaigns in China, they need pay due attention to the effects of product categories on cultural values portrayed in their advertising messages.

As documented in this study, for example, the cultural value "family" is used frequently in both Chinese and U.S. television commercials for medicine. So, a U.S. medicine commercial that stresses "family" value at home might also be effective in China if it still uses the same value in this different market. However, U.S. commercials for services that also use the value "family" quite often at home may not be as effective in the Chinese market if they resort to the same cultural value there. This is because the value "family," as indicated in our study, is seldom used by Chinese television commercials for services.

In our view, therefore, only when both differences in country origin and product category are taken into consideration could an advertising campaign work most effectively. Of course, this position needs to be further proved by more empirical studies, especially those based on consumer research.

Finally, we have found in this study that Chinese advertising is under a considerably strong influence of Western culture. Results indicate that all the cultural values used significantly more often for imported and joint-venture products are from Western culture. On the one hand, this again indicates that China is currently more open and tolerant of Western culture than ever before. On the other hand, this finding supports Anderson's (1984) assumption that China is "no longer immune from the influences of the transnational advertising."

Close attention should be paid to the similar finding that some Western values like "modernity" and "youth" are used far more often than other Western values like "enjoyment" and "sex" in Chinese television commercials. This implies that advertising in China is a "double-distorted mirror" of culture. The mirror is distorted the first time – as Pollay (1986) and Pollay and Gallagher (1990) used this metaphor for advertising in North America – due to the nature of advertising, which reflects only those values benefiting the advertisers and ignores those not benefiting them. The mirror is distorted in China a second time, however, because of the "idiosyncratic" social reality in the country, which favors certain Western cultural values and disfavors others.

The findings about the cultural "melting pot" and the "double-distorted mirror" discussed above indicate that advertising in China is still in a state of flux. This "idiosyncrasy" of Chinese advertising has important implications for both advertising researchers and advertising professionals. For the former, it presents a challenging but interesting research topic, which calls for an "idiosyncratic" treatment when compared with advertising in some other developing countries. For the latter, the opening feature of the "melting pot" and the closing tendency in the "double-distorted mirror" imply that those who want to enter and stay in the Chinese market may be both optimistic and cautious, trying to select the cultural values which not only aggressively promote their products but also fit neatly into Chinese social and political reality.

Notes

1. Although the requirement that all advertisements in China must be sanctioned by the Administration for Industry and Commerce at the national or local level was abolished in a few selected cities in 1993, advertising content still requires approval for certain product categories, which include household appliances, drugs, foodstuffs, alcoholic beverages and cosmetics (Miao, 1993). As consumer products make up the lion's share of the products advertised in China (Cheng, 1994), censorship of advertisements for consumer products virtually means censorship of most advertising content in the country.
2. The values "modernity" and "tradition" were treated as typical Western and Eastern cultural values, respectively, in several previous studies on cultural content in advertising (Lin, 1993; Mueller, 1987, 1992). The reason for regarding "patriotism" and "wealth" as Eastern cultural values here is that both of them were listed in the major scholarly works particularly devoted to the study of traditional Chinese cultural values (Bond et al., 1987; Chu and Ju, 1993). On the contrary, these two values were not mentioned in Pollay's (1983) widely cited typology for measuring cultural values manifest in advertising.

References

*These articles are published in Chinese. The English titles in the references are translated by the authors.

Advertising Age. "U.S. Advertising Volume." *Advertising Age*, May 2, 1994a.

Advertising Age. "World's Top 50 Advertising Organizations." *Advertising Age*, April 13, 1994b.

Anderson, Michael H. *Madison Avenue in Asia: Politics and Transnational Advertising.* London and Toronto: Associated University Press, 1984.

Baokan Guanggao Wenzhai [Advertising digest from the press]. "China's Advertising Media, 1990–1993." *Baokan Guanggao Wenzhai*, 5, May 1994.

Baudot, Barbara S. *International Advertising Handbook: A User's Guide to Rules and Regulations.* Lexington and Toronto: Lexington Books, 1989.

Beijing Review. "Advance Along the Road of Socialism with Chinese Characteristics." *Beijing Review*, November 9, 1987.

Beijing Review. "Communique of the Third Plenum of the Eleventh Party Congress." *Beijing Review*, December 29, 1978.

Belk, Russell W., Wendy J. Bryce, and Richard W. Pollay. "Advertising Themes and Cultural Values: A Comparison of U.S. and Japanese Advertising." In *Proceedings of the Inaugural Meeting of the Southeast Asia Region.* K. C. Mun and T. C. Chan, eds. Hong Kong: Academy of International Business, 1985.

———, and Richard W. Pollay, "Materialism and Status Appeals in Japanese and U.S. Print Advertising: A Historical and Cross-Cultural Content Analysis." *International Marketing Review* 2, 12 (1985): 38–47.

———, and Wendy J. Bryce. "Materialism and Individual Determinism in U.S. and Japanese Television Advertising." *Advances in Consumer Research* 13 (1986): 568–72.

Bond, Michael H. et al. "Chinese Values and the Search for Culture-Free Dimensions of Culture." *Journal of Cross-Cultural Psychology* 18, 2 (1987): 143–64.

Cheng, Hong. "Reflections of Cultural Values: A Content Analysis of Chinese Magazine Advertisements from 1982 and 1992." *International Journal of Advertising* 13, 2 (1994): 167–83.

China Daily (Beijing). "Party Accelerates Reforms: CPC Forges Politics for Socialist Market Economy." *China Daily*, November 15, 1993.

Chu, Godwin C, and Yanan Ju. *The Great Wall in Ruins: Communication and Cultural Change in China.* Albany, N.Y.: State University of New York Press, 1993.

Eisenstadt, S. N. *Tradition, Change, and Modernity.* New York: John Wiley & Sons, Inc., 1973.

Endicott, R. Craig. "U.S. Income Growth Outduels Foreign Side: Global Figure Stagnant at $14.5 Billion; WPP, McCann, Burnett Lead Rankings." *Advertising Age*, April 13, 1994.

Frith, Katherine T. "Analyzing Cultural Values in Advertising: An East/West Typology." Paper presented at the American Academy of Advertising annual conference, 1991.

———, and Subir Sengupta. "Individualism and Advertising: A Cross-Cultural Comparison." *Media Asia* 18, 2 (1991): 191–4, 197.

———, and David Wesson. "A Comparison of Cultural Values in British and American Print Advertising: A Study of Magazines." *Journalism Quarterly* 68, 1/2 (1991): 216–23.

**Guoji Guanggao* [International advertising]. "China's Advertising Industry Growth, 1981–1992." *Guoji Guanggao,* April 1993.

Hall, Edward T. *Beyond Culture.* New York, NY: Anchor Books, 1989.

Hinkelman, Edward G., ed. *China Business: The Portable Encyclopedia for Doing Business with China.* San Rafael, CA: World Trade Press, 1994.

Hong, Jae W., Aydin Muderrisoglu, and George M. Zinkhan. "Cultural Differences and Advertising Expression: A Comparative Content Analysis of Japanese and U.S. Magazine Advertising." *Journal of Advertising* 16, 1 (1987): 55–62, 68.

Hovland, Roxanne, and Gary B. Wilcox, eds. *Advertising in Society: Classic and Contemporary Readings on Advertising's Role in Society.* Lincolnwood, IL: NTC Business Books, 1989.

Kassarjian, Harold H. "Content Analysis in Consumer Research." *Journal of Consumer Research* 4, 1 (1977): 8–18.

Katz, Helen, and Wei-Na Lee. "Ocean Apart: An Initial Exploration of Social Communication Differences in US and UK Prime-time Television Advertising." *International Journal of Advertising* 11, 1 (1992): 257–67.

Leiss, William, Stephen Kline, and Sut Jhally. *Social Communication in Advertising: Persons, Products and Images of Well-Being*, 2nd ed. Ontario: Nelson Canada, 1990.

Lin, Carolyn A. "Cultural Differences in Message Strategies: A Comparison between American and Japanese TV Commercials." *Journal of Advertising Research* 33, 3 (1993): 40–48.

Lo, Thamis Wing-chun, and Amy Yung. "Multinational Service Firms in Centrally-Planned Economies: Foreign Advertising Agencies in the PRC." *Management International Review* 28, 1 (1988): 26–33.

Marquez, F. T. "The Relationship of Advertising and Culture in the Philippines." *Journalism Quarterly* 52, 3 (1975): 436–42.

Miao, Suzanne. "China Loosens Ad Guidelines in Cities: New Regulations for Direct Advertising and in Certain Product Categories." *Adweek,* April 19, 1993.

Mueller, Barbara. "Reflections of Culture: An Analysis of Japanese and American Advertising Appeals." *Journal of Advertising Research* 27, 3 (1987): 51–59.

Mueller, Barbara. "Standardization vs. Specialization: An Examination of Westernization in Japanese Advertising." *Journal of Advertising Research* 32, 1 (1992): 15–24.

Okechuku, Chike, and Gongrong Wang. "The Effectiveness of Chinese Print Advertisements in North America." *Journal of Advertising Research* 28, 5 (1988): 25–34.

Pan, Zhongdang, Steven H. Chaffee, Godwin C. Chu, and Yanan Ju. *To See Ourselves: Comparing Traditional Chinese and American Cultural Values.* Boulder, CO: Westview Press, 1994.

Parsons, Paul. "Marketing Revolution Hits Staid Giants . . . While in China, Advertising Blooms Like a Hundred Flowers." *Advertising Age*, July 19, 1993.

Pollay, Richard W. "The Distorted Mirror: Reflections on the Unintended Consequences of Advertising." *Journal of Marketing* 50, 2 (1986): 18–36.

———. "Measuring the Cultural Values Manifest in Advertising." In *Current Issues and Research in Advertising*, James H. Leigh and Claude R. Martin, Jr., eds. Ann Arbor, MI: University of Michigan Graduate School of Business Division of Research, 1983.

———, David K. Tse, and Zhengyuan Wang. "Advertising, Propaganda, and Value Change in Economic Development: The New Cultural Revolution in China and Attitudes Toward Advertising." *Journal of Business Research* 20, 2 (1990): 83–95.

———, and Katherine Gallagher. "Advertising and Cultural Values: Reflections in the Distorted Mirror." *International Journal of Advertising* 9, 4 (1990): 359–72.

Ramaprasad, Jyotika, and Kazumi Hasegawa. "Informational Content of American and Japanese Television Commercials." *Journalism Quarterly* 69, 3 (1992): 612–22.

Regulations for Advertising Management. Released by the State Council of the People's Republic of China, 1987.

Resnik, Alan, and Bruce L. Stern. "Analysis of Information Content in Television Advertising." *Journal of Marketing* 41, 1 (1977): 50–53.

Rokeach, Milton J. *The Nature of Human Values.* New York, NY: Free Press, 1973.

Rotzoll, Kim B., James E. Haefner, and Charles H. Sandage. *Advertising in Contemporary Society: Perspective Toward Understanding,* Columbus, OH: Copyright Grid, Inc., 1976.

Schmuck, Claudine. "Broadcast for a Billion: The Growth of Commercial Television in China." *Columbia Journal of World Business* 22, 3 (1987): 27–34.

Srikandath, Sivaram. "Cultural Values Depicted in Indian Television Advertising." *Gazette* 48, 3 (1991): 165–76.

Stempel, Guido H., III., and Bruce H. Westley. *Research Methods in Mass Communication*, 2nd ed. Englewood Cliffs, N.J.: Prentice Hall, 1989.

Stern, Bruce L., and Alan J. Resnik. "Information Content in Television Advertising: A Replication and Extension." *Journal of Advertising Research* 31, 3 (1991): 36–46.

Tansey, Richard, Michael R. Hyman, and George M. Zinkhan. "Cultural Themes in Brazilian and U.S. Auto Ads: A Cross-Cultural Comparison." *Journal of Advertising* 19, 2 (1990): 30–39.

Tse, David K., Russell W. Belk, and Nan Zhou. "Becoming a Consumer Society: A Longitudinal and Cross-Cultural Content Analysis of Print Ads from Hong Kong, the People's Republic of China, and Taiwan." *Journal of Consumer Research* 15, 4 (1989): 457–72.

Wall Street Journal. "China Expects to Boom." *Wall Street Journal* November 8, 1993.

Xu, Baiyi. "The Role of Advertising in China." Working paper, Department of Advertising, University of Illinois at Urbana-Champaign, 1989.

———. *Marketing to China, One Billion New Customers.* Lincolnwood, IL: NTC Business Books, 1990.

Yuan, Lao. "Annual Ad Bills to Hit $4.8b." *China Daily* (Beijing), November 8, 1993.

**Zhongguo Daobao* [China guide] Los Angeles. "China's Advertising Industry: A Vigorous Dragon Crossing the River." *Zhongguo Daobao,* June 2, 1994.

8

Controllable Factors of New Product Success: A Cross-National Comparison

Roger J. Calantone, Jeffrey B. Schmidt and X. Michael Song

1. Introduction

In most industries, the development and commercialization of successful new products are essential for a firm's survival. Innovations are financially important for firms since products introduced within the past 3–5 years account for more than 25% of firms' revenues (Wind, Mahajan, and Bayless 1990). Furthermore, new products can be a source of competitive advantage. While research over the past two decades has shed much light on the factors that are associated with the performance of new products in the market (see Montoya-Weiss and Calantone 1994, for a recent review), most of the literature focuses on a single country and provides no *direct* cross-national comparisons. As Cooper and Kleinschmidt state, "although there are hints that product development practices and success factors transcend national borders, few studies have been conducted in several countries concurrently" (1993, p. 91). In this study, we extend the literature by comparing factors of new product success in the United States and China.

The purpose of this paper is threefold. First, we develop a model of *managerially controllable* factors associated with new product success. Canadian NEWPROD data (Cooper 1979) are used to develop the model and to establish *initial* model parameters. We further validate the model using information we collected on 142 new products launched in the United States and 470 new products launched in China. Second, we directly compare the

Source: *Marketing Science*, 15(4) (1996): 341–358.

factors that managers perceive to be associated with new product success in the United States and China. After validating the model for each country separately, we perform a multiple-group path analysis to compare how perceived factors of new product success differ between the two countries. Third, we perform various statistical analyses to increase the confidence that may be placed in our findings and outline methods for assessing whether significant biases exist in cross-sectional data.

We specifically chose to study new product development in the United States and China. The United States was selected because it is an economically developed nation and has the world's largest economy. We chose China for three important reasons. First, with about one-quarter of the world's population, China is a very attractive market because of its vast size. Second, although Western interest in China is not new, recent changes have made it more accessible. "The Chinese economy is rapidly moving toward a market system and has grown by 13% in each of the past four years" (Parry and Song 1994, p. 16). Using a new measurement system, the Chinese economy has been ranked the third largest in the world (Song and Parry 1994, Parry and Song 1994). The combination of the swift growth rate and the size of the Chinese economy has attracted many Western companies to establish operations there. Third, whereas the United States is economically developed, China is still developing, and interesting differences may be found when the two types are compared.

This research is important for several reasons. First, this is the first large-scale study that directly tests the similarities and differences of the correlates of new product success in these countries. Since the Chinese economy is significant and will play an increasingly important role in the global economy, understanding the factors associated with new product success in that market is essential to venturing there. Second, a new model is tested with data from three countries, and a comparison of new product outcomes is made between the United States and China to determine any differences. Third, while much of the new product literature uses univariate or bivariate statistical techniques (Montoya-Weiss and Calantone 1994), we advance methodology by performing multiple-group structural equation modeling and examining the role of omitted firm effects which have been ignored in previous studies.

The organization of this paper is as follows. Section 2 presents the operationalized proposed model and specific research hypotheses. Section 3 describes the research design and data collection methods. In §4, we discuss the steps taken to analyze the data and investigate similarities and differences between the controllable factors of new product outcomes across countries. In addition, we test for various biases which potentially influence the results. Section 5 reports key findings, and §6 concludes the article with a discussion of implications and future research opportunities.

2. The Model and Research Hypotheses

This study focuses on managerial controllable variables for two reasons. First, the literature indicates that the success or failure of new products *is* under managers' control. In a meta-analytic review of the literature, Montoya-Weiss and Calantone (1994) conclude that the factors most strongly associated with new product success are controllable. Second, the factors over which managers exert some level of control offer the greatest opportunity for improving the success rate of new products.

Empirical research on new product performance has identified four categories of factors that affect success: market-related, product-related, new product development (NPD) process-related, and organization-related factors (Cooper 1979, Cooper and Kleinschmidt 1987). While organization-related factors may be difficult or impossible to change in the short term, they are under managerial control over the long run. Market-related factors are not controllable by managers and are therefore excluded from this study.

2.1. The Model

The model to be tested is shown in Figure 1. All paths are expected to have positive signs. The justification for these paths (i.e., βs) is given below. Note that all our hypotheses relate to association, not causation.

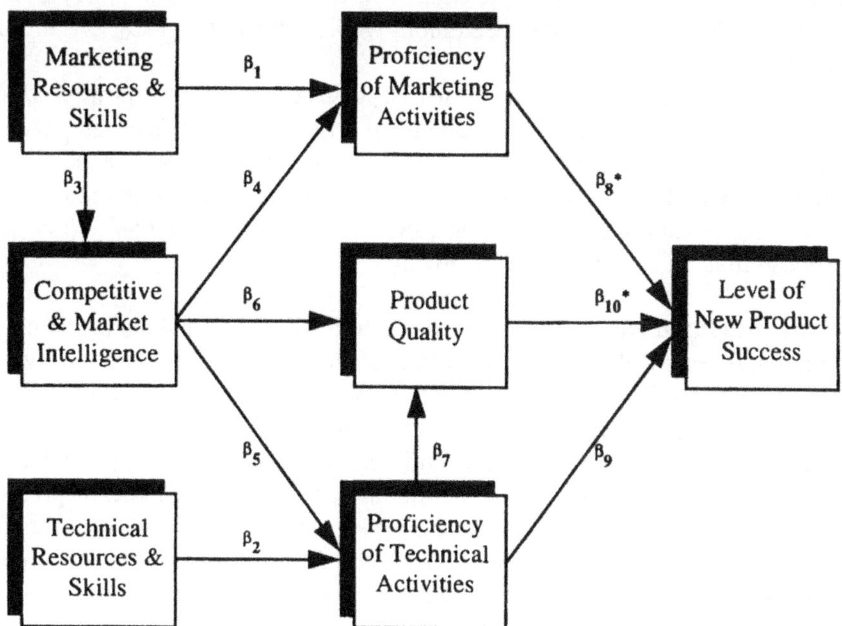

Figure 1: The proposed model

Organization-Related Factors. The NPD process primarily consists of marketing activities and technical activities. Past research suggests that firms must possess adequate resources and skills in both areas for successful NPD (Cooper and Kleinschmidt 1987; Song and Parry 1994, 1996), although this necessary condition does not guarantee NPD proficiency. Organizational factors (i.e., resources and skills) are hypothesized to be associated with new product success only indirectly through proficiency of NPD activities and product quality. The mere existence of resources and skills should not directly affect the degree of new product success. Furthermore, sufficient levels of marketing resources and skills are needed to enable firms to gather intelligence about competitors and the market. Thus, we hypothesize that β_1, β_2, and β_3 are positive.

New Product Development Process-Related Factors. In addition to the requisite organizational resources and skills, proficiency in performing marketing and technical activities requires information. Knowledge about customers' needs and wants, preferences, tastes, price sensitivities, and purchase behaviors are essential for successful marketing. To perform technical activities well, a firm needs information on competitors' product offerings and technological advances, as well as on the characteristics of the market. Marketing intelligence has been shown to be an important factor in new product success, and better competitive intelligence has been linked to higher levels of product quality (Calantone and di Benedetto 1988; Cooper 1979; Cooper and Kleinschmidt 1987; Song and Parry 1994, 1996). In light of the above discussion, we hypothesize that β_4, β_5, and β_6 are positive.

The proficiency of NPD activities is positively related to new product quality and success. In particular, technical activities and skills are important factors in success (Song and Parry 1994, 1996). Nevertheless, it has been shown repeatedly that a major cause of new product failure is inadequate marketing (Calantone and Cooper 1981, Song and Parry 1994). Thus, we propose that β_7, β_8, and β_9 are positive.

Product-Related Factors. While adequate resources and skills in the marketing and technical areas, along with proficiency in conducting these types of activities, are important ingredients in new product success, the product must have some advantage relative to competitors' offerings (Cooper and Kleinschmidt 1987). In an earlier study, Song and Parry (1994) concluded that product advantage and product quality are the most important predictors of new product success in China. Product quality is a major component of relative product advantage, and it has been found to relate to new product success. Thus, we expect that product quality is positively associated with the degree of new product success, as shown by β_{10}.

2.2. Cross-National Comparisons

Since the second objective of this study is to compare how the factors of new product success differ across nations, the 10 relationships shown in Figure 1 are dimensionally extended with regard to the United States and China. Below, we hypothesize which of the effects should be equal in these countries or relatively greater for one country.

As proposed above, marketing and technical resources and skills are required for proficient marketing and technical activities as well as competitive and market intelligence gathering. There is no reason, *a priori*, to believe that these factors are perceived to be more important for proficiently conducting NPD activities in either the United States or China. Thus, β_1, β_2, and β_3 are expected to be equal in both countries.

Information about customer preferences, markets, competitors and their products, and so on, is essential for effective NPD. This information is supplied through the intelligence gathering function. However, there is no reason to believe that the level of intelligence gathering is differentially associated with NPD proficiency and product quality in the United States and China; thus, β_4, β_5, and β_6 are hypothesized to be equal in both countries.

The association of the proficiency of marketing activities with new product success (β_8) is hypothesized to be greater in China than the United States. Compared to U.S. firms, most Chinese firms possess fewer marketing resources and have lower levels of marketing skills (Terpstra 1988). Before the 1979 economic reforms, Chinese firms had virtually no experience in Western marketing activities. While the reforms have introduced some forces of a market economy, marketing competency is still developing, and marketing is a fairly new phenomenon in China. On the other hand, U.S. marketing practices have been developing for nearly a century. In the United States, it is possible to hire outside experts, such as advertising agencies and consultants, to gather competitive and market intelligence, and secondary data are easily obtainable. In contrast, these opportunities are relatively scarce in China. In most U.S. industries, marketing resources, skills, and proficiency are so highly developed that they offer relatively less advantage over competitors than is the case in China. Thus, we expect increases in marketing proficiencies to have a greater effect on success in China than in the U.S.

Although marketing activities are important for successful NPD, technical activities are even more fundamental. Technical activities, such as product design and full-scale production, are essential for both market and planned economies, whereas marketing activities are not required in strictly planned economies since government agencies tell firms what, when, and how much to produce. Therefore, β_7 and β_9 are expected to be equal in both countries.

The quality of industrial products is generally high in the United States, but quite variable in China (Terpstra 1988). Consequently, firms that increase quality obtain a relatively greater competitive advantage in the Chinese market compared to the United States. Thus, we expect β_{10} to be greater in China than in the U.S.

3. Research Design and Data Collection

To determine the interrelationships among the factors of new product success, we use *historical* NPD projects data collected in Canada, the United States, and China. Our focus is on real decisions made by new product managers and the ultimate effects of those decisions, as viewed by them, irrespective of the theoretical correctness or incorrectness of those decisions. Consequently, all data were based on managers' perceptions. Managers involved with selected NPD projects were surveyed about factors leading to new product success and failure. While one could argue that focusing on managerial perceptions may miss the truth, this approach provides a balance by focusing on the real world business approach of making decisions on educated perceptions.

Across the three studies, product success was measured at the individual project level, which is preferable to measurement at the firm level. All variables were measured using 11-point bipolar scales (0 = strongly disagree, 10 = strongly agree), except for the new product performance variable which was measured at the individual product level on an 11-point scale (−5 = a great financial failure, +5 = a great financial success). A major advantage of using the perceived success measurement scale is that it permits comparisons across firms, based on each individual manager's assessments within their own particular industries, cultures, time horizons, economic conditions, and expectations. Moreover, it has been shown to be highly correlated with the objective measures of financial performance[1] (Song and Parry 1996). Consistent with the research design here, this scale captures the perceptions of the respondents that underlie their new product decisions, and it is easy and natural for the respondents to use. The appendix lists the variables and the scales used in this study. The research methods for each data set are described below.

3.1. Project NEWPROD: Baseline Canadian Study

Project NEWPROD data were used as the baseline model test in this research (see Cooper 1979 for study details). The NEWPROD sampling frame was industrial manufacturers in the Canadian provinces of Ontario and Quebec. Knowledgeable managers were asked to provide information on one successful and one failed new product developed within the past five years.

The selected product could be any that was new to the firm and was developed and commercialized by the firm, regardless of whether similar products already existed in the marketplace. Persistent follow-up yielded a response rate of 69% resulting in 195 new products from 103 firms.

3.2. The U.S. Sample

The U.S. sampling frame consisted of *Fortune 500* listed firms principally involved in the manufacture and sale of tangible products (346 firms). It contains a broad spectrum of industries, including manufacturing, construction, mining, agriculture, and others. Contact by telephone solicited cooperation, identified the appropriate respondent, and verified the mailing address. The data collection procedure for the NEWPROD study in Canada was followed with minor modifications. Several initial interviews were done on site to verify a realistic link between data in firm records and management perception and recall. Due to the nature of the information requested and from the results of the pretest, we asked each manager to provide information on the firm's most recent new product. Repeated follow-up telephone calls were made to increase the response rate, which was 41%. The final data consist of 142 NPD projects.

3.3. The Chinese Sample

In conducting any cross-national comparison, it is important to assess the validity of the comparison and the appropriateness of the data collection methodology before data collection begins. It is critical that researchers conduct a pretest in the target population. In order to make the comparison as meaningful as possible, we attempted to control for culture in measurement, both by maintaining the construct-item basis of the studies, as well as going through numerous steps to create reliable and valid measures in the Chinese (PRC sample) language and culture. In developing our research instruments, we adapted the procedures for conducting international research, as developed and outlined by Douglas and Craig (1983).

Four major steps were undertaken to assure the appropriateness of the research design: (1) problem formulation, variable specification, and categorization; (2) selecting appropriate research techniques; (3) developing appropriate research instrument design; and (4) developing sampling and survey administration techniques and procedures. Douglas and Craig (1983, p. 131) have emphasized the importance of establishing, "the comparability between data collected in different cultural contexts," where comparability "is defined as data that have, as far as possible, the same meaning or interpretation, and the same level of accuracy, precision of measurement, or reliability in all countries and cultures."

To this end, we followed Churchill's (1979) paradigm and the extensions of Mintu et al. (1994) for developing better measures of marketing constructs along with Gerbing and Anderson's (1988) updated paradigm. A multi-phase, iterative procedure was used to develop multiple items that characterize the hypothesized relationships to ensure the validity of the measurement scales. We began by reviewing the existing NPD literature and by identifying scales designed to measure the constructs in this preceding section. These scales were refined through in-depth case studies and focus group interviews with U.S. and Chinese NPD teams.

3.3.1. In-Depth Case Studies

We conducted six case studies in six Chinese companies to examine the appropriateness of the Canadian and U.S. data collection methods, to establish the content validity of the concepts, and to assess the usefulness of the measures and constructs in a Chinese context. We interviewed teams that had developed at least four new products in the three years preceding the interview and were developing a new product at the time of the interview. Following group interviews, interviews with individual team members were also conducted.

Several major lessons were learned from these case studies. First, although Chinese managers agreed that many of the original indicators were appropriate for measuring the NPD process in Chinese firms, some measures needed to be modified. Second, there was consistent knowledge about the intricacies of the NPD process among the team members for the selected projects. In every case, the team leader was always identified as the authority on information about the entire project. We also found that the team leader frequently asked opinions of the team members during the interviews and insisted on arriving at a consensus answer to each of the measurement items. It was recommended that, in our survey with a larger population, we should ask for team responses rather than individual responses to reflect the nature of the decision-making process in Chinese firms. Third, the items used in this article to measure the constructs were perceived to have face and content validity. Fourth, in terms of increasing response rates, including a business card of the researchers, getting endorsement from the appropriate government offices and promising a briefing of the results were found to be the most important steps in getting Chinese firms to participate.

To make sure that the original meaning was not altered, a rigorous, four-parallel double-translation method was used to translate the questionnaire. Eight Chinese nationals assisted. One was a visiting scholar at a prominent business school and an executive from a major Chinese trading company. Three had working experience in China, and four were Ph.D. students at prominent U.S. universities. All were fluent in both English and Chinese and had extensive translation experience. The process consisted of three steps. First, four of the eight people were asked to fill out the English version of the questionnaire in the presence of one of the authors and raise any questions about problems or ambiguities. After extensive discussion, each of the four was asked to prepare an independent Chinese translation of the English version. Second, each of the other four persons was asked to prepare an English translation of the Chinese version. They did not see the original English version until they finished. Third, although a comparison of the resulting questionnaires revealed considerable consistency, the third author met with the eight translators to resolve discrepancies in certain questions. When disagreements could not be resolved, this author selected the phrasing favored by a majority of the translators after consultation with some managers in the case studies.

Furthermore, to assess the appropriateness of the Chinese questionnaire for measuring the NPD process in Chinese firms, a pretest was also conducted among 19 managers in 19 Chinese firms. The final version of the questionnaire, which reflected several minor modifications suggested by participants in the pretest, was professionally printed. It should be noted that both the translators and the pretest participants indicated that the instrument was appropriate for studying NPD in Chinese firms and the items adequately measured the respective constructs.

The Chinese sampling frame consisted of firms in a variety of industries. Mailing lists were obtained from four Chinese ministries: Aviation, Electric Machinery-Building, Chemicals, and Electronics. From these lists, 300 firms were randomly selected. The first packet included a business card of the third author, a personalized letter to the president of the company in both English and Chinese, two identical questionnaires in Chinese, two postage-paid envelopes with individually typed address labels, and a research report of a related study. The cover letter acknowledged the endorsement of several government agencies and asked each president/contact person to forward the questionnaires to the firm's NPD manager. One week after the mailing, a personal telephone call was made to identify the responsible managers within each firm as well as possible NPD projects and procedures for collecting the data. This was found to be necessary for collecting the project-level data in China. After extensive conversations with the selected managers, two recently developed products were chosen by each participating firm.

To increase the confidence in the data collected, we requested that each responsible project manager obtain consensus from the team members on answers and that all team members and the project manager indicate how well each statement described the selected product(s). This is consistent with the literature on Chinese management and our case study interviews, which suggests that decision-making is based on consensus.

To increase the response rate, we noted the endorsements from four ministries, extended an invitation to a research seminar that would briefly present the results, and promised a summary report of the findings. Of the 300 questionnaires initially mailed, 11 were returned as undeliverable, yielding an adjusted sample size of 289. After one follow-up letter, usable responses were obtained from 147 firms.

A second wave of questionnaires was mailed to firms that had not yet responded to boost the response rate and to ensure representation of the four industries in China. Endorsement letters were obtained from several government agencies. The packet included the appropriate endorsement letter and all the contents of the first mailing. After two follow-up letters, usable responses were received from another 101 firms, resulting in an overall adjusted response rate of 85.8% at the firm level.

It is extremely difficult to obtain data about the operations of foreign companies, particularly at the division or project level. Data collection in a foreign country is more expensive and time consuming than in the United States. Foreign firms often distrust the researchers and are less willing to offer project data. This is especially true in China. In collecting data from these firms, we found that it is critical for researchers, first to understand how Chinese managers make their decisions. For example, it would not have been appropriate to ask for only individual responses and ignore the normal practice of consensus decision-making. However, doing "homework" to understand "normal" practices is not enough to gain cooperation. Researchers must go through proper channels and be patient, allowing time for managers to respond. Furthermore, *kuanxi* (that is, establishing connections, good relationships, and trust between the researchers and the responding firms) is essential to obtaining a high response rate.

To test for any nonresponse bias between the two waves of responses, a MANOVA analysis was performed for the 22 variables used in this study. No statistically significant differences were found at the 90% confidence level. Therefore, we do not expect any major problems with nonresponse bias (Armstrong and Overton 1977). The combined Chinese responses yielded an analysis sample of 470 NPD projects from 248 firms.

4. Analysis

Table 1 lists the steps taken in our analysis of the data. All the CFA and path models were tested using EQS software version 3.0 (Bentler 1992) with covariance matrices as input. In this section, we test the measurement model using CFA before assessing the structural relationships shown in Figure 1. As noted by Fornell and Larker, "before testing for a significant relationship in the structural model, one must demonstrate that the measurement model has a satisfactory level of validity and reliability" (1981, p. 45). Constructs must be unidimensional and reliable

Table 1: Steps in the data analysis

Steps	*Purpose*	*Selected references*
1. Performed confirmatory factor analysis for Canada, the United States and China individually.	Test construct validity. Eliminate factors with low loadings or loadings on multiple constructs.	Durvasula, Andrews, Lysonski, and Netemeyer (1993); Gerbing and Anderson (1988).
2. Performed two-group confirmatory factor analysis for the United States and China simultaneously.	Establish measurement equivalence across the U.S. and Chinese samples.	Bollen (1989), Song and Parry (1996).
3. Formed summated scales for constructs.	Overcome inherent limitations of single-item measures.	Churchill (1979), Gerbing and Anderson (1988).
4. Computed Cronbach coefficient alphas.	Assess the inter-item reliability of the summated measures.	Nunnally (1978).
5. Tested proposed structural model for Canada.	Provide a baseline model and validate the proposed model.	N/A
6. Tested proposed structural model for the United States and China individually.	Validate the model for the U.S. and Chinese samples.	Durvasula, Andrews, Lysonski, and Netemeyer (1993).
7. Tested proposed structural model for the United States and China simultaneously.	Determine cross-national similarities and differences.	Durvasula, Andrews, Lysonski, and Netemeyer (1993).
8. Performed theta-delta test and nomological validity test using confirmatory factor analysis for the United States and China individually.	Generalized test of specification errors, common method variance bias, and omitted variables.	Bollen (1989); Hughes, Price, and Marrs (1986).
9. Performed within/between analysis on Chinese sample.	Look for bias in parameters due to omitted firm variables.	Hausman (1978), Boulding and Staelin (1990, 1995).

before assessing the structural relationships among them (Anderson and Gerbing 1982). Furthermore, researchers must identify equivalent *phenomena* when conducting cross-national research (Mintu, Calantone, and Gassenheimer 1994). The extensive case studies, translation procedure, and pretests sought to insure that we were examining equivalent phenomena in China.

Based on theory, past research, and exploratory factor analyses, a separate CFA was performed for each of the three countries since CFA is a more rigorous method for assessing unidimensionality than coefficient alpha, exploratory factor analysis, and item-total correlations (Gerbing and Anderson 1988). The purpose was to ensure unidimensionality of the multiple-item constructs and to eliminate unreliable items from them. After eliminating items that loaded on multiple constructs or had low item-to-construct loadings, the Bentler-Bonett normed fit index (NFI), nonnormed fit index (NNFI), and comparative fit index (CFI) for all three analyses indicated good fits of the CFA models to the data.

Our CFA models show a high level of consistency in model form and measurement across the three countries. The results of these three individual country CFA models were very good, with fits ranging from 0.98 to 0.99. Furthermore, the factor loadings for each individual indicator to its respective construct (i.e., Λ_x) was highly significant ($p < 0.01$). All revised constructs in the three samples were composed of identical items except for the competitive and market intelligence construct. Douglas and Craig (1983) note that one must decide whether to use the same questions across different countries to tap the same concept. The key is to insure that the two sets of measures are actually measuring the same construct. The results from our extensive qualitative research and the pretests in China suggest that we are measuring the same underlying concept. The constructs and individual questionnaire items are shown in the appendix.

The equivalence of the measurement models across the U.S. and Chinese samples was tested using two-group CFA as outlined by Bollen (1989). If the measurement properties are the same for both samples, factor patterns and factor loadings should be equal. Therefore, the factor loadings for the two countries were set to be equal (invariant) for all questionnaire items that were identical for both groups. The results indicated that the factor patterns are identical, and the LM test indicated no difference between the groups for 14 of the 16 factor loadings ($p < 0.05$). Furthermore, the factor loading from each indicator to its respective construct was highly significant ($p < 0.01$). All three fit indices for the two-group CFA model were 0.98 or above. Consequently, since the measurement models were found to be invariant across the U.S. and Chinese samples, the respondents' ratings for the relevant items of each construct were summed and divided by the number of items to obtain the multiple-item measures. Construct reliability for each of the three samples was further assessed using Cronbach's coefficient alpha. As shown in the appendix, the coefficient alphas ranged from 0.79 to 0.90.

4.2. The Individual Path Models

Once the measurement issues were satisfactorily resolved, the structural model in Figure 1 was tested for each of the three countries individually. While the Canadian sample served as a baseline, a lack of model support by either the U.S. or Chinese sample would diminish the value of the two-group model results as a comparative tool (Bentler 1992). We briefly discuss the results of the individual model testing below.

4.2.1. Canada: The Baseline Model

The Canadian NEWPROD study was used as a baseline and for initial testing of the model. All paths were found to be statistically different than zero at the $p < 0.01$ level except for the path from competitive and market intelligence to product quality (β_6). The normed fit indices were 0.99, 0.98, and 0.99, for the NFI, NNFI, and CFI, respectively. The standardized residuals were below 0.21, and the LM test indicated that additional structural paths would not improve the fit of the model. Given the satisfactory results from the baseline Canadian model, the U.S. and Chinese samples were tested.

4.2.2. The U.S. Model

The model for the U.S. sample converged well. Nine of the ten paths were significantly greater than zero as hypothesized, the exception being the path from product quality to new product success (β_{10} in Figure 1). All fit indices for the U.S. model were 0.98 or above, and the standardized residuals were small (i.e., less than 0.30). The LM test indicated that no additional paths should be added to the model. Consequently, we were again unable to refute this model.

4.2.3. The Chinese Model

The Chinese model converged well and nine of the ten paths were statistically greater than zero, as hypothesized. The sole exception was the path from technical proficiency to product quality (β_7), which was not significantly different than zero. All the fit indices for the Chinese model equaled or exceeded 0.98, and the standardized residuals were below 0.33. Along with the LM test, these results indicated that additional paths would not improve the model. Thus, the results of the model for the China sample were also satisfactory indicating that this model could not be refuted.

4.3. The Two-Group Model: China versus the United States

As noted by Bollen (1989), the least demanding test of comparability of models (e.g., for the U.S. and China) is achieved when the models have the same form (i.e., same constructs/measures and relationships among constructs/measures). We found support for the model in each of the two countries. In the second step, we imposed strict constraints (that the path coefficients are equal across groups) across the measurement and structural models. We then used a Lagrangian Multiplier (LM) test to see whether, in fact, these constraints did not hold (i.e., that the overall model fit is substantially improved by releasing one or more of the constraints). To this end, we followed suggestions of many methodologists by assuming that (and then testing whether) the general form of the measurement and structural models underlying all countries was the same, but that the values of the specific parameters differed across the U.S. and China. Thus, this is a strong statistical test of inequivalence across the two countries, and it is the usual approach in multiple-group structural equation modeling (Bollen 1989).

Since the results of individual models for the United States and China were satisfactory, we performed a two-group simultaneous path analysis in order to test for similarities and differences in the factors of new product success between China and the United States. The objective of the two-group analysis was to determine if the path coefficients (i.e., βs) were invariant across the two countries. All paths except those from marketing proficiency to new product success (β_8) and product quality to new product success (β_{10}) were hypothesized to be equal for the U.S. and Chinese samples. To test these cross-cultural hypotheses, all ten structural paths shown in Figure 1 were constrained to be equal across the groups, and the path coefficients were then freely estimated. A comparison of the fully constrained and "free" models suggested that the model for China was different from the model for the United States.

The LM test in EQS was used to determine which paths differed. In multiple-group analysis, the LM test evaluates the null hypothesis that the *unstandardized* parameter is equal across the two groups. If the difference in chi-square (i.e., χ^2_{diff}) between the constrained and unconstrained models is significant with respect to the degrees of freedom, it suggests that the path coefficient is statistically different between the groups. The results indicated that four equality constraints should be released in the following order: (1) the path from product quality to new product success (β_{10}); (2) the path from marketing resources and skills to competitive and market intelligence (β_3); (3) the path from marketing resources and skills to marketing activities (β_1); and (4) the path from marketing activities to new product success (β_8). Each constraint was released in order, and the model was reestimated each time. Comparing the revised model (with the four equality constraints released) to the unconstrained model indicates that the fit cannot be improved by releasing any additional equality constraints ($\chi^2_{\text{diff}} = 11.82$, d.f. $= 4, p < 0.05$). Thus, it is concluded that six of the ten structural parameter estimates are invariant across the two countries, and the other four are different between the United States and China.

Following Bentler (1992), we evaluated the multiple-sample model in the same manner that the single-sample models were evaluated. With the four equality constraints released, no difficulty was encountered in estimating the model parameters. The final multiple-group model fit the data very well, as 17 of the 20 path coefficients were significantly greater than zero ($p < 0.01$), as expected, while the remaining three paths were not significantly different than zero. The three indices indicated a very good fit of the model to the data (NFI = 0.99, NNFI = 0.99, CFI = 0.99). All standardized residuals were below 0.43 for the U.S. sample and below 0.32 for the Chinese sample. Thus, we were unable to refute the model, and we conclude that the two-group model fits the data rather well.

4.4. Some Preliminary Specification Tests

Based on the results of all three samples, no additional paths were considered since there was no theoretical support for doing so. However, we were concerned about possible biases influencing the results. Under a structural equation modeling approach, a variety of unobservable variables can cause model specification errors (Bollen 1989; Hughes, Price, and Marrs 1986). In a preliminary fashion, we conducted two tests to insure that specification errors were not biasing our results: (1) a test of the theta delta (Θ_δ) matrix for each CFA and (2) an examination of nomological validity (Bagozzi and Yi 1988, Bollen 1989). Specifically, for both the U.S. and Chinese samples, the CFAs were rerun to allow the errors of the measures for both the marketing and technical resources and skills constructs (i.e., δs) to covary. In other words, we released the zero-correlation constraint for the relevant off-diagonal elements in the Θ_δ matrix. According to Hughes, Price, and Marrs (1986), one would expect that if an unobservable variable existed which biased the data, a common error variance would be generated between the items actually measured. The absence of a significant improvement in overall model fit when these constraints are released would demonstrate the absence of such a bias. Our results showed no significant difference between the fit of the new and original CFA models at a confidence level of $\alpha = 0.05$. Thus, the proposition that omitted variables were generating biases at the overall model level was tentatively rejected at $\alpha = 0.05$. We also examined the modification indices (LM tests) for the Λ_x vectors and Θ_δ matrices, and again we found no evidence to suggest a systematic bias overall.

5. Results

Since we are primarily interested in the cross-national similarities and differences between China and the United States, we focus our discussion on the results of the two-group model. Figure 2 contains the individual path coefficients and indicates whether each path differed significantly from zero. Essentially, each path represents a hypothesis that was or was not supported for either country. Both the standardized and unstandardized total effects parameter estimates for the multiple-group analysis are presented in Figure 2. The *standardized* estimates are useful for comparing the relative effects (i.e., βs) within a country while the *unstandardized* estimates are used to compare the effects across countries. The total effects consist of direct effects (i.e., βs) and indirect effects and help us understand the relationships between the managerially controllable factors associated with new product success.

As Figure 2 indicates, the results generally support the hypotheses in both the U.S. and Chinese samples. For the United States, eight of the ten paths are significantly greater than zero. The exceptions are the path from proficiency

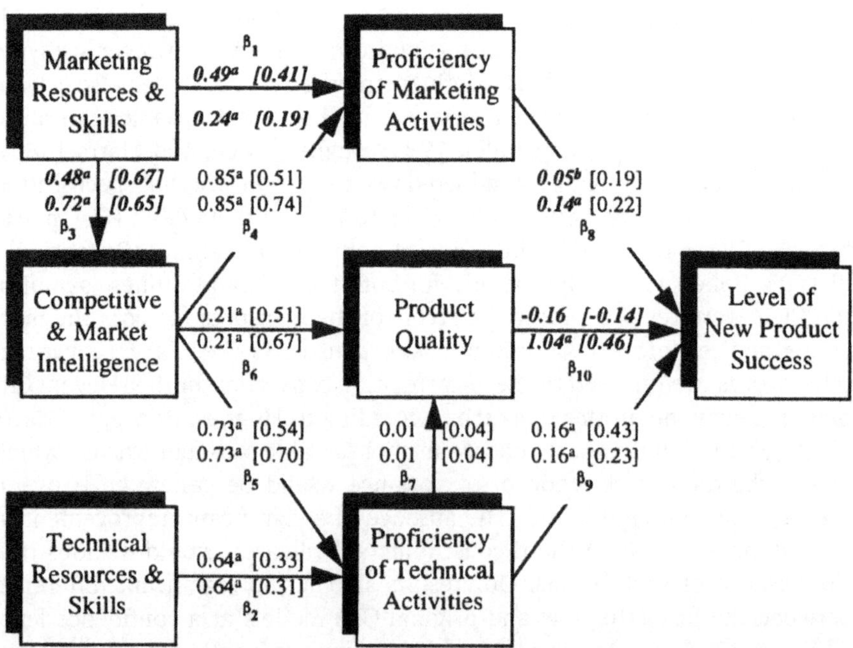

Notes: The top number represents the U.S. sample, the bottom number represents the Chinese sample. Number in brackets is standardized effect, number without brackets is unstandardized effect. [a]$p < .01$; [b]$p < .05$.

Figure 2: Path coefficients for the U.S. and China from the two-group model

of technical activities to product quality (β_7) and the path from product quality to new product success (β_{10}), which are not significantly different than zero. In China, nine of the ten paths are significantly greater than zero ($p < 0.01$), with the exception being the path from proficiency of technical activities to product quality (β_7). Thus, while the level of technical activity proficiency was significantly associated with the level of new product success in both China and the United States, it did not appear to be related to the level of product quality in either country. Figures 2 and 3 report the detailed results from testing the hypotheses in the two-group model. We focus our discussion on the key differences and similarities between the two countries in the following sections.

5.1. Cross-National Differences

Of the ten paths, four (β_1, β_3, β_8, and β_{10}) are significantly different between the U.S. and China. Furthermore, by examining the unstandardized estimates, several additional differences emerge which merit further discussion. First, it was hypothesized that product quality relates positively with new product success, and this relationship is stronger in China than the U.S. Our results support this hypothesis in the Chinese sample, but not in the U.S. sample. The finding that product quality is not significantly related to new product success in the U.S. runs counter to the conventional wisdom that product quality is a universal factor of new product success. It may be that since the majority of U.S. firms produce high quality products, the marginal effect on success due to changes in product quality does not obtain in the United States. In China, where quality levels among firms vary considerably, quality increases will more strongly impact success than in the United States.

Second, marketing resources and skills, as well as proficiency in gathering competitive and market intelligence and conducting marketing activities, are perceived by Chinese managers to relate more strongly to new product success than by U.S. managers. As expected, the relationship between the proficiency of marketing activities and the level of new product success is greater in China (0.14) than in the U.S. (0.05). For the Chinese sample, the association of marketing resources and skills with competitive and market intelligence is perceived to be greater than in the U.S. sample (0.72 versus 0.48, respectively). However, the association between marketing resources and skills on the proficiency of marketing activities is thought to be greater in the U.S. than in China (0.49 and 0.24, respectively). This apparent contradiction is explained by examining the unstandardized *total* effects in Figure 3 which reveals that marketing resources and skills, marketing activities, and competitive and market intelligence are all more highly related to the level of new product success in China than the U.S.

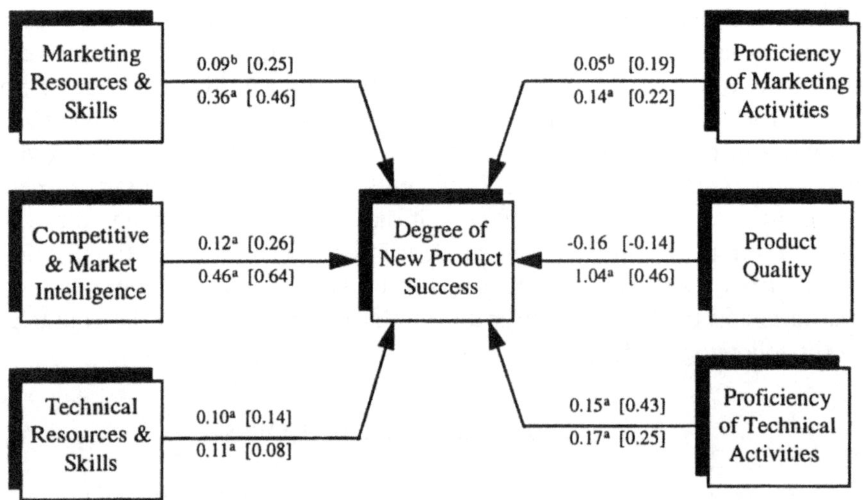

Notes: The top number represents the U.S. sample, the bottom number represents the Chinese sample. Number in brackets is standardized effect, number without brackets is unstandardized effect. $^{a}p < .01$; $^{b}p < .05$.

Figure 3: Total effects on new product success

Not surprisingly, marketing resources and skills are more associated with the proficiency of marketing activities in China. Since these skills are relatively less available in China, they offer a differential advantage in enabling Chinese companies to proficiently carry out technical activities such as product design and testing.

The proficiency of marketing activities involves the firm's understanding of customer needs, buyer behavior, and the competitive situation as well as the firm's execution of the preliminary market assessment, the prototype test with customers, the test market, and the market launch. A high level of such proficiency requires that project managers overcome the production orientation that prevails in many Chinese state enterprises due to the central planning system. Song and Parry (1993, 1994) suggest that unsuccessful NPD projects are due to engineers and technicians who resist the notion that marketing and selling are the central tasks of modern new product management and who ignore the needs of potential customers when making design decisions. Results in Figure 2 indicate that successful Chinese NPD project teams appear to concentrate their marketing resources and skills on gathering good information about the competition and the market. Based on that information, they develop products of higher quality than competing products (that is, with tighter specifications and more reliability), and the relatively higher quality strongly increases the level of new product success. In the United States, where product quality is not significantly associated with the level of new product success, firms focus their marketing resources and skills on differentiating the product in the marketplace through pretesting and positioning.

Finally, Figure 3 also reveals several differences in the relative importance of factors relating to new product success in China and the United States. In the United States, the order of importance of these factors is: proficiency of technical activities, competitive and market intelligence, level of marketing resources and skills, proficiency of marketing activities, and the level of technical resources and skills. In China, competitive and market intelligence emerges as the number one factor associated with new product success. Both product quality and marketing resources and skills have equivalent coefficients and thus are tied for position as the second most important factor. Proficiency of technical activities ranks fourth. While proficiency of marketing activities is the fifth key factor, technical resources and skills are the least important influences on new product success.

In both countries, it is important to collect and assess market and competitive information in order to understand customers' needs, wants, and specifications for the product; to know customers' price sensitivity; to understand customers' purchase decisions; and to learn about competitors' strategies, strengths, and weaknesses. In China, product quality is the second most highly correlated factor of new product success. To be successful in the Chinese market, products must be of higher quality, have tighter specifications, last longer, and be more reliable than competing products. Although Chinese consumers are accustomed to shoddy goods, a higher level of product quality is a competitive advantage that greatly increases the chance of success and is not easily copied by competitors. Therefore, firms competing in China should direct their marketing and technical efforts toward developing quality products. For example, firms should focus design and testing on the reliability of products, focus market assessment on studying key product attributes, and develop products that better meet these criteria.

5.2. Similarities between the United States and China

There are quite a few NPD similarities which were discovered between the United States and China despite several macro differences. The business cultures are different, the cultures of management and leadership differ, and the degree of government involvement in firm policies all differ greatly. Furthermore, the time orientation of individuals differs greatly between the countries' cultures as well as the general management orientation towards long-term results. Thus, almost counter-intuitively, a variety of similarities persist, perhaps aided by the strength of the method resisting rejection of the general null hypothesis that there are no differences.

As Figure 2 indicates, an adequate level of marketing resources and skills is perceived by both U.S. and Chinese managers to be positively associated with the proficiency of competitive and market intelligence.

It is surprising that marketing resources and skills correlate with higher levels of competitive and market intelligence in the Chinese sample since firms emerging from heavily state-managed competitive regimes would not, in our opinion, be proficient in such endeavors. Therefore, in both countries, adequate marketing research, sales force, distribution, advertising, and promotional resources and skills appear to be required for proficiently conducting market assessment studies, testing products, and introducing products. Furthermore, technical resources and skills are positively linked with proficiency in conducting technical activities. Sufficient R&D and engineering resources and skills relate to proficiency in performing technical assessments, developing and designing products, and manufacturing products. Thus, seeming universals obtain where one might not expect them.

Figure 3 reveals that these organizational factors also have significant and positive effects on the level of new product success in both countries. The total indirect effect of marketing resources and skills on new product success is 0.09 for the United States and 0.36 for China; the total indirect effect of technical resources and skills is 0.10 for the United States and 0.11 for China. These results imply that a firm's resources and skills relate to the types of information needed, its choice of markets, and its ability to develop a product with higher quality. These findings are consistent with previously cited literature. Thus, firms lacking sufficient resources and expertise are advised either to build the competencies internally or to develop reliable sources externally (for example, cultivate reliable suppliers who listen to the voice of the customer, conduct marketing research studies, and do product pretests).

In terms of NPD process-related factors, the results shown in Figure 2 support five of our seven hypotheses (β_4, β_5, β_6, β_8, and β_9) in both countries. Better information about the market and competitors positively relates to greater proficiency in conducting marketing activities and technical activities, as well as to better product quality. Understanding potential consumers' needs and specifications, their price sensitivities, and their purchase behaviors correlates with better implementation of product pretests, product manufacturing, and product introduction in both China and the United States. This understanding is also critical in developing higher quality products. For the same reasons, information about competitors' products and strategies is also important during the NPD process. While we did not hypothesize that competitive and market intelligence directly affect new product success, its total effect is substantial (0.12 for the United States; 0.46 for China; see Figure 3). Managers perceive it to be the top factor of new product success in China and the second most important factor in the United States. These findings support critical claims in the new product literature that information about the market and competition is key in influencing new product success. In fact, competitive and market intelligence becomes a differential source of success in China.

The results shown in Figure 3 also suggest that a higher proficiency in marketing and technical activities leads to a higher level of new product success in both countries. Though not hypothesized, the level of proficiency of technical activities appears to relate more to the level of new product success than do marketing activities.

Counter to our expectations, while the proficiency of technical activities has a significant and positive direct effect on new product success in both the United States and China, it does not have a significant effect on product quality in either country. It is possible that the data reflect managers' subjective perceptions of a product's quality level. Intuitively, such technical activities as product design and testing should affect the objective quality level of products. Furthermore, most Chinese operations take place at a different (lower) level of technical sophistication in process activities compared to U.S. firm operations, and these differences should carry through to affect overall product quality. An environment effect may be operating, however, such that differential results would not be obtained when all direct domestic competitors are working from the same technology bases.

Figure 3 provides the unstandardized total effects of each construct on the degree of new product success for the U.S. and China. While almost all of the effects are significantly different than zero, in several cases the magnitude of an effect differs greatly between the two countries. These results reinforce the results above and amplify the interesting divergence between the countries in the effects of product quality on success and of competitive and market intelligence on success. These relationships are logically supported by smaller yet still noteworthy differences in the effects of marketing resources and skills, where the Chinese coefficients are larger and proficiency of technical activities where the U.S. effects are greater. Overall, the results in Figure 3 concisely amplify the conclusions on differences one may draw from this analysis.

5.3. Possible Bias(es) in Results

One might omit variables which significantly bias results and interpretations (Boulding and Staelin 1990, 1995). Thus, there is a hidden threat to the validity of our results in this context. An important criterion to being "not wrong" is whether we can defeat an alternative explanation that firm level effects are operating as an "invisible hand" in our study and past studies of new product success. There exists the possibility that the "omitted" firm variables bias the effect on performance and, indeed, even the intermediate effects in all cross-sectional new product studies like this. While the test of Θ_δ in §4.4 may point to the lack of omitted variable bias, it has been attributed by some authors to the mere absence of a common method bias in measurement, and thus no definitive defense is available from that test alone. Thus, the challenge for all cross-sectional studies is to reject the hypothesis that many of the parameters associated with the dependent variable are biased by "omitted" firm level effects.

Since we collected two observations per firm in our Chinese sample we can examine whether bias exists due to omitted firm effects. As suggested by Hausman (1978), we compare the within estimates (i.e., the estimates based on deviations from firm means) to the between estimates (i.e., the estimates based on the firm means). If the omitted firm effect is correlated with the regressors, the between estimates will be biased and inconsistent, while the within estimates will be consistent (assuming no measurement error). Thus, our hope is that the between estimates are equivalent to the within estimates, suggesting a lack of omitted variable bias due to fixed firm effects.

Since our model in Figure 1 requires five equations, we reestimated them using OLS, for both the within and between estimates, using the Chinese sample. The results are presented in Table 2 below. The results indicate that all 10 of the coefficient pairs were within a 95% confidence interval of each other. In two cases (β_6, β_9) the confidence interval includes zero. Though not a formal application of the Hausman Test, the stability of the within and between estimates increases our confidence that our findings are robust to omitted firm effects.

Table 2: Within/between estimates (OLS)

Dependent variable	*Independent variable*	*Path*	*Between*	*Within*
Marketing Activities	Mktg. Resources & Skills	β_1	0.326	0.206
			(0.058)	(0.060)
	Competitive & Mkt. Intelligence	β_4	0.357	0.494
			(0.060)	(0.054)
Competitive & Mkt. Intelligence	Mktg. Resources & Skills	β_3	0.477	0.550
			(0.056)	(0.066)
Technical Activities	Technical Resources & Skills	β_2	0.156	0.232
			(0.037)	(0.046)
	Competitive & Mkt. Intelligence	β_5	0.464	0.319
			(0.045)	(0.053)
Product Quality	Competitive & Mkt. Intelligence	β_6	−0.048	0.054
			(0.069)	(0.065)
	Technical Activities	β_7	0.370	0.621
			(0.100)	(0.083)
Product Performance	Marketing Activities	β_8	0.078	0.034
			(0.042)	(0.039)
	Technical Activities	β_9	0.013	−0.108
			(0.045)	(0.041)
	Product Quality	β_{10}	0.253	0.288
			(0.024)	(0.028)

Note: The *b* and Standard error estimates are presented by the first and second number in each pair of estimates, respectively.

While an absence of omitted variable bias from a particular source alone cannot make a study right, it can help assure that it is "not wrong." Future research in the new product area should be especially cognizant of this possible bias, especially given the preponderance of single observation per firm cross-sectional studies.

6. Conclusion

This research advances the literature on new product performance in several ways. First, most previous work focused on a single country, whereas this study uses data from three. To our knowledge, this is the first cross-industry and cross-national comparative study of the controllable factors associated with new product success in the U.S. and China. Since modeling approaches offer less external validity than other statistical techniques (Bonoma 1985), multiple data sets can help overcome this problem. Cook and Campbell (1976, p. 226) note, "to infer a causal relationship at one moment in time, using one research setting, and with one sample of respondents, would give us little confidence that the demonstrated causal relationship is robust." Although it is impossible to prove causal relations within a structural equations model (Bollen 1989), we tested our model using data collected in *three* countries to increase the confidence that can be placed in our findings by means of general convergence. Second, the modeling approach used to study new product outcomes is more quantitatively sophisticated than techniques typically used in the literature. Typically, research emphasis progresses from theory building to theory testing, from qualitative to quantitative methods. While the literature in this field evolved somewhat in this manner, there is still too much reliance on descriptive research (Montoya-Weiss and Calantone 1994). Although less quantitative methods continue to offer richness, modeling approaches offer increased internal validity.

Yet, like all studies, this study is not without limitations. First, our sample only represents the U.S. and Chinese firms that are producing physical products, and the findings may not be generalizable to service industries and firms outside the sampled populations. Second, our data collection efforts use the retrospective methodology. Although self-assessment measures are prone to potential bias, they are the most commonly used method in marketing strategy research. Based on the extensive case study interviews before our survey study, we explicitly designed the research to limit the possibility of hindsight and halo effects.

We also conducted follow-up studies with selected Chinese firms. The original company records (including meeting minutes, recording books, company files of the entire NPD process for 62 selected projects) were examined. We found that the original data are highly reliable and accurately represent the historical descriptions of the development processes. While some new product development teams met to resolve discrepancies among the team members' ratings, others checked the company records before providing each individual response. We are confident about the reliability of our data in light of the follow-up studies.

While one may argue that we only measured managers' perceptions of reality, we used multiple, and rigorous methodological approaches to increase the confidence that can be placed in our findings. It is important to stress that causality cannot be proved using cross-sectional data. Since causal determinism is only really satisfied by an experimental design, the ordering of the directionality of influences was based on (1) past research findings in the literature and (2) theoretical reasoning. In our study we heavily relied on the new product literature and the two-year case studies in specifying the paths in the model. Our use of the structural equation models was designed to test whether we can reject the theoretical model we developed based on case studies and theory. While the directionality of the relationships was established theoretically, it is possible to argue that the directionality of the hypotheses could be reversed in some instances. Ideally, one needs to collect time-series data to test causal relationships. Yet, large-scale cross-national longitudinal data at the *project level* are difficult, if not impossible, to obtain. In this paper, while we have tested that our model is consistent with the data from three countries, we have not established absolute causality.

An important direction for further research is to replicate this study using the same methodology with other countries. Although our experience confirms several authors' conclusions that it is extremely difficult to obtain any data about a foreign company's operation, particularly at division or project level, it is a worthwhile objective to pursue. Models are also needed to incorporate the fourth category of new product success factors, market-related factors. Finally, future research is also needed to examine the potential moderating effects of environmental uncertainties and/or product innovativeness.

Appendix: Measurement items and reliabilities

	Cronbach's coefficient alpha		
	Canada	*U.S.*	*China*
Marketing Resources and Skills[1]	0.86	0.85	0.82
1. Our marketing research skills and people were more than adequate.			
2. Our sales force and/or distribution resources and skills were more than adequate.			
3. Our advertising and promotion resources and skills were more than adequate.			
4. Our management skills were more than adequate.			

	Cronbach's coefficient alpha		
	Canada	*U.S.*	*China*
Technical Resources and Skills[1]	0.90	0.85	0.84
1. Our R&D skills and people were more than adequate.			
2. Our engineering skills and people were more than adequate.			
Competitive and Market Intelligence[1]	0.80	0.86	0.84
1.[a] By the time we commercialized our product, we understood our potential customers' needs, wants, and specifications for this product.			
2.[a] We knew how much the customer would pay for such a product – his price sensitivity.			
3.[a] We understood the customers' purchase decision well – the "who, what, when, where, and how" of his purchase behavior.			
4.[a] We knew our competitors well – their products, pricing, strategies, and strengths.			
5.[b] Overall, we had superior intelligence on our competitors.			
6.[b] Overall, we had superior marketing information on our customers.			
Marketing Activities[2]	0.83	0.89	0.87
1. Preliminary assessment of the market – a cursory look at the market.			
2. Market study or market research – a detailed study of market potential, customer preferences, purchase process, etc.			
3. Prototype or sample testing – with the customer.			
4. Test marketing/trial sell prior to launch.			
5. Launching the product in the market – selling, promoting, and distributing.			
Technical Activities[2]	0.79	0.84	0.82
1. Preliminary engineering, technical, and manufacturing assessment or study.			
2. Product development – engineering, design, or R&D.			
3. Prototype or sample testing – in-house.			
4. Pilot production/trial or test production.			
5. Start-up of full-scale production.			
Product Quality[1]	NA	NA	NA
1. Our product was of higher quality – tighter specifications or stronger or lasted longer or more reliable, etc., than competing products.			
New Product Success or Failure	NA	NA	NA
1. Please indicate how successful the product was from a profitability standpoint.			

[1] This set of questions asked, "Do these characteristics describe your project?" Individual items were measured on a bipolar scale from 0 (strongly agree) to 10 (strongly disagree).
[2] This set of questions asked, "How well was each activity undertaken?" Individual items were measured on a bipolar scale from 0 (undertaken very poorly; mistakenly omitted) to 10 (done excellently).
[a] Individual item contained in summated measure for the China sample.
[b] Individual item contained in summated measure for the U.S. sample.

Note

1. Objective data were collected on several dimensions of product performance in the Chinese sample. The correlations between this measure and the objective measures range from 0.78 to 0.89.

References

Anderson, James C. and David W. Gerbing (1982), "Some Methods for Respecifying Measurement Models to Obtain Unidimensional Construct Measurement," *Journal of Marketing Research*, 19, November, 453–460.

——— and ——— (1988), "Structural Equation Modeling in Practice, A Review and Recommended Two-Step Approach," *Psychological Bulletin*, 103, 3, 411–423.

Armstrong, J. Scott and Terry S. Overton (1977), "Estimating Nonresponse Bias in Mail Surveys," *Journal of Marketing Research*, 14, August, 396–402.

Bagozzi, Richard R. and Youjae Yi (1989), "On the Use of Structural Equation Models in Experimental Designs," *Journal of Marketing Research*, 16, 3, 271–284.

Bentler, Peter M. (1992), *EQS Structural Equations Program Manual*, Los Angeles, CA: BMDP Statistical Software, Inc.

Bollen, Kenneth A. (1989), *Structural Equations with Latent Variables*, New York: John Wiley & Sons.

Bonoma, Thomas V. (1985), "Case Research in Marketing, Opportunities, Problems, and a Process," *Journal of Marketing Research*, 22, May, 199–208.

Boulding, William and Richard Staelin (1990), "Environment, Market Share, and Market Power," *Management Science*, 36, October, 1160–1177.

——— and ——— (1995), "Identifying Generalizable Effects of Strategic Actions on Firm Performance: The Case of Demand-Side Returns to R&D Spending," *Marketing Science*, 14, Summer, G222-G236.

Calantone, Roger J. and Robert G. Cooper (1981), "New Product Scenarios, Prospects for Success," *Journal of Marketing*, 45, Spring, 48–60.

——— and C. Anthony di Benedetto (1988), "An Integrative Model of the New Product Development Process," *Journal of Product Innovation Management*, 5, September, 201–215.

Churchill, Gilbert A. (1979), "A Paradigm for Developing Better Measures of Marketing Constructs," *Journal of Marketing Research*, 16, February, 64–73.

Cooper, Robert G. (1979), "Identifying Industrial New Product Success, Project NewProd," *Industrial Marketing Management*, 8, 2, 124–135.

——— and Elko Kleinschmidt (1987), "New Products, What Separates Winners from Losers," *Journal of Product Innovation Management*, 4, September, 169–184.

——— and ——— (1993), "Major New Products, What Distinguishes the Winners in the Chemical Industry," *Journal of Product Innovation Management*, 10, March, 90–111.

Cornwall, Christopher, Peter Schmidt, and Donald Wyhowski (1992), "Simultaneous Equations and Panel Data," *Journal of Econometrics*, 51, 151–181.

Douglas, Susan and C. Samuel Craig (1983), *International Marketing Research*, Englewoods Cliffs, NJ: Prentice-Hall.

Durvasula, Sriniva, J. Craig Andrews, Steven Lysonski, and Richard G. Netemeyer (1993), "Assessing the Cross-national Applicability of Consumer Behavior Models, A Model of Attitude toward Advertising in General," *Journal of Consumer Research*, 19, March, 626–636.

Fornell, Claes and David F. Larker (1981), "Evaluating Structural Equation Models with Unobservable Variables and Measurement Errors," *Journal of Marketing Research*, 18, February, 39–50.

Gerbing, David W. and James C. Anderson (1988), "An Updated Paradigm for Scale Development Incorporating Unidimensionality and Its Assessment," *Journal of Marketing Research*, 25, May, 186–192.

Griffin, Abbie and John R. Hauser (1992), "Patterns of Communication Among Marketing, Engineering and Manufacturing – A Comparison Between Two New Product Teams," *Management Science*, 38, March, 360–373.

Hausman, J. (1978), "Specification Tests in Econometrics," *Econometrica*, 46, 1251–1271.

Hughes, Marie Adele, E. Leon Price, and Daniel W. Marrs (1986), "Linking Theory Construction and Theory Testing: Models with Multiple Indicators of Latent Variables," *Academy of Management Review*, 11, 1, 128–144.

Mintu, Alma, Roger J. Calantone, and Jule Gassenhiemer (1994), "Towards Improving Cross-Cultural Research: Extending Churchill's Research Paradigm," *Journal of International Consumer Marketing*, 7, 2, 5–23.

Montoya-Weiss, Mitzi M. and Roger J. Calantone (1994), "Determinants of New Product Performance, A Review and Meta-Analysis," *Journal of Product Innovation Management*, 11, November, 397–417.

Nunnally, J. C. (1978), *Psychometric Theory*, 2nd Edition, New York: McGraw-Hill.

Parry, Mark E. and X. Michael Song (1994), "Identifying New Product Success in China," *Journal of Product Innovation Management*, 11, January, 15–30.

Song, X. Michael and Mark E. Parry (1993), "R&D-Marketing Interface in Japanese High-Technology Firms: Hypotheses and Empirical Evidence," *Journal of Academy of Marketing Science*, 21, 2, 125–133.

——— and ——— (1994), "The Dimensions of Industrial New Product Success and Failure in State Enterprises in the People's Republic of China," *Journal of Product Innovation Management*, 11, March, 105–118.

——— and ——— (1997), "The Determinants of Japanese New Product Successes," *Journal of Marketing Research*, forthcoming.

Terpstra, Vern (1988), "The Chinese Look to World Markets," *International Marketing Review*, 5, Summer, 7–19.

Wind, Yoram, Vijay Mahajan, and Barry L. Bayless (1990), *The Role of New Product Models in Supporting and Improving the New Product Development Process, Some Preliminary Results*, Cambridge, MA: The Marketing Science Institute.

9

Differences in "Cultural Values" and Their Effects on Responses to Marketing Stimuli: A Cross-Cultural Study between Australians and Chinese from the People's Republic of China

Anthony Chun-Tung Lowe and David R. Corkindale

Introduction

In the consumer behaviour literature values are recognised as a powerful force shaping consumers' motivations, life-styles, and product choices (Carman, 1978; Kluckhohn, 1969; McCracken, 1986; Yau, 1988). Differences in value systems across various cultures appear to be associated with major differences in consumers' behaviours (Grunert and Scherhorn, 1990; Jackson, 1973; McCracken, 1989; Tansuhaj *et al.*, 1991). Values can help to explain the differences in behaviour amongst people from different cultures (McCort and Malhotra, 1993) and these values tend to persist over time. The study of Taiwanese children's consumption behaviour by McNeal and Yeh (1989), for example, showed that centuries-old values continue to prevail. Furthermore, cultural values appear to have considerable effect on management decision making processes (Clark, 1990; Ken, 1985; Picken, 1987; Shane, 1988; Swierczek, 1991). A cross-cultural study by Tse *et al.* (1988) shows that home culture has predictable, significant effects on the decision making of executives from the People's Republic of China, Hong Kong and Canada.

Source: *European Journal of Marketing,* 32(9/10) (1998): 843–867.

Values became an active field of research from the late 1970s (e.g. Corfman *et al.*, 1991; Grunert *et al.*, 1989; Grunert and Scherhorn, 1990; Kamakura and Mazzon, 1991; Mitchell, 1983; Picken, 1987; Yau, 1986). Some marketers have become convinced that the role played by people's values is absolutely central to their personal development, to their actions as citizens and to their behaviour as consumers.

This is an exploratory cross-cultural study. It attempts to measure, in broad terms, the differences in cultural values between Australians and Chinese from the People's Republic of China. This study also seeks to show how the differences in responses by these two groups of people to some marketing stimuli are likely to be associated with the differences in cultural values.

For the purpose of this study, Australians are defined as those respondents who have stated that they were born in Australia, with their parents' country of origin either as Australia or "Anglo-Celtic"; Chinese from the People's Republic of China (PRC) are those respondents who have stated that they were born in PRC, with Chinese parents.

Developing the Measuring Instrument for "Cultural Values"

It appears that one of the difficulties in conducting cross-cultural studies is to develop a single measuring instrument which can be used for different cultures. For example, Grunert and Scherhorn (1990) compared List of Values (LOV) data from a German survey with survey data from the USA, Norway and parts of Canada. They found that the differences between the outcomes of the surveys appear to be for the most part explicable by cross-culturally differing connotations. In other words, the connotative meanings respondents have for the same values differ, sometimes considerably, thus leading to a certain measurement bias that makes cross-cultural comparisons more difficult. Additionally, there could be problems in translations, which might not in each case or in detail cover the general public's meaning associated with the LOV values. The measuring instruments of other studies, such as Values and LifeStyle research-VALS (Mitchell, 1983) and Rokeach Value Survey (RVS) (Rokeach, 1973) appear to have similar problems. On the other hand, Hofstede's (1980) cross-cultural work does not appear to be measuring the basic cultural values which is the purpose of this study

For this study, the concept of the Value Orientation framework (Kluckhohn and Strodtbeck, 1961) was adopted but not the measuring instrument. In conceptual terms, Kluckhohn and Strodtbeck (1961) have singled out five crucial and basic factors which are common to all human groups and these are:

(1) What is the character of innate human nature?
(2) What is the relation of human to nature (and supernatural)?
(3) What is the temporal focus of human life?
(4) What is the modality of human activity?
(5) What is the modality of a human's relationship to other humans?

Based on the above five questions, Kluckhohn and Strodtbeck formulated five basic Value Orientations, as follows:

(1) Human Nature Orientation;
(2) Man-nature (-Supernatural) Orientation;
(3) Time Orientation;
(4) Activity Orientation;
(5) Relational Orientation.

Kluckhohn and Strodtbeck (1961) postulated a range of variations for each of the five "Value Orientations", as follows:

(1) Human Nature Orientation: Evil; Neutral (i.e. mixture of good and evil); Good.
(2) Man-Nature Orientation: Subjugation-to-nature; Harmony-with-nature; Mastery-over-nature.
(3) Time Orientation: Past; Present; Future.
(4) Activity Orientation: Being; Being-in becoming; Doing.
(5) Relational Orientation: Lineality; Collaterality; Individualism.

Shively and Shively (1972) indicated that this schema for analysis of culture is most useful when the task is to differentiate between cultures, since Value Orientations are formulated with crucial and basic values which are common to all human groups. It is also useful when determining whether a society is undergoing changes. However, to avoid problems with the measuring instruments mentioned above and taking into consideration that this is a self-administered questionnaire, short concise statements with simple language were used. For example:

	Totally agree	Totally disagree
14. Marriage is an essential part of our society	1–2–3–4–5–6–7–8–9	
15. Marriage is a permanent contract and divorce should not be allowed	1–2–3–4–5–6–7–8–9	

These statements are less likely to be misinterpreted by the respondents from different cultures. Furthermore, if necessary, these statements can easily be translated into other languages.

Hypotheses

Advertising and Promotion

Tse *et al.* (1989) conducted a study which indirectly addressed the value systems of Hong Kong, PRC and Taiwan by assessing contents of existing advertising. In contrast, the present study attempted to establish the relationship between cultural values and responses to advertising/promotion directly rather than by inference. It attempts to relate the cultural values from two different countries (in this case, Australia and PRC) with their perceptions and attitudes towards advertising/promotion.

Generally, research indicates (e.g. McCracken, 1989; Tse *et al.*, 1989) advertising appeals do reflect the values of the culture that create them. In broad terms, value systems are different (see discussion below) between Australians and Chinese from the People's Republic of China and, therefore, one can hypothesise that:

> *H1*: The Chinese are likely to respond differently to advertising and promotion, when compared with Australians.

In order to measure the differences in response to advertising and promotion between these two cultural groups it is necessary to formulate sub-hypotheses for different situations.

A current television advertisement in Australia uses the sales pitch "for the most important person in the world!". The implication is that this description applies to the individual viewer. Advertising campaigns are but one sign in Australian society of the fact that we are in the midst of an age of increasing individualism. Furthermore, research by the Australian Institute of Family Studies (Vandenheuval, 1991b) indicates that there is an undercurrent of self-satisfaction when it comes to contemporary family values. Marriage is valued for the companionship it brings the individual. One reason advanced for having children is the fulfilment and enrichment they bring to the parents' lives. Children are also often seen as security against loneliness in old age (Vandenheuval, 1991a). In other words, many Australians have come to expect that family, marriage and children are instruments to satisfy individual, not institutional needs.

In contrast, the Chinese are collectivistic and the collectivistic nature of China is reflected in the Chinese family and kinship system (Hsu, 1970). The kinship system means continuous and long-lasting human ties which do not have clearly defined boundaries (Yau, 1986). To the Chinese, "family" means more than just father, mother and children, as is the case in Australia. In other words, the Chinese view "family" beyond the immediate members or "nuclear family" which (Anglo-Celtic) Australians tend to mean.

It is, therefore, important to note that unlike the Australian society, for the Chinese group, family welfare is more important than for an individual.

If necessary, the Chinese would sacrifice their own well-being for the benefits of the group or family. This value has a particular implication for advertising.

Furthermore, most of the Chinese have a stronger respect for authority than most Australians, because of the Chinese social system. Chinese society has a much more clearly defined hierarchical relationship than Australia's (Yang, 1959). For example, Confucius' "Five Cardinal Relations" constitute the foundations of traditional Chinese culture-values and they are: between father and son there should be solidarity and affection; between sovereign and minister, righteousness; between husband and wife, attention to their separate functions; between old and young, a proper function; and between friends, fidelity (Osland, 1990).

It is of highest value for a Chinese to be polite, obeying the rules, accepting and behaving according to the hierarchical system. For example, a Chinese student is less likely to query what the teacher has to say than the Australian student. Yau (1988) states that since the Chinese have such respect for authority which directs them to what is right or wrong, advertisements will tend to be more effective when opinion leaders stand up in commercials recommending products/services to their target consumers. Opinion leaders for Chinese consumers include older people, political leaders, family elders and authoritarian types. In contrast, some of the Western cultures (Australia is considered to be one of them) place higher values on youthfulness and ability (McCracken, 1988). Hence:

> *H1a*: Chinese are more likely to be influenced by models used in advertising which have characteristics such as family-orientation, authoritarian, older people and experts as opposed to model characteristics like celebrity, sexy, sports heroes etc. which are frequently found in advertising and promotional activities in Australia.

One of the major differences between Chinese and Australian consumers probably lies in their conception of products. This difference has conceivably stemmed from the Chinese placing high value on human relations and thus comparably less emphasis on things and animals. One of the consequences is that the Chinese have a relatively simpler and less differentiated concept of product. It is based primarily on product features since they do not attach as much affection to products as they do to human beings. The result of this tendency may be that the Chinese adopt a mostly utilitarian viewpoint towards products (Yang, 1989), particularly when compared with Australian consumers.

It is likely that:

> *H1b*: Chinese are likely to be less responsive than Australians to advertisements which consist of symbolic themes.

"Social orientation" is more important to the Chinese than Australians. In other words, the Chinese are more disposed to social conformity, submission to social expectations and worry about external opinions than the Australians. Yang (1989) indicates that it is very important for Chinese to have harmony maintenance, impression management, face protection, social acceptance and avoidance of punishment, embarrassment, conflict, rejection, ridicule and retaliation in a social situation. It represents a tendency for a Chinese to act in accordance with external expectations or social norms.

Chinese are strongly collective, which means that informal channels of communications are important in Chinese society. In other words, Chinese consumers tend to rely more on word-of-mouth communication because of the high contact rate among group members. Furthermore, given that informal channels of communication carry facts and rumour, Chinese consumers are much more likely to rely on, and make use of rumour from the informal channels, rather than what is actually claimed for the product officially (Kindel, 1982).

Therefore, one can hypothesis that:

> *H1c*: Chinese make relatively more use of informal channels of communication than Australians.

Chinese regard human beings as part of nature and believe that one's life is predetermined by some external force: one should accept what is given and not try to overcome or master it. On the other hand, Australians regard natural forces of all kinds as phenomena to be overcome and put to the use of human beings. It is, therefore, understandable that Chinese have a greater tendency to attribute failure of products/services to fate rather than to the producer or supplier (Yau, 1986). In other words, warranties may not be able to assist, since fate has already predetermined the outcome.

Hence:

> *H1d*: Chinese are less likely to be attracted by product warranties than Australians.

Branding

The Chinese tend to put more value on "past-time" orientation and "continuity" than Australians. This implies that the Chinese would tend to be more brand loyal than Australians. Unless the product or brand being used proves very unsatisfactory they are not likely to switch to purchasing other brands or products. In addition, Chinese consumers, especially married ones, are likely to consider opinions, values and influences of deceased relatives and respected figures in their current consumption choices (Yau, 1988).

Furthermore, Chinese consumers are more likely to conform to group norms than Australians, therefore, the Chinese consumers have a higher tendency to purchase the same brand of product that their other group members recommend. In other words, if a reference group has established a brand or product as the normative standard, Chinese consumers are less likely to deviate from it than the Australians.

Based on the above discussion, therefore, it could be concluded that:

H2: Chinese tend to be more brand loyal than Australians.

The fact that the Chinese place more importance on "past-time" orientation and "continuity" than Westerners has lead many Western researchers to infer that the Chinese may be more brand loyal than Westerners. However, this may be a rather simplistic assessment of the situation, since one also needs to take other cultural values into consideration.

The Chinese are very socially and situationally dependent and this may result in their using different decision criteria, when evaluating product alternatives, for products with different levels of social significance (Yang, 1989). In a low-involvement situation when products are used for private consumption, the Chinese may adopt a rather more down-to-earth approach to purchasing than Westerners. The cognitive domain for these products is likely to consist of strictly physical functions of the product. Consequently, for this type of product, the Chinese may be less brand conscious and more oblivious to marketing efforts to establish brand image than Westerners. Price and quality would be the main criteria for purchase.

In a high-involvement situation where products are used as social symbols, such as to reflect social status, to maintain social relationships, to express gratitude, to return a favour and to signal approval and disapproval for the Chinese the choice of a product is often based on its ability to express precisely the social meaning a purchaser intends to convey. It is important to the Chinese to follow what society prescribes as appropriate and meaningful as the selection criteria. Under such circumstances, prestige, brand name and packaging become the prevailing criteria for purchase; whereas the intrinsic quality of the products is considered almost irrelevant. For example, Hong Kong held the world record for per capita consumption of cognac. This is mainly because the Chinese consider that it follows the principle of *Li* (i.e. ritual action) to bring expensive gifts when invited to a dinner to show to the host their gratitude for the invitation, and cognac has long been established in Hong Kong as "the thing" to bring for, and to drink during, an important dinner. The fact that cognac is for Westerners an after dinner drink and that the strong taste destroys the good taste of food does not bother the Chinese at all (Yang, 1989).

The following two hypotheses express the discussion above:

H2a: Chinese are less price conscious and more brand conscious than Australians when social occasion or ceremony demand a gift to be given to someone.

H2b: Chinese are more price conscious and less brand conscious than Australians, when purchasing goods for their own private use.

Sales and Retailing

Perceived risk is one of the major factors influencing consumers' purchasing behaviour. Loudon and Della Bitta (1988) indicate that there are several kinds of risk which consumers may perceive in a purchase situation:

- *Financial risk*: the consumer may lose money if the brand/product does not work at all or cost more than it should to keep it in good shape.
- *Performance risk*: the brand/product may not work properly or as expected.
- *Physical risk*: the brand/product may be or become harmful or injurious to one's health.
- *Psychological risk*: the brand/product may not fit in well with the consumer's self-image or self-concept.
- *Social risk*: the brand/product may negatively affect the way others think of the consumer.
- *Time-loss risk*: the brand may fail completely, thus wasting the consumer's time, convenience and effort getting it adjusted, repaired or replaced.

Owing to the cultural differences between the Chinese and Australians, the perception of the above risks will also differ. For example, in a gift giving situation, for the Chinese the financial and performance risks are less important than purchasing a product which is acceptable or which conforms with the social norm, when compared with Australians.

Even if we assume that all the risk factors are perceived to be the same by Australians and Chinese except for Psychological and Social risk, these two risk factors are likely to cause differences in consumers' purchasing behaviour between the two cultures.

In broad terms, therefore, one can postulate that:

> *H3*: The factors influencing Chinese consumers' purchasing behaviour are likely to be different from those influencing Australians.

In marketing terms, Chinese consumers' value of "abasement" may have possible implications for sales force management. If an effective salesperson has to be interventionist and positive minded by American standards, a Chinese would tend to be judged as a bad salesperson. However, in Chinese society, an aggressive salesperson might frighten customers who may be humiliated. For example, Chinese buyers like to do their shopping in a free environment without interference. If a salesperson in a retail store is too eager to help and approaches a customer who has not decided what to buy, the customer will feel uneasy and go away. The proper thing to do is to keep a distance from the customer, but at the same time let him/her know that one is always ready to help (Yau, 1988).

Therefore:

> *H3a*: Chinese consumers prefer to deal with a less interventionist salesperson than Australians.

There are at least four basic Chinese cultural values that determine the way Chinese consumers handle dissatisfaction. They are the values of social harmony, moderation, "face" and the concept of *Pao*. All four of them have adverse effects on Chinese consumers taking action when dealing with their dissatisfaction, especially when dissatisfaction is handled by way of public confrontation. The desire to maintain social harmony in a public situation often deters Chinese consumers from voicing their dissatisfaction. The need to maintain "face" in public also serves as a negative force for complaint behaviour because not getting a satisfactory result from the complaint means losing "face" in front of people, even if these people are not significant to them (Yang, 1989).

The principle of moderation obviously elevates Chinese consumers' level of tolerance for product dissatisfaction and their threshold for taking action against bad business practices. The concept of *Pao* (i.e. reciprocity) often prevents Chinese consumers from taking direct actions because they believe that manufacturers who exercise bad practices will be automatically retributed (Yang, 1989).

The values of social harmony, moderation, "face" and the concept of *Pao* are much more important to the Chinese than Australians. It is, therefore, possible to hypothesise that:

> *H3b*: Chinese are less likely to complain about products that do not meet with their expectations than Australians.

The Chinese have a stronger belief in "continuity" than Australians, particularly in terms of human relationships. In addition, the Chinese believe in *T'ien Ming* (i.e. the Chinese believe that each one of our lives is predetermined by some external force). The Chinese believe nothing is likely to happen by accident, even friendship. To the Chinese, therefore, once a friendship has been developed, it will continue to be nurtured. One can expect to maintain long-term personal loyalty and affection, irrespective of political and economic upheavals (Osland, 1990).

Therefore:

> *H3c*: The Chinese will show a higher preference for dealing with a salesperson with whom they have had previous dealings than Australians.

As indicated earlier, the Chinese place more importance on interpersonal and social relationships than Australians. Other people's opinions are very important to the Chinese. If one's behaviour is unacceptable, then one will risk losing "face" which is an important factor for one's survival within a social group (Osland, 1990). In addition, the Chinese tend to be more "situational" orientated than Australians. In a purchasing situation, for the Chinese it is more important to ensure that the purchase meets the approval of others than expressing one's individuality (Hsu, 1970). For example, following the formation of PRC in 1949, Chairman Mao's uniform was readily adopted by both males and females of the population in PRC. Although it was encouraged by the government, one feels that it was the social rather than political pressure which produced such rapid adoption.

Socially unacceptable behaviours or purchases tend to be perceived as more detrimental to the Chinese than Australians. Chinese will try to seek other people's prior opinion within their social group, whenever and wherever possible.

Therefore:

> *H3d*: Chinese tend to show a higher preference to shop with others than Australians.

Introduction of New/Innovative Products or Services

The Chinese place greater emphasis on tradition and are less likely to take risks than the Australians, particularly for new or innovative products or services. The Chinese are less likely to change merely for the sake of change. New things are often viewed with great scepticism and may only be accepted after long resistance (Yang, 1989). A cross-cultural study conducted by Tansuhaj *et al.* (1991) concludes: "there is some indication that understanding of fundamental cultural values of a country can help to explain the differences in innovation (especially those related to media and to entertainment) in the global marketplace".

One can, therefore hypothesise that:

> *H4*: The rate or process of adoption for new/innovative products or services among the Chinese is different from that of Australians.

The rate of adoption of a new/innovative product or service appears to be directly related to one's belief in "Fate" and "Tradition".

There have been a few studies that related fatalism to innovativeness and perceived risks. Rogers (1983) found "earlier adopters" to be less fatalistic than later adopters. Fatalism or fate-orientation is tied conceptually to one's relationship with nature. The Chinese believe in luck, chance, and fate to a greater extent than Americans (Hsu, 1961).

Traditionalism, on the other hand, is linked conceptually with "Time Orientation". The Chinese tend to be past-orientated and place greater value on tradition, while Australian society has a strong future orientation. Thus the Chinese are less willing to initiate changes than Australians.

In addition, the doctrine of "mean" (i.e. not going to the extremes) may also influence the Chinese consumers' attitudes towards a new/innovative product or service because they may regard adopting or using this new/innovative product or service as an extreme behaviour which may not be acceptable to the group.

Therefore, one could hypothesise that:

H4a: The Chinese are less willing to try or adopt a new/innovative product or service than the Australians.

The Chinese tend to have a global perception towards objects and situations. Yang (1957) believes that the concept of "familism" and *Pao* are the major causes for the Chinese to develop such tendencies. A Chinese individual needs to consider not only themselves but also their family before initiating an action. They have to consider the behavioural consequence not just in terms of its effect on themselves but also on their family members and their offspring. They have to perceive and conceptualise things from a larger and more holistic point of view.

Some studies (e.g. Nakamura, 1964; Northrop, 1946) indicate that the Chinese way of thinking tends to be synthetic, concrete and contextual; whereas the western style is more analytical, abstract and imaginative. It is much more difficult for the Chinese to change one whole model for another than to change parts of a model. Hence there is a tendency to reject the unknown and to stay carefully within the known.

Based on the above discussion, therefore:

H4b: New/innovative products with familiar or well-known brand names will be diffused more rapidly than new/innovative products with unknown brand names for the Chinese when compared with Australians.

The concept of "mean" stresses that the Chinese believe in the importance of exercising self control and not letting oneself go to the extremes (Loudon and Della Bitta, 1988). In terms of consumption behaviour, particularly for new/innovative products, the Chinese tend to be more conservative than Australians. Furthermore, the concept of "abasement" is also likely to reinforce this more conservative consumption behaviour, since this concept tends to make the Chinese perceive "modesty" to be more important than do Australians (Yau, 1988). To purchase a product and make a mistake is a loss of "face" to the Chinese consumer and is to be avoided (Kindel, 1982). For example, if someone has purchased a new/innovative product which is much more complex than an existing product and the product failed to perform, others may not sympathise with that person. In fact, often others may say: "He/she deserves to have such problems, because he/she tries to show off; or he/she tries to be smart; or he/she thinks that he/she knows everything". These factors are likely to cause the Chinese to be more cautious and to take less extreme action in their purchasing behaviour than Australians.

Thus:

H4c: When compared with Australians, the Chinese are more likely to avoid purchasing a new and complex product when an existing and simpler product can perform the same function.

Research Design

To test the above hypotheses, samples of Australians and Chinese from the PRC were asked to complete a questionnaire. The questionnaire contained questions which would enable cultural-values to be established and claimed behaviour towards marketing stimuli measured. The samples were drawn from the university student population as described below.

Sample Population

Australian

The Australian sample population was drawn from three groups of students from The University of South Australia who were:

(1) A daytime-class of first year Physics students; the majority of this group were studying full-time and in a younger age group (i.e. less than 23-years old).
(2) An evening-class of first year Accountancy students; the majority of this group were studying part-time, in an older age group (i.e. more than 23-years old) and working full-time.
(3) A group of post-graduate, mainly MBA students, was randomly selected; all the students within this group were working full-time and studying the post-graduate degree on a part-time bases. This group of students were within the older age group (i.e. more than 23-years old).

Chinese from PRC

The sample population consisted of all the overseas PRC students who were studying at University of South Australia, The University of Adelaide and The University of Sydney, Australia.

Data Collection Methods

We adopted three different methods of collecting the data.

(1) *Australian sample – undergraduate students*. The questionnaires were handed out at the beginning of a lecture and the students were asked to complete the questionnaire at home. The questionnaires were collected at the same time at the beginning of the same lecture

the following week. A pre-addressed and reply-paid envelop was handed to those students who had not completed or did not bring the questionnaire.

(2) *Australian sample – postgraduate students.* We have randomly selected a group of postgraduate students and placed the questionnaire in their "pigeonholes". We requested the students to place their completed questionnaire in the postgraduates' assignment box.

(3) *Sample for Chinese from PRC – undergraduate and postgraduate students.* A questionnaire was mailed to all the PRC students who had enrolled at the Australian universities stated above. In all cases, a covering letter which explained the purpose of the study and an endorsement from the appropriate person within these universities was placed in front of the questionnaire. A pre-addressed and reply-paid envelop was also included. After one month, a "reminder" letter with the same questionnaire was again mailed to all of them. Those who had already responded were asked to ignore the "reminder" letter and thanked for their cooperation.

All the questionnaires were self administered. The questionnaire was pre-tested and revised many times before the final version was produced for this study.

Response Rate

Australian Sample

Table I indicates that we received 160 responses which accounted for 50.5 percent of the total Australian sample population. However, we rejected 46 of the returned questionnaires (or 14.5 percent of the total Australian sample population) which did not meet the preset criteria. The final 114 useable questionnaires accounted for 36 percent of total Australian sample population.

Table I: Response rate of sample population

	Australian		*PRC Chinese*		*Total*	
	(n)	%	*(n)*	%	*(n)*	%
Total hand/mail out	317		320		637	
Wrong address			15		15	
Net hand/mail out	317	100.0	305	100.00	622	100.0
Total response	160	50.5	138	45.2	298	47.9
Unusable questionnaires	46	14.5	12	3.9	58	9.3
Net response	114	36.0	126	41.3	240	38.6

Sample of Chinese from PRC

We mailed out a total of 320 questionnaires but 15 were returned because of "wrong address". A total of 138 questionnaires (or 45.2 percent of the "net mail-out") was received and 12 of them were rejected (or 3.9 percent of the net mail-out) during editing. The 126 usable questionnaires accounted for 41.3 percent of the net mail-out.

Demographic Profile of Respondents

Table II indicates that the Chinese sample from the PRC is generally male, older and has higher educational qualifications than the Australian sample. This is understandable, since the majority of the PRC students who have enrolled in an Australian university are scholarship holders who are undertaking some form of post-graduate studies.

Data Analysis

The questionnaire consists of a number (110) of short concise statements in simple language to avoid misinterpretation by the respondents. An English version of the questionnaire was administered to all the respondents. If necessary,

Table II: Demographic profile of respondents

	Australia (%)	*PRC (%)*
Gender		
Male	52.6	68.3
Female	47.4	31.0
N/A		0.7
Total (n)	(114)	(126)
Age		
<18	20.2	0.0
19–21	22.8	7.1
22–25	7.9	19.0
26–30	14.9	26.2
31–34	15.8	18.3
35–40	11.4	23.8
41–45	7.0	5.6
Total (n)	(114)	(126)
Education		
Undergraduate	64.9	21.4
Post-graduate	27.2	50.0
Has a post-graduate	7.9	28.6
Total (n)	(114)	(126)
Years in Australia		
<2		25.4
>2		(126)
Total (n)		

these statements could easily be translated into other languages and are likely to be interpreted the same way by people from different cultures.

In order to reduce and summarise the large number (90) of statements used to measure "Values", factor analysis was used. Factor analysis addresses the problem of analysing the interrelationship among a large number of variables (e.g. test scores, test items questionnaire responses) and then explaining these variables in terms of their common underlying dimensions (factors) (Hair *et al.*, 1992).

In the first instance, the factor analysis was carried out according to the five pre-established "Value Orientation" framework. After scrutinising the results produced by the initial factor analysis, it appeared that the research objectives would be better served by factor-analysing the "Person to Oneself Orientation" and "Personal Activity Orientation" as one unit (i.e. combining them). This is because some of the variables within these two groups appear to be related or likely to measure the same construct or factor.

In order to ascertain the relative difference between the two different cultural groups in this study, we have factor analysed the two groups' responses together. In other words, we intend to measure the relative differences between the two cultural groups based on the same value orientation factors.

Following varimax rotation, it produced a total of 22 factors that had Eigenvalues of greater than 1. Only those variables with factor loadings greater than 0.4 were used to develop descriptions for each of the 22 factors (Hair *et al.*, 1992). All the 22 factors were retained and no further factors reduction procedure was carried out (e.g. "Scree Test"), because at this exploratory stage of the research, it will be useful to examine as many "Value Factors" as possible. The labels given to the factors, based on the common underlying dimensions of the variables, are as follows:

Factor 1: Relationship with one's parents.
Factor 2: Relationship with social hierarchical system.
Factor 3: Relationship with authority.
Factor 4: Importance of "Face Saving".
Factor 5: Relationship with family.
Factor 6: Relationship with "Social others".
Factor 7: Relationship with "Institutions".
Factor 8: Relationship between "Marriage" and "Society".
Factor 9: Concept of "Self-training".
Factor 10: Concept of "Modesty".
Factor 11: Concept of "Mean" (or not to take extreme action).
Factor 12: Importance of "Social harmony".
Factor 13: Importance of "Socially acceptable behaviour".
Factor 14: Concept of "Pragmatism".
Factor 15: Concept of "Situational" behaviour.
Factor 16: "Tradition".

Factor 17: "Continuity" – family.
Factor 18: "Continuity" – others.
Factor 19: Attitude to "Changes".
Factor 20: Dealing with "Nature".
Factor 21: Concept of "Fatalism".
Factor 22: Concept of "Status quo".

In order to ascertain the differences in the "Value Factors" and the responses to the Marketing Variables between Chinese from PRC and Australians, all the data were analysed by ANOVA (two-tailed) and Discriminant Analysis. The results of these two analyses showed consistent patterns between the two groups of respondents for the Value Factors as well as the Marketing Variables. We will, therefore, only present the results from Discriminant Analysis because the results can be presented more easily and clearly.

Furthermore, Pearson's correlation analysis was used to ascertain whether the "Value Factors" held by respondents are associated with the respondents' attitudes and perceptions towards the marketing variables.

Findings

Differences in Cultural Values

In overall terms, the result indicates that these 22 factors have excellent discriminating power between Australians and Chinese from PRC (Table III). It has an "Eigenvalue" of 2.4. In addition, its "Canonical Correlation" has a value of 0.84 and 70 percent of the differences between the two groups are accounted for by these Value Orientation factors (Wilks' Lambda = 0.30). Furthermore, the differences between the two groups are far in excess of those expected by chance ($P < 0.0000$).

The results show that the most important discriminating factors for the two groups are:

(1) Relationship with one's parents (factor 1) (i.e. filial piety) is more important to the Chinese from PRC than the Australians.
(2) Chinese from PRC tend to be more "modest" (factor 10) when compared with Australians.
(3) Chinese from PRC are less likely "to go to the extremes" (i.e. the concept of "Mean") (Factor 11), when compared with Australians.
(4) To behave in a "socially acceptable manner" (factor 13) appeared to be more important to the Chinese from PRC than for the Australians.
(5) "Tradition" (factor 16) is more important to the Chinese from PRC than to Australians.
(6) "Continuity" of the family (factor 17) is more important to the Chinese from PRC than for the Australians.

Table III: Standardised canonical discriminant function coefficients of the "Value Orientation" factors

Factors	*Australia/PRC*
Relationship with:	
1. One's parents	0.843
2. Hierarchical system	−0.064
3. Authority	−0.186
4. Concept of "Face"	−0.157
5. Family	−0.190
6. "Social others"	−0.154
7. "Institutions"	−0.137
8. Marriage and society	−0.142
Person to oneself:	
9. "Self-training"	0.016
10. "Modesty"	0.377
11. "Mean"	0.254
Personal activity:	
12. "Social harmony"	0.014
13. "Social behaviour"	0.315
14. "Pragmatism"	−0.178
15. "Situational"	−0.008
Time orientation:	
16. "Tradition"	0.264
17. "Continuity" – family	0.237
18. "Continuity" – others	−0.088
19. Attitudes to changes	−0.209
Person to nature:	
20. With "nature"	−0.206
21. "Fatalism"	0.111
22. "Status quo"	0.57
Eigenvalue	2.393
Canonical correlation	0.840
Wilks' lambda	0.295
Chi-squared	276.1

Differences in Attitudes/Perceptions towards Marketing Variables

The respondents were asked to indicate their attitudes and perceptions towards a range of statements which describe the activities undertaken by companies in the course of marketing their products or services (Table IV). These activities, such as content of advertising, sales and retailing procedures, are called the "marketing variables".

The results indicate that these marketing variables have excellent capability to discriminate between Australians and Chinese from PRC. These marketing variables have an overall "Eigenvalue" of 1.02. In addition, its "Canonical Correlation" has a value of 0.71 and 50 percent of the differences between the two groups are accounted for by these marketing variables (Wilks' Lambda = 0.50). Furthermore, the differences between the two groups are far in excess of those expected by chance ($P < 0.0000$).

Table IV: Standardised canonical discriminant function coefficients of marketing variables

Marketing variables	*Australia/PRC*
1. I prefer to go shopping with someone, rather than go shopping alone	0.057
2. When I buy a new product, I always choose the one with a well-known brand name	0.190
3. Generally, advertisements featuring older people are more persuasive than advertisements with well-known actors/actresses, sexy models etc.	0.506
4. Generally, advertisements featuring family groups are more persuasive than advertisements with well-known actors/actresses, sexy models etc.	0.092
5. When I buy a gift, I always make sure that it is a well known brand, irrespective of cost	0.033
6. I do not understand how the Coca-Cola advertisements can help to sell more of this drink	0.243
7. The brand of ice-cream I buy is more likely to be influenced by my relatives and friends recommendations than by advertisements	−0.021
8. The brand of refrigerator I buy, is more likely to be influenced by my relatives and friends recommendations than by advertisements	−0.127
9. Generally, advertisements featuring recognised experts are more persuasive than advertisements with well known actors/actresses, sexy model etc.	0.107
10. I like to browse around the shop without any interference from salespeople, until I am ready to buy or ask questions	−0.162
11. I always avoid being the first person to try a new product	0.213
12. I always avoid purchasing new and complex products, if an older and simpler product can do the same	0.259
13. Trying out new products is a waste of time	0.196
14. I always buy new products with brand names that I am familiar with	0.469
15. I prefer to deal with a salesperson that I have dealt with before than someone unknown to me	−0.257
16. I have favourite brands for most things I buy and I tend to stick to them	−0.496
17. I do not usually lodge a formal complaint if a product was faulty	0.253
18. Generally, product warranty is not an important factor and it will not influence my purchasing decision	−0.031
Eigenvalue	1.018
Canonical Correlation	0.708
Wilks' Lambda	0.498
Chi-Square	158.90

This research indicates that the most important discriminating marketing variables for the two groups are:

(1) Advertisements featuring "older people" or "experts" tend to be more persuasive to the Chinese from PRC than the Australians (Supports *H1a*).

(2) Advertisements with a "practical theme" (i.e. stresses benefits/features), tend to be more persuasive to the Chinese from PRC than the Australians (Supports *H1b*).

(3) The Chinese from PRC are less likely to lodge a formal complaint for a faulty product, when compared with Australians (Supports *H3b*).

(4) Chinese from PRC have less tendency to purchase "new products", when compared with Australians (Supports *H4a*).

(5) When purchasing a "new product", the "new product" with a familiar brand name is more influential to the purchasing decision making

process for the Chinese from PRC than for the Australians (Supports *H4b*).

(6) When compared with the Australians, the Chinese from PRC are more likely to avoid purchasing a new and complex product, if an older and simpler product can perform the same function (Supports *H4c*).

(7) When compared with the Chinese from PRC, the Australians are more likely to have favourite brands for most products they purchase and they have a higher tendency to continue purchasing their favourite brands (Contradicts *H2*).

(8) The Australians showed a higher preference than the Chinese from PRC to deal with a salesperson that they have had dealing with before than someone unknown to them (Contradicts *H3d*).

Measures of Association

As Table IV indicates, in overall terms, these marketing variables have excellent capability to discriminate between Australians and the Chinese from PRC. However, this does not mean that the value orientation factors which will have an influence on these marketing variables are likely to be different between Australians and the Chinese from PRC. One can hypothesise: "the value orientation factors that influence these marketing variables are going to be the same". In other words, the same value orientation factors will influence the perceptions and attitudes towards the marketing variables stated.

The results from Pearson's correlation analysis suggest that the set of values which influence the attitudes and perceptions towards a marketing activity in one country, may be a totally different set for those in another country. As discussed in hypothesis *H1a*, family, hierarchical relationships and social systems are likely to have an effect on the response to personalities used in the advertising and promotional activities.

For Australian respondents, advertising featuring "older people" (Table V) is positively correlated with "social harmony" ($P < 0.05$).

Table V: Pearson's correlation coefficients of "persuasiveness of advertisements featuring older people" with "value orientation" factors

Factors	*Australia*	*PRC*
Relationship with		
Hierarchical system	0.016	0.203*
Family	−0.003	0.223*
Personal activity		
–"Social harmony"	0.204*	0.000

Note: *Signif. level 0.05; (two-tailed).

Table VI: Pearson's correlation coefficients of "purchasing new products with familiar brand names" with "value orientation" factors

Factors	*Australia*	*PRC*
Relationship with		
Concept of "face"	0.040	0.221*
"Social others"	0.71	0.191*
"Institutions"	0.212*	0.114
Personal activity		
"Situational"	0.34	0.194*
Time orientation		
"Continuity" – family	0.295**	0.080
"Continuity" – others	0.86	0.251**
Person to nature		
"Status quo"	−0.241**	−0.057

Note: *Signif. level 0.05; ** Signif. level 0.01 (two-tailed).

In contrast, for the Chinese respondents, the same advertising variable is positively correlated with the "hierarchical system" ($P < 0.05$) and relationship with one's "family" ($P < 0.05$).

Similarly, for Australian respondents, the marketing variable "Purchasing new products with familiar brand names" (hypothesis *H4b*) is positively correlated with the following values (Table VI):

- Relationship with "institutions" ($P < 0.05$);
- "Continuity" of family ($P < 0.01$).

and negatively correlated with the "Concept of Status Quo" ($P < 0.01$).

For the Chinese respondents, on the other hand, this same marketing variable is positively correlated with:

- Importance of "face" saving ($P < 0.05$);
- Relationship with "social other" ($P < 0.05$);
- Concept of "situational" behaviour ($P < 0.05$).
- "Continuity" – others ($P < 0.01$).

In order to substantiate the above findings, Pearson's correlation analysis was also carried out on those marketing variables which did not indicate any differences between Australians and the Chinese from PRC.

For example, although statistically there was no significant difference in their attitudes and perceptions towards "shopping with others" for the respondents from these two countries, the cultural values influencing these two groups' attitudes and perception towards this marketing variable are different (Table VII).

For Australians, "shopping with others" is negatively correlated with:

- Concept of "mean" i.e. not to take extreme action ($P < 0.01$);
- Concept of "situational" behaviour ($P < 0.05$);

Table VII: Pearson's correlation coefficients of "shopping with someone" with "value orientation" factors

Factors	*Australia*	*PRC*
Relationship with		
Family	−0.027	0.192*
Person to oneself		
"Mean"	−0.261**	0.008
Personal activity		
"Social harmony"	−0.56	0.177*
"Situational"	−0.226*	0.031
Time orientation		
"Continuity" – family	−0.118	−0.220*

Note: *Signif. level 0.05; ** Signif. level 0.01 (two-tailed).

However, for the Chinese, the same variable is positively correlated with:

- Relationship with "family" ($P < 0.05$);
- Importance of "social harmony" ($P < 0.05$).

and is negatively correlated with "Continuity" – family ($P < 0.05$).

Discussion

In general terms, this research indicates that there are differences in cultural values between Australians and Chinese from the PRC. On the other hand, we have found some similarities in factors which have been suggested should be different by a number of other commentators, e.g. "Relationship with Hierarchical System", the importance of "Social Harmony".

The findings also indicate that there are differences in the attitudes and perceptions towards various marketing stimuli between the two groups. These research findings also contradicted some of the commonly held beliefs about the Chinese attitudes and perceptions towards various marketing stimuli. For example, several commentators have stated that "Chinese tend to be more brand loyal than Westerners" which would include Australians. The present findings suggest that this is not the case, the Australians tend to be more brand loyal than the Chinese. However, when purchasing a new product, familiarity with the "Brand Name" did appear to be more important to the Chinese than Australians.

The observed differences in attitudes and perceptions towards some of the marketing stimuli were associated with cultural differences in the respondents' value systems. However, the cultural values which influence attitudes and perceptions towards the marketing stimuli are more complex than just the differences in cultural values. While one set of values influenced the attitudes and perceptions towards marketing stimuli among one group of consumers (e.g. Australians), there may be a totally different set for the other group of consumers (e.g. Chinese). One cannot assume that the same set of values will influence two different groups of consumers' responses for the same marketing stimuli. This is particularly important for research studies across different countries. We cannot assume that causes for behaviour in one country are the same as in another.

Limitations of the Study

An important and often crucial decision in cross-cultural research design is the extent of population coverage. To be truly representative there is a need for comparable samples. Owing to resource and time constraints, our sample population has put some limitations on the scope and the results of this study.

The study uses a convenience sample, since university students were selected as respondents. They cannot be considered to be truly representative samples of the Chinese and Australian populations because:

(1) Australian university students tend to represent the Australian population who are better educated and within a higher social-economic group.
(2) The majority of the students in Australia from PRC are also likely to represent a higher social-economic and better educated group of the population within their own country.

However, one could argue that the results of the research from these groups of respondents could represent the "trend" of these cultural groups, since they are likely to be influential in future in their respective countries. From the marketers' point-of-view, the findings can provide an indication of those cultural-values that marketers need to influence and those cultural values that they need to remain in harmony with.

The research instrument is always the subject of discussion in quantitative research. The instrument of this study is no exception.

First of all, an English questionnaire was administered to all the respondents. Although none of the Chinese respondents indicated any problems with understanding and filling out the questionnaire, it nevertheless may raise some concern. We do not think that this problem is a serious one because precautions were taken in the development of this research instrument (i.e. each statement was made to be as simple as possible). Furthermore, the Chinese students must achieve a pre-set standard of English skills prior to being admitted into any university in Australia.

Second, the respondents' attitudes and perceptions towards the marketing variables in this study are based on their responses to some simple statements. To accurately examine these marketing variables, one would need to have a more complex experimental design which was beyond the scope of this study.

The study was also cross-sectional and so no cause-effect relationships can be claimed, just associations. Despite the limitations stated above, this study provides an indication of the key differences in cultural-values and their relationship to responses to certain marketing variables between the two groups that were studied. In addition, this study can be used to indicate some of the directions for future research.

Suggestions for Future Research

This was an exploratory study. To verify this study's findings utilising the same measuring instrument it could be replicated by selecting the same groups of students from universities in Australia and in PRC.

Second, data from more representative samples of the whole population of Chinese from PRC and Australians need to be drawn. The instrument used in this study could then be repeated to further test our findings.

Finally, this is a quantitative research study where the respondents' attitudes and perceptions towards the marketing variables are measured by their reactions to single statements only. In order to further understand and substantiate these initial findings it would be desirable to express the marketing variables in more comprehensive ways and to gather responses to them via appropriate experimental design methodologies.

References

Carman, J.M. (1978), "Values and consumption patterns: a closed loop", *Advances in Consumer Research*, Vol. 5, pp. 403–07.

Clark, T. (1990), "International marketing and national character: a review and proposal for an integrative theory", *Journal of Marketing*, October, pp. 66–79.

Corfman, K.P., Lehmann, D.R. and Narayanan, S. (1991), "Values, utility and ownership: modeling the relationships for consumer durables", *Journal of Retailing*, Vol. 67 No. 2, pp. 184–204.

Grunert, K.G., Grunert, S.C. and Bealty, S.E. (1989), "Cross-culture research on consumer value", *Marketing and Research Today*, February, pp. 30–9.

Grunert, S.C. and Scherhorn, G. (1990), "Consumer values in West Germany underlying dimensions and cross-cultural comparison with North America", *Journal of Business Research*, Vol. 20, pp. 97–107.

Hair, J.F. Jr, Anderson, R.E., Tatham, R.L. and Black, W.C. (1992), *Multivariate Data Analysis*, 3rd ed., Macmillan Publishing Company, New York, NY.

Hofstede, G. (1980), *Culture's Consequences*, Sage Publication, Beverly Hills, CA.

Hsu, F.L.K. (1961), "American core value and national character", in Hsu, F.L.K. (Ed.), *Psychological Anthropology: Approaches to Culture and Personality*, Dorsey Press, Homewood, IL.

Hsu, F.L.K. (1970), *Americans and Chinese: Reflections on Two Cultures and Their People*, Doubleday, National History Press, New York, NY.

Jackson, R.G. (1973), "A preliminary bicultural study of value orientations and leisure attitudes", Journal of Leisure Research, Vol. 5, pp. 10–22.

Kamakura, W.A. and Mazzon, J.A. (1991), "Value segmentation: a model for the measurement of values and value systems", *Journal of Consumer Research*, Vol. 18, pp. 208–18.

Ken, T. (1985), "Japan's matrix of nature, culture and technology", *Management Review*, May, pp. 42–7.

Kindel, T.I. (1982), "A partial theory of Chinese consumer behaviour: marketing strategy implications", *Hong Kong Journal of Business Management, Vol.* 1, pp. 97–109.

Kluckhohn, C. (1969), "Value and value orientations in the theory of action", in Parsons, T. and Shills, E.A. (Eds), *Towards a General Theory of Action*, Harvard University Press, Cambridge, MA, pp. 388–433.

Kluckhohn, F. and Strodtbeck, F. (1961), *Variations in Value Orientations*, Row, Peterson, Evanston, IL.

Loudon, D.L. and Della Bitta, A.J. (1988), *Consumer Behaviour-concept and Application*, 3rd ed., McGraw Hill, New York, NY.

McCort, D.J. and Malhotra, N.K. (1993), "Culture and consumer behaviour: towards an understanding of cross-cultural consumer behaviour in international marketing", *Journal of International Consumer Marketing*, Vol. 6 No. 2, pp. 91–127.

McCracken, G.D. (1986), "Culture and consumption: a theoretical account of the structure and movement of the cultural meaning of consumer goods", *Journal of Consumer Research*, Vol. 13, pp. 71–84.

McCracken, G.D. (1988), *Culture and Consumption: New Approaches to the Symbolic Character of Consumer Goods and Activities*, Indiana University Press, Bloomington, IN.

McCracken, G.D. (1989), "Who is the celebrity endorser? Cultural foundations of the endorsement process", *Journal of Consumer Research*, Vol. 16, pp. 310–21.

McNeal, J.U. and Yeh, C.-H. (1989), "Taiwanese children as consumers", *European Journal of Marketing*, Vol. 23 No. 8, pp. 32–43.

Mitchell, A. (1983), *The Nine American Lifestyles*, MacMillan, New York, NY.

Nakamura, H. (1964), *Ways of Thinking of Eastern Peoples: India, China, Tibet, Japan* (English Translation), Wiener, P.P. (Ed.), East-West Center Press, Honolulu, Hawaii.

Northrop, F.S.C. (1946), *Meeting of East and West: An Inquiry Concerning World Understanding*, The MacMillan Co., New York, NY.

Osland, G.E. (1990), "Doing business in China: a framework for cross-cultural understanding", *Marketing Intelligence & Planning*, Vol. 8 No. 4, pp. 4–14.

Picken, S.D.B. (1987), "Values and value-related strategies in Japanese corporate culture", *Journal of Business Ethics*, Vol. 6, pp. 137–43.

Rogers, E.M. (1983), *Diffusion of Innovations*, The Free Press, New York, NY.

Rokeach, M.J. (1973), *The Nature of Human Values*, Free Press: New York, NY.

Shane, S. (1988), "The role of obligation in the Japanese marketing system", *Business Quarterly*, Spring, pp. 92–5.

Shively, A.M. and Shively, S. (1972), "Value changes during a period of modernization – the case of Hong Kong", The Chinese University of Hong Kong, Social Research Centre, Hong Kong.

Swierczek, F.W. (1991), "Culture and negotiation in the Asian context: key issues in the marketing of technology", *Journal of Managerial Psychology,* Vol. 5 No. 5, pp. 17–24.

Tansuhaj, P., Gentry, J.W., John, J., Manzer, L.L. and Cho, B.J. (1991), "A cross-national examination of innovation resistance", *International Marketing Review*, Vol. 8 No. 3, pp. 7–20.

Tse, D.K., Belk, R.W. and Zhou, N. (1989), "Becoming a consumer society: a longitudinal and cross-cultural content analysis of print ads from Hong Kong, The People's Republic of China and Taiwan", *Journal of Consumer Research*, Vol. 15, pp. 457–72.

Tse, D.K., Lee, K.H., Vertinsky, I. and Wehrung, D.A. (1988), "Does culture matter? A cross culture study of executives' choice, decisiveness and risk adjustment in international marketing", *Journal of Marketing*, Vol. 53, October, pp. 81–95.

Vandenheuval, A. (1991a), "In a class of our own? – an international comparison of family values", *Family Matters*, Vol. 29, pp. 20–1.

Vandenheuval, A. (1991b), "The most important person in the world", *Family Matters*, Vol. 29, pp. 8–13.

Yang, C.F. (1989), "A conception of Chinese consumer behavior", in Yang, C.F., Ho, S.C. and Yau, H.M. (Eds), *Hong Kong Marketing Management at the Cross-Roads*, Commercial Press, Hong Kong, NY, pp. 317–42.

Yang, C.K. (1959), *The Chinese Family in the Communist Revolution*, Harvard University Press, Cambridge, MA.

Yang, L.S. (1957), "The concept of *Pao* as a basis for relation in China", in Fairbank, J.K. (Ed.), *Chinese Thought and Institutions*, University of Chicago Press, Chicago, IL.

Yau, O.H.M. (1986), "Consumer satisfaction and cultural values – an investigation of the relationships between Chinese cultural values, expectations from performance of and satisfaction with consumer products", PhD dissertation, University of Bradford.

Yau, O.H.M. (1988), "Chinese culture values: their dimensions and marketing implications", *European Journal of Marketing*, Vol. 22, pp. 44–57.

10

Guanxi: Connections as Substitutes for Formal Institutional Support

Katherine R. Xin and Jone L. Pearce

Although executives spend substantial time interacting with others outside their organizations, theories of organizational behavior are surprisingly silent on the meaning of these contacts. Sociologists and organizational theorists have studied structural connections among executives for years (Granovetter, 1985; Larson, 1992; Macaulay, 1963; Powell, 1990; Yan & Gray, 1992). However, formal structure provides an incomplete picture of how executives develop connections. Executives also meet with others in settings of their own choosing and strive to build personal dependence in addition to formal structural dependence. As others have noted, informal relations help employees work around formal constraints within organizations (e.g., Crozier, 1964; Pfeffer, 1992). We propose that one reason executives seek out connections and cultivate close personal relationships is to obtain resources or protection not otherwise available.

Such personal connections seem particularly important to executives in countries without a stable legal and regulatory environment that allows for impersonal business dealings (Redding, 1990; Zucker, 1986). For example, without an impartial judiciary, executives are reluctant to develop business relationships with those they do not personally trust. The importance of good personal relationships to doing business in developing countries has been discussed widely in popular writings for managers (cf. *Asian Advertising and Marketing*, 1989; Fox, 1987), yet the advice given in business periodicals has rarely been analyzed in management scholarship. We drew on the

Source: *Academy of Management Journal*, 39(6) (1996): 1641–1658.

work of Redding (1990), Putnam (1993), and Nee (1992, 1989) to develop hypotheses about which executives in the People's Republic of China will find personal relationships more important for business and invest more in their cultivation.

In China, interpersonal connections are called *guanxi*. In her comprehensive study, Yang stated that *guanxi*

> means literally "a relationship" between objects, forces, or persons. When it is used to refer to relationships between people, not only can it be applied to husband-wife, kinship and friendship relations, it can also have the sense of "social connections," dyadic relationships that are based implicitly (rather than explicitly) on mutual interest and benefit. Once guanxi is established between two people, each can ask a favor of the other with the expectation that the debt incurred will be repaid sometime in the future (1994: 1–2).

In China, *guanxi* usually does not carry negative connotations, whereas allowing something to be decided by open competition instead of by using connections may be considered stupid and disloyal (e.g., Alston, 1989; Chen & Pan, 1993; Hwang, 1987; Lockett, 1988; Yau, 1988). Despite its importance, we know of no empirical tests of guanxi or of the circumstances that shape when, where, and with whom such relationships should be most important to managers.

Framework and Hypotheses

Guanxi as a Substitute for Formal Institutional Support

We suggest that managers cultivate personal connections to substitute for reliable government and an established rule of law, characteristics we merge under the label "structural support." This idea is hardly new (cf. Boisot, 1986; Coleman, 1993; Fallers, 1965; Putnam, 1993; Riggs, 1964; Walder, 1986), but it has not been systematically tested. Redding observed that networks in China are useful in "the regulation of transactions in the absence of state institutions for that purpose" (1990: 56). Certainly, many observers have noted that *guanxi* is endemic in Chinese business (Alston, 1989; Hall & Xu, 1990; Jacobs, 1980; Leung & Yeung, 1995; Lockett, 1988; Yang, 1994; Yau, 1988), yet Walder noted that "the concept is by no means culturally unique [to China]; the terms *blat* in Russia and *pratik* in Haiti refer to the same type of instrumental-personal tie. *Guanxi* is not a sociologically precise term: it refers to instrumental-personal ties that range from strong personal loyalties to ceremonial bribery" (1986: 179). A weak rule of law is problematic for all who do business in China, but such unreliability would prove particularly burdensome for newer, smaller private businesses. China today provides a context in which we can study the role of connections as manager-initiated substitutes for the kind of formal institutional support taken for granted in countries with more stable business environments.

Nee (1992) classified Chinese organizations into three types: state (federal)-owned, privately owned, and collective-hybrids, enterprises typically owned by local governments that produce products for competitive markets. He noted that China's transitional economy is characterized by weak capital market structures, poorly specified property rights, and institutional instability, of which a lack of coherent business laws is an example. These characteristics make market exchanges uncertain and costly. Under these circumstances, private companies have difficulty getting capital, because the banks, which are state-owned, favor state-owned companies. Further, in a country with uncertain property rights, the potential for threatening interference and expropriation from party and governmental officials is great. According to Nee, collective-hybrids have structural advantages over both privately owned and state-owned companies, because being affiliated with local governments protects them from government interference. At the same time, collective-hybrids sell in competitive markets, so they face "hard budget constraints" (Kornai, 1989) that encourage efficiency, unlike state-run companies. As Nee noted, Chinese state-owned companies, which face substantial regulatory restraint on wages, prices, capital expenditures, and product mix, are at a substantial organizational disadvantage. Similarly, Chinese private companies, which do not have the institutional protection of government ownership that state-owned and collective-hybrid companies do, are subject to arbitrary extortion by officials and others since the society lacks a reliable rule of law.

We take Nee's insights as a point of departure and suggest that Chinese private-company executives operating without the structural protection of governmental support, which is more available to state-owned and collective-hybrid organizations, will not passively await their fate. Rather, by developing *guanxi* as a substitute for the formal institutional protection government ownership offers their counterparts, they will cultivate close personal relationships with people useful to business. Certainly, all Chinese managers will use *guanxi*, but these connections will be seen as even more important by those with less structural support – that is, by private-sector managers.

Controlling for the Liability of Newness and Smallness

Before proceeding, it is necessary to discuss a potential alternative explanation for the greater importance of personal connections to executives in Chinese private companies. Private companies are relatively new and small in a country that is still, at least nominally, communist. Their executives may cultivate connections to counteract liabilities of newness and smallness, not as a substitute for structural protection.

Stinchcombe (1965) claimed that new organizations generally face greater risks than older organizations, because they lack external legitimacy. Empirical studies have tended to support the idea that newness is a liability for organizations (e.g., Delacroix & Carroll, 1983; Freeman, Carroll, & Hannan, 1983; Hannan & Freeman, 1989; Singh, Tucker, & House, 1986). Further, Freeman and colleagues (1983) showed that smallness presents its own liabilities to organizational survival. Aldrich and Auster (1986) suggested this is because new, small organizations have executives with fewer ties with others. Further, Singh and colleagues (1986) and Aldrich and Fiol (1992) found that as the number of ties held by executives of new and small organizations increased, the chances of their survival increased. Thus, in China, it is possible that executives in private companies stress the importance of their personal connections simply to counteract liabilities that result from their organizations' youth and smallness, not as a substitute for formal structural support via ownership. Therefore, to conduct a stronger test of the structure-substitution hypothesis, we needed to control for organizational age and size.

> *Hypothesis 1: With the age and size of their companies controlled, executives in private Chinese companies will report that their business connections are more important to their success than will executives in either state-owned or collective-hybrid companies.*

Using *Guanxi*

If *guanxi* is more important to managers with great need for a substitute for formal structural support, this importance should be reflected in the ways these managers characterize their relationships. In particular, we would expect such a substitution to be reflected in greater reliance on connections as a defense against threats, a greater reliance on connections in government, and reports of deeper and closer connections on the part of private executives. Those who rely on their business connections as a substitute for a stable rule of law would also be expected to see them as primarily defensive. That is, rather than reporting the usefulness of connections in obtaining customers, market information, or securing credit, as managers in stable developed-market economics might, managers in less developed countries may report needing connections to help them face fundamental threats, such as expropriation and extortion (Nee, 1992; Redding, 1990; Yang, 1994).

> *Hypothesis 2: Executives in private Chinese companies are more likely to report that their business connections are useful as a defense against threats than are executives in either state-owned or collective-hybrid companies.*

Further, threats to companies in such societies can come from a misuse of ill-defined power or the absence of governmental protection from extortionists and thieves. In addition, private companies need access to resources controlled by government. Thus, we would expect good connections in government to be of paramount importance to those in societies with a weak rule of law. In China, executives of state-owned and collective-hybrid companies secure their government protection structurally, via government ownership. To substitute for such protection, private-company managers will use personal connections to government officials.

> *Hypothesis 3: Compared to executives in either state-owned or collective-hybrid Chinese companies, executives in private Chinese companies will report more connections with individuals who hold positions in government.*

Finally, we propose that private-company executives will seek to build relationships that are deeper in trust (closer *guanxi*) than those sought by executives with structural protection. Sociologists long have argued that "modern" forms of impersonal bureaucratic organization provide substitutes for the particularistic trust relationships characteristic of premodern societies (Coleman, 1993; Riggs, 1984; Walder, 1986; Weber, 1947; Zucker, 1986). Clear property rights, an independent judiciary, and predictable impersonal enforcement of regulations provide institutional protection that does not depend on the particularistic knowledge of others. People need only assume that others are following the known rules (Coleman, 1993; Weber, 1947; Zucker, 1986). However, without this form of structural protection, business executives must fall back on particularistic relations (Redding, 1990; Zucker, 1986). Because the kind of protection required may involve risks for both parties, risks such as bending or ignoring laws, managers would seek to develop business relationships that are as trustworthy as possible. This depth of relationship should be reflected in reports of greater trust in connections among those who most depend on them for protection.

> *Hypothesis 4: Executives in private Chinese companies will report that their business connections are characterized by more trust than executives in either state-owned or collective-hybrid companies will report as characteristic of their relationships.*

Building *Guanxi*

How can executives build good connections with people who can provide resources and protection? Although many ways of doing this may be possible, in China normative expectations are clear, as they are built on long traditions of *guanxi* (Redding, 1990; Yang, 1994). How is *guanxi* developed in China? Jacobs (1980) suggested that *guanxi* depends primarily on shared identification with family, hometown, region, school, or place of work. The possibilities are varied enough that people motivated to build *guanxi* can find a common basis. This is not to suggest that common background will necessarily lead to good *guanxi* between people. It does imply that individuals who do not share some of these common backgrounds will have less of basis for developing *guanxi* than individuals who do. However, *guanxi* varies in its closeness, and Jacobs argued that it can be made closer either by a social interaction that contributes to positive affect (*ganqing*) or by helping, both of which rely, to some extent, on gift giving as an indication of goodwill and respect:

> If, for example, a township leader wishes to make his *guanxi* with a village leader closer, the township leader will attempt to increase the social interaction between them by inviting the village leader to banquets on such occasions as weddings in the township leader's family and festivals in his home village. Should a wedding occur in the village leader's family, the township leader will be sure to send a wedding gift (1980: 228).

In building *guanxi*, gift giving continues over time. As Alston noted "*Guanxi* ties have to be continuously reinforced" (1989: 28). Two of the most frequently used tactics to enhance *guanxi* in Chinese society are presenting a gift to and holding a banquet for the other party (Hwang, 1987).

Although *guanxi* often involves the exchange of gifts, these gifts are viewed as investments in the relationship. The emphasis in China is on the relationship being built (Hwang, 1987; Yang, 1994). They are not fee-for-service bribes, as they often are in other countries where import licenses or construction contracts have well-known "prices" (cf. Gupta, 1992). This is not to say that straightforward bribery does not occur in China. It does, and participants in such an act may call it *guanxi*, but Chinese society widely scorns such *guanxi* (cf. Yang, 1994). Therefore, given the general expectation in China that gift giving will cultivate connections, we expected private-company executives to invest more in building the quality of their *guanxi* to protect themselves from the risks inherent in China's uncertain legal environment, and their expectations will be reflected in their gift-giving patterns.

> *Hypothesis 5: Executives in private Chinese companies will report giving more nonreciprocated gifts to those with whom they have business connections than executives in either state-owned or collective-hybrid companies.*

Methods

Sample

The sample for this study was composed of managers in various industries from state-owned, collective-hybrid, and private companies in an interior Chinese city with a population of half a million people in late 1992. In China, it is difficult to find executives willing to talk openly about their *guanxi*. To overcome this problem, the first author drew the sample from the business connections of a close relative who is an executive for the state-owned insurance company in that city. Since all businesses in that particular region are required to obtain insurance policies from this insurance company, the manager of the insurance company had close connections with local businesses. The sample included heads and directors of key functional units (operations, finance, and marketing) in financial services, industrial manufacturing, textile manufacturing, transport, retail, and wholesale trade organizations. Only one executive declined to be interviewed. Interviewees were 15 state-owned-company executives, 8 collective-hybrid-company executives, and 9 private-company executives. We selected as wide a variety of industries as possible given the used to have all three types of company ownership possible in China in 1992 represented. We initially identified ownership status and industry using insurance company records and then confirmed them during interviews. We are aware that the demarcation lines between these legal ownership categories in China may, in practice, have become quite murky (for example, an executive of a state-owned company may direct the organization's resources to his private company, or a collective-hybrid may be a convenient legal designation for a privately controlled company). However, although such practices make it more difficult to find the hypothesized effects, they should not confound interpretations of supportive results. The average age of the interviewees was 41.7 years, and their mean tenure with their companies was 7.2 years. Eighty-one percent of the interviewees were men.

Procedures and Measures

Data were collected by means of a structured interview we first developed in English. In line with Brislin's (1986) recommendations, the instrument was translated into Chinese and back-translated into English to ensure accuracy of translation. To ensure use of up-to-date terminology and correct meanings for each item, we conducted two field tests with business students from China. Each interview, which lasted 60 to 90 minutes, started with the following statement: "We are interested in learning how managers develop their businesses and solve problems. In particular, this study focuses on ways managers work with others to get things done. . . . You and your organization will be completely anonymous. We are interested in general trends and will never release any information that could be used to identify you or the organization." Then, descriptive information was obtained about the managers and their companies (e.g., enterprise ownership, age, size). Next, the interviewer told the respondent this: "All managers rely on help from others outside their 'unit.' Managers deal with nonsubordinates, or those they have no hierarchical authority over, in efforts to develop their organizations as well as solve the day-to-day problems. Therefore, for the following questions, please be brutally honest. Your information will be used solely for research. Think of 8 to 10 individuals who are most useful in helping you succeed in this job. Think of those who are useful for day-to-day problems of your current job and those who are helpful to your long-run career success. These individuals are not necessarily the ones you 'like' the most or are close friends with, but those most necessary to your job and career success. Please exclude your direct subordinates from the list." All the interviewers but one identified eight individuals, with one collective-hybrid executive identifying ten. At this point the interviewees were asked to write a nickname for each connection onto a card the size of a business card (to provide anonymity for connections). A series of 27 questions was presented, and for each question the interviewees were asked to assign each of the "relationships" (the 8 or 10 cards in their hands) into the appropriate response category (e.g., 1 = deeply distrust, 5 = trust completely). The questions and response options relevant to this study are reported below.

Interviewees sometimes elaborated on an individual relationship with examples and comments. From the 32 interviews, we obtained data on 258 business connections. Table 1 gives means, standard deviations, and correlations among the studied variables.

The *importance of a connection* was assessed with the question, "How important is the relationship to you?" Executives rated relationships on a range from 1, "not important," to 4, "vitally important."

Whether a connection was a *defense against threats* was assessed by the executives' responses to the following statement: "This relationship is useful as a defense against threats," (1 = strongly disagree, to 5 = strongly agree). Whether a person offered a *government connection* was measured by responses to "What is the primary reason for the person's usefulness?"

Table 1: Means, standard deviations, and correlations among variables[a]

Variables	*Mean*	*s.d.*	*1*	*2*	*3*	*4*	*5*	*6*	*7*
1. Importance of connection	3.34	0.89							
2. Connection defends against threats	4.18	0.92	.51**						
3. Government connection[b]	0.37		.15*	.26**					
4. Trust in connection	3.94	0.86	.35**	.25**	.11				
5. Give connection gifts[c]	0.37		.29**	.19**	.35**	−.00			
6. Organizational age	14.06	12.17	−.13*	−.10	−.17**	−.07	−.00		
7. Organizational size	55.88	83.56	−.04	.11	.04	.07	.04	.28**	
8. State-owned company[d]	0.47		−.18**	−.13*	−.25**	−.12	−.13*	.77**	.21*
9. Collective-hybrid company[d]	0.25		−.11**	−.10	.16**	−.08	.04	−.32**	.07

[a] $N = 258$.
[b] Mean indicates that 37 percent of the relationships were useful for their connections in government.
[c] Mean indicates that 37 percent of the connections received nonreciprocated gifts.
[d] The three types of organizational ownership were dummy-coded, resulting in two variables. State-owned companies are coded as 1 in variable 8, and collectives are coded as 1 in variable 9.
* $p < .05$.
** $p < .01$.

Responses were coded as 1 for "important connections in government" or as 0 for any of the following: "important connections in key companies," "important connections elsewhere in this company," "controls financial resources," "access to customers," "technical or professional knowledge," and "I have to go through this person." *Trust in the connection* was measured by asking, "To what extent do you trust the person?" (1 = deeply distrust, 5 = trust completely). The variable called *give connection gifts* was assessed by the following question: "People in business relationships often give one another gifts. Could you categorize these relationships by the form of gift giving between you and the other?" (1 = give connection nonreciprocated gifts or 0 = do not give connection gifts or give mutual gifts.) Because we were testing the hypothesis that executives in less structurally secure situation would have more need to strengthen their guanxi via giving gifts than those in more structurally secure environments, we focused on nonreciprocated gift giving.

Organizational age and *size*, the control variables, were assessed by asking for descriptive information in the first section of the interview. It is important to note that the organization referred to here is the business unit (e.g., an ink-manufacturing plant), not an entire company.

Validity Issues

Since data were collected by interview, all variables are single-item scales. Therefore, it was not possible to compute interitem reliability coefficients. Nor was it possible to tape interviews about such a delicate subject in a country with little tradition of confidential, disinterested social science research; thus, we could not compute interrater reliability coefficients for these measures. However, since interviewees sorted cards into categories visible to them on the desk, the interviewer was not required to make any assessments or inferences, a circumstance that provides some modest confidence in measure reliability.

As for construct validity, no prior information on the validity of these measures was available since they are new. We derived information on construct validity first through the responses and elaborations of interviewees, which provided a qualitative check on the executives' understanding of questions. We share some interviewee elaborations in the Results section, both to reflect the executives' understanding of the concepts being measured and to provide illustrations of the way business connections operate in China. Second, we sought preliminary support for the construct validity of these measures from confirmation of this study's hypotheses. Nunnally (1967) argued that an important test of measures' construct validity is whether the network of theoretically expected relationships is supported, and therefore, construct validity accrues over time from many studies.

Since each executive reported multiple connections, one potential problem is nonindependence of measures: there may be less variance within than between interviewee responses. We used a within-and-between analysis (WABA) (Dansereau, Alutto, & Yammarino, 1984; Yammarino & Markham, 1992) to test this potential problem. The corrected *F* from the WABA analysis was not significant for any variables. Variance existed both within and between interviewees on each variable, suggesting that it is appropriate to treat each connection as an independent unit. This test also contributed to evidence for the measures' construct validity.

Finally, since managerial level might affect the kinds of connections executives have (we sampled from two levels), we tested for effects of such differences on the study variables for each of the ownership types. Results of *t*-tests indicated no significant differences on any study variable between general managers and functional managers, the two types of interviewees.

Results

To test Hypotheses 1, 2, and 4 and to identify specific differences on each variable across the three different ownership types, we performed oneway analysis of variance using Scheffé's multiple range test for comparing pairwise means. The first hypothesis predicts that executives in private companies will report that their business connections are more important to their success than will executives in either state-owned or collective-hybrid companies, given controls for company age and size. As Table 2 indicates this hypothesis was supported. Private companies in China were more likely to be newer and smaller than the collective-hybrids and state-owned companies,

Table 2: Results of analysis of variance and cell means[a]

Variables	*State-owned company connections*	*Collective-hybrid company connections*	*Private company connections*	*Sum of squares*	df	F	η
Importance of connection[b]	3.17	3.18	3.79	19.59	2	13.63*	.31
Error	(0.96)	(0.91)	(0.50)	181.73	253		
Connection defends against threats	4.05	4.03	4.53	11.99	2	7.03**	.23
Error	(0.99)	(1.02)	(0.67)	218.48	256		
Trust in connection	3.83	3.82	4.23	8.61	2	6.00**	.21
Error	(0.81)	(1.05)	(0.68)	183.53	256		
N	120	66	72				

[a] Numbers in parentheses are standard deviations. For all variables, private-company executives' values are significantly higher than those of state-owned and collective-hybrid executives at $p < .01$.

[b] This was an ANCOVA test with controls for the covariants organizational age and size. However, these covariates were not significant.

* $p < .05$.

** $p < .01$.

with the state-owned companies significantly older than the other two (mean age was 24 years for state-owned vs. 7 years for collective-hybrids and 3 years for private companies, $F = 198.23, p < .01$), and the private companies were significantly smaller (a mean of 16 employees, vs. 75 in state-owned and 66 in collective-hybrid companies; $F = 13.02, p < .01$). Nevertheless, we found that, even after we controlled for the companies' relative youth and small size, executives in private companies apparently did seek to compensate for their relative lack of formal structural support by relying more on their *guanxi*.

Similarly, data reported in Table 2 support Hypothesis 2. Executives in private companies reported significantly more use of their connections to protect against threats than did either collective-hybrid or state-owned company executives.

Logistic regression analysis was used to test Hypotheses 3 and 5 because the dependent variables in these cases were dichotomous (Norusis, 1990). This test partially supports Hypothesis 3. The model chi-square tests the null hypothesis that the coefficients for all of the terms in the current model except the constant would equal zero. This procedure is comparable to the overall *F*-test for regression analysis. In this case, the model chi-square for government connections is 16.34 ($p < .01$), which indicates the main effect in this model is significant. Since there are three categories of independent variables, we used a two-parameter coding in this analysis. When ratings by private executives were compared to those of state and collective executives, the coefficient was 0.99 ($p < .01$). When ratings by collective executives were compared to those of state and private executives, the beta was 4.15, $p < .001$. From the two parameters (two dummy variables for three different ownership structures), it can be seen that managers from privately and collectively owned companies are more likely to have government connections than executives from state-owned companies. The collectively owned companies may need government connections as much as the private companies because many scarce resources are still controlled by the central government, and the local government officials with whom the collectives typically have close ties are not of much help in gaining these critical resources. The following interviewee quotations illustrate how private companies' executives use government connections. The first is from the general manager of a private computer company. "X," his administrative assistant, is the one of a high government official. The general manager hired X in order to strengthen his guanxi with the father.

> My company had bad luck. We were audited for income tax fraud. The Auditing Bureau has Red Eye Disease [jealousy]. Whenever they see a private company making money, they come and find trouble.
>
> The tax auditor just showed up one day and wanted to see company books. There are no standardized rules on how to keep books in China, especially for private companies like ours. If they want to find fault with

> your income tax, they will always find something wrong. If we had been found guilty of tax fraud, we could have faced thousands of yuan in fines and the possible suspension of our business license. All our hard work would have been gone like the wind. Our accountant was very worried. I called my administrative assistant, X, into my office and told him the situation. He smiled and said, "Give me a 2,500 yuan allowance [equivalent to a middle managers' six-month salary] and I will take care of everything." I had no choice. So I said, "I will give you 2,500 yuan, but you will lose your job if you cannot handle this crisis."
>
> By noon, my phone rang. X asked me to go to lunch with the auditors, at the best restaurant in the city. We hired a Mercedes Benz and went to lunch. The auditors kept saying that they only needed a working lunch. I was worried that X had gone overboard, but X was right. After expensive drinks and Peking duck, the head auditor started to praise our accounting system, saying how good and efficient it looked. This lunch lasted three hours and cost plenty, but it saved my company. After lunch the head auditor left me a notice requesting a 2,500 yuan income tax supplement. The reason he had to force us to pay the supplement was that he had to report to his boss on what he accomplished that day. Later on I found out that X's father is a good friend of the head auditor.
>
> There are too many threats for small companies like mine. There are no laws to protect you. The only way we can protect ourselves is through personal connections, trust, and being flexible. I hired X, a high school graduate, with his father's connections in mind. It does not sound right but everyone does it; you have to be open-minded.

Hypothesis 4 states that private-company executives would report closer *guanxi* with their business connections as reflected in executives' reports of greater trust in them. The results in Table 2 show that executives in private companies in fact reported their business relationships as characterized by greater trust than did the executives in state-owned or collective-hybrid companies. The following quotation from the founder and owner of a private textile trading company illuminates how important Chinese private-company executives feel it is to have trustworthy, responsive connections:

> In my mind, all business is connections and trust. That is all it is. No trust, no connections, no business. If you do not have connections to look after you at different levels of government, they can find excuses to suspend your business. The key connections I have are very close relationships. We have a kind of bond among us. As to how I maintain these relationships, I use various ways. I regularly invite people out to dinner, good food. You establish a good relationship, and help comes naturally – sometimes you don't have to ask. Relationships take a long time to build, and you need to maintain them.

Finally, executives in private companies were significantly more likely to report giving their business connections nonreciprocated gifts than were the executives of either state-owned or collective-hybrid companies, supporting

Hypothesis 5. Although the overall model chi-square is only marginally significant ($\chi^2 = 4.673, p < .10$), with logistic regression analysis the two parameters indicate that private-company executives are more likely to engage in gift giving than executives from state-owned companies (private vs. state-owned and collective, $\beta = 0.63, p < .05$; collective vs. state-owned and private, $\beta = 0.45$, n.s.). By their own reports, these private business executives sought to use gift giving to build closer guanxi.

Discussion

In interviews with executives in Chinese state-owned, collective-hybrid, and private companies we found, as expected, that private-company executives in this developing economy sought to compensate for their lack of formal institutional support by cultivating personal connections. Even after controlling for organizational age and size, we found that private-company executives' business connections were more important to them than the connections of collective-hybrid and state-owned company executives were to them. Further, as expected, private-company executives relied significantly more on building connections with government officials to defend themselves against threats like appropriation or extortion. Finally, the private executives made more extensive use of gift giving to build these connections and maintained business connections of greater trust than did executives in the more structurally secure collective-hybrid and state-owned companies. Private-company executives counteracted their formal structural disadvantages by building good *guanxi* with government officials as protection from unstable conditions. Thus, this test provides independent empirical confirmation of observations about the role of particularistic personal relationships as substitutes for formal structural supports in business relationships made by historians and sociologists such as Weber, Redding, Walder, Fallers, and Zucker. Although many have written of the necessity for good *guanxi* when doing business in China, few have placed this business practice into a theoretical context, and we are not aware of any empirical data systemically testing the role of gift giving in Chinese business relations.

Although the cultural role of gift giving has been analyzed extensively by anthropologists (e.g., Bell, 1991; Ekeh, 1974; Malinowski, 1922), not enough attention has been paid to the role of gift giving in business relationships (Bruhn, 1996). We hope this preliminary study of connections and gift giving in one society demonstrates the value of a better understanding of patterns of gift giving for those interested in international management research.

These results also offer potential insights into non-Chinese business settings. They support the idea that the "corruption" often decried by Westerners doing business in many developing and transitional societies (cf. Blunt &

Jones, 1992; *Economist*, 1993a, 1993b; Gupta, 1992) is in part a consequence of weakly institutionalized structural protection for private business. As legal protection for private firms becomes established in China, tracking the changes there may provide a future experimental test of these ideas.

A structural approach to the issue of personal relationships in business has important practical implications. It suggests that forbidding what the West calls bribery in societies in which gift giving is the expected way of building personal relationships would simply drive such actions further underground. If laws and reliable government cannot provide protection to those wishing to conduct business, businesspeople will seek to create their own protection, drawing on the means available to them. The interesting question is the extent to which a "culture of corruption" might be functionally autonomous, perpetuating such forms of gift giving beyond their structural utility. Future research might test these arguments in other developing countries.

Finally, this study opens up a relatively unstudied area of organizational behavior. Heretofore, the study of cross-organizational connections among executives has primarily focused on structural studies of formal interlocks or the "boundary-spanning" of scientists and engineers. As valuable as that work is, we hope this study demonstrates that cross-organizational connections are a fertile source of insights regarding organizations. As reliance on alliances and other forms of network organizations increases, cross-organizational connections also promise to assume increasing importance.

Several limitations of the current research should be acknowledged. First, although the WABA analysis indicated that it was appropriate to treat each connection as an independent unit, it did not remove the potential threat of nonindependence of observations in this study. Second, our use of many single-item measures makes it difficult to tease out the different dimensions of constructs such as trust. Also, the reliability of these single-item measures is unknown. Third, the sample used in this study was not randomized, so caution needs to be taken in generalizing its results.

In conclusion, this is a small, preliminary, empirical study addressing a large issue. Its context is a society undergoing massive economic upheaval, and it relies on single-item measures that are not independent. We hope future research will be able to address these questions in other settings with measures in which we can have more confidence. Nevertheless, these initial data do suggest promising new directions for international management research. They provide a provocative glimpse of the ways in which managers in structurally weak developing and transitional societies may build substitutes for the formal rule-of-law that managers in the developed world can take for granted. Patterns of gift giving, too, may be a rich vehicle for learning about business relations in different institutional contexts and could enlighten researchers as to the potential rewards of studying executives' connections outside their organizations.

References

Aldrich, H., & Auster, E. R. 1986. Even dwarfs started small: Liabilities of age and size and their strategic implications. In B. M. Staw & L. L. Cummings (Eds.), *Research in organizational behavior*, vol. 8: 165–198. Greenwich, CT: JAI Press.

Aldrich, H., & Fiol, C. M. 1992. *Fools rushing in? The institutional context of industry creation.* Working paper, sociology department, University of North Carolina, Chapel Hill, NC.

Alston, J. P. 1989. *Wa, guanxi, and inhwa:* Managerial principles in Japan, China, and Korea. *Business Horizons*, 32(2): 26–31.

Asian Advertising and Marketing. 1989. Graft: An ugly fact of life in China. January 28.

Bell, D. 1991. Modes of exchange: Gift and commodity. *Journal of Socio-Economics*, 20(2): 155–167.

Blunt, P., & Jones, M. L. 1992. *Managing organizations in Africa.* New York: de Gruyter.

Boisot, M. H. 1986. Markets and hierarchies in a cultural perspective. *Organization Studies*, 7: 135–158.

Brislin, R. W. 1986. The wording and translation of research instruments. In W. J. Lonner & J. W. Berry (Eds.), *Field methods in cross-cultural research:* 137–164. Beverly Hills, CA: Sage.

Bruhn, M. 1996. Business gifts: A form of non-verbal and symbolic communication. *European Management Journal*, 14(1): 61–68.

Chen, M., & Pah, W. 1993. *Understanding the process of doing business in China, Taiwan and Hong Kong.* Lewiston, UK: Mellen.

Coleman, J. S. 1993. The rational reconstruction of society. *American Sociological Review*, 58: 1–15.

Crozier, M. 1964. *The bureaucratic phenomenon.* Chicago: University of Chicago Press.

Dansereau, F., Alutto, J. A., & Yammarino, F. J. 1984. *Theory testing in organizational behavior: The varient approach.* Englewood Cliffs, NJ: Prentice-Hall.

Delacroix, J., & Carroll, G. R. 1983. Organizational foundings: An ecological study of the newspaper industries of Argentina and Ireland. *Administrative Science Quaterly*, 28: 274–291.

Economist. 1993a. The road to Ayodha. February 6: 21–23.

Economist. 1993b. Nigeria. August 21: Supplement.

Ekeh, P. P. 1974. *Social exchange theory.* Cambridge, MA: Harvard University Press.

Fallers, L. A. 1965. *Bantu bureaucracy.* Chicago: University of Chicago Press.

Fox, M. 1987. In China, "*guanxi* is everything." *Advertising Age*, November 2: S-12, S-14.

Freeman, J., Carroll, G. R., & Hannan, M. T. 1983. The liabilities of newness: Age dependence in organizational death rates. *American Sociological Review*, 48: 692–710.

Grnaovetter, M. S. 1985. Economic action and social structure: The problem of embeddedness. *American Journal of Sociology*, 91: 481–510.

Gupta, S. B. 1992. *Black income in India.* New Dehli: Sage.

Hall, R. H., & Xu, W. 1990. Run silent, run deep – Cultural influences on organizations in the Far East. *Organization Studies*, 11: 569–576.

Hannan, M. T., & Freeman, J. 1989. *Organizational ecology.* Cambridge, MA. Harvard University Press.

Hwang, K. 1987. Face and favor: The Chinese power game. *American Journal of Sociology*, 92: 944–974.

Jacobs, J. B. 1980. The concept of *guanxi* and local politics in a rural Chinese cultural setting. In S. L. Greenblatt, R. W. Wilson, & A. A. Wilson (Eds.), *Social interaction in Chinese society:* 209–236. New York: Praeger.

Kornai, J. 1989. The Hungarian reform process: Visions, hopes, and reality. *Journal of Economic Literature*, 24: 1687–1737.

Larson, A. 1992. Network dyads in entrepreneurial settings: A study of the governance of enchange relationships. *Administrative Science Quarterly*, 37: 75–104.

Leung, T., & Yeung, L. L. 1995. Negotiation in the People's Republic of China: Results of a survey of small business in Hong Kong. *Journal of Small Business Management*, 33(1): 70–77.

Lockett, M. 1988. Culture and problems of Chinese management. *Organization Studies*, 9: 475–496.

Macaulay, S. 1963. Non-contractural relations in business: A preliminary study. *American Sociological Review*, 28: 55–69.

Malinowski, B. 1922. *The argonauts of the western Pacific.* London: Routledge & Kegan Paul.

Nee, V. 1989. A theory of market transition: From redistribution to markets in state socialism. *American Sociological Review*, 54: 663–681.

Nee, V. 1992. Organizational dynamics of market transition: Hybrid firms, property rights, and mixed economy in China. *Administrative Science Quarterly*, 31: 1–27.

Norusis, M. J. 1990. *SPSS/PC + advanced statistics.* Chicago: SPSS.

Nunnally, J. C. 1967. *Psychometric theory.* New York: McGraw-Hill.

Pfeffer, J. 1992. *Managing power.* Cambridge, MA: Harvard Business School Press.

Powell, W. W. 1990. Neither market nor hierarchy: Network forms of organization. In B. M. Staw & L. L. Cummings (Eds.), *Research in organizational behavior*, vol. 12: 295–336. Greenwich, CT: JAI Press.

Putnam, R. D. 1993. *Making democracy work.* Princeton, NJ: Princeton University Press.

Redding, S. G. 1990. *The spirit of Chinese capitalism.* New York: de Gruyter.

Riggs, F. W. 1964. *Administration in developing countries.* Boston: Houghton Mifflin.

Singh, J. V., Tucker, D. J., & House, R. J. 1986. Organizational legitimacy and the liability of newness. *Administrative Science Quarterly*, 31: 171–193.

Stinchcombe, A. 1965. Organizations and social structure. In J. G. March (Ed.), *Handbook of organizations:* 142–193. Chicago: Rand McNally.

Walder, A. G. 1986. *Communist neo-traditionalism.* Berkeley: University of California Press.

Weber, M. 1947. *The theory of social and economic organization* (A. M. Henderson & T. Parsons, trans. & eds.). New York: Oxford University Press.

Yammarino, F. J., & Markham, S. E. 1992. On the application of within and between analysis: Are absence and affect really group-based phenomena? *Journal of Applied Psychology*, *77*: 168–176.

Yan, A. & Gray, B. 1992. *A bargaining power approach to management control in international joint ventures: A multi-case study of U.S.-Chinese manufacturing joint ventures.* Paper presented at the annual meeting of the Academy of Management, Las Vegas.

Yang, M. M. 1994. *Gifts, favors and banquets: The art of social relationships in China.* Ithaca, NY: Cornell University Press.

Yau, O. H. M. 1988. Chinese cultural values: Their dimensions and marketing implications. *European Journal of Marketing*, 22(5): 44–57.

Zucker, L. 1986. Production of trust: Institutional sources of economic structure. In B. M. Staw & L. L. Cummings (Eds.), *Research in organizational behavior*, vol. 8: 53–101. Greenwich, CT: JAI Press.

11

A Relationship Marketing Approach to *Guanxi*

José Tomás Gómez Arias

Introduction

In recent years there has been a growing interest among both academics and businessmen regarding business practices in Asia, and particularly in China (Björkman and Kock, 1995; Davies *et al.*, 1995; Pluchart, 1996). Four constants have been found that differentiate Asian management from Western management (Cova and Pras, 1995):

(1) The base economic actor is the family rather than the firm.
(2) A long-term time horizon.
(3) A risk reduction approach.
(4) A consensus approach to decision making.

This interest is to a great extent due to the changes in China's position as a market and the difficulties of European and American companies to address it. It has been argued that doing business in China is particularly difficult because of the higher relative importance of personal relationships (*guanxi*), as opposed to the specification and enforcement of contracts in the West (Davies *et al.*, 1995). The establishment of these networks of trust relationships is often a lengthy, complex, time consuming effort (Thorelli, 1990). In this paper we propose a new approach to *guanxi* from a relationship marketing perspective. Relationship marketing has emerged during the last decade as an alternative to exchange as the foundation of the concept of marketing,

Source: *European Journal of Marketing*, 32(1/2) (1998): 145–156.

stressing the importance of managing relationships between buyer and seller in the long term. It sees marketing as relationships, networks and interaction (Gummesson, 1996) and provides an appropriate conceptual framework for the study of *guanxi*. Some authors (Björkman and Kock, 1995), have suggested that *guanxi* represents a traditional form of relationship marketing. We will show that, although there are some relevant connections, relationship marketing refers to a particular way of doing business that includes not only the establishment and management of personal and business relationships (the domain of *guanxi*), but also how the business is defined from a service perspective, and the management of the service delivery process (Grönroos, 1996).

In the first section of this article we introduce the concept of *guanxi* and its most relevant elements. The second section is dedicated to the concept of relationship marketing. The third section explores the commonalities and differences between the different elements of *guanxi* and relationship marketing. In the fourth section, we outline the changes in the economic importance of *guanxi*. Finally, in the last section we offer our conclusions and the implications for management.

The Phenomenon of *Guanxi*

Guanxi is briefly translated as personal connections/relationships on which an individual can draw to secure resources or advantage when doing business as well as in the course of social life (Davies, 1995b), and constitutes an important transaction mode in China (Wu, 1994). Although it refers to the status and intensity of an ongoing relationship between two parties, it has become synonymous with the network of social and business connections necessary to do business in this part of the world. However, its meaning is laden with more powerful implications, some of them deeply rooted in Chinese tradition and culture (Ambler, 1995; Davies *et al.*, 1995):

(1) It includes the notion of continuing reciprocal obligation over an indefinite period of time, involving the fulfilment of specifications of the agreement, and also personal favors and sustaining each other's reputation and social status.
(2) Favors are banked, to be repaid when the time is right, if ever.
(3) It goes beyond the relationship between two parties (Björkman and Kock, 1995), and is extended to include other parties within the social network of the interacting parties (Kirkbride *et al.*, 1991). For instance, if A owes a favor to B, and B owes a favor to C, A can balance his position with a favor to C.
(4) The network of relationships is built among individuals, not among organizations. If an individual moves to a different organization or department, the connections move with him or her.

(5) Therefore, it is essentially a social network built on interactions consisting mainly of social exchanges, but information and business exchanges can also take place. As social networks, *guanxi* networks have two components: the personal network, or contacts and bonds with specific individuals; and the cultural component in which the individual actors are embedded (Björkman and Kock, 1995).
(6) Status matters. Relationships with a senior will extend to his subordinates, but not the reverse. From a network perspective, seniority can be defined as the centrality of the position occupied. A position can be locally central if it has a large number of connections with other positions in its immediate environment, or globally central if it is strategically significant in the overall structure of the network (Mizruchi, 1994; Scott, 1991).
(7) The social relationship is prior to and a prerequisite for the business relationship (Björkman and Kock, 1995).

Guanxi is not unique to China, and is a universal phenomenon (Davies, 1995b). It also pervades the business cultures of Japan, Korea, India, Russia and other managed economies where intimacy with those in authority, be they political, military or bureaucratic, is important (Lehtinen, 1996; Robins, 1996). However, since 1949 in China, in a highly centralized bureaucratic state, the use of personal connections was often the only way to get things done. Even after the recent economic reforms leading to more market openness, access to the Chinese market is conditioned by the reliance on trust relationships rather than on the enforcement of contracts, since commercial law is almost non-existent (Ambler, 1995), and often arbitrarily enforced. Thus, *guanxi* can be described as a result of Chinese culture, institutional weakness and corruption:

(1) As a cultural product, *guanxi* is a third relational way between very close expressive ties within the extended family, wherein relationships are based on need, and very loose instrumental ties with strangers, with transactions based on equity. *Guanxi* ties are of a mixed nature, and controlled by equality. Face and shame, the equilibrium and propriety in personal behavior in the five Confucian directions (with superiors, inferiors, peers, the self and the environment), also play an important role in sustaining these relationships (Hwang, 1987).
(2) With the dismantling of the Chinese legal and judicial system after 1949, and the consequent difficulty to enforce contracts, relations are an economically better mode of governance of transactions than contracts (Davies, 1995b).
(3) In a system with abundant requirements for licenses, permissions and approvals, these become rent yielding assets with loosely defined property rights, thus creating incentives for corrupt behaviors ranging from simple lubrication to subornation of Civil Servants/party officials suppossedly empowered to decide over those rights (Davies, 1995b).

The Concept of Relationship Marketing

During the last decade we have witnessed a paradigm shift in marketing from a transaction approach based upon the concept of exchange (Bagozzi, 1974), to relationship marketing where the focus is to "establish, maintain, and enhance relationships with customers and other partners, at a profit, so that the objectives of the parties involved are met. This is achieved by mutual exchange and fulfilment of promises" (Grönroos, 1990, p. 138).

Origins of Relationship Marketing

This new trend has its origin from the convergence of four different approaches (Grönroos, 1994):

(1) *The interaction and network approach to industrial marketing advocated by the industrial marketing and purchasing (IMP) group.* In a network of buyers and suppliers of industrial products and services, various interactions take place including the flow of goods and services, financial and social exchanges (Johanson and Mattsson, 1985). These interactions may not be necessarily initiated by the seller and may continue for a long period of time. Even more, the positions of buyer and seller may not be clear cut when exchanges of resources flow in both directions. The management of these relationships requires the involvement not only of the marketing department, but of all the employees of the firm, the part-time marketers (Gummesson, 1990). In business-to-business exchanges, the points of contact between organizations also occur in non-marketing functions such as research and development, design, deliveries, customer training, invoicing and credit management.

(2) *The marketing of services.* Researchers from the Nordic School of Services look at the marketing of services as something that cannot be separated from overall management (Grönroos and Gummesson, 1985). The consumer of a service typically interacts with systems, physical resources and employees of the service provider. The consumer is deeply involved in the production of the service – what Langeard and Eiglier (1987) called "servuction". Like in the case of industrial marketing, a long-lasting relationship often develops between the service provider and its customer. The success of this relationship is determined both by the full-time and the part-time marketers.

(3) *The interest in customer relationship economics.* Research results in several industries (Reicheld, 1993; Reicheld and Sasser, 1990) show that other than economies of scale, companies can obtain market economies, achieving better economic results by understanding the customer (Heskett, 1987). A mutually satisfactory continuing relationship makes it possible to reduce transaction costs and quality costs (Grönroos, 1994).

(4) *International marketing.* The transaction approach to marketing is primarily based on the mass marketing of packaged consumer goods in the USA. However, when we move those concepts to overseas markets we find they may not be applicable under a different culture, tradition, economic structure, legal system or institutional setting (Gummesson, 1996). Research from scholars in Europe and other parts of the world suggests that a relational approach to marketing is better suited to the cultural, economic and institutional characteristics of most countries.

Shift in Marketing Axioms

Behind the development of relationship marketing there is a shift in two basic axioms of marketing (Sheth and Parvatiyar, 1995a):

(1) *From competition and conflict to mutual cooperation.* In transactional marketing, value creation is driven by competition and self-interest. This competition happens at the dyad level – the relationship between a customer and a supplier; at the triad level – the relationship among the customer, its present supplier and its competitors; and at the network of physical distribution level (Gummesson, 1996). At the three levels, exchange is assumed to be a zero sum game, and therefore gains are obtained at the expense of other actors in the exchange relationship. Proponents of relationship marketing believe that under some circumstances cooperation leads to higher value creation.

(2) *From choice independence to mutual interdependence.* While transactions marketing is based on the belief that efficiency in the creation and distribution of value is achieved only if marketing actors keep their freedom to choose their transactional partner at each decision point, it has been shown that transaction costs and quality costs can be reduced through interdependence and partnering (Williamson, 1975).

Promises and Trust

There are two essential elements in relationship marketing: promise and trust (Grönroos, 1994). These two elements determine how a relationship is established, maintained and enhanced:

(1) A firm may attract customers by giving promises, thus persuading them to behave in some desired way. These promises may be explicit or implicit in the image of a brand. A new customer may be attracted and a new relationship built. Long-term profitability requires that the relationship be maintained and enhanced in order to retain the customer base. The fulfilment of the promises given is essential to achieving customer satisfaction.

(2) Trust has been defined as "a willingness to rely on an exchange partner in whom one has confidence" (Moorman *et al.*, 1993, p. 3). This definition implies: belief that the other partner will follow the desired course of action; intention to behave and commit its resources according to that belief; uncertainty, since the trustor cannot control the trustee's behavior; and vulnerability to the consequences of the actions of the trustee. As Grönroos (1994) points out, in many situations it is not clear who is the trustee and who is the trustor; more likely, both parties are in both positions. It is important to remark that trust requires personal relationships that transcend the individual contact, and is reinforced by face-to-face relationships (Malecki and Tootle, 1996).

Strategic and Tactical Issues

Adopting a relationship marketing approach involves changing the traditional way of managing marketing at the strategic and tactical level. We can distinguish three important strategic issues in the relationship marketing approach (Grönroos, 1996):

(1) Redefining the business as a service business, and the key competitive element as service competition.
(2) Looking at the organization from a process management perspective, and not from a functional perspective.
(3) Establishing partnerships and a network to be able to handle the whole service process.

At the tactical level there are three typical elements (Grönroos, 1996):

(1) Seeking direct contact with customers and other stakeholders.
(2) Building a database covering necessary information about customers and others.
(3) Developing a customer-oriented service system.

The Elements of *Guanxi* in the Light of Relationship Marketing

Social and Business Relationships

Relationship marketing stresses the building and management of relationships in a social context (Grönroos, 1994). It means a change in focus from products and firms as units of analysis to people and organizations (Webster, 1992). However, the fundamental object is the business interaction among the actors, while the social processes appear as a consequence of ongoing business relationships. Here lies an essential difference with *guanxi*, which is a network of social relationships (Ambler, 1995; Björkman and Kock, 1995; Davies *et al.*, 1995) often related to a common background such as having studied together, coming from the same part of China, having worked together or having family ties, but sometimes deliberately built via visits, gifts, giving face, or the use of an intermediary of high status (Björkman and Kock, 1995). Hence, we have two different directions of causality. Ongoing business relationships are the cause of social processes from a relationship marketing perspective. In *guanxi* networks, the social relationship is a prerequisite to get involved in a business relationship. However, this direction of causality is not exclusive to doing business in China. Initial contacts from social networks evolve into business-focused networks, and then into strategic networks (Malecki and Tootle, 1996) in both Western and Far Eastern countries.

From a relationship marketing perspective, relationships are not only created by people in organizations, but also by symbols, images and brands (Gummesson, 1996). However, a *guanxi* perspective is limited to social relationships which cannot be embedded in a brand name because of their personal nature. It may be argued that family names act as brand names in this context. However, they do not possess an independent personality distinguishable from the personality of the members of the family, as product and service brands do.

The Relevance of Promises and Trust

Both in the concept and practice of relationship marketing and in the traditional Chinese business and social networks, we find that the exchange and fulfilment of promises, and the development of trust are of central importance. However, the content of those promises, the timeframe over which they must be fulfilled, and the importance of trust development differ significantly:

(1) The promises exchanged in a marketing relationship are of an economic nature concerning goods, services, systems of goods and services, financial solutions, material administration, transfer of information, social contacts and a number of future commitments (Grönroos, 1991). As such, it is possible (albeit often difficult) to measure customers' expectations and levels of satisfaction for most of the promises given. Since *guanxi* networks are of a fundamentally social nature, promises are often implicit and go beyond their economic content to include reciprocal personal favors and mutual protection and enhancement of reputation and social status.

(2) Marketing promises usually have a well defined deadline when they must be fulfilled. They are certainly meant to extend profitably over a long period of time, but the relationship is evaluated over discrete periods.

On the other hand, in a *guanxi* network favors are banked and create an obligation (promise) of reciprocity. Although obligations are recognized by both parties, the relationship may never become balanced.

(3) The relatively higher importance of trust in *guanxi* networks is due to structural and cultural reasons:
- Chinese culture, as in other Asian cultures, is based on cooperation rather than competition. Trust is not only a supplement to contractual arrangements, but also often substitutes them as the preferred form of governance of business exchanges (Ambler, 1995; Palmer, 1995; Thorelli, 1990). In Confucian terms, the "rule of man" prevails over the "rule of law" (Jacobs *et al.*, 1995). Breach of trust encompasses a social sanction that goes beyond damaging the two-party relationship and extends to the relationships, both personal and business, with the whole network. Once a relation has been established it can hardly be broken, but once a relation has been broken it is very difficult to re-establish (Yau, 1988).
- Commercial law in China has traditionally been non-existent (Ambler, 1995), partly because of the traditional Chinese preference for uncodified and undiffused information (Boisot and Child, 1988). Under these conditions, the legal and judicial system cannot be relied upon for the enforcement of business deals. Furthermore, people and organizations in charge of enforcing regulations and deals are often a party in those deals. Therefore, the reputation and trust of the parties involved and their business and personal connections are far more important when engaging in a business relationship and managing its development than the reliance on a legally or contractually defined set of rules and an external referee.
- China is a very interventionist bureaucratic state where administrative processes are ill-defined and decision authority is spread across a number of overlapping central, provincial and local government bodies, party officials and the army. Often, the only way to get things done within a reasonable time frame is to bypass the formal system of official licenses and approvals. These relations may involve elements which are illegal to some extent. Therefore, it is essential to develop mutual trust prior to any business or information exchange (Björkman and Kock, 1995).

Network Integration

There is a strategic rationale for building business networks under a relationship marketing approach. It involves redefining the business as a provider of services or solutions for the customer, and rethinking the whole process of delivering the service from an integrated process management perspective.

Partnerships and business networks are necessary in order to manage the whole service process.

Guanxi networks, in contrast, have a more limited role. They are a source of particularly scarce resources in the Chinese market, with a particular emphasis on information on market trends, government policies, regulations and business opportunities, and licenses and approvals (Davies *et al.*, 1995), but also basic commodities, energy, skilled labor, and other inputs typically in short supply in planned economies.

The Case of Consumer Product Markets

Although the application and study of relationship marketing in consumer product markets is in a nascent stage, Sheth and Parvatiyar (1995b) find that there are both personal motivations, sociological reasons and institutional bases for the consumers to engage in relational market behavior. However, we found no mention of the use or relevance of *guanxi* networks in the marketing of consumer products. Yan (1994) points out that Chinese buyers are brand conscious and brand loyal, and reluctant to pioneer new brands. However, once their neighbors have tried the product they follow suit promptly, perhaps because the cohesiveness of the Chinese society. This indicates that there are sociological reasons to believe that social networks are also relevant in the marketing of consumer products and services (Yau, 1988).

Trends in the Economic Importance *Guanxi*

From a strategic point of view, it is interesting to question what will be the importance of *guanxi* for marketers in the future. While the cultural bases of *guanxi* can be expected to change slowly as the experience in advanced Chinese societies like Hong Kong and Taiwan shows (Yau, 1988), we have detected some trends indicating important changes that will erode the structural foundations of *guanxi* and its relevance in doing business in China.

The Economic Liberalization of China

As China moves towards a market economy, the level of government intervention and the importance in GDP terms of large state-owned companies is expected to decrease even more, while the importance of collective and other forms of companies will keep growing (Davies, 1995a). Thus, there will be a reduced need of connections within the party-government-industry system to gain access to licenses and approvals on one hand, and resources such as supplies and energy on the other, since more and more areas will be subject to market (or *quasi*-market) mechanisms (Deng and Dart, 1995). Of particular importance will be the (expected) liberalization of the market for information, one of the basic commodities flowing through *guanxi* networks.

Changes in the Civil Service

Since 1993, there are changes under way in the Chinese Civil Service with three basic goals: scientific management of state Civil Servants; excellence, by means of an objective merit-based system; and honesty of Civil Servants (Aufrecht, 1995). Although the new system will not be fully in place until several years have passed, it implies a stricter separation of political and administrative power, and therefore reduces the possibility of discretionary decisions.

The Rule of Law

Partly due to the pressures of Western countries and international institutions like the World Trade Organization, and also because of the requirements of a growing, dynamic and increasingly open and sophisticated economy, China is developing a Western-style system of commercial law and independent judiciary. This is a substantial change from traditional decision making based on interpretations of Confucian philosophy and, more recently, Marxist philosophy, to a strict rule of law. Therefore, we can expect a change in the traditional rule of man towards a greater influence of the rule of law.

The New Chinese Managers

A new breed of managers is joining the Chinese companies. The emergence of Western-style managers with MBAs, increased job hopping, more discretionary spending, and time available for family and leisure activities away from the company limits the extension and depth of their social networks within the company (Ambler, 1995). This increasingly numerous sort of managers is more prone to rely on hard data than on social relationships.

Conclusions

We have shown that there are some important commonalities between *guanxi* as a typical way of doing business in China, and relationship marketing. Both of them have to do with managing relationships, networks and interactions. However, identifying *guanxi* with relationship marketing would be misleading. *Guanxi* is essentially a cultural construct with a particular value in doing business in China under its present structural, legal, institutional, political and economic conditions. These conditions are changing and are expected to change even further in the future. By contrast, relationship marketing involves a thorough strategic reconsideration of the business as a service business from a process management perspective. The establishment and management of networks (business and personal) is a means to delivering a whole solution to the customer by pulling resources from a variety of actors.

The basic managerial implications of these distinctions are twofold:

(1) Having the right personal connections is useful to open the right doors, in China as elsewhere. However, the management of personal connections must be a coherent part of the customer-oriented service delivery process to be successful in the long term.
(2) *Guanxi* as a social construct can be expected to last, but the economic and structural conditions that make it particularly relevant in doing business in China are changing. In particular, legal changes are making it more difficult (not to say illegal) to "pull *guanxi*" to obtain access to certain controlled resources as more and more of them are becoming subject to market forces.

In short, the evolution of the Chinese market is bringing about the need for a relationship marketing approach to serve more sophisticated consumers who demands better products and services. Understanding the role *guanxi* plays in Chinese society and business is part of the process of learning about the Chinese market that Western (and Asian) companies must follow. It is expected to lose its role as a means to obtaining rent yielding assets while retaining its importance in facilitating and smoothing business transactions.

References

Ambler, T. (1995), "Reflections in China: re-orientating images of marketing", *Marketing Management*, Vol. 4 No. 1, pp. 22–30.

Aufrecht, S.E. (1995), "Reform with Chinese characteristics: the context of Chinese Civil Service reform", *Public Administration_Review*, Vol. 55 No. 2, pp. 175–82.

Bagozzi, R.P. (1974), "Marketing as an organized behavioral system of exchanges", *Journal of Marketing*, Vol. 38, October, pp. 77–81.

Björkman, I. and Kock, S. (1995), "Social relationships and business networks: the case of western companies in China", *International Business Review*, Vol. 4 No. 4, pp. 519–35.

Boisot, M. and Child, J. (1988), "The iron law of fiefs: bureaucracy failure and the problem of governance in the Chinese systems reforms", *Administrative Science Quarterly*, Vol. 33, pp. 507–27.

Cova, B. and Pras, B. (1995), "Que peut-on apprendre du management asiatique?", *Revue Française de Gestion*, Vol. 103, March-April-May, pp. 20–32.

Davies, H. (1995a), "The nature of the firm in China", in Davies, H. (Ed.), *China Business: Context and Issues*, Longman, Hong Kong, pp. 135–54.

Davies, H. (1995b), "Interpreting *guanxi*: the role of personal connections in a high context transitional economy", in Davies, H. (Ed.), *China Business: Context and Issues*, Longman, Hong Kong, pp. 155–69.

Davies, H., Leung, T.K.P., Luk, S.T.K. and Wong, Y.H. (1995), "The benefits of "guanxi". The value of relationships in developing the Chinese market", *Industrial Marketing Management*, Vol. 24, pp. 207–14.

Deng, S. and Dart, J. (1995), "The impact of economic liberalization on marketing practices in the People's Republic of China", *European Journal of Marketing*, Vol. 29 No. 2, pp. 6–22.

Grönroos, C. (1990), "Relationship approach to the marketing function in service contexts: the marketing and organizational behavior interface", *Journal of Business Research*, Vol. 20 No.1, pp. 3–11.

Grönroos, C. (1991), "The marketing strategy continuum: towards a marketing concept for the 1990s", *Management Decision*, Vol. 29 No.1, pp. 7–13.

Grönroos, C. (1994), "From marketing mix to relationship marketing: towards a paradigm shift in marketing", *Management Decision*, Vol. 32 No. 2, pp. 4–20.

Grönroos, C. (1996), "Relationship marketing: strategic and tactical implications", *Management Decision*, Vol. 34 No. 3, pp. 5–14.

Grönroos, C. and Gummesson, E. (1985), "The Nordic School of Service marketing", in Grönroos, C. and Gummesson, E. (Eds), *Service Marketing – Nordic School Perspectives*, Stockholm University.

Gummesson, E. (1990), *The Part-time Marketer*, Center for Service Research, Karlstad.

Gummesson, E. (1996), "Broadening and specifying relationship marketing", *Asia-Australia Marketing Journal*, Vol. 2 No. 1, pp. 31–43.

Heskett, J.L. (1987), "Lessons in the service sector", *Harvard_Business_Review*, Vol. 65, March-April, pp. 118–26.

Hwang, K.K. (1987), "Face and favour: the Chinese power game", *American Journal of Sociology*, Vol. 92 No. 4, pp. 944–74.

Jacobs, L., Guopei, G. and Herbig, P. (1995), "Confucian roots in China: a force for today's business", *Management Decision*, Vol. 33 No. 10, pp. 29–34.

Johanson, J. and Mattsson, L.G. (1985), "Marketing investments and market investments in industrial networks", *International Journal of Research in Marketing*, Vol. 4, pp. 185–95.

Kirkbride, P.S., Tang, S.F.Y. and Westwood, R.I. (1991), "Chinese conflict preferences and negotiating behaviour: cultural and psychological influences", *Organization Studies*, Vol. 12 No. 3, pp. 365–86.

Langeard, E. and Eiglier, P. (1987), *Servuction. Le Marketing des Services*, Wiley, Paris.

Lehtinen, U. (1996), "Relationship marketing approaches in changing Russian markets", *Journal of East-West Business*, Vol. 1 No. 4, pp. 35–49.

Malecki, E.J. and Tootle, D.M. (1996), "The role of networks in small business competitiveness", *International Journal of Technology Management*, Vol. 11 No. 1/2, pp. 43–57.

Mizruchi, M.S. (1994), "Social network analysis: recent achievements and current controversies", *Acta Sociologica*, Vol. 37, pp. 329–43.

Moorman, C., Deshpandé, R. and Zaltman, G. (1993), "Relationships between providers and users of market research: the role of personal trust", Working Paper No. 93–111, Marketing Science Institute.

Palmer, A.J. (1995), "Relationship marketing: local implementation of a universal concept", *International Business Review*, Vol. 4 No. 4, pp. 471–81.

Pluchart, J.-J. (1996), "Négociation: leçons chinoises", *Revue Française de Gestion*, Vol. 104, March–April–May, pp. 5–11.

Reicheld, F.E. (1993), "Loyalty-based management", *Harvard Business Review*, Vol. 71, March–April, pp. 64–73.

Reicheld, F.E. and Sasser, W.E. Jr (1990), "Zero defections: quality comes to service", *Harvard Business Review*, Vol. 68, September-October, pp. 105–11.

Robins, F. (1996), "Marketing in a 'managed' economy", *Marketing Intelligence & Planning*, Vol. 14 No. 3, pp. 45–56.

Scott, J. (1991), *Social Network Analysis – A Handbook*, Sage, London.

Sheth, J.N. and Parvatiyar, N. (1995a), "The evolution of relationship marketing", *International Business Review*, Vol. 4 No. 4, pp. 397–418.

Sheth, J.N. and Parvatiyar, N. (1995b), "Relationship marketing in consumer markets: antecedents and consequences", *Journal of the Academy of Marketing Science*, Vol. 23 No. 4, pp. 255–71.

Thorelli, H.B. (1990), "Networks: the gay nineties in industrial marketing", in Thorelli, H.B. and Cavusgil, S.T. (Eds), *International Marketing Strategy*, Pergamon, Oxford.

Webster, F.E. (1992), "The changing role of marketing in the corporation", *Journal of Marketing*, Vol. 56, October, pp. 1–17.

Williamson, O.E. (1975), *Markets and Hierarchies: Analysis and Antitrust Implications*, The Free Press, New York, NY.

Wu, W.P. (1994), "*Guanxi* and its managerial implications for Western companies in China – a case study", paper presented at the International Conference on Management Issues for China in the 1990s, University of Cambridge, 23–25 March.

Yan, R. (1994), "To reach China's consumers, adapt to Guo Qing", *Harvard Business Review*, Vol. 72, September-October, pp. 66–74.

Yau, O. (1988), "Chinese cultural values: their dimensions and marketing implications", *European Journal of Marketing*, Vol. 22 No. 5, pp. 44–57.

12

Does Culture Matter? A Cross-Cultural Study of Executives' Choice, Decisiveness, and Risk Adjustment in International Marketing

David K. Tse, Kam-hon Lee, Ilan Vertinsky and Donald A. Wehrung

An understanding of how cultural differences affect international marketing decisions is important to a firm's external operation. It can be used to predict strategic moves and responses of competitors and hence to design effective competitive strategies. This understanding is also salient to international sales negotiations (e.g., Pye 1983).

In addition, a knowledge of the impact of culture on marketing decisions is important to the internal conduct of multinational firms. Internal coordination in these firms requires well-orchestrated responses from executives with different cultural backgrounds. Even in organizations with elaborate standard operating procedures, the interpretation of environmental cues may vary among executives from different nations as a result of their cultural differences. A knowledge of cultural influences enables the firms to accommodate and adapt to such differences, hence reducing "noisy" communications among executives and errors in decision making (Montgomery and Weinberg 1979). In the past multinational firms were dominated by "Western managerial culture." Recent trends in international trade and foreign direct investment have increased significantly the global role of Asian multinational firms and North American subsidiaries operating in Asia, thus

Source: *Journal of Marketing*, 52(4) (1988): 81–95.

increasing the salience of understanding cultural impact on a firm's internal operations.

We describe a study of the effects of a manager's home culture on the marketing decisions of Chinese and Western (Canadian) executives. The study also provides some preliminary indications of whether cultural effects on marketing decisions diminish as a consequence of intercultural exposure, interdependence, and learning. To accomplish this, two populations of Chinese executives, one from the People's Republic of China (PRC) and the other from Hong Kong were studied. PRC business executives have been relatively isolated from contacts with international markets for many years. Hence, cultural effects on their marketing decision processes, if present, would represent a relatively pure form of cultural influence on business behavior. The Chinese executives in Hong Kong represent an Oriental business community with intense and continuous interactions with the Western business world. If globalization of markets has eroded the impact of ethnicity on marketing decision making, one would expect Hong Kong executives to behave similarly to North American executives. The Canadian executives, whose decision processes in risky situations have been found to be similar to those of U.S. executives (MacCrimmon and Wehrung 1986), represent the Western managerial culture.

The executives were asked to respond to four hypothetical marketing situations. An "in-basket" format (Frederiksen, Saunders, and Wand 1957; Gill 1979) was selected to investigate the impact of culture on executives' decision making because of its realism and its rich context (see Appendices A through D). In comparison with conventional tools for studying executives' decisions, such as belief statements, this approach provides more relevant decision variables to the respondents. In addition, because executives representing different cultural backgrounds and organizations are responding to some common decision situations, their behavior can be compared. In the past researchers have used the technique to study executive decisions toward trade unions and customer threats (e.g., MacCrimmon and Wehrung 1986).

In the four hypothetical marketing situations, the outcome variables of prime concern were (1) choice, (2) decisiveness, and (3) adjustment of the decision environment. The decisions involve elimination of a current product line, mode of entry into a new market, new product design, and response to a malfunctioning product. The cultural traits addressed include some of those commonly cited in the literature as distinguishing Western from Chinese managers, in particular (1) individual face saving (Lee 1982; Redding 1982), (2) repayment of "dues" and attitude toward competition (Meade and Barnard 1973; Redding 1982; Tung 1981), (3) participation in decision process (Cascio 1974; Han 1983; Meade 1969; Tung 1981), (4) pan-ethical orientation to problems (Ch'ien 1973; Yin 1976), (5) quest for harmony, and (6) fatalistic views (Chan 1967).

Culture and Decision Making

Some recent studies reported in the marketing literature have confirmed the importance and dynamics of cultural influence on consumer behavior (e.g., Erickson, Johansson, and Chao 1984; Tse, Belk, and Zhan 1988). Other studies such as the work of Wallendorf and Reilly (1983) have focused specifically on ethnic differences. Studies using Singaporean subjects found that traditional Chinese values were fading slowly because of Western influences (e.g., McCullough, Tan, and Wong 1986; Tan and Farley 1987). We examine how home cultural values affect managerial decisions in risky situations.

Hofstede (1980, p. 19) defined culture as "... the interactive aggregate of common characteristics that influence a group's response to its environment." Culture may be reflected in general tendencies of persistent preference for particular states of affairs over others, persistent preferences for specific social processes over others, and general rules for selective attention, interpretation of environmental cues, and responses. It is generally known that culture may provide detailed prescriptions (norms) for specific classes of situations while leaving other domains relatively unregulated. National and ethnic cultures are thus distinguished in their degree of regulation of behavior, attitudes, and values, the domain of regulation, and the consistency and clarity of regulation and tolerance of other cultures.

Comparative studies of Chinese and North American cultures have underscored several distinctive general norms that are dominant in one culture and absent in the other. Hence it is possible to find distinctions among societies having the same ethnic but different national cultures, such as those in the PRC and Hong Kong.

The prime distinction between Chinese and North American cultures appears to be the collective orientation of the former and the individualistic orientation of the latter (see e.g. Chan 1986; Ch'ien 1973; Moore 1967; Yin 1976). A collective orientation implies (1) an emphasis on diffused relationships, that is, relationships not limited to a particular domain or function, (2) a pan-ethical approach to action, emphasizing social objectives in decisions, (3) an intergenerational time perspective that considers the rights of both current and future generations, and (4) an emphasis on collective harmony and discipline. In contrast, an individualistic orientation implies (1) the specific or functional definition of relationships, (2) a utilitarian concept of problem solving, (3) a shorter time perspective, and (4) an emphasis on freedom of choice and competition. A collective orientation also implies a tendency to submit to one's individual fate – fatalism (Chan 1967) – whereas the individualistic orientation, in the quest for freedom, implies a desire to seek control over one's fate.

Specific norms have been proposed in the literature as dominant in one culture and absent in the other. Four such norms that are relevant to the decision situations are discussed next.

Face Saving

"Face" refers to the respect, pride, and dignity of an individual as a consequence of his or her position in society. This principle influences many facets of Chinese life and is regarded as a means for fostering harmony (Moore 1967). The norm regulates responsibilities and interpersonal relationships in the family and society. It prescribes that the dignity of the individual, even in trivial matters, must be defended and respected (Chan 1967). This responsibility for the preservation of dignity ensures the maintenance of hierarchies and elucidates the responsibilities of persons within the hierarchy. To a large extent this norm is similar to the notion of shame in Japanese culture.

In a marketing context, a product represents part of the person who initiated it. Hence the initiator is psychologically tied to the product and any criticism of the product would mean damage to his or her "face." It is reasonable, therefore, to expect Chinese executives to be more inclined to persist in investing in their products even if weakness is demonstrated. Studies of how Japanese managers react to product failures have found this characteristic in Japan (Johansson 1986).

Repayment of "Dues" and Attitude toward Competition

Exchange relationships are present in both cultures. In Western culture they are based on principles of balance, clearance, and specific relationships. In Chinese culture exchanges create long-term moral obligations. This intricate system of long-term moral obligations of repayment, without explicit rules for termination of the obligations, buttresses collective survival and increases harmony.

In the marketing context, the Chinese system may place limits on destructive competition and may induce certain market imperfections. For example, some preferential treatment may be given to the "insiders" and barriers may be erected against the "outsiders."

Participation in Decision Making and the Significance of Consensus

Closely related to the Chinese face-saving norm is subordinates' lack of involvement in key decisions. Within the Chinese value system a subordinate is expected to obey, sometimes without question. A leader is consistently regarded as the most intelligent member of the group (Wu 1967). Consequently a question – or worse, a difference of opinion – may bring about loss of face of superiors. Authoritarian behavior by superiors and passive obedience by subordinates are expected. In contrast, consensus and participation in key decisions are valued in most Western cultures. They are also important elements of the Japanese system through the *ringi* (Cascio 1974).

In the marketing context, this tighter coordination is important to both the effectiveness of the marketing department and its contribution to the firm. It may lead to a quicker product development process and more effective brand management.

Pan-Ethical versus Utilitarian Approach to Problems

The key paradigm guiding behavior in the West is utilitarianism. In an extreme form, utilitarianism encourages a cost-benefit approach to the decision by the decision maker based on his or her own preferences. The alternatives are assessed from an individual's perspective rather than from a societal point of view. This approach tends to shorten the time horizon considered and increase the time discount rate. Ethical obligations are sometimes viewed more as social costs and constraints to be satisfied than as objectives to be fulfilled. In contrast, Confucian teachings emphasize moral ideals and place the virtue of social justice above any considerations of utility (Wu 1967, p. 223). This virtue is also emphasized in PRC's organizational guidelines (Tung 1981).

In the marketing context, the pan-ethical approach implies a concern for consumers that exceeds the usual rational considerations of costs and benefits (the basic decision criterion of the utilitarian approach). It may mean that a "moral" product warranty is stronger than either legal obligations or requirements for maintaining the firm's reputation.

Effects of Cultural Norms

The prime question we address is to what extent these cultural characteristics are reflected in the marketing decision process. The "ideal" business decision model in Western culture presumes rationality – a choice among feasible alternatives so as to maximize the decision maker's utility. In a risky situation the choice must reflect the risk-taking tendency of the decision maker, that is, the tradeoff between risks and returns.

Culture may affect the validity of such a model as a prescription for behavior in several ways.

1. Cultural norms may influence problem definitions. What appears in the functional orientation to be a generic marketing problem may be interpreted as another type of problem because of the presence of features that trigger distinct cultural interpretations.
2. Cultural norms may affect problem definition by providing standard operating procedures and programs for processing information. Thus, for example, some cultures promote the absorption of uncertainty by encouraging a "black and white" external description of uncertain situations.

3. Cultural norms that regulate control beliefs may influence the generation of alternatives before and after a choice.
4. Some cultures may encourage individuals to take strong positions on alternatives whereas other cultures may value caution and ambiguity in positions.
5. Some cultures emphasize the processes of decision making (e.g., obtaining a consensus) more than the quality of the decisions reached.
6. A culture may affect business decisions by generally influencing risk-taking patterns (e.g., promoting caution and discouraging gambling) or prescribing a pattern of tradeoffs between risk and return.
7. A culture also may prescribe patterns of reward and punishment that affect what executives do to make the decision situation more favorable (i.e., risk adjustment) before and after the choice is made. Thus, if the Chinese culture tightly regulates how Chinese executives make decisions in the international marketing domain, a diffused orientation would imply susceptibility of problem definitions to concerns outside the scope of "risks and returns." Face saving may dominate functional organizational objectives related to risks and returns in certain decision situations. Fatalism may reduce willingness to generate alternatives and other risk-adjustment activities of Chinese executives in comparison with North Americans. A quest for harmony may decrease decisiveness among Chinese executives (i.e., strength of preference between alternatives).

Hypotheses

The basic hypothesis of this study is that general cultural differences significantly affect marketing decision making. We expect to find differences between PRC and Canadian executives in (1) choice, (2) decisiveness, and (3) adjustment of decision environment – the dependent variables investigated. A corollary to this hypothesis is that, as international contacts intensify (as in the case of Hong Kong executives), the influence of ethnic culture diminishes. Hence we hypothesize that the behavior of Hong Kong executives will be between that of PRC and that of Canadian executives. This hypothesis and the others discussed in this section are summarized in Table 1.

On the basis of the cultural effects discussed in the preceding section, we hypothesized that the choices adopted by Canadian and PRC executives would differ in several ways. In comparison with Canadian executives, PRC executives would choose decision alternatives involving (1) greater face saving, (2) longer term repayment of obligations, (3) more authoritarian and less consensual decision processes, and (4) greater focus on a pan-ethical viewpoint. This hypothesis (H_1) was examined in four decision situations designed to allow cultural effects to influence the decision options under consideration, as described in the next section.

Table 1: List of hypotheses[a]

Decision situations and other dependent variables	*Cultural norm investigated*	*Hypothesis*
H_{1a}: Eliminating an unprofitable product line	Face saving	PRC executives: Continue HK executives: Between CND executives: Eliminate
H_{1b}: Joint venture with competitor who is in trouble	Repayment of "dues"	PRC executives: Joint venture HK executives: Between CND executives: Enter alone
H_{1c}: Adoption of a new design without subordinates' consensus	Leader authority	PRC executives: New design HK executives: Between CND executives: Standard design
H_{1d}: Recall malfunctioning product	Pan-ethical view	PRC executives: Recall product HK executives: Between CND executives: Send reminder
H_2: Decisiveness	Harmony	PRC executives: Least decisive HK executives: Between CND executives: Most decisive
H_3: Willingness to adopt risk-adjustment strategies	Fatalism or control of the environment	PRC executives: Least willing HK executives: Between CND executives: Most willing
(a) Willingness to control decision environment		PRC executives: Least preferred among all adjustment strategies CND executives: Most preferred among all adjustment strategies
(b) Willingness to consult superiors		PRC executives: Most preferred among all adjustment strategies

[a]PRC denotes People's Republic of China, HK denotes Hong Kong, and CND denotes Canadian.

Most marketing decisions involve a choice among alternatives. An individual executive may (1) choose among the alternatives presented or (2) engage in what MacCrimmon and Wehrung (1986) call "risk adjustment" before making a choice. If one of the alternatives is clearly superior to other alternatives, the decision maker is likely to have a stronger preference for that decision. Similarly, in screening the options, a decision maker may find alternatives that can be rejected with strong confidence. The degree of conviction held for a particular alternative or, as Wehrung et al. (1988) termed it, "decisiveness," could be a function of the choice situation (e.g., its riskiness) or the culture of which the individual is a member.

The literature on decision making of PRC executives emphasizes their slowness in reaching a decision (Hendry 1986; Pye 1983), which could be explained as a result of either the executives' indecisiveness or the necessity of deferring the decision to consult with superiors (one of our subsequent hypotheses). We chose to hypothesize that culture affects the executive's individual decisiveness (H_2) and that PRC executives would be less decisive than the Canadians.[1] As a corollary to this hypothesis and as a test of the presence of globalization effects of decisiveness, we expected Hong Kong executives to be similar in their responses to the Canadians (this corollary is general to all our hypotheses about cultural differences and is not repeated).

Managers frequently try to modify the situations they face to make them more favorable as part of their decision process. Four important types of adjustment identified by MacCrimmon and Wehrung (1986) are (1) gaining control of the environment, (2) gaining information, (3) gaining time, and (4) reducing one's personal exposure to risk. Chinese, like other Orientals, tend to accept their environments rather than seeking to change them (Chan 1967; Moore 1967). They seek to fit or harmonize with the environment. In contrast, Western cultures reject fatalistic perceptions, encouraging executives to seek means for controlling their environment. These control beliefs are part of the North American myth about the unlimited possibilities open to each individual.

Thus we hypothesized that PRC executives would be less inclined than Canadians to engage in risk-adjustment strategies (H_3). Among the four adjustment strategies, the PRC executives would avoid the use of risk-adjustment strategies to increase control over the decision environment, gather information, or develop alternative courses of action (H_{3a}). They would be most likely to reduce both their personal and the firm's exposure to risk by consulting superiors (H_{3b}).

Research Design

We used three subject groups (i.e., executives from three cultures) and four international marketing decisions as repeated measures. Two independent variables – country (i.e., manager's home culture) and situation (i.e., type of international marketing decisions) – were investigated.

The "In-Basket" Instrument

An in-basket format was used to ascertain how executives behave in risky marketing situations. In this method, developed first by Frederiksen, Saunders, and Wand (1957), hypothetical scenarios solicit managerial decisions. The method has been used in studies of decision making (e.g., MacCrimmon and Wehrung 1984) and other managerial topics. See Gill (1979) for a review.

The executives were asked to play the role of a newly promoted vice-president of a large multinational corporation based in their home country – in Shenzhen (one of the four experimental economic zones in the PRC) for PRC executives, Hong Kong for Hong Kong executives, and Toronto for Canadian executives. The decision problems each subject considered consisted of four international marketing situations. These problems were described by memoranda in the subject's in-basket and required immediate response. The decisions were whether to (1) continue or drop an unprofitable product line, (2) enter a new market alone or through a joint venture with a competitor, (3) adopt a new product design or use a current one, and (4) recall a malfunctioning product or send warning letters to buyers of the product. Appendices A through D are the memos used for the four situations.

The participants were asked to respond using the materials at hand. No outside information was allowed. To discourage delay, the exercise stated that the participant was scheduled to leave for an important business meeting in San Franscisco within a couple of hours and would not return for a week, before which decisions would have to be made. None of the materials could be taken on the trip. Each participant was instructed to read through the materials and use his or her own experience as the basis for decisions.

As each situation presented a choice between two alternatives whose expected values were the same, the basis for a choice involved consideration of factors other than expected returns. This method has been used and tested by MacCrimmon and Wehrung (1984). In the decision to continue or drop an unprofitable product line, dropping the product could involve a "loss of face for the decision maker" because the executive had developed the product him- or herself. In the decision to enter a new market, either alone or through a joint venture with a financially troubled competitor who had helped the firm before, going alone might destroy a competitor whereas a joint venture would repay an obligation. The adoption of an innovative product design could be interpreted as making an authoritarian decision because there was no consensus on the design among subordinates, whereas the current design would promote continued harmony in the firm. Finally, in the decision whether to recall a malfunctioning product or send reminders, a pan-ethical orientation would require a complete correction of the problem through recall and a utilitarian orientation would permit a partial, short-run solution. See Table 1 for a summary of the specific hypotheses examined in each of these situations.

The entire questionnaire was translated into Chinese by a doctoral student from the PRC. The translated questionnaire was reviewed by a panel consisting of another PRC doctoral student and two of the authors whose mother tongue is Chinese. The Chinese version was used in a pretest conducted in the PRC and in the major study for PRC executives, whereas the English version (with appropriate changes in names of characters and addresses for each location) was used in Hong Kong and Canada.

The in-basket instrument seemed appropriate for investigating the impact of cultural differences on decision making. In contrast to belief scales (e.g., Anderson and Coughlan 1987) and descriptive techniques (e.g., Lazer, Murata, and Kosaka 1985; Naor 1986), the in-basket instrument provides a rich contextual narrative for each stylized marketing problem, thus permitting cultural influence to be studied across subjects from different cultures. Special care was taken in the design of the instrument to ensure that the tasks were familiar and within the competence of the subjects (see Chakravarti,

Mitchell, and Staelin 1981; Little 1970; Little and Lodish 1981). The situations were designed to provide a broad cross-section of marketing decisions that did not require detailed, specific know-how.

Pretest

Three pretests were conducted, with (1) 45 PRC teachers in business, (2) 16 MBA students enrolled in a West Coast Canadian university, and (3) 20 Canadian Chinese executives from Vancouver's Chinatown. The first and second pretests were designed to show whether the decision situations were perceived as appropriate for PRC and Canadian subjects. The third pretest assessed whether the situations and the amount of investment involved in each situation were realistic. The first pretest used the Chinese language version of the instrument and the latter two pretests used the English version. Subsequent to the pretests, the situations and some questions in the questionnaire were modified.

Sample

A total of 145 executives from Canada, Hong Kong, and the PRC formed the sample. The PRC sample consisted of 50 working executives from the PRC who participated in an executive training program in international marketing management in Hong Kong. The Hong Kong sample consisted of 45 working executives from Hong Kong who participated in an executive program in marketing and international business at a major university in Hong Kong. The Canadian sample was pooled from two sources. It consisted of 34 executives attending an evening MBA program at a West Coast university and 16 executives identified by a local international trade association who agreed to participate in the study. Aside from differences in age and work experience, the two Canadian samples showed no marked differences in the dependent measures and hence were combined.

Research Procedure

Each participant was asked to respond to each in-basket memorandum presenting the decision situations without consulting others. Once the subjects had read a memorandum they were asked to write a memorandum in response, describing what they would do and the reasons for their actions. After completing each memorandum the subjects were asked to provide additional judgments on 9-point bipolar scales. They were instructed to respond completely to one decision situation before beginning the next one.

The six scales can be divided into three types. The first type assessed the subject's perception of the riskiness of the situation to the organization (from 1 = very risky to the company to 9 = not risky to the company). The second type consisted of four scales measuring the participant's inclination to engage in four types of risk-adjustment strategies. They included the participant's inclination to (1) use resources to change the environment (from 1 = accept whatever outcomes occur from the decision to 9 = try to influence situation through bargaining and spending resources), (2) collect additional information (from 1 = use the available information to make the decision to 9 = gain as much additional information as possible), (3) develop more options (from 1 = decide among the options currently available to 9 = try to develop new options), and (4) consult superiors (from 1 = make decision by myself without counsulting my superiors to 9 = make decision in consultation with my superiors).

The third type of scale measured the strength of the participant's preference between the two decision options specified in each situation. These alternatives formed the two ends of a 9-point scale. Higher values corresponded to a preference for the alternative consistent with the hypothesized Chinese perspective as summarized in Figure 1. Some additional scales indicated sociodemographic characteristics of participants. The entire response to the four decision situations took about one hour to finish.

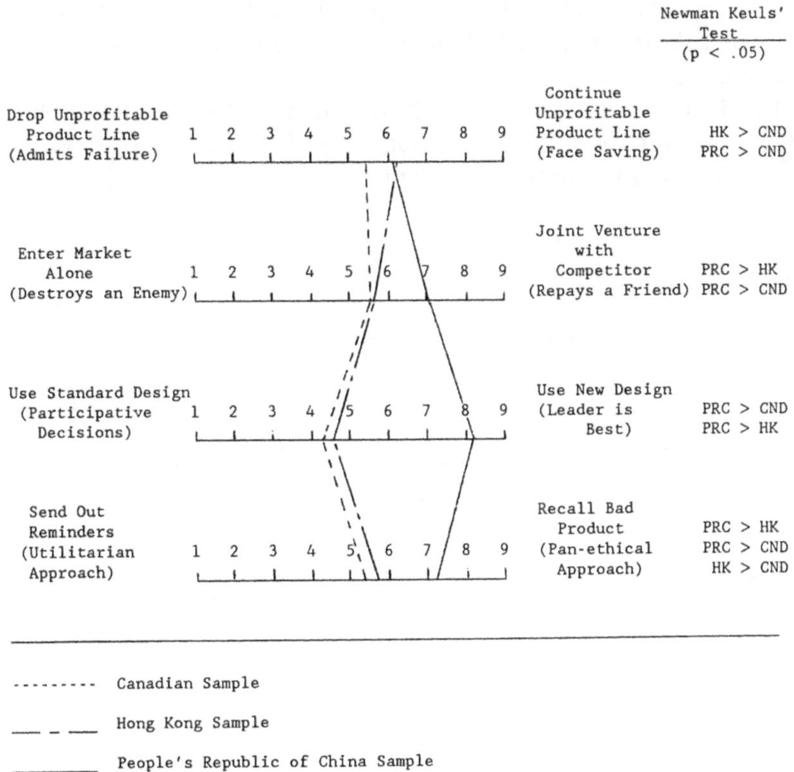

Figure 1: Choice in four situations by subject groups

Findings

Manipulation Checks

The data first were checked to ensure that (1) each situation connoted similar levels of riskiness to the executives across cultures so that comparisons among the executives were meaningful and (2) the four situations represented different levels of riskiness so that a wide range of risky marketing decisions were considered.

Subjects' perceived riskiness for each situation was used as a manipulation check. Analysis of variance was performed with subjects' perceived riskiness as the dependent variable and country (i.e., subjects' home country) and situation as independent variables. The country effect and the country by situation interaction were insignificant, whereas the situation effect was highly significant ($P < .01$). The mean perceived riskiness ratings for the four situations were, respectively, 5.1, 6.9, 6.0, and 4.4 on a scale that ranged from 1 (very risky) to 9 (not risky to the company). The Newman-Keuls tests indicated that each situation was perceived to be significantly ($P < .05$) different from another. Hence, though the four situations differed in their perceived riskiness, executives from all three cultures perceived about the same degree of riskiness in each situation.

The data were analyzed mainly by ANOVA with country and situation as independent variables. Table 2 is a summary of the tests of the three formal hypotheses and some of their corollaries.

Table 2: Results of ANOVA on different dependent variables

	Dependent variables						
Effects	*Choice (n = 144)*	*Decisiveness (n = 144)*	*Use resources to change environment (n = 141)*	*Gather information (n = 144)*	*Develop alternatives (n = 142)*	*Consult superior (n = 143)*	*Overall*[a] *(n = 140)*
Country (C)							
Sum of squares	406.97	128.07	590.54	173.76	550.45	23.14	3650.11
F-value	19.16**	33.00**	22.42**	6.87**	27.74**	1.02	23.40**
Situation (S)							
Sum of squares	8.94	20.11	84.98	39.97	433.05	212.36	3519.54
F-value	.38	8.03**	5.98**	19.32**	24.39**	11.09**	29.41**
C × S							
Sum of squares	187.08	3.94	35.64	84.46	12.86	70.80	434.29
F-value	3.96**	.79	1.25	2.04	.36	1.85	1.82
r^2	.39	.55	.57	.45	.49	.41	.53

[a]Sum of all four types of risk adjustment.
*$p < .05$.
**$p < .01$.

Choice

The ANOVA results on the subjects' choices are summarized in the first column of Table 2. As expected, the country effect is significant, confirming H_1 that cultural difference affects subjects' decisions. The situation effect, which was not a central theme in the study, is insignificant. The country by situation interaction is significant at the .01 level, suggesting that a situation by situation analysis is necessary. A closer examination suggests the significance of this interaction probably is caused by the choices of Hong Kong executives in situation 1 (see Figure 1).

Figure 1 displays the subjects' mean choice scores in the four situations with the results of the Newman-Keuls tests on the right. In summary, all the corollaries in H_1 that pertain to Canadian and PRC executives are confirmed; Hong Kong executives differ from the other two groups, depending on the situation.

The first situation involved the influence of face saving on decision making. Both Hong Kong (mean score 6.21) and PRC (6.10) executives were more sensitive to saving-face concerns than Canadian executives (5.35), and hence persisted with the unprofitable product line. Similar persistence was reported by Johansson (1986), who described Japanese reactions to product failures.

In the second situation, PRC executives (7.00) were significantly more inclined to maintain long-term exchange relationships by agreeing to a joint venture with a competitor than either the Hong Kong (5.64) or Canadian (5.47) executives, who were less inclined to repay their friends.

The results for situation 3 confirm our hypothesis about the impact of preferences for different decision processes. PRC executives (8.06) reflected in their choices a preference for authoritarian decision styles, whereas Canadian (4.37) and Hong Kong (4.70) executives revealed a preference for participative management.

Situation 4 involved a test of the impact of cultural differences stemming from pan-ethical versus utilitarian orientations. PRC executives (7.10) were more inclined to follow a pan-ethical approach to the problem and take complete remedial action when a faulty product was discovered than were Hong Kong executives (5.71), who were in turn significantly more inclined to do so than the Canadian executives (5.28).

Except in situation 1, where Hong Kong executives had a greater though insignificant tendency to continue an unprofitable product line, Hong Kong executives always scored between their PRC and Canadian counterparts. Three of the four situations studied, however, showed Hong Kong executives to be more similar to Canadian executives than to PRC executives. This finding suggests the important impact of continuous interactions with the Western business world in contrast to the influence of the ethnic culture.

However, the significance of the country by situation interaction suggests that the globalization process is uneven along different cultural norms. Hong Kong executives appear to adhere to the "face-saving" norm as strongly as the PRC executives but are similar to the Canadian executives on other norms investigated.

Decisiveness

An executive was regarded as decisive if one of the two decision alternatives specified in a situation was clearly chosen. An executive's degree of decisiveness therefore was operationalized as the absolute difference between the score given on the choice scale and the midpoint of that scale. Hence the decisiveness variable ranges from 0 (totally indecisive) to 4 (strongly committed to a particular course of action).

The ANOVA result (Table 2, second column) with decisiveness as the dependent variable shows that both the country and situation effects are significant but the interaction effects are not. The Newman-Keuls test results indicate that the PRC executives were significantly more decisive (mean score 3.6) than either Hong Kong (mean score 2.8) or Canadian (mean score 2.5) executives, whereas the latter two show no significant difference.

This finding contradicts H_2 and the common views in the literature. It can be explained by the PRC executives inclination to classify the world into extremes – "black or white," "evil or good" (Moore 1967) – which implies a tendency to resolve ambiguity quickly and hence be more decisive.

Adjustment of the Decision Environment

Three indicators were used to understand how the subjects adjust their decision environment: the strength (or magnitude), the number, and the type of adjustment used.

First, each subject's responses to four adjustment scales in four situations were used as dependent variables in an ANOVA. The independent measures were country, situation, and type of adjustment. Table 3 shows that all three main effects and three two-way interactions are significant at .01 but the three-way interaction is not. The significant country main effect confirms H_3 and its corollary. PRC executives were significantly (Newman-Keuls test $P < .05$) less inclined to adjust their environment (mean score 3.94 on a 9-point scale) than those from Hong Kong (5.17) and Canada (5.46). The latter two groups show no significant difference. Though they are not the principal foci of the study, types of adjustment, situation, and all two-way interactions of the three main effects are also significant in understanding the executives' risk-adjustment behavior.

Table 3: ANOVA on risk adjustment with country, type of adjustment, and situation as independent variables (N = 143)[a]

Effects	*Sum of squares*	*F-value*
Country (C)	991.95	25.21**
Type of adjustment (A)	276.31	13.91**
Situation (S)	971.86	48.93**
C × A	418.25	10.51**
C × S	130.70	3.29**
A × S	151.87	2.55**
C × A × S	71.65	0.60
r^2	.29	

[a]Here subjects' responses to four adjustment scores in four situations were used as repeated measures in the dependent variable; hence the number of observations is 143 × 4 × 4 = 2288.
**$p < .01$.

The results of the ANOVA with total adjustment scores as the dependent variable are given in the last column of Table 2. They show that the sum of the four adjustment strategies depends significantly on country and situation effects but not on interaction between them. This sum ranges from 4 to 36, with higher values corresponding to a greater use of risk adjustments. Examining the country effect, we find that PRC executives (mean score 15.7) were significantly (Newman-Keuls test $P < .05$) less likely to try to adjust their environment than Canadian (mean score 20.7) and Hong Kong (21.9) executives. Similar results are obtained when the four adjustment scores are analyzed by MANOVA, confirming H_3. No significant differences are found between Hong Kong and Canadian executives. As found in the preceding test, the situation effect also is significant in explaining this measure of executives' risk-adjustment behavior.

When the four adjustments are analyzed separately (Table 2, columns 3 to 6), similar results are obtained for three adjustment strategies, namely using resources to change the environment, gathering information, and developing additional alternatives. Again the main effects are significant but the interaction is not. The mean score also reflects the fact that PRC executives were less likely than other executives to adopt these three risk-adjustment strategies (Table 4), as predicted by H_{3a}. The insignificant country main effect on consulting superiors disconfirms H_{3b} and suggests that PRC and Canadian executives preferred this mode of adjustment at similar levels. The Newman-Keuls test on the types of adjustment among the PRC executives (Table 4, last row) suggests that consulting superiors was the most preferred among the four risk-adjustment strategies.

Number of Adjustment Strategies

A related measure for the degree of adjustment is the number of adjustment strategies adopted by an executive. An indicator variable was developed that recorded an adjustment as having been adopted (scored 1) if the

Table 4: Mean score on types of adjustment across three countries

	Country groups[a]			
	Canada (n = 50)	*Hong Kong (n = 45)*	*People's republic of China (n = 50)*	*Newman-Keuls test (p < .05)*
Use resources to change environment (B)	5.69	5.91	3.52	CND > PRC HK > PRC
Gather information (I)	5.31	5.75	4.44	CND > PRC HK > PRC
Develop alternatives (A)	4.99	4.96	2.89	CND > PRC HK > PRC
Consult superior (S)	4.75	5.24	4.91	No sig. difference
Newman-Keuls test (p < .05)	B > A, B > S I > S	B > A, B > S I > A	S > B, S > A I > B, I > A B > A	

[a]Mean score averaged across four situations on a scale ranging from 1 = least likely to 9 = very likely to engage in the particular risk-adjustment strategy.

Table 5: Zero, single, and multiple risk-adjustment strategies across three countries (number of responses = 640)

Number of strategies committed[a]	*Canada (%)*	*Hong Kong (%)*	*People's republic of China (%)*
Zero	27	13	33
One	15	22	30
Multiple (2–4)	58	65	37
Total	100	100	100

$\chi^2 = 43.62$ with 4 d.f., significant at .001.

[a]A strategy was recorded as a 1 if the raw score (from 1 to 9) on the adjustment strategy was more than 5.

corresponding raw score (from 1 to 9) exceeded the midpoint value of 5. The sum of these indicator variables across the four adjustments then was analyzed by ANOVA with country and situation as independent variables. These results confirm that PRC executives adopted significantly (P < .001) fewer adjustment strategies (1.32) than Hong Kong (2.23) and Canadian (2.18) executives. The latter two do not differ significantly (P < .05).

More importantly, results in Table 5 show that more than half of Hong Kong and Canadian executives used multiple risk adjustments, in contrast to only slightly more than a third of PRC executives (the chi square score is significant at .001).

Preferences among Adjustment Strategies

Table 6 reports the ANOVA result with the scores on all four adjustment strategies in each situation as dependent variables and type of adjustment and situation as independent variables. In general, both main effects (types of adjustment and situation) are significant for all countries whereas the

Table 6: ANOVA on risk adjustment with type of adjustment and situation as independent variables across three countries

Effects		*Canada (n = 50)*	*Hong Kong (n = 45)*	*People's republic of China (n = 50)*
Type of adjustment (A)	Sum of squares	101.17	106.72	493.67
	F-value	5.96**	5.13**	16.99**
Situation (S)	Sum of squares	335.79	240.98	541.47
	F-value	19.78**	11.58**	18.63**
A × S	Sum of squares	95.82	67.64	62.44
	F-value	1.88*	1.08	0.72
r^2		.11	.08	.13

*$p < .05$.
**$p < .01$.

interaction is marginally significant only for Canadian executives. The results reconfirm H_3. As shown in the first column of Table 4, the Canadian executives ranked highest the spending of resources to change the environment (Table 4, last row), followed by information gathering and development of new alternatives. Consulting a superior was the least preferred adjustment.

Hong Kong executives also rated highest the strategy of spending resources to change the environment (Table 4, last row). This alternative was followed by gathering information. Like the Canadian executives, Hong Kong executives show no significant differences in their preferences for consulting superiors to the options of developing new alternatives. In contrast, the PRC executives rated the option of consulting superiors as the most preferred, confirming H_{3b}. They rated the option of developing new alternatives as the least preferred whereas gathering additional information and the use of resources to change the environment were rated between these two options.

Implications

One important consideration underlying many international marketing plans is the extent to which traditional cultural values persist in a rapidly changing environment. This question is especially crucial when managers approach the world's most populated and underexplored market, China. One motive of our study was to investigate how much of the traditional Chinese value system persists after 38 years of communist philosophy and more than eight years of modernization.

We hypothesized and found that all four Chinese values investigated not only persist, but influence PRC executives' decisions and their reactions to the environment. The values of saving face, long-term exchange relationships and restricted competition, unquestioned respect for leaders, and panethical views are well reflected in their market entry and product decisions.

Their tendencies to hold dichotomous and fatalistic views of their environment are evident in their decision process.

We discovered, contrary to common views held by other authors as well as our own hypothesis, that PRC executives are more decisive than either Hong Kong or Canadian executives. Though we assumed that the Chinese acceptance of hierarchy and quest for harmony would reduce their willingness to make a decision, perhaps their inclination for uncertainty absorption leads to increased decisiveness.

Another interesting finding is the effect of culture on risk-adjustment behavior. PRC executives engaged to a lesser degree in adjusting their decision environment than either Hong Kong or Canadian executives. They preferred strategies that would reduce their personal exposure to failure. In contrast, both Hong Kong and Canadian executives showed marked preference for strategies to control their environment.

Traditional cultural influences are consistently challenged by exposure to different values. Executives from Hong Kong were influenced more by their exposure to Western business practices than by their Chinese heritage, though some residual influence of such deep-rooted values as face saving and pan-ethical views is reflected in their choices. We thus find that the process of globalization is uneven in its effect on different cultural norms. The persistence and dynamism in cultural values clearly suggest the need to trace, monitor, and understand cultural factors in international marketing plans.

Conclusion

Our findings suggest that ethnic cultures do matter (at least for Chinese and Canadian executives) in marketing decision making. A general comparative analysis of cultures may help marketing executives to anticipate the responses of their rivals, understand more accurately their customs in business transactions, and deal with colleagues of different nationalities in joint decision making. Culture makes a difference in problem identification and in the objectives motivating choice. Culture also may make a difference in the communication of problems and recommendations, and particularly in the decisiveness of recommendations. Failure to understand these differences may lead to "noisy" communication, misinformation, and misunderstanding. Culture also makes a difference in individual strategies to adjust decision situations to facilitate choice and mitigate undesirable consequences for the organization and the decision maker.

Our investigation also demonstrates, however, that in a marketing world characterized by intensive communications, standardization, and the employment of similar decision technologies, cultural differences tend to diminish. Indeed, the process of globalization (Levitt 1983) on the supply side has already begun.

Appendix A

General Products International, Inc.
Memorandum

To: Mr. Chan Wing-Tat

From: Lee Ka-Keung
Assistant to V.-P.,
International Operations

Date: June 4, 1986

We have completed our annual review of the European Division's product line for the upcoming meeting of the Executive Committee. There were no real surprises and in general the European Division has had a good year. One issue that is sure to come up in the Executive Committee meeting, however, is what to do with the Natural Beauty Care product line that has been losing money since it was introduced a year ago.

I don't need to go into the background of this line because you initiated and managed the Natural Beauty Care line when you were Marketing Manager with the European Division. The President of the Division has expressed his concern about this product's losses of $500,000 (U.S.) during its first year of sales in Europe. The feeling seems to be that the use of traditional Asian beauty aids derived from natural ocean vegetation and sea life has a difficult time catching on with Europeans.

It seems that we have two options with this product line. We can scrap it now with no future consequences except incurring our past losses. Alternatively, we can invest another $600,000 (U.S.) in marketing the natural beauty idea. The chances of success do not seem too good and are estimated by the European Division to be maybe one chance in five. However, if successful, we would receive an expected profit of $3 million (U.S.) net of the marketing expenses. If unsuccessful, we would lose another $150,000 in addition to the $600,000. These figures do not include last year's loss of $500,000.

You will likely be called on at the Executive Committee meeting on June 15th to express your views on this product line, so let me know if I should do anything else to help you on this issue before the meeting.

Appendix B

Mr. Lee Shing-Tak
Vice-President
International Operations
General Products International, Inc.
2300 Alexandra House
5000 Queen's Road
Hong Kong

Dear Mr. Lee:

Last week the president of Tak On's Brazilian Division called me to see whether General Products International might be interested in a joint venture with them in South America. I am not surprised at this suggestion because they must still be hurting from the major losses they incurred in their failed venture in the Middle East. Tak On is General Products International's closest competitor and we haven't had a joint venture with them in quite some time.

However, remember that Tak On helped us out in our European venture in the late 1970s and we have had good relations with their management for many years. So far they have always competed with us fairly.

The proposed joint venture sounds quite promising. We and Tak On would jointly produce our standard water pumping equipment in our respective Hong Kong factories and market this equipment under a single new brand name in Brazil. All costs, revenues, and profits would be shared equally and both firms would put up half of the estimated initial investment of $1 million (U.S.). Tak On said they needed our participation in the joint venture to obtain the needed investment capital and to share the risks of a new market entry. They also had heard that we have been considering an independent entry into Brazil's water pump equipment market and believe a cooperative joint venture would make both companies better off than a competitive battle for this new market.

Our analysis shows that a joint venture would yield a 20% return on investment for both firms. Tak On has already acquired strong support from the Brazilian government and this market should continue to expand. We have the necessary production capacity and we would be helping Tak On to get back on its feet after the difficult period it has been facing.

Alternatively, we can enter this market alone as we have been planning. In a competitive venture against Tak On, however, there is uncertainty about how much of the market we could capture. If Tak On doesn't have the resources to make a strong independent entry, we should gain a large market share. In this case we would earn a 25% return on our somewhat higher investment. On the other hand, Tak On might focus its energy on this new market because we had rejected their offer of a joint venture. Under this scenario, we could get only a small share of the market and perhaps only a 10% return on investment. Because of Tak On's situation, we believe the chances are two out of three that we could get a larger market share in a competitive venture and there is a one-third chance of getting a small market share.

Tak On has asked us to decide on their offer of a joint venture by June 12. Please let me know your thinking on this question so a formal reply can be made.

Yours truly,

Cheung Yee-Ching
President
South American Division
General Products International

Appendix C

May 30, 1986

Mr. Chan Wing-Tat
Vice-President, International Operations
General Products International
2300 Alexandra House
5000 Queen's Road
Hong Kong

Dear Mr. Chan:

Congratulations on your new appointment. I am sorry to greet you with a problem so early in your new position, but we have a pressing situation in the North American Division that requires your recommendation and you asked to be consulted on all international contracts.

Six months ago the Division began negotiating a contract to supply a robot toy to a New York wholesaler. During this period we have been investigating two alternative designs for the toy. One design is a standard one we have used successfully in several similar toys marketed throughout the world. The technology for producing this standard toy is well-known and we are sure to make a return of about 25% on our investment because the market for this design is large and stable. The vast majority of the engineering and marketing people in the Division recommend going with this standard design.

However, a couple of very knowledgeable people from the research and marketing departments support a new design they have extensively researched; but there is little experience in marketing the new design though the costs in producing both designs are roughly the same. They argue the market for the standard design is not expanding and the Division needs to produce innovative products. The new design has its problems also. The major uncertainties seem to be whether this design will allow the toy to hold up under hard use and whether the North American market will accept the new design. Advocates of both designs agree that the new design has a much greater potential than the standard design. If it is accepted in the market and stands up to use, the new design could lead to a 40% return on investment. If not, the new design would yield only a 10% return, well below our Division's average return of 20%. Both groups also agree that the chances of success for this new design are 50–50.

The urgency on this issue is caused by the New York wholesaler's requirement that we complete the contract (with the design specified) no later than June 10, 1986. Starting production later than this date would jeopardize Christmas sales in North America. The wholesaler has no preference on the two designs because its fees are fixed as our foreign agent.

Shall we go with the standard design that has the support of the majority of our engineers and marketing people, or with the new design even though it has few advocates? Please let me know your recommendation on this issue as soon as possible.

Yours truly,

Raymond Lee
President
North American Division
General Products International

Appendix D

General Products International, Inc.
Memorandum

To: Mr. Chan Wing-Tat

From: Frank Chin
Head, Customer Service
Date: May 31, 1986

We have received three complaint letters within the last week from customers who have had serious problems with our new household electronic control panel. Two letters were from U.S. customers and one was from a Canadian customer. It seems that if the buttons are pushed in one particular sequence all appliances hooked up to the panel are automatically shut down. I checked with the manufacturing group that produces these units and they have confirmed the problem. It seems to be a programming flaw in the design of the control unit.

Although there appears to be no safety problem, the malfunction could seriously inconvenience customers by shutting down refrigerators, freezers, air conditioning units, and the like. We must take some action quickly to correct the problem. Two options have been suggested by the manufacturing group. First, they could recall all the units and replace the programming unit. We have already sold over 100,000 of these units internationally which retail for about $500 (U.S.). The recall and replacement costs would be about $50 for each unit. This adjustment would therefore cost the firm about $5 million (U.S.).

A more cost effective solution would be to mail each customer who sent in his warranty card a notice advising him of this problem and cautioning him against pushing the butttons in this particular sequence. This option would cost only $500,000 U.S. because we have the warranty list on our computerized database. The problem is that not all customers sent in their warranty cards so they would not receive our correction notice and even those who do receive the notice might not read it. If the problem occurs frequently enough, our customers might think our products are of poor quality and our reputation as a high quality producer might be tarnished. Our expected profits of $20 million for this year should not be affected. However, if our image as a quality producer deteriorates our expected profits of $20 million per year for the remaining four year life expectancy of the product will likely drop to only $15 million. I hope this doesn't happen, but the sales people I have contacted here estimate about one chance in four that the sales drop could occur.

The production, marketing, and design people at headquarters have all put their heads together on this problem, but these two options are all that we could come up with. What do you think? We need to come to a decision by June 12.

Note

1. It may seem contradictory to hypothesize that the Chinese are both authoritarian and indecisive. In the Chinese culture "harmony" is the ideal state (i.e., the "end") whereas "authoritarian style" is the accepted way of handling things (i.e., the "means"). A Chinese executive therefore can be indecisive but still regarded as authoritarian within an organization. Thus there is no contradiction between the two hypotheses.

References

Anderson, Erin and Anne T. Coughlan (1987), "International Market Entry and Expansion via Independent or Integrated Channels of Distribution," *Journal of Marketing*, 51 (January), 71–82.

Cascio, Wayne F. (1974), "Functional Specialization, Culture, and Preference for Participative Management," *Personnel Psychology*, 27 (4), 593–603.

Chakravarti, Dipankar, Andrew Mitchell, and Richard Staelin (1981), "Judgement Based Marketing Decision Models: Problems and Possible Solutions," *Journal of Marketing*, 45 (Fall), 13–23.

Chan, Wing-tsit (1967), "The Individual in Chinese Religions," in *The Chinese Mind*, Charles A. Moorehead, ed. Honolulu: University of Hawaii Press.

——— (1986), *Chu Hsi and Neo-Confucionism*. Honolulu: University of Hawaii Press.

Ch'ien, Mu (1973), "On the Systems of Academic Knowledge," in *Higher Education and University Students*, Philip Shen, ed. Hong Kong: University Press, 15–32 (in Chinese).

Erickson, Gary M., Johny K. Johansson, and Paul Chao (1984), "Image Variables in Multi-Attribute Product Evaluations: Country-of-Origin Effects," *Journal of Consumer Research*, 11 (September), 694–700.

Frederiksen, N., D. R. Saunders, and B. Wand (1957), "The In-Basket Test," *Psychological Monographs*, 76, 438.

Gill, R. W. T. (1979), "The In-Tray (In Basket) Exercise as a Measure of Management Potential," *Journal of Occupational Psychology*, 52 (June), 185–97.

Han, Xinlan (1983), "Democratic Management in China's State-Owned Industrial Enterprises," in *China's Management Reforms*, K. C. Mun and K. Y. Wong, eds. Hong Kong: New Asia College, The Chinese University of Hong Kong, 117–32.

Hendry, Steven R. (1986), "The China Trade: Making the Deal Work," *Harvard Business Review*, 64 (July–August), 75– 84.

Hofstede, Geert H. (1980), *Culture's Consequences*. Beverly Hills, CA: Sage Publications, Inc.

Johansson, Johny K. (1986), "Japanese Marketing Failures," *International Marketing Review*, 3 (3), 33–46.

Lazer, William, Shoji Murata, and Hiroshi Kosaka (1985), "Japanese Marketing: Towards a Better Understanding," *Journal of Marketing*, 49 (Spring), 69–81.

Lee, Kam-hon (1982), "Personal Values and Consumption Behavior, a Comparison Between Chinese and Western Managers," in *The Sinicization of Social and Behavioral Science*

Research in China, Institute of Ethnology Academic Sinica Monograph Series B, No. 10 (April), 441– 67 (in Chinese).

Levitt, Theodore (1983), "The Globalization of Markets," *Harvard Business Review,* 61 (May–June), 92–102.

Little, John D. C. (1970), "Models and Managers: The Concept of a Decision Calculus," *Management Science,* 16 (April), B466–B485.

——— and Leonard M. Lodish (1981), "Comments on Judgement Based Marketing Decision Models," *Journal of Marketing,* 45 (Fall), 24–9.

MacCrimmon, Kenneth and Donald A. Wehrung (1984), "The Risk In-Basket," *Journal of Business,* 57 (July), 367–87.

——— and——— (1986), *Taking Risks.* New York: The Free Press.

McCullough, James, Chin Tiong Tan, and John K. Wong (1986), "Effects of Stereotyping in Cross Cultural Research: Are the Chinese Really Chinese?" in *Advances in Consumer Research,* Vol. 13, Richard J. Lutz ed. Provo, UT: Association for Consumer Research, 576–8.

Meade, Robert D. (1969), "An Experimental Study of Leadership in India," *Journal of Social Psychology,* 79 (December), 283–4.

——— and William A. Barnard (1973), "Conformity and Anticonformity Among Americans and Chinese," *Journal of Social Psychology,* 89 (February), 15–24.

Montgomery, David B. and Charles B. Weinberg (1979), "Toward Strategic Intelligence Systems," *Journal of Marketing,* 43 (Fall), 41–52.

Moore, Charles A. (1967), *The Chinese Mind.* Honolulu: University of Hawaii Press.

Naor, Jacob (1986), "Toward a Socialist Marketing Concept – The Case of Romania," *Journal of Marketing,* 50 (January), 28–39.

Pye, Lucian (1983), *Chinese Commercial Negotiation Style.* Cambridge, MA: Oelgeschlager, Gunn and Hain.

Redding, S. G. (1982), "Cultural Effects in the Marketing Process in Southeast Asia," *Journal of the Market Research Society,* 24 (2), 98–114.

Tan, Chin Tiong and John U. Farley (1987), "The Impact of Cultural Patterns on Cognition and Intention in Singapore," *Journal of Consumer Research,* 14 (March), 540–4.

Tse, David K., Russell W. Belk, and Nan Zhan (1988), "Learning to Consume: A Longitudinal and Cross-Cultural Content Analysis of Print Advertisements from Hong Kong, People's Republic of China and Taiwan," *Journal of Consumer Research* (forthcoming).

Tung, Rosaline L. (1981), "Patterns of Motivation in Chinese Industrial Enterprises," *Academy of Management Review,* 6 (July), 481–9.

Wallendorf, Melanie and Michael D. Reilly (1983), "Ethnic Migration, Assimilation and Consumption," *Journal of Consumer Research,* 10 (December), 292–302.

Wehrung, Donald A., Kam-hon Lee, David K. Tse, and Ilan Vertinsky (1988), "Adjusting Risk Situations: Theory and an Empirical Test," working paper, University of British Columbia.

Wu, John C. H. (1967), "Chinese Legal and Political Philosophy," in *The Chinese Mind,* Charles A. Moore, ed. Honolulu: University of Hawaii Press.

Yin, Hai-kuang (1976), *The Future of Chinese Culture.* Hong Kong: The Arts Book Store.

13

Partner Selection and Venturing Success: The Case of Joint Ventures with Firms in the People's Republic of China

Yadong Luo

Choosing alliance partners is always challenging. It is even more challenging when choosing partners in developing economies. This paper takes received theory and applies it in understanding the performance implications of choosing alliance partners in the People's Republic of China.

Jay B. Barney

A major challenge for global management in the 1990s lies in the way that multinational corporations (MNCs) become competent and attain sustained superior performance. In an attempt to do so, MNCs have in recent years turned increasingly to the use of international joint ventures (IJVs) as a means of global expansion (Harrigan 1988, Kogut 1988, Parkhe 1991). However, the intercultural and interorganizational nature of IJVs results in enormous complexities, dynamics, and challenges in managing this cross-border, hybrid form of organization (Parkhe 1993). One popular argument is that interpartner comparative or configurational features, variously termed as strategic symmetries (Barney and Hansen 1994, Harrigan 1988), interfirm diversity (Parkhe 1991), or complementary resources and skills (Geringer 1991), create an interpartner "fit" which is expected to generate a synergistic effect on IJV performance (Buckley and Casson 1988).

Although the analysis of IJV performance and its determinants has commanded considerable attention, few researchers have investigated the

Source: *Organization Science*, 8(6) (1997): 648–662.

systematic relationship between local partner selection and IJV performance. This question is critical, however, because the strategic and organizational characteristics of local partners influence the degree of resource complementarity or indivisibility, and the extent of organizational and strategic fit, between local and foreign partners (Buckley and Casson 1988, Luo 1996, Zeira and Shenkar 1990). Because the strategic traits of a local partner (e.g., absorptive capacity and product relatedness) will affect strategic fit between partners while the organizational traits of a local partner (e.g., organizational form and collaboration experience) will influence organizational fit between partners (Tallman and Shenkar 1994), this study intends to assess the impact of both strategic and organizational traits of local partners on IJV performance.

Local partner selection is even more critical for the success of IJVs investing in newly emerging economies. On the one hand, such economies have in recent years become major hosts of direct investment by MNCs because these rapidly expanding economies, characterized by an exploding demand previously stifled by ideologically-based government intervention, provide tremendous business opportunities that MNCs can preempt. On the other hand, transnational investors in such economies face the challenges of structural reform, weak market structure, poorly specified property rights, and institutional uncertainty. Local partners can be of utmost value to foreign investors by helping boost market expansion, obtaining insightful information, mitigating operational risk, and providing country-specific knowledge (Beamish 1987, Luo 1996). This study addresses the issue of the relationship between local partners' strategic and organizational traits and IJV performance in the context of an emerging economy. Because of the particular importance of China as the World's largest emerging market economy and fastest-growing market, this research uses China as its analytical setting.

The underlying premise of this study is that different strategic or organizational traits may have a heterogeneous effect on an IJV's overall and unidimensional performance; each trait may affect different aspects of IJV performance idiosyncratically. MNCs need to know not only about the important partner selection criteria in general but also which criteria may be crucial to their specific strategic goals. We expect that our results will help define partner selection criteria in emerging economies, identify their impact on multidimensional performance, and offer useful implications for MNCs pursuing crossborder venturing activities in emerging economies. In the following pages, a presentation of the theoretical foundations and hypothesis development will be followed by a brief discussion of methodological issues. Next, the empirical results will be discussed, and the major findings summarized. Finally, possible theoretical and practical implications and directions for future research will be suggested.

Theory and Hypothesis Development

Despite high instability, propensity for failure, and a complex governance structure (Morris and Hergert 1987), MNCs continue to engage in IJVs at a rapid pace. IJVs have been widely considered as vehicles for joining together complementary skills and know-how (Contractor and Lorange 1988). The IJV form of organization does, however, entail additional costs due to shared decision making and the need for coordination between partners (Killing 1983, Schaan 1983). It is therefore assumed that firms establish IJVs only when the perceived additional benefits of exercising the IJV option outweigh its expected extra costs (Geringer 1991, Beamish and Banks 1987). One of the key notions in the IJV literature is that these additional benefits will accrue only through the retention of a partner who can provide the complementary skills, competencies, or capabilities that will assist the firm in accomplishing its strategic objectives (Buckley and Casson 1988, Hamel 1991, Harrigan 1985). Partner selection determines an IJV's mix of skills, knowledge, and resources, its operating policies, processes, and procedures, and its vulnerability to indigenous conditions, structures, and institutional changes (Hamel et al. 1989, Harrigan 1985, Luo 1996). In a dynamic, complex, or hostile environment, the importance of local partner selection to an IJV's success is magnified because the right partner can spur an IJV's adaptability, improve the strategy-environment configuration, and reduce operational uncertainty (Teagarden and Von Glinow 1990, Zeira and Shenkar 1990).

During the process of IJV formation, foreign parent firms must identify what selection criteria should be employed as well as the relative importance of each criterion (Geringer 1991). The criteria for local partner selection are both extensive and divergent across firms, settings and time (Beamish 1987). Broadly, the criteria can be classified into two categories: task or operation-related and partner or cooperation-related (Geringer 1991). While operation-related criteria are associated with the strategic traits of partners, cooperation-related criteria often mirror organizational traits. Examples of the former include absorptive capacity, product relatedness, market position, and industrial experience. Examples of the latter include previous interpartner collaborations, foreign experience, organizational form, and size. A partner's strategic traits influence the operational skills and resources needed for the joint venture's competitive success. At the same time, a partner's organizational traits affect the efficiency and effectiveness of interfirm cooperation. Conceptually, both strategic and organizational traits are crucial for IJV performance. A partner with superior strategic traits but lacking strong organizational characteristics can make the joint venture unstable, while the possession of desirable organizational attributes without corresponding strategic competence leaves the joint venture unprofitable. From a process perspective, the mid-range linkage between partner selection and IJV success may lie in interpartner fit (Parkhe 1993). While strategic attributes may affect strategic fit between partners (Shenkar and Ellis 1995), organizational traits are likely to influence organizational fit (Li and Shenkar 1996). In contrast to previous studies in the literature which focus on either strategic or organizational traits (e.g., Geringer 1991), this study assesses the effect of both. Empirically, in order to alleviate result bias and increase the power of the test, all relevant constructs have to be incorporated in the model as either predictor or control variables.

Business opportunities in newly emerging economies are both promising and challenging. MNCs entering these economies are likely to face higher barriers and more uncertainties than when entering other, more familiar environments (Child 1994). The more promising the industry appears, the more restrictions or interventions the host government is likely to make (Shenkar 1990). It has been argued that MNCs investing in such economies need to collaborate with local partners in order to facilitate market access, improve government relations, acquire culture-specific knowledge, and gain access to scarce resources (Beamish 1987, Luo 1995).

In newly emerging economies, even where some economic sectors have been decentralized and privatized, governments still hinder industrial and market structural adjustments. Indeed, the "invisible hand" in the reform process often causes unexpected social, political, or economic turmoil that may go beyond the tolerance level of the government or society. Under these circumstances, the visible hands of administrative, fiscal, and monetary interventions are called to the rescue. The administrative option is often the most expedient, allowing for swift action that will be promptly reflected in the market. In this situation, local partners can be of great value to the foreign firms. They make investment in restricted industries possible and help MNCs gain access to marketing channels and meet government requirements for local ownership. In addition, having recourse to an IJV as a means of reducing political risks or achieving political advantages is a logical choice for many MNCs operating in strategic sectors in such economies (Kobrin 1982). Moreover, local partners can assist foreign partners in obtaining insightful information and country-specific knowledge concerning governmental policies, local business practices, operational conditions, and the like (Inkpen 1992). Furthermore, the IJV form helps MNCs gain access to, or secure at a low cost, locally-scarce production factors such as labor force, capital, or land. Some of these various needs are unique to emerging market economies, while others are applicable to all contexts. In the context of market economies, local partners also assist MNCs in achieving local knowledge (Beamish and Inkpen 1995, Raveed and Renforth 1983), meeting human resource needs (Stopford and Wells 1972), sharing costs and risks (Roulac 1980), and gaining market access (Killing 1983).

Interpartner fit is multidimensional, and consequently generates a multifaceted synergistic effect (Luo 1996). According to the literature, IJVs gain cooperative and strategic benefits from sharing highly specialized resources which are complementary between partners (Buckley and Casson 1988), while they achieve competitive and financial benefits from increasing economies of scale, improved learning, risk reduction or global integration synergies (Harrigan 1988, Ghoshal 1987). Because the advantages are multifaceted, it stands to reason that IJV performance must be a multidimensional construct, including not only accounting return and risk reduction but also local market expansion, export growth, and interpartner learning. For a given IJV, the performance measurement should match the strategic roles. While the resource-based view suggests that the nature and strength of investment resources determine IJV roles (Prahalad and Hamel 1990), FDI theory stresses the importance of host environmental conditions for determining IJV roles (Brewer 1993), and the IJV literature emphasizes the corresponding relationship between the parent's strategic objectives and the venture's roles (Kogut 1988). This study proposes that the strategic roles of an IJV are determined by the integration of all three factors – resources, environment, and the parent firm's strategic objectives.

To further develop the relationship between local partner selection and the multidimensional performance of IJVs in an emerging market economy, the effects of the strategic and organizational traits of local partners on specific dimensions of IJV performance are examined below. The strategic traits diagnosed include: (1) absorptive capacity, (2) market power, (3) product relatedness, and (4) industrial experience. The organizational traits include: (1) organizational form, (2) number of employees, (3) foreign experience, and (4) organizational collaboration.

Strategic Traits

Absorptive Capability. It has been noted in the IJV literature that complementary needs create interpartner "fit" that is expected to generate a synergistic effect on IJV performance (Geringer 1991, Parkhe 1991). However, complementarity is not likely to materialize unless a certain threshold of skills is already in place. Local partners in emerging economies generally seek technological and innovational skills from foreign partners (Shenkar 1990). The success of an IJV's local operations and expansion in these economies will largely depend upon its local partner's absorptive capability, or its ability to acquire, assimilate, integrate, and exploit knowledge and skills. The firm's ability to process, integrate, and deploy new knowledge and skills closely depends on how these relate to the skills already established (Li and Shenkar 1996). This skill base is expected to influence both strategic and organizational fit between IJV partners (Beamish 1987), which in turn influence the IJV's accomplishment in economic rent (Geringer 1991). This rent, according to Buckley and Casson (1988), contains both financial synergies and operational synergies. As a result, a local partner's absorptive capability is likely to be positively associated with the IJV's profitability and sales growth. Because absorptive capability is more important in capital- or technology-intensive projects, which are often oriented to the local market in China (Luo 1995), the sales growth effect is likely to be revealed in the IJV's local market expansion rather than in export. Therefore:

> Hypothesis 1. *In a newly emerging market economy, ceteris paribus, a local partner's absorptive capacity will have a favorable influence on return on investment and local market expansion for the IJV in which it participates.*

Market Power. Because a major objective of foreign investors in emerging economies is to preempt market opportunities and business potentials, a local partner's market power is a key asset for IJV development. A local partner's market power often represents its industrial and business background, market position, and established marketing and distribution networks (Beamish 1987, Kumar 1995). Market power also enables the firm to mitigate some industry-wide restrictions on output, increase bargaining power, and offer the advantages of economies of scale (Scherer and Ross 1990). Over the last few years, the Chinese government has relinquished control over a growing number of industries. The rapidly expanding Chinese economy, together with the existence of a pent-up demand long stifled by ideologically-based government intervention, has made market position extremely important for the success of any business in the country. In such circumstances, a local partner's market strength is key to the IJV's financial return and indigenous market growth. Moreover, a local partner's strong market power can strengthen an IJV's commitment to local market expansion (Adler and Hlavacek 1976). This commitment will make the IJV less inclined to increase the export ratio in its business operations. Furthermore, stong market power can lead to greater bargaining power with the government (Brewer 1993). This can help the IJV reduce political risks and business uncertainties. Therefore:

> Hypothesis 2. *In a newly emerging market economy, ceteris paribus, a local partner's market power will be positively related to return on investment, local market expansion, and risk reduction for the IJV in which it participates.*

Product Relatedness. The product diversification relationship between a local partner and the IJV in which it participates can influence the venture's economies of scale and scope, and efficiency of transaction costs (Harrigan 1985). This relationship may also affect the IJV's ability to develop the market and products in the host country because product relatedness between the local firm and the venture implies how much the joint venture can utilize the existing distribution channels, product image, industrial experience, and production facilities already established by the local partner domestically

(Geringer et al. 1989). Although a Chinese partner can help the IJV better its relationship with the government, gain access to scarce production factors, increase administrative efficiency, and reduce financial and operational risks in either related or unrelated diversification, some unique values or synergies in related diversification (vertical or horizontal) are not expected to be present where the local parent's products are unrelated to the venture's. Economic rents arising from economies of scale and from a local partner's existing distribution channels, marketing skills, consumer loyalty, and production facilities are predicted to be greater in related product diversification than in unrelated diversification. In the Chinese industrial environment, competitors, buyers, suppliers, and various governmental institutions interact with each other in extremely complicated ways (Perkins 1994). The related product link between a local partner and the venture can be very helpful in building up the IJV's long term stable relationships with suppliers, buyers, local government, and other entities in its value chain. Therefore:

> Hypothesis 3. *In a newly emerging market economy, ceteris paribus, an IJV with a product related with that of its local partner will outperform an IJV with an unrelated product, in terms of return on investment, local market expansion, and risk reduction.*

Market Experience. When operating in a transitional economy characterized by a weak market structure, poorly specified property rights, and institutional uncertainty, an IJV seeking efficiency and growth needs an adaptive orientation, a solid supply relationship, comprehensive buyer networks, and a good organizational image (Luo 1996). A local partner's market experience and accumulated industrial knowledge are of great value for the realization of these goals. A local partner's established history and strong background in the market often result in a good reputation or high credibility in the industry. Lengthy industrial/market experience signifies that the local firm has built an extensive marketing and distribution network, a badly needed competence for IJV market growth in China. In addition, because China has a stronger relationship-oriented culture compared to industrialized market economies (Luo anc Chen 1996), IJV business activities in China can be immensely facilitated by local partners' connections with the domestic business scene and good relations with influential persons. Firms with longer market experience are expected to have developed a better business relationship network. Having such a relationship constitute country-specific knowledge, which enhances a firm's competitive advantage, economic efficiency, and risk reduction capability. Therefore:

> Hypothesis 4. *In a newly emerging market economy, ceteris paribus, the length of a local partner's market experience will have a favorable influence on return on investment, local market expansion, and risk reduction for the IJV in which it participates.*

Organizational Traits

Organization Form. Economic transition has given birth to a new diversity of organizational forms (Child 1994). The spectrum spans the continuum from state-owned (private and collective businesses) (Nee 1992). A local partner's organizational form influences not only its motivation for forming an IJV, but also its commitment and contribution to the operation of the IJV (Luo 1996). This in turn affects the IJV's local performance (Beamish 1987). During structural reforms in the Chinese economy, characterized by weak market structure, poorly specified property rights, and strong governmental interference, state-owned firms have the advantage in gaining access to scarce resources, materials, capital, information, and investment infrastructure (Perkins 1994). In addition, state-owned organizations usually have an advantage over privately or collectively-owned firms in terms of industry experience, market power, and production and innovation facilities (Child 1994). Moreover, it is fairly common for state-owned enterprises to have privileged access to state-instituted distribution channels (Rawski 1994). These channels play a dominant role in product distribution in the Chinese market. State-owned businesses are also treated preferentially by the government in selecting market segments. This organizational form may hence facilitate the market growth in new domains. Finally, given that they are state-owned, hierarchical state firms tend to have a better relationship with various governmental institutions. This relationship is expected to result in a greater problem-solving capacity for these firms (Child 1994). For all these reasons, state-owned organizations are likely to contribute more to IJV's local market expansion than non-state-owned organizations.

Privately or collectively-owned enterprises are typically operated and managed by entrepreneurs. They have fewer principle-agent conflicts and greater strategic flexibility (Nee 1992). The existence of many unfulfilled product and market niches in the Chinese economy increases their chance for survival and growth. Their simple structure and small size have positioned them for speed and surprise, giving them a greater ability to react quickly to opportunities in the environment and proactively out-maneuver more established firms (Tan and Litschert 1994). In addition, private and collective businesses are constrained by a "hard budget", forcing them to be more efficient and oriented on profit (Rawski 1994). In contrast, state firms lack self-motivation and operational autonomy, yet are highly vulnerable to bureaucratic "red tape". It is reported that over 60 percent of state-owned enterprises in China have shown a loss, whereas private or collective businesses have been showing continuous profit (Jefferson et al. 1992). IJVs with efficiency-oriented private or collective partners are thus likely to have a superior return on investment. Therefore:

Hypothesis 5a. *In a newly emerging market economy, ceteris paribus, IJVs with state-owned local partners will have a high performance in local market expansion;*

Hypothesis 5b. *In a newly emerging market economy, ceteris paribus, IJVs with privately or collectively-owned local partners will have a high performance in return on investment.*

Number of Employees. A local partner's ability to contribute to its IJV's survival and growth is positively associated with its organizational size (Kumar 1995, Luo 1996). Organizational size with respect to the number of employees makes an important contribution to economies of scale, market power, process innovation, and organizational image (Geringer 1991). It also influences an IJV's ability to overcome entry barriers stemming from minimum efficiency scale (Scherer and Ross 1990), a factor which is critical to an IJV's profitability and market growth (Killing 1983). Organizational size may also affect the degree of organizational fit between two partners, which in turn impacts the magnitude of the synergistic effect (financial and operational) on the IJV they establish (Li and Shenkar 1996). Moreover, greater organizational size implies a higher capability to reduce risks and mitigate uncertainty (Scherer and Ross 1990). The number of employees in a given Chinese firm is positively linked with its bargaining power in the course of negotiations with local authorities (Luo 1995), which may be conducive to risk reduction for the IJV it initiated. Thus, a local partner's organizational size is also likely to have a positive effect on the IJV's risk reduction. Therefore:

Hypothesis 6. *In a newly emerging market economy, ceteris paribus, a local partner's number of employees will have a favorable influence on return on investment, local market expansion, and risk reduction for the IJV in which it participates.*

International Experience. The international experience of local partners is critical to the success of intercultural and cross-border venturing activities (Luo 1995). International experience affects the organizational fit between partners in the early stages of joint venturing (Zeira and Shenkar 1990) and the changes of fit over time as the venture evolves (Geringer 1991). Because the business atmosphere and commercial practices in emerging economies such as China are quite different from those in developed countries, mistrust and opportunism often occur during IJV operations. A local firm's international experience, through import and export business or cooperative projects with other foreign investors, proves to be a very desirable attribute because this experience represents superior knowledge, skills, and values regarding modern management methods (Kumar 1995). Contact with foreign companies and business people can sharpen sensitivity toward competitiveness in the international market. A long history of business dealings with foreign markets can increase receptivity toward maintaining quality standards, customer responsiveness, and product innovation (Beamish 1987). As foreign experience is accompanied by exposure to foreign (Western) values, it also increases a local firm's ability to effectively communicate with its foreign partner (Zeira and Shenkar 1990). This acquired knowledge stimulates the trust and collaboration between partners. As a consequence, the international experience of local partners is likely to have a positive impact on IJVs' financial return, risk reduction, and sales growth in the domestic as well as export markets. Therefore:

> Hypothesis 7. *In a newly emerging market economy, ceteris paribus, a local partner's length of international experience will have a favorable influence on return on investment, local market expansion, risk reduction, and export for the IJV in which it participates.*

Orgnizational Collaboration. As the length of the interaction between partners increases, the economic transactions become increasingly embedded within the social relations of the two partners, which in turn deters opportunism (Barney and Hansen 1994, Grannovetter 1985). Previous contact between partners leads to the development of specialized skills and routines adapted to the exchange. These include specific knowledge about the structure and operation of the partner organization, and the abilities of the personnel within the partner firms (Levinthal and Fichman 1988). Such skills and routines constitute an investment in specific assets adapted to interpartner cooperation. These are at risk if cooperation breaks down. Hamel et al. (1989) assert that the operation and management of IJVs involve daily interactions which can be greatly facilitated if the partners have correctly assessed each other's strengths and weaknesses. Past and existing long-term relationships between partners based on previous import/export experience, investments, or even on private grounds can therefore prove to be a fine asset to economic efficiency and export growth (Luo 1996). Such relations also foster the climate of openness which is essential for discussing behavioral problems that may be a barrier to learning (Buckley and Casson 1988). This type of background is especially important in newly emerging economies where a relationship-oriented culture is more prevalent than a task and job-oriented culture (Luo and Chen 1996). It is hence expected that the length of past collaboration between partners has a favorable effect on risk reduction. Therefore:

> Hypothesis 8. *In a newly emerging market economy, ceteris paribus, a local partner's length of past collaboration with its foreign partner will have a favorable influence on return on investment, risk reduction, and export for the IJV in which it participates.*

Research Methodology

Background

China officially opened its door to foreign investment in 1979. By the end of 1996, Chinese authorities had approved the establishment of over 283,793 FDI projects involving $469.33 billion in foreign capital. About half of these ventures representing $177.22 billion in investment have commenced operations (*Bulletin of MOFTEC* 1997). The formation and operation of these ventures have played a major role in shaping the new economic environment and have turned China into the second largest FDI absorbing country in the world, only behind the United States. The industrial output and import/export volume of foreign ventures have recently reached 13% and 37% of the nation's total respectively, employing about 17 million Chinese people in these ventures in 1996 (*Bulletin of MOFTEC* 1997).

Among the FDI entry modes, the international equity joint venture constitutes a dominant mode which accounts for 50.26% of total FDI value in 1996 (*Bulletin of MOFTEC* 1997). Foreign parent firms of IJVs are mostly from Hong Kong, Taiwan, the United States, Japan, South Korea, and European countries. In the early 1980s, the Chinese government had certain restrictions on FDI entry mode and the selection of local partners. As a result of an unabated opening up and, particularly, the decentralization of FDI control since the late 1980s, transnational investors are now free, in most economic sectors, to opt for the entry mode and choose local partners if the IJV form is selected.

Data and Sampling

The data were collected from China during a pivotal time in the transition to a maket economy. The secondary data regarding local partners' attributes and IJV performance in China are available only from local authorities such as commissions of foreign economic relations and trade, foreign exchange administrations, and taxation bureaus. Foreign researchers who attempt to access this resource for scholarly purposes can obtain it through local state-owned international consulting companies. In this study, cross-sectional data for 116 IJVs operating in manufacturing industries from 1988 through 1991 in Jiangsu Province were obtained from the Provincial Commission of Foreign Economic Relations and Trade. Based on an estimated two-year time lag from formation to operation for IJVs in China (National Council 1991), this study focused on those IJVs formed as of the end of 1986. Among a total of 277 IJVs established in the province by that time, 116 were left after deducting those investing in non-manufacturing sectors or having multiple partners. In order to avoid the confounding effect of having multiple partners (≥ 3), this study focuses on single local-single foreign partnerships. Among these 116 IJVs, there were 18 ventures that had discontinued operations before the end of 1991. In order to ensure the reliability and validity of the test results, these discontinued IJVs are also included in the sample. We use their last four years' financial figures to measure their performance. In cases where they were in business for less than four years (3 IJVs), we measure their performance based upon the actual length of operations. For all 116 sample firms, with the exception of operational risk, three other performance measures are entered in SAS after being averaged over multiple years.

The data about performance figures (except operational risk) were obtained from the balance sheets and income statements that IJVs submitted to the above commission. These statements had been audited by independent certified public accountants before they were submitted. The information about local partners' attributes and control variables (country of origin and equity distribution) was obtained from the *Directory of Foreign-Invested Enterprises in Jiangsu Province* and other relevant documents obtained from the above Commission. Jiangsu now ranks second in China in terms of GDP and FDI absorption, only surpassed by Guangdong province. The policies, rules and measures adopted in the province vis-à-vis FDI have been widely applied elsewhere in the country. In addition, each industry's growth index (control variable) was obtained by calculations (see Appendix 1) based on the figures in four consecutive editions of *China Statistical Yearbook* (industry section), compiled by the State Statistical Bureau, PRC, covering the years 1988 through 1991. For discontinued IJVs, we computed the relevant industry's growth index for the period covering their last four years of operations (or last two or three years for those IJVs which ran less than four years).

Variable Measurement

As noted earlier, no single measure can capture the diverse goals of IJVs, thus multidimensional performance measures have to be used. Moreover, the specific dimensions of performance selected must be in harmony with the strategic objectives of foreign investors and the corresponding role of their subsidiaries. In IJV literature, the commonly accepted objectives of foreign parent firms and corresponding roles of subsidiaries include efficiency, market growth, cost-minimization (via export), risk reduction, and interpartner learning (Ghoshal 1987). Based on the above criteria, four measures have been retained finally and will be used in this study. These are return on investment, local sales revenue/investment, export revenue/investment, and operational risk. Because the interpartner learning effect often contributes to the parent firm performance rather than that of IJVs (Luo 1995), this study didn't use a learning measure for IJV performance.

This study measures the operational risk facing IJVs by computing the geometric average of the standard deviations of venture performance measures (see Appendix 1). In essence, this index is equivalent to the accounting-based risk calculation used in the strategic management literature (Amit and Livnat 1988, Bettis 1981). Because the result of the multiplication of standard deviations of performance measures could be very large (extreme scores) for observations in a highly dynamic environment, thus leading to skewed distributions, this study uses a geometric average instead of simple multiplication of performance variations. Given the inherent drawbacks of the standard deviation approach (e.g., a fast growing firm will show high variations), future research should also use a subjective approach to verify the risks as perceived by managers, and capture a longer time frame to assess uncertainties. It should also be noted that market-based risk measure, namely, systematic risk or *beta*, is not applicable to IJVs in China because foreign-invested enterprises are restrained by the Chinese government from being listed in the exchanges or buying the "**B**" shares of other listed companies.

In his study on Chinese firms' absorptive ability, Jia (1991) finds that this ability is mirrored in the percentage of professional and technological personnel amongst the total number of employees for the firm under investigation. Similarly, Kumar (1995) reports that the percentage of these personnel in the firm in developing countries reflects the ability to learn technological and organizational skills from developed countries. This study hence uses this percentage to measure a local firm's absorptive ability. Additionally, we use the categorical approach to measure product relatedness between a local partner and the IJV in which it participates. This is a dummy variable indicating if an IJV is related (vertical or horizontal) to its local parent firm (1 if related; 0 otherwise). This information is obtained from the aforementioned *Directory*. The measurement of other predictor variables is relatively staight-forward and is detailed in Appendix 1.

Control Variables

Equity status owned by local partners is treated as a control variable in this study because it represents the firm's resource commitment and may influence its relative power, the extent of control over the IJV, and the degree of the IJV's local dependence (Shan 1991). Interindustry variance affects strategic roles and subsequent performance of IJVs (Kogut and Singh 1988). The moderating effect of interindustry variance on the relationship between firm attributes and performance is likely to be greater in transitional economies than in other contexts because industry structure imperfections in the former are more evident and dynamic. Industry characteristics hence constitute the second control variable in the study. Finally, country of origin of investment affects the cultural distance between home and host countries (Shan 1991), the correlation between home and host market structures (Brewer 1993), and the degree of financial synergies due to different currency and dividend policies (Hagedoorn and Schakenraad 1994). These influences justify the incorporation of country of origin in the model as the third control variable.

Model and Analysis

The generalized multivariate regression model used in SAS can be summarized as:

$$Y_n = B_0 + \Sigma\, b_i X_i + \Sigma\, b_j C_j + E$$

where: Y_n (criterion variables) refers to the multidimensional IJV performance; X_i (predictor variables) stands for a set of partner selection criteria; C_j denotes control variables. Because some estimates reveal high standard errors (> 0.5) as displayed in the GLM test, the ORTHOREG regression method was used to analyze the effect of strategic and organizational traits of local partners on IJV financial and operational outcomes. The ORTHOREG procedure performs linear-square regression using the Gentleman-Givens computational method. It produces more accurate estimates than other regression procedures when data is not well conditioned, as reflected by high standard errors (*SAS/STAT User's Guide* 1990; p. 1211). In order to assess the multivariate effect of a strategic or organizational trait on overall performance of MNC subunits, a MANOVA test was also conducted. Because MANOVA requires that the criterion variables be correlated, the appropriateness of the multivariate technique was validated by a test for sphericity. The test (Mauchly's criteron $= 0.44$, $x^2 = 68.77$, $p < 0.001$) indicated that the data have a Type H covariance structure for the criterion variables, suggesting that MANOVA is appropriate for analyzing the data. The combination of ORTHOREG and MANOVA can present both multivariate and univariate effects of a strategic or organizational trait on multifaceted performance.

Results and Discussion

Strategic Traits

Descriptive statistics revealed in Table 1 indicate high standard deviations for various IJV performance measures and partner selection criteria. It seems that IJVs behave and perform heterogeneously given the diversity of the Chinese economy and the uncertainty of the task and institutional environment. As shown in Table 2, the ORTHOREG and MANOVA tests suggest that a local partner's absorptive capacity is important for the IJV's overall performance ($F = 2.16, p < 0.1$) as well as its financial return ($T = 1.93, p < 0.05$) and sales growth ($T = 1.69$, $p < 0.1$). These two performance dimensions are found to be an increasing function of the local firm's ability to acquire,

Table 1: Descriptive statistics and correlation coefficient ($N = 116$)

Variable	*Mean*	*St.d.*	*1*	*2*	*3*	*4*	*5*	*6*	*7*	*8*	*9*	*10*	*11*	*12*	*13*	*14*	*15*
1. Return on Invest.	10.97	5.61	1.00														
2. Local Sales	29.77	11.84	0.69***	1.00													
3. Export Sales	9.50	6.27	0.25**	−0.20*	1.00												
4. Operational Risk	3.89	4.04	0.19*	0.25**	0.08	1.00											
5. Organization Form	0.61	0.44	−0.06	0.29**	0.13	0.17	1.00										
6. Number of Employee	5.99	1.90	0.08	0.21*	0.12	−0.05	0.39***	1.00									
7. Absorp. Capacity	9.72	2.66	0.26**	0.37***	0.22*	0.03	0.16	−0.04	1.00								
8. Market Power	4.25	3.22	0.33***	0.42***	0.23*	−0.19*	0.39***	0.16	0.27**	1.00							
9. Produ. Relatedness	0.63	0.28	0.22*	0.25**	0.19*	−0.15	0.09	0.10	0.48***	0.13	1.00						
10. Foreign Experience	3.53	1.84	0.26**	0.22*	0.38***	−0.17	0.23*	0.16	0.53***	0.13	−0.03	1.00					
11. Org. Collaboration	1.91	0.90	0.23*	0.09	0.28**	−0.37***	0.11	0.07	−0.02	0.06	0.20*	0.26**	1.00				
12. Ind. Experience	11.33	4.75	0.17	0.33***	0.10	−0.29**	0.40***	0.18	0.10	0.29**	0.06	0.20*	0.15	1.00			
13. Local Equity	54.68	5.59	−0.05	0.11	0.16	0.44***	0.06	0.13	0.17	0.05	0.22**	−0.04	−0.14	0.10	1.00		
14. Industry Growth	8.14	13.45	0.36***	0.28**	−0.19*	0.16	−0.02	0.21*	0.14	0.12	0.07	0.13	0.10	−0.06	0.15	1.00	
15. Country of Origin	0.47	0.46	0.08	0.15	−0.26**	0.18	0.17	0.19*	0.06	0.22*	0.13	0.11	0.15	0.14	−0.17	0.07	1.00

*$p < 0.05$.
**$p < 0.01$.
***$p < 0.001$.

Table 2: The relationship between local partner traits and IJV performance: ORTHOREG and MANOVA analysis

	Univariate effect				*Multivariate effect*	
Variables	*ROI*	*SALE*	*EXPT*	*RISK*	*Wilks' λ*	*F*
Intercept	1.37	−1.97*	2.47*	1.76*		
Strategic Traits						
Absorptive Capacity	1.93*	1.69†	0.87	−0.27	0.88	2.16†
Market Power	3.34**	4.85***	−1.84†	−2.13*	0.75	6.10***
Product Relatedness	1.78†	1.85†	1.68†	0.88	0.89	1.84
Industry Experience	1.44	2.66**	0.71	−2.33*	0.91	1.55
Organizational Traits						
Organizational Form	−1.19	2.70**	0.35	0.72	0.93	1.46
Number of Employees	1.39	1.82†	0.79	−1.18	0.95	1.17
Foreign Experience	1.99*	3.25**	4.51***	1.68†	0.86	2.47*
Org. Collaboration	1.77†	1.30	2.08*	3.01**	0.88	2.13†
Control Variables						
Local Equity	−0.84	1.09	1.35	2.20*	0.91	1.61
Industry Growth	2.68**	2.05*	−1.17	1.36	0.86	2.46*
Country of Origin	0.22	0.71	−2.29*	0.94	0.94	1.39
Sum of Squared Errors	57.05	37.48	44.82	49.34		
Degree of Freedom	104	104	104	104		
Mean Squared Error	0.55	0.36	0.43	0.47		
Root Mean Sqr Error	0.74	0.60	0.66	0.69		
R-square	0.62	0.70	0.67	0.65		
N	116	116	116	116		

Note: The entries in the table (univariate effect) are T-Ratios (parameter estimates divided by their standard error) and their significance levels (two-tailed).
†$p < 0.10$.
*$p < 0.05$.
**$p < 0.01$.
***$p < 0.001$.

assimilate, and integrate the foreign partner's distinctive technologies or tacit knowledge. H_1 is hence supported. Indeed, prior knowledge permits the assimilation and exploitation of new knowledge. This evidence corroborates Hamel's (1991) assertion that a local firm must have a minimal level of knowledge and understanding if it is to learn effectively from a foreign partner. It seems that an IJV's sustained competitive advantage in emerging economies may not necessarily depend upon the advanced technologies that its foreign parent has contributed, but rather on how appropriate the contributed technologies are, relative to the absorptive capacity of the local partner.

It is found that a local partner's market power before IJV formation is an essential determinant of the venture's overall performance ($F = 6.10$, $p < 0.001$), as well as of the various narrowly-defined dimensions of performance (Table 2). Because this attribute is positively associated with IJVs' financial return, sales growth and risk reduction, the above evidence lends support to Hypothesis 2. The local partner's superior market power and favorable market position constitute a key factor in the joint venture's success. This is not surprising, because a local firm's large market share represents not only great market power but also signals superior product quality, higher levels of goodwill, and better relationships with the government, customers, suppliers, and others in the value chain (Porter 1986). These advantages are crucial for an IJV's efficiency, local market growth, and risk reduction. Table 2 also shows a negative relationship between market power and export sales, suggesting that a local partner's large market share contributes to the IJV's level of commitment to local market expansion at the expense of exports.

Consistent with our prediction, product relatedness between the local partner and the IJV is found to be related to the venture's ROI, local sale, and export at a significant level. Because this attribute is measured by a mutually exclusive dummy variable, the positive signs of T_s suggest that related diversification between local parent firms and IJVs are superior to an unrelated product linkage in promoting financial and market performance. Hypothesis 3 is thus supported. In China, where IJVs encounter both a complex task environment and a turbulent institutional environment, those IJVs maintaining related links with their local parents appear to benefit more from economies of scale, existing distribution networks, and industry-specific or product-specific knowledge, information, and experience. These expected benefits are of utmost importance not only for boosting market growth in the host country but also for exploiting internalization advantages within the MNC network.

The MANOVA and ORTHOREG tests demonstrate that a local partner's market experience has a profound and positive influence on the IJV's local sales ($T = 2.66$, $p < 0.01$) and risk reduction ($T = -2.33$, $p < 0.05$). Nevertheless, this attribute is not systematically associated with IJV's return on investment nor on overall performance. Hypothesis 4 is thus partly supported. Indeed, rich market experience often signals a strong production and marketing background and high popularity and visibility in the industry. As noted earlier, in many emerging economies, especially China, business dealings are strongly relationship-oriented. Therefore, a local partners' strong industrial background can greatly assist IJVs in boosting indigenous sales and reducing operational uncertainties.

Organizational Traits

As shown in Table 2, although a local partner's organizational form is not critical for the IJV's overall performance, it has a significant and positive impace on the venture's local market expansion ($T = 2.70$, $p < 0.01$). In other words, state firms appear to contribute to sales growth for the IJVs in which they participate. This finding lends support to Hypothesis 5a. This suggests that state-owned local partners can effectively assist the IJVs in enhancing market power and facilitating market development. Although they have inherent weaknesses in operation and management processes, their advantages in marketing and distribution channels can be of great value for IJVs in search of indigenous market growth. Because organizational form is a mutually exclusive dummy variable, the negative regression sign for the relationship between this trait and ROI suggests that a privately-owned or collectively-owned local partner is positively associated with the IJV's financial return. Nevertheless, this linkage is not statistically significant (Table 2). Hypothesis 5b is hence not supported. As export and risk reduction are not significantly related to this selection criterion, the organizational form of local partners seems not important to those foreign firms pursuing risk reduction and cost-minimization (via export).

Organizational size with regard to the number of employees is not found to have a multivariate effect on IJV's overall performance. Nevertheless, a local partner's number of employees has a positive impact on an IJV's local sales ($T = 1.82$, $p < 0.1$). Because the number of employees is not significantly associated with IJV profitability and risk reduction, Hypothesis 6 is only partially supported. These results suggest that a local firm's organizational size in terms of number of employees is not a fundamental factor to take into account unless a local market share is sought.

A local partner's international experience is shown to have a significant multivariate effect on an IJV's overall performance ($F = 2.47$, $p < 0.05$) and have a significant univariate influence on all the IJV's unidimensional performance measures (Table 2). The T ratios indicate a positive association between this experience and the IJV's accounting return, local sales, risk reduction and export. Hypothesis 7 is thereby supported. In emerging economies, foreign experience constitutes a distinctive competence not given to most local firms. Prior to liberalization, local manufacturers had been strictly prohibited from dealing in international markets. At that time, all import and export operations were controlled by the central government and handled exclusively by a few state-owned foreign trade companies. During the transitional state, although foreign trade operations had been decentralized to a large extent, local manufacturers were still subject to a variety of restrictions and regulations when conducting business with foreign markets. Under these circumstances, those manufacturers who were authorized by the government to deal with international markets must have been highly qualified in all the operation and management arenas. Not surprisingly, IJVs having such local partners are likely to outperform others in terms of accounting and market-based performance measures. Moreover, a local partner's international experience is conducive to trust, forbearance, and collaboration between the partners (Buckley and Casson 1988), and to understanding the dynamics of international markets (Johanson and Vahlne 1977). This further enhances an IJV's risk reduction and export growth.

Table 2 also suggests that interpartner collaboration before IJV formation is important for a venture's overall performance ($F = 2.13$, $p < 0.1$). This selection criterion also leads to a low level of operational risk ($T = 3.01$, $p < 0.01$) and a high level of export sales ($T = 2.08$, $p < 0.05$). Moreover, it shows a moderately positive relationship to IJV profitability ($T = 1.77$, $p < 0.1$). These findings support Hypothesis 8. This evidence suggests that interpartner collaboration before IJV formation facilitates future understanding, fruitful interaction, and cooperation between partners, and yields a better operational outcome in reducing risks and uncertainties and promoting exports for the venture.

As a control variable, equity distribution is found to be systematically related to an IJV's risk level. Table 2 reveals that equity status owned by local partners is positively associated with IJV operational risks ($T = 2.20, p < 0.05$), suggesting that when a foreign partner has a dominant ownership position, the IJV will demonstrate low operational volatility. This confirms the theoretical argument that the majority status of foreign partners enables them to maintain more control over the venture and low dependence upon local context, thus leading to fewer operational uncertainties (Beamish and Banks 1987, Yan and Gray 1994). In IJV literature, Killing (1983) observed a positive correlation between a foreign partner's dominant control and high IJV performance. In contrast, Shenkar (1990) and Beamish (1987) report that dominant control leads to poor IJV performance in China because having a foreign partner making nearly all the decisions in a complex and uncertain environment is extremely risky. Alternatively, Kogut (1988) observed no relationship between equity control and performance. Some new insights seem to be offered by this study, which may help shed light on the above controversy: a foreign partner's dominant equity may not be systematically related to the IJV's overall performance (multivariate effect) but still has a favorable effect on some (not all) dimensions of IJV performance (univariate effect). The Chinese evidence found in this study suggests dominant ownership by foreign partners leads to low risks and uncertainties. Although the equity percentage owned by foreign investors is positively related to profitability (Table 1), the relationship is not significant.

Industry growth is found to have a significant multivariate effect on an IJV's overall performance and a positive univariate effect on an IJV's financial return and domestic sales (Table 2). This result is consistent with observations made by other researchers (Berg et al. 1982, Hagedoorn and Schakenraad 1994), based on the advanced market economy context, that industry characteristics independently impact IJV performance in a significant manner. Another control variable, namely country or origin, has no apparent multivariate impact on an IJV's overall performance but a significant effect on export growth. When the foreign partner in the IJV originates in the developed world, the venture tends to focus more on the exploitation of local market possibilities.

Conclusion

This study explored the systematic relationship between various strategic and organizational traits of a local partner and the performance of the IJV it participates in, in China. The key results of this work suggest that partner selection criteria are important not only for overall performance of international expansion of foreign businesses (multivariate effect), but also for several different aspects of IJV performance such as financial return, local market expansion, export growth, and risk reduction (univariate effect). The results indicate enormous differences in the effect that different criteria have on IJV's overall and unidimensional performance. Each selection criterion affects individual dimensions of IJV performance differently. Overall, cooperation-related criteria, or organizational traits (such as organizational collaboration and international experience), are found to be important for an IJV's overall performance and have a positive effect on uncertainty reduction and profitability. Operation-related criteria, or strategic traits (such as absorptive capacity, product relatedness, and market power), are found to be more important for an IJV's sales growth and financial return. Some country-specific criteria such as organizational form are also linked with some aspects of IJV performance.

The major findings can be summarized as follows. First, product relatedness and market position are critical strategic traits affecting all the major dimensions of IJV performance. Related product linkage between local partners and IJVs outperforms unrelated diversification in terms of both financial return and sales growth. The superior market position of local partners is an essential determinant for IJV success in accomplishing economic efficiency, risk diversification, and market growth. Second, the strategic fit between partners depends not only upon the resource complementarity they actually contribute, but also on the absorptive capabilities of partners. A local partner's high capacity to absorb and assimilate its counterpart's tacit knowledge will lead to better overall performance in general and better ROI and local sales in particular for the IJV. Third, a local partner's organizational experience is of utmost importance in facilitating strategic or organizational fit between partners and hence contributing to the IJV's efficiency and effectiveness. A local firm's market and international experience are both found to have a favorable influence on the IJV's risk reduction, market development, and accounting return. Fourth, the greater length of inter-partner collaboration in the past leads to superior overall performance and in particular to risk reduction, export sales, and profitability. This collaboration spurs fruitful interfirm trust and mutual forbearance, which in turn result in a better operational outcome and serve as a stabilizing device for venturing activities in a dynamic and complex environment. Finally, organizational form and size are not found to be significant to an IJV's overall performance. Nevertheless, hierarchical state enterprises can assist IJVs greatly in enhancing market power and facilitating market development. Organizational size in terms of the number of employees positively influences IJV local sales.

Because of the theoretical importance of interpartner fit, along with the widely shared practical interest in this issue, we expect that this exploratory study may be of interest for both theory and practice. We have established a systematic linkage between partner selection criteria, both strategic and organizational, and the multidimensional performance of IJVs in a dynamic and complex environment. This linkage lies at the core of IJV theory. The primary results of this study have confirmed a key notion in IJV literature, that is, selection of "complementary" partners results in improved IJV performance (Buckley and Casson 1988, Harrigan 1985). In contrast to some previous studies which hypothesize that operation-related criteria (strategic traits) may be necessary conditions while cooperation-related criteria (organizational traits) only constitute sufficient conditions for venture success (e.g. Geringer 1991), this study seems to suggest that both groups of criteria are necessary conditions. From a methodological perspective, our results validate the multidimensional approach to IJV performance as pertinent and promising. The multidimensional approach is clearly needed to capture the heterogeneous impacts of predictor variables on the various aspects of performance, to clarify the trade-offs that are often involved, and to underline the importance of the venture's strategic roles in identifying relevant performance dimensions.

At a more practical level, this study offered some useful implications for MNCs operating in newly emerging economies which have become major hosts for MNCs' offshore investments. Based on this study's findings, MNCs will be able to determine what criteria they should use in opting for local partners and what criteria are vital to their goal accomplishment. For example, those investors seeking local market expansion should select those local partners that have rich industrial experience, superior market position, high absorptive capacity, and/or related product diversification. Those seeking profitability and stability should select local firms that have superior international experience, longer interpartner collaboration in the past, and/or greater market power. From the standpoint of MNCs, the critical partner-selection criteria can ensure partner traits that are favorable for the achievements of their strategic goals. The host government or local partners, on the other hand, can try to make these traits available to attract more stable and profitable foreign direct investment.

Despite some contributions to the literature and practice, this research has several limitations that should be addressed in future research. First, the sample IJVs studied here may not be fully representative of all IJVs in China. In order to truly appreciate the robustness and generalizability of the empirical results reported here, future work needs to use a larger sample of firms with a more recent time frame. The lessons drawn from China could possibly be extended to other emerging economies; however, this needs to be empirically verified. Second, the degree of congruence in strategic motivations of

IJV formation and the degree of complementarity in rentgenerating skills between foreign and local partners are areas well worth investigating. Finally, this study did not address the dynamic effect of interpartner fit once a local partner is selected. It would be a worthy effort to assess how fit or misfit changes over time as the venture evolves (i.e., how fit, once reached, is maintained, and misfit, once created, is corrected by the partners over time).

Appendix 1

Variable measurement and calculation

Variable	*Measurement*
Performance:	
Return on Investment (ROI)	Net income after tax/total investment (%)
Local Sale (SALE)	Local sales revenue/total investment (%)
Export (EXPT)	Export value/total investment (%)
Operational Risk (RISK)	$[\text{Std(ROI)Std(SALE)Std(EXPORT)}]^{1/3}$
Strategic Traits:	
Absorptive Capacity	Percentage of professional and technical personnel in the total number of employees
Market Power	Firm sales/industry sales (1/10,000) in the prior year of IJV formation
Product Relatedness	Dummy variable: if related; 0 otherwise (unrelated)
Market Experience	Years operated in the market before IJV formation
Organizational Traits:	
Organizational Form	Dummy variable: 1 if state-owned; 0 otherwise (Privately- or collectively-owned)
Number of Employees	Total number of employees (in 100)
International Experience	Years involved, directly or indirectly, with international trading or investment before IJV formation.
Org. Collaboration	Years for which the two partners have cooperated before IJV formation
Control Variables:	
Local Equity	Equity percentage owned by the local partner
Industry Growth	Each industry's growth index[#]
Country of Origin	Dummy variable: 1 if from developed countries; 0 otherwise

[#] $GI_j = \Sigma\,\{[(1 + r_{ijt1})(1 + r_{ijt2})(1 + r_{ijt3})]^{1/3} - 1\}/6$ where GI_j = growth index of industry j; r_{ijt} = annual growth rate of industry growth indicator i for industry j at year t; $t_1 = 1989$, $t_2 = 1990$, $t_3 = 1991$; $i = 1, \ldots 6$, standing for number of enterprises, new output value of industry, sales revenue; net value of fixed assets, total pre-tax profits, and total after-tax profits, respectively.

References

Adler, L. and J. D. Hlavacek (1976), *Joint Ventures for Product Innovation*, New York: American Management Association.

Amit, R. and J. Livnat (1988), "Diversification and the Risk-Return Trade-off," *Academy of Management Journal*, 31, 154–166.

Barney, J. B. and M. H. Hansen (1994), "Trustworthiness as a Source of Competitive Advantage," *Strategic Management Journal*, 15, Winter Special Issue, 175–190.

Beamish, P. W. (1987), "Joint Ventures in LDCs: Partner Selection and Performance," *Management International Review*, 27, 23–37.

——— and J. C. Banks (1987), "Joint Ventures and the Theory of the Multinational Enterprises," *Journal of International Business Studies*, 18, 1–16.

——— and A. C. Inkpen (1995), "Keeping International Joint Ventures Stable and Profitable," *Long Range Planning*, 3, 28, 26–36.

Berg, S. V., J. Duncan and P. Friedman (1982), *Joint Venture Strategies and Corporate Innovation*, Cambridge, MA: Oelgeschlager.

Bettis, R. A. (1981), "Peformance Differences in Related and Unrelated Diversified Firms," *Strategic Management Journal*, 2, 379–393.

Brewer, T. L. (1993), "Government Policies, Market Imperfections, and Foreign Direct Investment," *Journal of International Business Studies*, 24, 101–120.

Buckley, P. J. and M. C. Casson (1988), "The Theory of Cooperation in International Business," in F. Contractor and P. Lorange (Eds.), *Cooperative Strategies in International Business*, Lexington, MA: Lexington Books, 31–34.

Bulletin of MOFTEC (1997), The Bulletin of the Ministry of Foreign Trade and Economic Cooperation of the People's Republic of China, Issue #1, 1–19.

Child, J. (1994), *Managing in China During the Age of Reform*, Cambridge, England: Cambridge University Press.

Contractor, F. and P. Lorange (1988), "Why Should Firms Cooperate? Strategy and Economic Basis for Cooperative Ventures," in F. Contractor and P. Lorange (Eds.), *Cooperative Strategies in International Business*, Lexington, MA: Lexington Books, 31–34.

Foreign Investment in China (1996), China Foreign-Invested Enterprises Association, Issues No. 4 and No. 6.

Geringer, J. M. (1991), "Strategic Determinants of Partner Selection Criteria in International Joint Ventures," *Journal of International Business Studies*, First Quarter 1991, 41–62.

———, P. Beamish and R. C. daCosta (1989), "Diversification Strategy and Internationalization: Implications for MNE Performance," *Strategic Management Journal*, 10, 109–119.

Ghoshal, S. (1987), "Global Strategy: An Organizing Framework," *Strategic Management Journal*, 8, 425–440.

Grannovetter, M. (1985), "Economic Action and Social Structure: The Problem of Embeddedness," *American Journal of Sociology*, 91, 481–510.

Hagedoorn, J. and J. Schakenraad (1994), "The Effect of Strategic Technology Alliances on Company Performance," *Strategic Management Journal*, 15, 291–309.

Hamel, G. (1991), "Competition for Competence and Inter-Partner Learning Within International Strategic Alliances," *Strategic Management Journal*, Special Issue, 83–104.

———, Y. L. Doz and C. K. Prahalad (1989), "Collaborate with your Competitors – and Win," *Harvard Business Review*, 67, 133–139.

Harrigan, K. R. (1985), *Strategies for Joint Ventures Success*, Lexington, MA: Lexington Books.

——— (1988), "Joint Ventures and Competitive Strategy," *Strategic Management Journal*, 9, 141–158.

Inkpen, A. C. (1992), "Learning and Collaboation: An Examination of North America-Japanese Joint Ventures," Unpublished Ph.D. Dissertation, University of Western Ontario.

Jefferson, G. H., T. G. Rawski and Y. Zheng (1992), "Growth, Efficiency, and Convergence in China's State and Collective Industry," *Economic Development and Cultural Change*, 40, 239–266.

Jia, L. (1991), "A Quantitative Analysis of Chinese Industrial Structure and Technological Change: Production Functions for Aggregate Industry, Sectorial Industries and Small Scale Industry," *Applied Economics*, 23, 1733–1740.

Johanson, J. and J. E. Vahlne (1977), "The Internationalization Process of the Firm – A Model of Knowledge Development and Increasing Foreign Market Commitments," *Journal of International Business Studies*, 8, 23–32.

Killing, J. P. (1983), *Strategies for Joint Venture Success*, New York: Praeger.

Kobrin, S. J. (1982), *Managing Political Risk Assessment*, Berkeley, CA: University of California Press.

Kogut, B. (1988), "Joint Ventures: Theoretical and Empirical Perspectives," *Strategic Management Journal*, 9, 319–332.

Kogut, B. and H. Singh (1988), "Entering US by Joint Venture: Competitive Rivalry and Industry Structure," in F. J. Contractor and P. Lorange (Eds.), *Cooperative Strategies in International Business*, Lexington, MA: Lexington Books.

Kumar, B. N. (1995), "Partner-Selection-Criteria and Success of Technology Transfer: A Model Based on Learning Theory Applied to the Case of Indo-German Technical Collaborations, *Management International Review*, 35, Special Issue, 65–78.

Levinthal, D. A. and M. Fichman (1988), "Dynamics of Interorganizational Attachments: Auditor-Client Relationships," *Administrative Science Quarterly*, 33, 345–369.

Li, J. and O. Shenkar (1996), "In Search of Complementary Assets," in J. Child and Y. Lu (Eds.), *Management Issues in China*, London: Routledge, 52–65.

Luo, Y. (1995), "Business Strategy, Market Structure, and Performance of International Joint Ventures: The Case of Joint Ventures in China," *Management International Review*, 35, 241–264.

——— (1996), "Evaluating Strategic Alliance Performance in China," *Long Range Planning*, 29, 532–540.

——— and M. Chen (1996), "Managerial Implications of Guanxi-based Business Strategies," *Journal of International Management*, 2, 293–316.

Morris, D. and M. Hergert (1987), "Trends in International Cooperative Agreements," *Columbia Journal of World Business*, 22, 2, 15–21.

National Council for US-China Trade (1991), *Special Report on US Investment in China*, Washington, DC: Department of Commerce.

Nee, V. (1992), "Organizational Dynamics of Market Transition: Hybrid Forms, Property Rights, and Mixed Economy in China," *Administrative Science Quarterly*, 37, 1–27.

Parkhe, A. (1991), "Interfirm Diversity, Organizational Learning, and Longevity in Global Strategic Alliances," *Journal of International Business Studies*, 22, 579–601.

——— (1993), "Strategic Alliance Structuring: A Game Theoretic and Transaction Cost Examination of Interfirm Cooperation," *Academy of Management Journal*, 36, 794–829.

People's Daily (1994), Overseas Edition March 2, 1994, Statistics for Economy and Social Development of 1993.

Perkins, D. (1994), "Completing China's Move to the Market," *Journal of Economic Perspective*, 8, 23–46.

Porter, M. E. (1986), *Competition in Global Industries*, Boston, MA: Harvard Business School Press.

Prahalad, C. K. and G. Hamel (1990), "The Core Competence of the Corporation," *Harvard Business Review*, 90, 79–91.

Raveed, S. R. and W. Renforth (1983), "State Enterprises – Multinational Corporation Joint Ventures: How Well Do They Meet Both Partners' Needs?" *Management International Review*, 1, 24–41.

Rawski, T. G. (1994), "Chinese Industiral Reform: Accomplishments, Prospects, and Implications," *American Economic Review*, 84, 271–275.

Roulac, S. E. (1980), "Structuring the Joint Venture," *Mergers and Acquisitions*, Spring 1980, 18–33.

SAS/STAT User's Guide (1990), SAS Institute Inc., Version 6, 4th ed., Cary, NC: SAS Institute.

Schaan, J. L. (1983), "Partner Control and Joint Venture Success: The Case of Mexico," Unpublished Ph.D. Dissertation, University of Western Ontario.

Scherer, F. M. and D. Ross (1990), *Industrial Market Structure and Economic Performance*, 3rd ed., Boston, MA: Houghton Mifflin Company.

Shan, W. (1991), "Environmental Risks and Joint Venture Sharing Arrangements," *Journal of International Business Studies*, 22, 555–578.

Shenkar, O. (1990), "International Joint Ventures' Problems in China: Risks and Remedies," *Long Range Planning*, 23, 3, 82–90.

——— and S. Ellis (1995), "Death of the Organization Man: Temporal Relations in Strategic Alliances," *The International Executive*, 37, 537–554.

Stopford, J. M. and L. T. Wells (1972), *Managing the Multinational Enterprise*, New York: Basic Books.

Tallman, S. and O. Shenkar (1994), "A Managerial Decision Model of International Cooperative Venture Formation," *Journal of International Business Studies*, 25, 91–114.

Tan, J. J. and R. J. Litschert (1994), "Environment-Strategy Relationship and Its Performance Implications: An Empirical Study of the Chinese Electronics Industry," *Strategic Management Journal*, 15, 1–20.

Teagarden, M. B. and M. A. Von Glinow (1990), "Sino-Foreign Strategic Alliances Types and Related Operating Characteristics," *International Studies of Management and Organization*, 20, 99–108.

Wernerfelt, B. (1984), "A Resource-Based View of the Firm," *Strategic Management Journal*, 5, 171–180.

Yan, A. and B. Gray (1994), "Bargaining Power, Management Control, and Performance in United States–China Joint Ventures: A Comparative Case Study," *Academy of Management Journal*, 37, 1478–1517.

Zeira, Y. and O. Shenkar (1990), "Interactive and Specific Parent Characteristics: Implications for Management and Human Resources in International Joint Ventures," *Management International Review*, 30, Special Issue, 7–22.

14

Selling Machinery to China: Chinese Perceptions of Strategies and Relationships

Norman McGuinness, Nigel Campbell and James Leontiades

In the decade prior to the violent suppression of student demonstrations in 1989, China had greatly reformed its economic system. This drive to modernize and to decentralize economic decisionmaking created industrial market structures that featured much of the autonomous customer decisionmaking that is characteristic of Western markets. Although major purchase decisions could still be centralized within key ministries, most other equipment purchases were influenced primarily by local plant personnel and local government agencies [Grow 1986; Wang 1986]. Western firms selling to these markets could no longer focus only on key centralized personnel; they now had to establish broad marketing programs to cope with the needs of a large number of somewhat independent plants, throughout a vast and complex country.

Since Tiananmen Square, the government has tried to maintain the essence of these economic policies while simultaneously clamping down severely on those urging political change [Huan Guocang 1989]. Although China may still be on the verge of political instability, it appears that its government wants the "open door" to remain open and that industrial purchase decisions may continue to be made in a fairly decentralized fashion. As a market that imported more than $55 billion in 1988, many Western firms will continue to regard China as an attractive opportunity.

Source: *Journal of International Business Studies*, 22(2) (1991): 187–207.

The purpose of this paper, therefore, is to examine the effectiveness of various marketing strategies for building product preference among local plants in China. In doing so, special attention will be devoted to the importance of developing strong customer relationships. The Peoples Republic of China is a market whose cultural traditions suggest that relationships between customers and suppliers may be more important than they are in Western markets [Lockett 1987; Sheng 1979; Walls 1986; Pye 1982]. Although various studies have recommended that Western firms take pains to build strong relationships with Chinese customers, that advice has typically been given from the point of view of how to negotiate more effectively [Tung 1982; Pye 1982; Wang 1986; Campbell and Adlington 1988]. Thus some of this advice reflects times when business in China was done in a much more centralized fashion and most of it tends to ignore the role played by marketing factors other than the behaviour of the negotiators themselves. This paper, therefore, will focus on assessing the effectiveness of various marketing strategies, and on evaluating the importance of relationships in the context of those strategies.

Traditional Relationships in China

Chinese culture attaches a very high value to continuing relationships based on family and other ties such as clan, home village, education, and other shared experiences [Lockett 1987]. Unlike the West where commercial transactions are made binding through legal contracts, in China it has been traditional to subsume the business relationship under the "moralistic notion of friendship" [Sheng 1979; Walls 1986]. By friendship is meant much more than just a pleasant and rewarding relationship. In China, friendship implies a longer term, holistic relationship of trust and loyalty where, unlike the West, obligations to the other are not cleared in utilitarian fashion through performance on a particular transaction. Instead the Chinese ideal sets an indefinitely long-time horizon that requires that one always be obligated to one's friends. In negotiations, therefore, it is understandable why the Chinese constantly revert to the theme of friendship [Pye 1982, p. 31]. For the Chinese, friendship is intended to provide the basic framework within which agreement can be reached. And the agreement itself is regarded less as the conclusion of a transaction, than as another significant step in the building of the "friendship" framework.

Such cultural inclinations imply that good customer relationships will be more enduring in China, that Chinese customers will be more loyal to their suppliers than Western customers. Certainly there is evidence that relationships are important in China. Grow [1986] cites a case where a Japanese company, regarded as an "old friend," won a major contract against U.S. and Russian competitors, who each offered better performance. Additional evidence for the importance of traditional Chinese relationships is the finding that the long-term obligation to friends felt by mainland Chinese was stronger than that found for Canadians and Hong Kong Chinese [Tse et al. 1988]. This adds weight to Tung's [1982] earlier finding that U.S. negotiators had more success when they exhibited prior preparation, patience, and sincerity – factors valued in Chinese relationships.

There is also evidence from business practices. Prior to the Open Door policy when all business was done through fourteen Foreign Trade Corporations, these corporations displayed great loyalty to their suppliers. Thus the Japanese trading companies which did business with China during the '50s and '60s became known as the Friendship companies, and the British companies which went on the 1954 Icebreaker mission are still warmly regarded today. More recently when Western business people were queried, two-thirds of a sample of a Beijing-based group thought Chinese customers to be very loyal to old established suppliers [Campbell 1986].

However, in spite of all the evidence stressing the importance of relationships in China, there is some data that suggests relationships there may be no more important in business dealings than they are in other countries. In one experiment, for instance, negotiations between Chinese were found to produce better results when there was an element of interpersonal attractiveness present. But that was true of all the nationalities, including Americans, in the negotiation experiment [Graham and Kim 1988]. Business people themselves have reported that the need for personal rapport and friendship in China is no different from elsewhere, since in their view "all successful negotiations call for a high level of trust and respect" [Pye 1982, p. 32].

Gauging the importance of relationships in China becomes even more difficult when the effects of other marketing variables are included in the mix. It has been argued that the Chinese concept of "face" may encourage them to buy only products with a well-known brand name or reputation [Wong 1986]. Chinese culture tends to rank everything hierarchically so that it is highly desirable to buy what is at the top. Should buying the best come into conflict with the desire for friendship, then buying the best will generally win out, especially since Chinese officials leave themselves open to criticism if they do not [Pye 1982, p. 32]. That opinion seems to be confirmed in a recent survey where business people indicated that economic and technical factors were considerably more important than relationships to Chinese customers [Campbell and Adlington 1988].

Complicating these issues is the likelihood that Chinese buying criteria are changing. With a better understanding of transactions with foreigners, Chinese patterns seem to have gone through an adaptation process that could be interpreted as a sort of westernization. As early as 1982, it was noted that the Chinese had moved away from an initial emphasis on friendship to a concern for buying the very best and latest technology. Difficulty in absorbing and making good use of that advanced technology shifted the emphasis in turn to an awareness that somewhat less advanced technologies may be more appropriate to China's needs and capabilities [Pye 1982, pp. 32–33].

It appears that the Chinese have been willing to moderate their traditional cultural inclinations in favour of greater functionality. Could that same shift have also affected the traditional Chinese emphasis on "friendship" as the basis for commercial relationships? Could the Chinese now have a more utilitarian (and Western) approach where their relationships with Western firms reflect mainly the perceived value of the supplier's overall product and service package? Do Chinese buyers, in other words, now deal with suppliers in much the same way as Western buyers?

This is an important issue when considering how best to market in China. The research model that follows incorporates both relationships and marketing variables so that the role played by relationships in various marketing strategies can be empirically evaluated.

Research Model

The research model in Figure 1 shows marketing variables influencing customer preferences in two ways. The first is through a direct impact on Preference, which is equivalent to saying that customer preferences are due solely to such things as the perceived quality of the product and service offered. The second mode of influence shown in the model is an indirect one whereby marketing activities are hypothesized to be instrumental in building good Customer Relations which in turn influence Preference in a positive way.

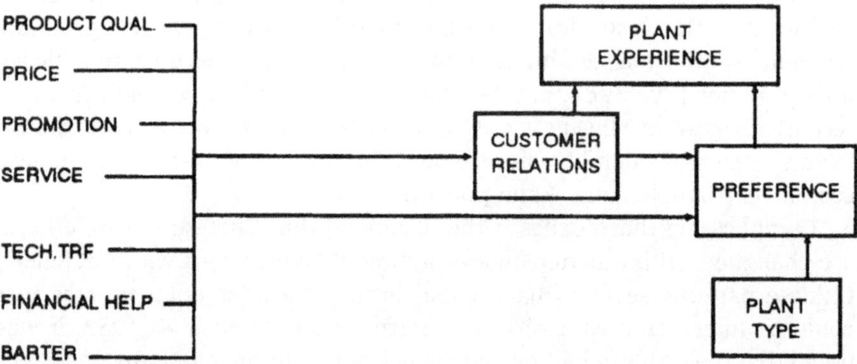

Figure 1: Research model

The model also incorporates two other sources of impact on Preference. The first of these is "Experience." The greater the amount of experience the Chinese customer has had with a particular supplier's equipment, or the longer the firm has been operating in China, the more familiar the Chinese plant is likely to be with the supplier. Hence Experience is expected to result in both stronger relationships and preferences. Preferences may also vary according to the "Plant Type." Large plants may opt for more sophisticated equipment (higher quality) than smaller plants. The same might be true for plants competing in export markets with higher quality standards. The Plant Type element is included in the model to control for these influences.

The position of relationships in the model is derived from the interaction, or network, approach to analyzing industrial markets where supplier-customer relationships are given a central role [Hakansson 1982, p. 14]. Extensive case study-type research in a number of industrial countries by the International Marketing and Purchasing (IMP) group has done much to validate and illuminate this emerging view of industrial marketing and purchasing [Turnbull and Cunningham 1981; Hakansson 1982; Turnbull and Valla 1986]. According to the interaction model, each interaction, or exchange, between buyer and seller is regarded as just one episode in what is often a series of episodes. Should these episodes be mutually rewarding they tend to result in a close long-term relationship between the two parties. Thus many industrial markets can be conceptualized as a network of fairly stable systems of interactions where suppliers and customers are bound together by the mutually dependent relationships between them. Since each marketing exchange of any sort has a longer term impact on the relationship, the strategy of a supplier can be regarded as a process of marketing investment that strengthens its relationships with customers [Johanson and Mattsson 1985]. Or, in Jackson's [1985] terms, such market investments serve to attract new customers and to keep existing ones more loyal by raising their switching costs.

The Customer Relations element in Figure 1, therefore, corresponds to the element called Atmosphere in Hakansson's [1982, p. 24] interaction model. Although Atmosphere in that model is only loosely defined, it is intended to reflect the quality (closeness, cooperation, expectations, etc.) of the supplier-customer relationship that has resulted from prior transactions, and which therefore sets the atmosphere within which subsequent transactions take place.

Relationships are motivated by the desire of both parties for economic gain and to reduce uncertainties [Hakansson and Ostberg 1975]. For customers, economic gain results from the value of the product and service package and from the efficiencies and more effective communication that result from dealing with a restricted number of suppliers. With increasing trust between the partners, joint problem solving and mutual adaptation results in each becoming more intricately interwoven into the value-added chain of the other. The relationship may become institutionalized and structured into a set of roles whereby each party divides responsibility for such things as inventory and product development [Hakansson 1982, p. 14]. Much of the uncertainty in the relationship derives from the power differentials in it and the vulnerability of each partner to the actions of the other. The trust required to reduce these and other sources of uncertainty tends to be built over time as each partner meets the performance expectations of the other [Dwyer, Schurr and Oh 1987]. Also important in this trust-building process is interpersonal social exchange and the building of the norms and shared values that will guide the relationship [Hakansson and Ostberg 1975; Dwyer, Schurr and Oh 1987].

The research model in this paper assumes that all these relationship-building activities happen in the course of performing various marketing efforts. Although the supplier is portrayed as driving the process, customers in the interactive model are also active participants. In fact, the initiative in building a relationship may be taken by the partner feeling the greatest uncertainty and sense of dependency [Dwyer, Schurr and Oh 1987]. That could well be the Chinese customer. Chinese purchasers of machinery typically lack trained installation, operating, and maintenance personnel, do not have alternate local suppliers, and cannot obtain technical support and repair parts locally. Their anxiety about such heavy dependence on the foreign supplier for these services makes them fearful that the supplier may not have a long-term interest in China and could stop servicing it. Thus the strategy of the Chinese customer may be the utilitarian one of deliberately choosing to build a good relationship with the most preferred supplier to encourage ongoing interest and support.

Whatever the circumstances, the logic of the model is that both parties invest in the relationship to optimize mutual economic gain. They will continue to do so as long as the benefits seem worthwhile. In a utilitarian sense the relationship is valued only for its economic merits. Cunningham [1982] documents an instance where a single episode, a 35% price increase, destroyed a relationship that had been in effect for fifty years. Similarly, it was found in a U.S. study that relationships based mainly on social interaction and interpersonal attraction were not perceived to be a substitute for providing the customer with real value [Crosby and Stephens 1987]. However, if the nature of the relationship corresponds to Chinese "friendship," it should take on a value above and beyond its perceived instrumentality for economic gain. Such relationships are valued for their own sake and are hypothesized to have an influence on preferences that exceed just the perceived value of the supplier's product and service package. In those circumstances, the Customer Relations element in the model will have a separate affect of its own on Preferences after the influence of other factors is accounted for. Conversely, if a traditional type Chinese relationship is not present, the Relationship element will not have a separate influence of its own.

Data Collection

Data for the research was collected as follows:

Phase 1: During February 1987, British companies operating in China were asked about their practices and problems. Data were collected from a total of nineteen companies, eleven of whom were interviewed in Hong Kong, and the balance of eight in Beijing. Most of these companies were large, well-known manufacturers of industrial or electronic equipment, but the group interviews also included an accounting firm, two banks, and several sales agencies representing large firms. The data were collected both through interviews and by having one or more respondents from each firm complete a written questionnaire.

Phase 2: To capture the Chinese view, a second visit was made to Beijing in June 1987 to interview Chinese plant managers, and ministry and bureau officials. This time the interviewing focus was narrowed to consider primarily textile, flour milling, and food processing machinery. These industries were chosen because most of the European nations and Japan were active in them and therefore comparisons of their marketing strategies could be made. The aim of the interviewing was to gather information on Chinese buying processes, buying criteria, influences on the buying process, and to assess how well different marketing strategies were meeting Chinese needs. To get a comparative view, the Chinese were asked to compare the performance of firms from Italy, Germany, Britain, UK, France, and Switzerland.

It was not easy to get access to the Chinese for interviews. In spite of the Open Door policy and decentralization, the Chinese system still consists of huge bureaucracies where there seemed to be a strong tendency to avoid being interviewed by a foreigner. However, in a two-week period nine interviews were completed: three in textiles, three in flour milling, two dealing with a broad range of machinery, and one in food processing. In addition to an interpreter and a note-taker, there were always at least two and sometimes six Chinese present at these interviews. They usually lasted at least two hours, and some, especially plant visits, went on much longer.

During interviews it was found that the Chinese were inclined to discuss equipment differences in terms of country of origin. Company names were mentioned now and then with respect to particular instances but usually the Chinese were more comfortable in comparing Italian equipment with Japanese, and so on. Even when the person interviewed noted that all the suppliers from a particular country were not the same, there was no difficulty in comparing one country with another. The country of origin was treated much like a brand name by the Chinese to characterize the typical equipment and marketing approach used by foreign suppliers.

Phase 3: During this second visit, the services of a market research operation within MOFERT (Ministry of Foreign Economic Relations and Trade) were used to mail a questionnaire to a sample of plant managers throughout

China. The covering letter indicated that the information was being gathered by the research agency for its own purposes. Without this official involvement it would have been impossible to get a mail list, or to get anyone to respond even if a mail list had been available.

The questionnaire was written first in English, translated into Chinese, then retranslated back to English to make sure the translation was accurate. Using 5-point Likert-type scales, plant managers were asked to give their perceptions of attributes of product, service, and promotional activities, of suppliers of machinery from six countries of origin: Italy, Germany, UK, Japan, Switzerland and France. They were also asked to rate their preference for the machinery from each country.

Although the mail list provided by Chinese officials was several years old and acknowledged to be somewhat out of date, it was the best available. From it a sample of the larger plants was drawn because the larger plants purchase most foreign equipment. The sample was divided to roughly reflect the industries in the research according to the import priorities that seemed to be given to them by the Chinese. About 800 questionnaires were mailed of which about 250 were sent to textile plants, and 125 to 150 were sent to each of flour mills, grain oil producers, baking operations, and plants in the dairy industry. Of these, 216 were returned for a response rate of 27%.

Variable Definitions

The measures used and their grouping into composite variables are shown in Table 1. The design of the scale measures was heavily influenced by the information already collected in the interviews. It had become clear that the Chinese valued such things as technical seminars staged by suppliers, invitations to visit suppliers' plants abroad, and visits by specialists to China. The Chinese regarded such activities as a form of technology transfer, but from a marketing point of view it seemed more appropriate to treat them as promotional factors.

During the interviews the Chinese were very reluctant to say they had a better relationship with suppliers from one country than another. Usually they would only say that they got along well with everybody. Yet in the interviews statements such as "They understand us very well," or, "They must want to help China," or "They are familiar with our needs and were the only country to bring the right equipment," would crop up. Further information came from the interviews with business people who attached great importance to persistence, a long-term interest, and the need to be flexible. To the Chinese such qualities and attitudes seemed to reflect a long-term commitment by the supplier that helped to build a relationship of trust. Since the Chinese seemed quite willing to respond to these kinds of attributes, they were used

Table 1: The variables used in the study

		Cronbach alpha's					
Composite variable	*Individual scale items*	*Italy*	*Germany*	*UK*	*Japan*	*Switzerland*	*France*
Product quality	How advanced the technology Number of unique features Expected life of machine Maintenance required How advanced control system Overall quality	.85	.87	.86	.81	.88	.86
Price	Relative price level						
Adv. & Promotion	Frequency of technical seminars Salesmen's technical ability Amount of advertising Frequency of supplier visits to China Frequency of inviting Chinese to supplier's country	.79	.80	.72	.80	.80	.63
Service	Willingness to adapt products Speed of response to inquiries Quality of maintenance service Length of delivery time	.80	.68	.68	.81	.70	.51
Technical Transfer	Willingness to consider technical transfer						
Financial Help	Ability to offer special financing for purchase						
Barter	Willingness to consider barter						
Customer Relations	Enthusiasm for business with China Knowledge of Chinese customers Ability to build good relations Degree of long-term interest in China Interest in helping China Flexibility in negotiations	.81	.78	.85	.71*	.82	.84
Plant Experience**	Was first country to enter (re-enter) China after 1978. % of equipment in plant bought from Western country.						
Plant Type**	Plant size (no. of employees in plant) % of plant output exported						
Preference	Likelihood of buying from Western country in future.						

*Does not include the "interest in helping China" measure.
**Not a composite variable. The individual measures were used as separate variables.

in the questionnaire as a somewhat indirect method of measuring the quality of customer relationships.

Table 1 shows that the Cronbach alpha's for the composite variables are all well above the range considered acceptable for research [Peter 1984]. Factor analysis was useful in confirming the structure of the variables, especially across countries. Although there were differences in the factor loadings between countries, the factors derived from each country paralleled each other quite well. Only the Price variable posed some difficulty. The price dimension for almost all the countries loaded on the factor representing product quality which indicates that the Chinese equated the two. However, because of the importance the Chinese are reputed to attach to getting a good price, it was decided to retain Price as a separate variable.

Results

The presentation of results will begin with descriptive data showing how the Chinese perceived the strategies of the six countries. Then multiple regression will be used to evaluate the impact of the marketing variables on the preference for each country's products. Finally the impact of customer relationships will be assessed along with an analysis of the determinants of good customer relationships.

Perceived Country Strategies

It is clear from the data in Table 2, that in the eyes of the Chinese, the suppliers from different countries pursued distinctly different strategies.

The suppliers from two countries, Germany and Switzerland, were perceived by the Chinese to occupy the high quality part of the market using very similar strategies. Both countries showed a relatively early interest in China

Table 2: Country comparisons (means of variables)[1]

Variable	*Germany*	*Switzerland*	*U.K.*	*Italy*	*Japan*	*France*
Product Quality	4.18	4.27	3.67	3.66	3.40	3.44
Price	4.19	4.34	3.74	3.35	3.44	3.45
PROM	3.26	3.19	2.76	3.13	3.44	2.48
Service	3.60	3.59	3.15	3.55	3.72	3.10
Technical Transfer	2.98	2.80	2.73	2.99	2.59	2.55
Financial Help	2.61	2.67	2.35	2.83	2.52	2.40
Barter	2.33	2.20	2.04	2.49	2.60	2.32
First to Enter (Re-enter)	3.72	3.33	2.70	3.24	4.49	2.17
Percent of Equipment in Plant from Country	28.41	24.48	20.95	33.33	37.50	14.67
Customer Relationship	3.57	3.51	3.02	3.59	4.03	2.99
Customer Preference	4.02	3.98	3.47	3.76	3.50	3.07

[1]All variables except the percentage of equipment installed in the plant range from a low of 1 to a high of 5.

after 1978, although both were well behind the Japanese, and the Swiss lagged the Germans. On product quality, no other country came close to their high ratings of 4.18 and 4.27, respectively, on a scale of 5, or their equally high price ratings. Also strong were Chinese perceptions of their promotional and service efforts. These were second only to the Japanese. None of the countries were regarded as being very enthusiastic about technology transfer, providing special financial help, or barter arrangements. Even though Germany and Switzerland were not perceived as being the most receptive to such deals, they were still regarded as being flexible enough to be rated second to either Italy or Japan. Through their activities the Germans and the Swiss gained middle-range customer relationship ratings, which are about the same as the Italians, but considerably lower than the Japanese. The overall result of these various factors was that equipment from Germany and Switzerland realized the top preference ratings of all the countries in the study.

Material gathered from the interviews confirmed this strategic picture, but drew more attention to the effort both countries seemed to exert in familiarizing the Chinese with their products. The Germans, especially, were described as staging many technical seminars, and through government contacts arranging, on a regular basis, many visits by the Chinese to Germany for technical training. In negotiations, Germany and Switzerland were not regarded as particularly flexible on pricing. They tended to quote a price and stick to it. But there was evidence that the Germans were willing to consider longer term technology transfer arrangements earlier in the relationship than other European nations. Comments during the interviews suggested that they tended to establish customer relationships based more on respect and reliability than on warmth and familiarity.

At the low quality, low price end of the market are found French and Japanese equipment. However, the Chinese perceived the strategies of suppliers from these two countries to differ greatly on other marketing dimensions. The Japanese were the first to pursue sales in China after 1978 whereas the French were last, entering long after all the other countries in the sample. The Japanese put more effort into promotion and service than any country; the French were perceived as doing the least. Overall, the Japanese realized the highest ratings on customer relationships but gained only moderate buying preference ratings. The French were rated lowest on both – about the same as England on customer relationships but well below the other countries on buying preferences.

Again, the interview material tended to confirm the data from the written questionnaire. The Chinese noted that there was a lack of familiarity with the French equipment and that the French were not putting enough effort into promoting it. On the other hand, the Japanese seemed to be admired more for their business acumen than for their products. The lower quality Japanese equipment tended to be regarded as more suited to applications not requiring much complexity, or when foreign exchange was scarce. But the Japanese, themselves, were praised for their understanding of Chinese customer needs, their aggressive marketing, their knowledge of China and Chinese ways, and their shrewdness at doing business. Although the Chinese never made negative comments about their relationships with the Japanese, interviews with experienced sales agents indicated that there were potentially strong undercurrents of distrust due to Japanese business practices that had been a little too sharp, and longer term, historic tensions between China and Japan.

In the middle of the product quality spectrum, and almost evenly matched in quality ratings, were Italian and British equipment. In every other respect except quality, however, the Italian marketing program was perceived as being much more competitive than the UK's. The Italian approach resembled the Japanese strategy with low prices (lower than the Japanese), accompanied by strong promotional and service efforts (in the same range as Germany and Switzerland). In contrast, the UK was perceived as having middle-range prices which were much higher than the Italian level. To make matters worse, the promotional and service efforts of the UK were perceived as being well below those of the Italians. The Italians were also rated as being much more flexible than the UK in such matters as technology transfer, special financing, and barter. The UK, therefore, seems to have been caught in the middle: not competitive in quality at the high end, and unable to match the low prices, and strong promotion and service, of the Italians and the Japanese at the low end. As a result the Italians exceeded the rating of the UK significantly on both customer relationships and buying preferences.

During interviews the Chinese noted that some of the machinery from the UK was excellent. However, it was more common to hear comments that the UK did not seem to be keeping up with the latest technology. One of the Chinese interviewed told of visiting textile plants in Britain and of being disappointed with the calibre of the operations. Even so, the people interviewed usually rated the UK equipment at a higher quality level than the Italian. The Italian equipment was regarded as robust, but less refined and sophisticated than the British machines. Because the Italian prices were low, the Chinese considered their equipment seriously. In one instance, the Chinese seemed to have made a trial purchase to find out just how well the Italian equipment did perform. The Italians were regarded as being much more active at marketing their equipment than the English. In terms of relationships, the British were described variously as serious, gentlemanly, concerned with dignity, and as too rigid about contractual matters. For the Italians terms such as gentle, and flexible, came up. Some of the Chinese acknowledged that they seemed to have an easier rapport with the Italians, or as one put it, "They make us feel good."

Impact of Marketing Variables on Preferences

To test the impact of the individual elements of these marketing strategies on Chinese preferences, multiple regression models were tested for each country using customer preference as the dependent variable. Customer relationships were omitted from these models to focus only on the direct impact of the marketing programs on preferences.

Although each of the regression models in Table 3 explained a significant amount of the variance in country preferences, the adjusted R^2 levels of between .229 and .327 are not particularly high. It seems surprising that more of the variance in preferences would not have been accounted for by models that seem to contain most of the key factors affecting them. Political factors and customer relationships seem to be the main omissions. However, when customer relationships are included in a later section, it will be seen that the R^2 values did not change significantly.

The pattern of beta coefficients in Table 3 indicates that perceived product quality had the most important influence on preferences, regardless of the country's marketing strategy. This result must be interpreted with some care as product quality, for every country except Japan and Italy also had

Table 3: Multiple regression results for each country (customer relationships omitted)

Independent variables	*Standardized beta coefficients*					
	Germany	*Switzerland*	*U.K.*	*Italy*	*Japan*	*France*
Product Quality	.396[1]	.266[1]	.280[2]	.402[1]	.429[1]	.250[3]
Price				−.104	−.112	.122
Promotion			−.108	.165[3]		
Service		.146	.294[1]		.203[1]	.260[1]
Technical Transfer	−.144[3]			−.179[3]		
Financial Help }		.138				
}	.203[3]					
Barter }					.088	.255
First to Enter (Re-enter)	.187[2]	.259[1]	.280[1]	.165[3]		.191
% of Equipment in Plant from Country	.095	.088	.096			
Plant Size				.138[3]	.207[1]	−.121
% of Plant Output Exported		.099	−.160	.133		
R^2	.259	.269	.377	.317	.277	.336
ADJ R^2	.229	.236	.327	.271	.249	.268
SIG F	8.730	8.095	7.476	6.799	9.875	4.975
F	.0000	.0000	.0000	.0000	.0000	.0004
N	131	161	81	126	135	66

Dependent Variable = Customer Preference
[1]Significance ≤ .01.
[2]Significance ≤ .05.
[3]Significances ≤ .10.

Table 4: Correlations of each variable with the preference rating of each country

Independent variable	*Germany*	*Switzerland*	*U.K.*	*Italy*	*Japan*	*France*
Product Quality	.40[1]	.41[1]	.49[1]	.40[1]	.39[1]	.47[1]
Price	.22[1]	.09	.23[1]	.05	−.03	.27[2]
Promotion	.16[2]	.33[1]	.35[1]	.31[1]	.13[3]	.30[1]
Service	.25[1]	.32[1]	.40[1]	.23[1]	.29[1]	.49[1]
Technical Transfer	−.01	.12	.14	−.05	.19[2]	.13
Financial Help	.17[3]	.14	.09	.21[3]	.21[2]	.05
Barter	.06	.10	.03	.29[1]	.18[2]	.37[1]
First to Enter (Re-enter)	.27[1]	.38[1]	.39[1]	.26[1]	.01	.23[3]
% of Equip in Plant from Country	.10	.15	.57[1]	.24[2]	.10	.06
Plant Size	.19[2]	.16[3]	.04	.14[3]	.15[3]	−.06
% of Plant Output Exported	.03	.22[2]	−.16	.17[3]	−.10	.15
Customer Relationships	.33[1]	.31[1]	.36[1]	.37[1]	.13[3]	.28[1]

[1]Significance of correlation ≤ .01.
[2]Significance of correlation ≤ .05.
[3]Significance of correlation ≤ .10.

strong correlations with promotion and service that ranged between .33 and .54 and were mostly higher than .40. Because of this collinearity, the product quality variable tended to overwhelm the effect of promotion and service, even though it is apparent in Table 4 that promotion and service, themselves, had very significant correlations with product preferences. Therefore, although product quality had a very important influence on preferences, the beta coefficients for product quality overstate that influence to some degree.

Price, on the other hand, did not emerge as a strong influence, even for the low pricers, Italy and Japan. Again price was highly correlated with product quality, and that must be what it represents in the correlations in Table 4, where it shows significant positive (not negative!) relationships with preferences for Germany and the UK, neither of which were noted for low prices.

These results appear to confirm Grow's [1986] opinion that price may not be that important in the final decision. However, a more likely explanation is that the Chinese are value rather than price sensitive, and that the best price at the desired quality level might well win the day. During interviews the Chinese acknowledged that they typically had a preferred supplier and quality level in mind before starting the purchase process. The Chinese also noted in the interviews that they had enough purchasing experience to know what the price ought to be at various quality levels. Although these prior preferences and targets could change, the Chinese were obviously conscious of the quality-price trade-off from the beginning. It is possible that what Westerners have perceived as an excessive emphasis on a low price may have been only a tactic aimed primarily at squeezing down the price of an already preferred supplier. In the minds of the Chinese, quality and price level may have been closely related.

In negotiating price, the Chinese were also conscious that they had to take different approaches with different countries. They did not anticipate that the Germans or Swiss would move much from their initial position, whereas the Japanese and Italians might move considerably. That the Chinese gave the highest preference ratings to German and Swiss equipment suggests that price alone may not have been that crucial a purchase criteria.

For countries with medium or low quality levels, either promotion or service emerged as a more salient influence on preference than for the countries with high quality. Again multicollinearity raised problems as promotion and service were also highly intercorrelated and fought with each other for statistical significance in the regression runs. However, using the data from both Tables 3 and 4, it seems reasonable to tentatively conclude that promotion and service probably had an important influence for all countries, but that their influence was relatively more important when product quality levels were lower.

Except for Germany and Italy, technology transfer, financial help, and barter, did not seem to have much of a relationship to preferences. Possibly plant managers left those considerations to personnel in the bureaus or ministries. It is curious, however, that technology transfer was negatively related to preferences for Italy and Germany. This implies that a greater willingness to transact technology transfer agreements reduced their preference levels – which does not seem likely. A more probable explanation is that these countries resisted technology transfer when they enjoyed a strong market position, and used it as a means of gaining sales when their position was weak. When interviewing British firms, one company was found to be doing just that. To get an edge on a better entrenched Swiss competitor, it was proceeding as quickly as possible with technology transfer negotiations.

The regression results show that stronger preferences were won by those suppliers who entered China early after 1978. From the interviews it became apparent that once they were familiar with the equipment, plant managers were reluctant to switch to another type, unless they had very good reason. Moreover, other plants were inclined to emulate the purchase if the equipment performed well. The practice in China was for plant managers to exchange information on the merits of different kinds of equipment and to visit plants where quite new equipment had been installed. All the European countries except France benefited to some degree from this process.

However, Japan, who was the earliest of all to enter after the Cultural Revolution, and had more equipment already installed than any other country, gained no increase in preference thereby. From the interviews we learned that textile factories were switching away from less sophisticated

Japanese machinery to the more advanced European machines they needed to help them upgrade their products for the export market. The preference rating for Japanese equipment (Table 2) was not particularly low, so there may also have been other factors, such as political influence, at work too.

The Impact of Customer Relationships

The simple correlations in Table 4 show relatively strong connections between customer relationships and customer preferences. For the European countries, these correlations range between .28 for France and .37 for Italy. Yet those countries with the highest ratings on customer relationships, did not necessarily get the most influence from them. The discrepancy between the magnitude of the relationship rating and the influence of the rating on preferences was most pronounced for the Japanese. No country approached their high 4.03 rating on customer relationship, and no other country had their very low .13 correlation between relationship and customer preference. A clue as to why this correlation is so low may be provided by the make-up of the Japanese composite relationship variable. For Japan only it was necessary to omit the "interest in helping China" item because it was insufficiently correlated with the other elements. In other words, the Japanese were perceived as being enthusiastic about sales in China, but as not being particularly interested in "helping" China. The Chinese clearly had some concerns about longer term Japanese objectives.

For the European countries, however, these correlations suggest that relationships were important, and that echoes material collected from British firms doing business in China. Twenty questionnaires were completed by seventeen different firms. When asked to state the three most important factors leading to success, thirty-eight out of the fifty-two reasons given related to some aspect of customer relationships. The comments touched on personal characteristics with words such as honesty, integrity, respect, and trust. They also touched on knowledge factors with comments about knowing the Chinese system, understanding the problem, having contacts. Very commonly mentioned (seventeen out of the fifty-two reasons) were the desirable attitudinal traits of patience, perseverance, and flexibility. While only indirectly related to relationships, such attitudes would seem to be important in building the kind of long-term relationships valued by the Chinese.

The question remains, however, as to whether relationships added something to preferences beyond the perceived value of the package of products and services being offered. To try to answer that question, the customer relationship variable for each country was added to the model for each country that resulted from the previous regression runs to see how much the explanatory power of the regressions increased. From Table 5 it can be seen that the resulting changes in the R^2 values were too small to be significant for

Table 5: Multiple regression models – with customer relationships added[1]

Independent variables	*Standardized beta coefficients*					
	Germany	*Switzerland*	*U.K.*	*Italy*	*Japan*	*France*
Product Quality	.356[2]	.265[2]	.303[3]	.357[2]	.429[2]	.250[4]
Price				−.068	−.122	.122
Promotion			−.177	.050		
Service		.063	.188		.203[2]	.206[3]
Technical Transfer	−.152[4]			−.206[3]		
Financial Help }	.182[3]			.126		
Barter }					.088	.255
First Enter (Re-enter)	.152[4]	.250[2]	.279[2]	.142[4]		.191
% Equipment in Plant from Country	.082		.060			
Plant Size				.135[4]	.207[2]	−.121
% Plant Output Exported		.098	−.160	.103		
Custom Relationship	.129	.119	.191	.219[4]	.000	.000
R^2	.271	.276	.391	.339	.277	.336
ADJ R^2	.236	.236	.333	.287	.249	.268
SIG F	7.682	6.917	6.709	6.602	9.875	4.975
F	.0000	.0000	.0000	.0000	.0000	.0004
N	131	116	81	126	135	66
R^2 Change[5]	.012	.077	.014	.021	.000	.000
F of Change	2.070	1.018	1.688	3.751	.000	.000
SIG F Change	.153	.315	.198	.055	1.000	1.000

Dependent Variable = Customer Preference.
[1]Relationship variables added to the model which emerged when only the marketing variables were considered.
[2]Significance $< .01$.
[3]Significance $< .05$.
[4]Significance $< .10$.
[5]R^2 Changes from adding customer relationships to the model.

any of the countries except Italy. For most of the countries, therefore, it seems that customer relationships tended to reflect primarily the value attached to past transactions and services and contributed nothing additional. That the Italians did seem to gain something extra, may have been due to the greater warmth that seemed characteristic of the relationships they built.

These results indicate that the Chinese most frequently evaluated relationships in a utilitarian manner that reflected the value of the product and service package. However, unless the Italian result is a statistical aberration, it at least shows the possibility of building relationships that add something extra to product preferences. To that degree it is still an open question as to whether the Chinese continue to approach relationships with Western suppliers in the traditional Chinese way.

Given the weight of evidence supporting the importance of relationships in China, it was surprising that relationships did not emerge more strongly as having a separate impact of their own on preferences. One speculation as to why this occurred is that good relationships may be a required state with a supplier before their offering will be seriously considered. Hence good relationships become a given that do not enter into the final decision. Yet the fact remains that the Germans and the Swiss had the highest preferences but not the highest relationship ratings which suggests that other factors are more potent in influencing preferences than relationships. To probe for other possibilities, the result was discussed with a Chinese who had spent many years in purchasing activities in MOFERT and who had also worked in plants. To him the finding was not surprising because he distinguished between suppliers who operated essentially outside the Chinese system from those who were within it. Inside the Chinese system, according to this view, relationships continue to be critical. However, those outside the Chinese system are treated differently. In the early days of the Open Door policy the Chinese did stress relationships in transactions with foreign suppliers because they were unfamiliar with the companies. But now that China has learned much about Western suppliers, they tend to deal with them in much the same way as Western buyers. Relationships in the full Chinese sense, he believed, would only apply should these Western companies begin to operate in China and *within* the Chinese system.

To examine the determinants of customer relationships, another series of regressions were run using customer relationships as the dependent variable. The results in Table 6 yield reasonably high R^2 levels that range between .51 and .63. There seems to be no doubt that promotional and service activities had the major influence on customer relationship ratings. That should not be surprising as these are the activities that generate interaction between suppliers and customers.

For some reason, technology transfer, special financial help, and barter emerged as more important factors in building customer relationships than in gaining higher customer preferences. Could this simply indicate that the Chinese appreciate such offers as a sign of commitment to a longer term relationship, but when the purchase decision is to be made they still opt for the best equipment?

Not surprising, though, is to find that customer relationships were rated higher when the country entered earlier, or had a large amount of equipment installed in the plant. These were the hypothesized relationships in the research model and tend to confirm that plant personnel were more familiar and comfortable with the suppliers they had been dealing with the longest and most frequently. In that sense Chinese personnel seem no different than their Western counterparts.

Table 6: Multiple regression results: Impact of marketing variables on customer relationships

Independent variables	*Standardized beta coefficients*					
	Germany	*Switzerland*	*U.K.*	*Italy*	*Japan*	*France*
Product Quality	.138	−.132	−.125			
Price	−.117				−.091	
Promotion	.315[1]	.420[1]	.342[1]	.351[1]	.501[1]	.184[3]
Service	.390[1]	.485[1]	.512[1]	.412[1]	.277[1]	.432[1]
Technical Transfer		.128[3]	.137[3]	.059		.332[1]
Financial help }				.050		.224
}	.128[2]					
Barter }		.117[3]		.142[2]		
First to Enter (Re-enter)	.164[2]		.070	.149[2]		
% of Equip in Plant from Country	.066		.185[2]	.108[3]		.240[1]
Plant Size		.059				
% Plant Output exported	−.081				.056	
R^2	.564	.660	.632	.644	.515	.637
ADJ R^2	.535	.641	.607	.623	.496	.608
SIG F	19.721	35.257	25.752	30.513	27.392	21.061
F	.0000	.0000	.0000	.0000	.0000	.0000
N	131	116	81	126	135	66

Dependent Variable = Customer Preference.
[1]Significance < .01.
[2]Significance < .05.
[3]Significance < .10.

Conclusions

The aim of the research was to examine the impact of marketing strategies and customer relationships on Chinese purchasers of machinery. Since data was collected only in textile manufacture, food processing, flour milling, and grain oil production, the results cannot be safely generalized beyond those industries. Indeed, the results actually represent a composite average of the industries sampled and hence each of the specific industries sampled may deviate somewhat from that average. Using a Western-style data collection technique in China (a mail questionnaire with Likert-type scales) may also have introduced a variety of unexpected response errors and biases.

Given these limitations and uncertainties, the results do strongly suggest that the most important factors in winning sales in China are product quality, promotional effort, and service. Competitors whose quality levels are not of the highest, may have to exert more than average promotional and service efforts to capture sales. An entry strategy of being first, ahead of other Western competitors, also seems to have paid handsome dividends.

Cutting prices and offering special terms does not necessarily influence preferences. The Chinese plant managers seem to demand mainly that prices be in keeping with the quality being offered, and that there be some flexibility on matters such as technology transfer and countertrade.

Customer relationships seem to have emerged naturally as a result of promotional and service efforts that have been appreciated by the Chinese. Efforts to gain higher preferences through developing an extremely close rapport based on personal attractiveness may pay off, providing the company's services are also good. However, for Western companies with only limited knowledge of the Chinese language, customs, and systems, it would seem difficult, if not impossible, to depend heavily on building traditional type "friendships" with the Chinese. The indication from this study is that the Chinese, themselves, may be taking a more utilitarian approach to commercial relationships with Western firms. For most firms, the best strategy may be to concentrate on doing the basic marketing job well, which includes building relationships similar to what they would aspire to in Western markets. Even if such relationships do not meet the traditional Chinese "friendship" standard, they may still be adequate for marketing success.

At the country level, it seems to be suppliers from the quality-oriented nations that are in the strongest position and beginning to supplant the Japanese. However, there may also be a demand for lower quality, lower priced equipment, and in this study it was the Italians who were moving strongly into that niche. The worst place is where the British firms are perceived to be: in the middle, with rather high prices, and weak promotional and service activities.

Finally, the research demonstrates that there is much more to doing business in China than simply being skillful at negotiations. The most important marketing job for any would-be exporter of machinery to China is to familiarize potential customers with the company's product. That can no longer be done on a centralized basis. Potential customers throughout the country must be visited, informed, and their special needs understood. That calls for marketing programs with breadth and depth. Representation by agents aimed primarily at establishing contact and building personal rapport is only a beginning. It will not suffice by itself to create strong customer preferences.

Obviously more research is needed to develop a better understanding of Chinese purchasing criteria and decisionmaking processes. Relationship building, itself, is well deserving of more attention since so much of the material on doing business in China points to its importance. Important contributions could be made by exploring in more detail the nature of relationships formed with Chinese customers, the relationship building process itself, and the importance of relationships to both suppliers and customers.

References

Campbell, Nigel. 1986. *China strategies: The inside story.* University of Manchester/ University of Hong Kong.

——— & Peter Adlington. 1988. *China business strategies.* Pergamon Press.

Crosby, Lawrence A. & Nancy Stephens. 1987. Effects of relationship marketing on satisfaction, retention, and prices in the life insurance industry. *Journal of Marketing Research*, 24: 404–11.

Cunningham, Malcolm T. 1982. Sprinter. In Hakan Hakansson, ed., *International marketing and purchasing: An interaction approach.* New York: John Wiley & Sons.

Dwyer, Robert F., Paul H. Schurr & Sejo Oh. 1987. Developing buyer seller relationships. *Journal of Marketing*, 51 (April): 11–27.

Graham, John L., Dong Ki Kim & Michael Robinson. 1988. Buyer-seller negotiations around the Pacific rim: Differences in fundamental exchange processes. *Journal of Consumer Research*, 15 (June): 48–54.

Grow, Roy F. 1986. Japanese and American firms in China: Lessons of a new market. *Columbia Journal of World Business*, Spring: 49–56.

Hakansson, Hakan, ed. 1982. *International marketing and purchasing: An interaction approach.* New York: John Wiley and Sons.

——— & Claes Ostberg. 1975. Industrial marketing: An organizational problem? *Industrial Marketing Management*, 4: 113–23.

Jackson, Barbara Bund. 1985. Build customer relationships that last. *Harvard Business Review*, 63(3): 120–28.

Johanson, Jan & Lars-Gunnar Mattsson. 1985. Marketing investments and market investments in industrial networks. *International Journal of Research in Marketing*, 2:185–95.

Lockett, M. 1987. Culture and the problems of Chinese management. Paper presented at the conference on "The China Enterprise," Manchester Business School, June 1–2.

Peter, J. Paul. 1984. Reliability: A review of psychometric basics and recent marketing practices. *Journal of Marketing Research*, 16 (February): 6–17.

Pye, Lucian. 1982. *Chinese commercial negotiating style.* Santa Monica, Calif.: Rand Corporation.

Sheng, Richard. 1979. Outsiders' perception of the Chinese. *Columbia Journal of World Business*, Summer: 16–22.

Tse, David K., Kam-hon Lee & Donald A. Wehrung. 1988. Does a manager's home country matter? *Journal of Marketing*, 52 (October): 81–95.

Tung, Rosalie L. 1982. U.S.-China trade negotiations: Practices, procedures and outcomes. *Journal of International Business*, Fall: 25–37.

Turnbull, P.W. & M.T. Cunningham. 1981. *International marketing and purchasing: A survey among marketing and purchasing in five European countries.* London: Macmillan.

Turnbull, P.W. & Jean-Paul Valla. 1986. *Strategies for international industrial marketing.* London: Croom Helm.

Walls, Jan. 1986. China: Cross cultural business skills. *Issues,* Spring: 1–8.

Wang, N.T. 1986. United States and China: Business beyond trade – An overview. *Columbia Journal of World Business*, Spring: 3–11

Wong, John. 1986. The concept of 'face' in Asian culture: Its implications for marketing. In Chin Tiong Tan, William Lazer & V.H. Kirpilani, eds., *Emerging international frontiers,* 183–86. Chicago: American Marketing Association.